INDEX

which describes typical conflict flows and comparisons are made.

Relative status-field theory is applied to conflict data for the time period indicated. Implications for policymaking are generated from a world model constructed out of the empirical results.

Discriminant function analysis is applied to nations exhibiting positive vs. negative weights, across all of the dimensions of a- and d-space, for distance theory. Thus, the attribute characteristics of nations exporting a particular way, say to those distant from them in respect to economic development, are identified and compared with the characteristics of those exporting in the opposite way.

A second stage factor analysis is applied to the parameter weights for distance theory. The analysis determines whether behavioral tendencies tend to cluster. That is, to illustrate, if a nation tends to export conflict to other nations distant from it in respect to economic development, does it also tend to do so in respect to power base? All nations are rank sorted in terms of the variable clusters that develop so that it is possible to determine whether any two nations, or, any group of nations, share the same "export profiles."

GENERATING A-SPACE FOR THE MID-1960'S: WITH AN EXAMPLE OF POSSIBLE USAGE

By: Jack E. Vincent

Professor of Political Science

Florida Atlantic University

Boca Raton, Florida 33432

GENERATING A-SPACE FOR THE MID-1960'S: WITH AN EXAMPLE OF POSSIBLE USAGE[1]

Introduction.

Many scholars would like to have a convenient index which summarizes the positions of states on groups of related variables. For example, in respect to those variables that are frequently used to define "economic development" where does Brazil stand relative to Mexico?, Great Britian to France? Factor analysis of course is frequently used to identify groups of variables, but, the summarizing index that could be used to answer the kinds of questions posed above, the factor scores, are seldom provided.

The purpose of this effort is to create a set of useful indexes defining national position on factors derived from a set (144) of attribute variables measured in the mid-1960's. As will be seen, such an analysis not only conveniently summarizes a great deal of information about the states, but, sets the stage for subsequent analyses which can employ the factor scores as predictor variables, such as relating to the behavior patterns of states. Since the term, "a-space," (Rummel, 1969a) has been used to describe attribute collections, both actual and theoretic, using this terminology, the purpose can be restated as -- to define the dimensions of a-space (mid-1960's) and locate each state on the dimensions of that space and to illustrate possible usage.

Before presenting the results, that such an analysis generates, it might be useful to summarize some of the major aspects of the factor analytic approach.

Factor analysis: a brief summary.

Factor analysis refers to certain mathematical techniques, the purpose of which is to reduce a large number of indices (variables) into a smaller number of factors. Factors may be viewed as intervening variables which emerge from the pattern of intercorrelation among variables. Various techniques of factor extraction have been employed. In the principal axis method, operations are performed upon a matrix consisting of the intercorrelations of the variables with one another. The first "factor" (or "component") is that which accounts for the greatest proportion of the intercorrelations. Successive operations upon successive, residual matrices generate the second factor, the third factor, etc. Each factor is mathematically defined so that it is orthogonal[2] to the other factors. Each variable "loads"[3] differently upon the factors. These loadings or weights may be viewed as correlations of the variables with the factors and may be utilized to generate "factor scores" which express each subject's position on each factor. Factors are sometimes rotated to maximize the loadings for certain indicators and minimize the loadings for others. Rotated factor loadings present the simplest possible picture of the contributions of the variables to the factors. Once factor scores have been calculated, it is possible to correlate them with other variables to facilitate prediction and description.

Factor scores.

Subjects can be located on factor dimensions in a manner conceptually similar to the way that they are located on original variables.

If estimates of communalities (less than 1)[4] are placed in the principal diagonal,[5] factor scores can only be estimated, that is, not precisely calculated. One estimation formula is F=ZR-1A, WHERE F IS A MATRIX OF FACTOR SCORES, Z IS A MATRIX OF SCORES ON THE ORIGINAL VARIABLES IN STANDARD SCORE[6] FORM, R-1 IS THE INVERSE OF A MATRIX OF INTERCORRELATIONS AMONG VARIABLES,[7] AND A IS THE FACTOR STRUCTURE MATRIX. This formula yields scores for both the orthogonal and oblique[8] cases. In this connection it is necessary to distinguish between factor pattern and factor structure. Factor structure refers to the correlations of the original variables with the factors, while factor pattern refers to the coefficients assigned to the factors in predicting the original scores. It is the factor structure, not the factor pattern, which is employed in this formula, when the factors are oblique. It does not matter which is employed in the orthogonal case because, in such a case, factor pattern and factor structure coincide. If the original scores are correlated with the factor scores, using this formula, they usually come close but do not perfectly agree with the factor structure. That

PROJECT THEORY:

INTERPRETATIONS AND POLICY RELEVANCE

Jack E. Vincent
Department of Political Science
Florida Atlantic University

University Press of America, Inc.™
4710 Auth Place, S.E., Washington D.C. 20023

Printed in the United States of America

ISBN: 0-8191-0551-1

Library of Congress Catalog Card Number: 78-59172

is, such factor scores predict the original variable almost to the extent they should, as given by the factor structure. How far off they are becomes an empirical question and depends upon the magnitude of the communalities. As they approach unity, such correlations come closer and closer to the factor structure.

If unities are placed in the principal diagonal, factor scores may be calculated precisely (orthogonal case) and have the quality of predicting the original variables exactly to the extent they load on the factors. A proper formula is F = ZA (A'A)-1, WHERE F IS A MATRIX OF FACTOR SCORES, Z IS A MATRIX OF SCORES ON THE ORIGINAL VARIABLES IN STANDARD SCORE FORM, A IS A MATRIX OF FACTOR COEFFICIENTS (LOADINGS).

This formula applies to both the unrotated and rotated cases. In the unrotated case, A refers to the unrotated matrix of loadings, and in the rotated case, the rotated matrix of loadings. In the unrotated case, the mathematical operation for one case is equivalent to multiplying each z-score for a subject by the appropriate variable loadings, given in the factor matrix for a particular factor, summing, and then dividing the obtained quantity by the variance explained (sum of column entries squared) by the factor. In the rotated case, the procedure is more complicated because A'A does not, as in the unrotated case, produce a diagonal matrix. That is, values other than 0 occur as entries off the principal diagonal and these affect the magnitude of the factor score as well as the variance explained, given in the principal diagonal. In both cases, however, the scores have exactly the same properties after calculation, that is, they are standardized, they predict the original variables exactly to the extent that the variables load on the factors and they are uncorrelated.

Variable selection.

The justification for the inclusion of a certain number of variables in a factor analysis, out of the potential universe of available variables, usually varies somewhat from one investigator to another.

It should be understood, in this connection, that the size of a factor, in terms of variance explained,[9] is a direct function of the degree to which the original variables correlate with one another. For example, say three factor dimensions emerge from the study of a number of variables, that is, the dimensions of "development," "authoritarianism," and "U.S. relations." If most of the variables loaded heavily (average .90) on "development," it would explain most of the original variance. If the second largest number of variables loaded heavily (same average) on "authoritarianism," it would explain the second most variance, and so forth. It should be apparent that either of the second two dimensions could be made "most important" simply by variable manipulation. For example, newspaper circulation, radios per 1,000 population, number of inhabitants per physician, per cent literate in population, per capita gross national product, and similar variables tend to load very heavily on a "development dimension," which emerges from a number of studies. If all of the heavy loading variables except one, say, newspaper circulation, were dropped from a "modified study," then "development" would emerge as a very weak factor, "authoritarianism" would become the most important factor, "U.S. relations" the second most important, and, of course, "development" the third most important. Similarly, if a number of variables loading heavily on "authoritarianim," such as competitive electoral system, representativeness of the regime, freedom of group opposition, and so forth, were dropped, leaving only one or two political indices, authoritarianism would drop greatly in importance, and U.S. relations would now emerge as the "most important" factor.

Put in these terms, then, even the smallest factors can have considerable "importance" in the sense of allowing understanding of the original correlation matrix. This is because the factor analysis is telling us, in the case of the smaller factors, that the variables that load on them do not correlate well with any of the other variables in the analysis, although those on the same dimension correlate fairly well with each other if their loadings are quite high. Further, if only one variable loads heavily on a dimension, the analysis indicates that this single variable correlates poorly with all of the other variables considered. As predictors, such "small" factors may be extremely important. This is why factor scores are frequently computed for all the rotated dimensions.

Factor loadings.

If a researcher has used the principal components solution of factor analysis, the result will be an unrotated factor loading matrix where the first factor accounts for the maximum variance that any one factor can account for, the second factor the maximum of the remaining variance, and so forth. If the objective of the analysis is to identify the factor with the greatest predictive power in respect to the original variables, the factor with the second greatest predictive power, etc., this solution can be considered final. That is, the first two or three factors emerging from a battery of 15 or 20 variables could possibly account for something in the order of 70 per cent to 80 per cent of the original variance. The factor analyst, at this point, could compute factor scores and these scores have the property, if unities were placed in the diagonal, that they will predict (explain the variance of) the original variables to the extent of their loadings. For example, if the first variable loaded on the first factor .90, the first factor, that is, factor scores, can account for .90 squared or 81 per cent of the variance of the first variable. In the unrotated matrix loadings tend to be moderately high on the first principal component, less high on the second principal component, and so forth, until, depending on how far out the principal components are computed, the loadings may become very small. The predictive power of the last principal component in respect to the heaviest loading variable might be something on the order of 5 per cent of the variance of the variables, or less. Because of this, many researchers feel that it is desirable to rotate the factors in such a way that each has important predictive power for at least one or more of the variables.

Rotation may be thought of as an effort to realign the factors through closely related clusters of variables. At first, rotation was accomplished through analytical and graphic techniques that incorporated subjective evaluations on the part of the investigator. The first completely objective technique was developed by Carroll in 1953 and is referred to as the quartimax method.

One of the main limitations of the quartimax technique is its tendency to develop a general factor and to simplify rows rather than columns. Dissatisfactions with this solution led Kaiser in 1958 to develop the varimax technique which is based on an effort to maximize the sum of the squares of the columns.

Oblique solutions which have been developed include oblimax, quartimin, covarimin, biquartimin, and direct oblimin. Each criterion yields somewhat different results. For example, in comparing quartimin, biquartimin, and covarimin, the quartimin solution tends to produce the most oblique factors, biquartimin somewhat less oblique factors, and covarimin the least oblique factors, when used on the same data.

The selection of one of these various technique depends in part upon the research needs of the investigator. Depending on the data input, all techniques may lead to fairly similar or divergent results. For example, rotation to an oblique solution may still leave the factors basically uncorrelated. The primary value of oblique rotation is that it may reduce the number of moderate loadings more than orthogonal rotation. In short, oblique rotation offers the possibility of even simpler structure than it is possible to achieve in the case of orthogonal rotation. The primary difficulty of oblique rotation concerns the possible problem of using correlated factor scores in further analysis.

The value of uncorrelated predictor variables.

One of the principal (possible) values of factor analysis is to reduce correlated variables into a set of uncorrelated variables or factor scores. Uncorrelated factor scores are highly desirable in two ways. First, if such scores are correlated with some third variable, the variance explained in each case is known to be unique. Say, for example, a factor analysis yields two uncorrelated factor dimensions which we label "development" and "democracy." If factor scores are calculated and the two sets are correlated with another variable, say, "number of riots, " we know that any variance accounted for by "democracy" cannot be accounted for by "development" and vice versa. This will not be the case if the predictors are correlated, that is, are redundant. In this case the predictors may be "explaining" the same variance in the dependent variable.

Second, uncorrelated scores facilitate the use of techniques such as multiple regression analysis and canonical[10] correlation.[11] If correlated variables are inserted, in either case, interpretation can become difficult.

All of this is to say that orthogonal rotation has many advantages over oblique rotation when the purpose is to use factor scores as variables in further analysis.

Communalities.

After a factor analysis has been performed, the term communality refers to the amount of variance explained in a variable by all of the factors taken collectively. The communality for a particular variable may be computed by squaring its loading on each of the factors and summing the results. If the communality for a variable equals .75, this means that seventy-five per cent of the information in the variable is contained within the factors and twenty-five per cent is not.

The factor analysis.

In line with the above discussion, the purpose here is to create an orthogonal set of factor scores from the original attribute variables (144 in number), based on Kaiser's varimax criterion and using a 1.0 eigenvalue cut-off.[12]

Variable selection for a-space construction.

The variables of a-space were taken, for the most part, from the

Cross-Polity Time Series (Banks, 1971) and the World Handbook of Political and Social Indicators (Taylor and Hudson, 1971). The exact variable list will shortly. Variables were selected on the following grounds: first, they had to clearly pertain to the attributes of states. Second, the information (total collection used) was required to be 90% complete. Where information was missing, or ambiguous, regression estimates were used. The regression estimate routine employed searches the entire collection of variables to find that variable on which the subject has information most closely related to the variable on which the information is missing. Simple regression is then used to estimate the missing value. Since many variables had skewed distributions, a rank transformation was also employed. Thus, number sequences, such as 1 3 7, were changed to sequences such as 1 2 3. This transformation gives basic agreement between the mean and median of a distribution, so that there are as many cases above the mean as below it.

Results.

The following presents an analysis of the rotated loadings of a-space. That is, a-space was generated by factor analyzing 144 attribute variables, which resulted in 22 factors. The 22 factor loadings are listed with the variable names. For example, total population loads -.23 on the first factor. The last entry or the 23rd indicates the communality. In the case of total population the communality is .95. This means that 95% of the variance of total population is accounted for by the 22 factors. The entry, column sums of squares, gives the amount of variance explained by each factor in aggregate variance terms. For example, the first factor accounts for 31.17 -units of variance out of the 144 possible units of variance. All column sums of squares exceed 1.0 because a 1.0 eigenvalue cut-off was employed.

Following the column sums of squares analysis, each factor is named and variable loadings .49 or larger on each factor are grouped and presented in order of decending magnitude. For example, national government revenue per capita is the largest positive loading on the factor of economic development. This means that .92 squared or 85 percent of the variance of national government revenue per capita is accounted for by the factor of economic development. A nation with a high factor score on this factor, then, would tend to have high scores on all of the positively loading variables and low scores on the negatively loading variables. A similar interpretation pertains for the remaining factors. For example, states scoring high on power base tend to have high scores in respect to total primary school enrollment, total school enrollment, total population etc. In case of a factor, such as factor 4, non-competitive political system, which has all negative loadings, interpretation should be equally as clear. In this case, a state with a high factor score tends to have low scores in respect to aggregate competition index, party legitimacy, competitiveness of nominating process, legislative effectiveness, etc.

Put table 1 about here., I 1

The above analysis, then, shows the variable clusters generated by the factor analysis. To determine where a state stands in respect to these clusters the factor scores were computed (F=ZA(A'A)-1 formula).

The following presents an analysis of the a-space factor scores, with a rank sort on three of the factors.

Put table 2 about here., I 2

As explained above, after the loadings of a-space are computed, they are used, in conjunction with the subjects original standardized scores on the variables to generate the factor scores. For example, Afghanistan has a factor score of -.97 on the first factor. Since the first factor is economic development, this indicates that Afghanistan is below the system average in respect to its economic development in the sense that we predict that Afghanistan will have low scores on the positive loading variables on this factor, and high scores on the negative loading variables. That is, compared to other states, Afghanistan should have low national government revenue per capita, low national government expenditure per capita, low imports per capita, low gross national product per capita in U.S. dollars, a high percentage of gross domestic product originating in agriculture, a late beginning year of modernization and high crude birth rates, 1960. A check on Afghanistan's actual scores, in this respect, shows that the predictions are accurate.

After the block listings of the scores, they are sorted for three factors in terms of decending magnitude. Thus, the prediction (for economic development) of high scores on positively loading variables and low scores for negatively loading variables is most pertinant for states such as Kuwait, Iceland, Luxumbourg, New Zealand, Australia and so forth. As factor scores move towards 0, we expect average variable scores, that is, 0, when such variables are standardized, considering the heavily loading variables. In the case of the large negative factor scores, for states like India, Pakistan, Nigeria, Ethiopia and Indonesia, we make a prediction opposite to that for the states with large positive scores. Such states tend to have low scores on positive loading variables and high scores on negative loading variables.

Some may question why the United States does not stand higher on the economic development factor. It should be understood that these scores predict the variables to the extent of their loadings and are the best possible solution, to account for a variable cluster, in variance explained terms, given the restraints of requiring orthogonal factors and rotation according to Kaiser's varimax criterion. In other words, there is no other way of assigning the factor scores, given these restraints, if the factor scores are to predict the original variables to the extent of their loadings. The only way national government revenue per capita can correlate .92 with these factor scores is to make these factor score assignments, if the factor loadings are to remain the same in the remainder of the analysis.

Since these factors express the information contained in the original 144 variables with the fewest possible dimensions in orthogonal terms, (1.0 eigenvalue cut-off) we can look at these scores as a rearrangement of the original information with some information loss. In this particular case, 15% of the original information was lost. That is, when we correlate the 22 sets of factor scores with the original variables the aggregate variance explained by the factors in the variables is 15% less than the aggregate variance originally contained within the variables. Instead of 144 original variables, which have highly confusing interrelationships, which make subsequent analysis extremely difficult, we have, instead, 22 factors retaining 85 percent of the original information. Since the factors are mutually orthogonal they cannot have, by definition, confusing interrelationships. The factors can be used, in place of the original information, for numerous types of analyses of the international relations system.

Uses.

The value of the above analysis can be demonstrated by asking five hypothetical questions, and then answering them in terms of the results.

1. In respect to the variable cluster, economic development, which state stands higher Great Britain or France? Answer: Great britain stands slightly higher (.98 vs. 95). 2. Are both above the system average? Answer: Yes, the system average is 0. 3. Is East Germany above or below the system average in respect to the variable cluster "power base"? Answer: It is considerable above the system average (1.20). 4. How does Sweden compare with France in respect to the variable cluster "non-competitive political system"? Answer: Sweden has a more competitive political system than France (Sweden = -1.08, France = -.74). 5. Are both different from the system average? Answer: Yes, they are quite different, the system average = 0.

Many questions of this type can be posed and answered quickly and conveniently by examination of the above tables.

What other uses does this type of analysis facilitate? In many studies a researcher must work with the sample rather than the universe of states. He is frequently in the dark, however, in respect to knowing whether or not the the sample deviates significantly from the universe, in respect to key characteristics, such as attributes. If attributes are a concern, this can be ascertained by correlating the factor scores, given above, for the sample. To the extent that the correlations depart from 0, the sample is not representative of the universe of states treated in this study. Thus, the first step in any kind of sampling problem in the mid-60's, where attributes are a concern could be to simply correlate the factor scores generated in this study, for the sample, to answer the "representativeness" issue, at least in respect to attributes.

The factor scores can also be used to predict other international relations phenomena. As explained above, since the factor score are orthogonal, a considerable simplification in analytical procedures can be obtained. In fact, simple correlation analysis can generate all of the information and predictive statements that multiple correlation analysis is capable of generating. Obviously, if a researcher intends to factor analysis attribute variables, he can save himself a great deal of time by simply using the factor scores presented here, since they represent state standing, for this time period, on a larger group of variables than any other study presently published.

An illustration.

To illustrate such usage, the scores will be used to predict WEIS (McClelland, 1972) conflict data spanning, basically, the same years as the attribute data.

WEIS data construction.

See Paper 2 discussion, Inserts 3,9

The above factor scores of a-space were then correlated with the WEIS data to complete the analytical steps for the illustrative example.

Put table 5 about here., I 4

In this table all correlations above .23 are significant at the .01 level.

The following generalizations, then, are in order. The higher the power base, per capita school enrollment, energy production, domestic violence and military personnel and the smaller the Christian community, the higher the total conflict score tends to be. Because the predictors are orthogonal factor scores, the square of each correlation defines the unique variance explained, ie., that variance explained by power base is not also explained by few military personnel per capita and the total of all the correlation squares is equal to R square, which in this case is equal to .38. In other words, all the predictors together account for 38% of the variance of the total conflict scores. One might note the simplicity of this interpretation compared to the obvious difficulties that would arise in attempting to correlate the original variables with the total conflict scores, instead of the factor scores.

It is interesting that these findings raize doubts concerning McGowan and Shapiro's Proposition 29 "there is little or no relationship between various national attributes, taken together, and a state's foreign conflict and cooperation behavior."(1973:98) Also, domestic violence is found, here, to be associated with total conflict in apparent contradiction to Proposition 15 " there is little or no relationship between domestic conflict and foreign conflict at one point in time."(1973:79). On the other hand, these findings support Proposition 26 "there is no correlation between the degree of democracy or autocracy and the violent foreign conflict behavior of a state."(1973:94), Proposition 27 "there is a positive relationship between the military power of a state and its foreign conflict behavior."(1973:95) and Proposiition 28 "a nation's length of independence is not related to its foreign conflict behavior."(1973:97)

It is suggested that various studies along such lines can be developed, although the purpose at this point is to illustrate rather to complete an extensive analysis in respect to such behavioral data.

Summary.

The purpose of this analysis was to locate states on the dimensions of a-space as determined by variables measured in the mid-1960's. Such an analysis has several advantages. First, it can answer a host of questions about the relationships of states to one another, and, to the system, in terms of primary variable clusters, such as "economic development." Second, a researcher using a sample of states in this time period can use the factor scores generated to determine the degree to which the sample is representative (in respect to attributes). If the sample factor scores deviate significantly from 0, the sample is not representative of the universe. Third, the factor scores can be used in attribute based studies focusing on the mid-1960's. For example, they can be used to predict conflict or cooperation data. A sample analysis, focusing on WEIS data, was presented in this regard.

NOTES

(1). The assistance of Jim Slitor, Wes Kranitz and Carol Jones was greatly appreciated.

(2). An orthogonal factor analysis refers to one where the resulting factors are uncorrelated. If the factors are thought of as vectors, the vectors are at right angles (90 degrees) in the space.

(3). The principal components factor loadings of a correlation matrix may be computed by the formula: L = V'S, WHERE L IS A MATRIX OF PRINCIPAL COMPONENTS LOADINGS, V IS AN ORTHOGONAL EIGENVALUE MATRIX OF THE CORRELATION MATRIX R, AND S IS A DIAGONAL MATRIX CONSISTING OF THE SQUARE ROOT OF THE EIGENVALUES OF R.

(4). See the treatment of communalities below.

(5). The principal diagonal of a square matrix are those elements which lie on the diagonal from the upper left hand corner to the lower right hand corner.

(6). See the discusion of z-scores in Paper 5.

(7). Every variable is correlated with every other variable as a starting point of a factor analysis. The resulting matrix is called the correlation matrix and it is a square, symmetric matrix having as many rows or columns as there are variables in the analysis. Since variables correlate perfectly with themselves, it has unities (1.0's) in the principal diagonal. Hence, the trace of the correlation matrix is equal to the number of variables in the analysis.

(8). An oblique factor analysis refers to one where the resulting factors can be correlated. If the factors are thought of as vectors, oblique analysis allows them to assume some angle other than a right angle, i.e., 90 degrees.

(9). The variance explained by a factor in a factor analysis may be ascertained by squaring the loadings on the dimension and then summing them. That is, computing V = SUM A SQUARED, WHERE V IS THE VARIANCE EXPLAINED AND A ARE THE LOADINGS ON A DIMENSION. The number of the variables treated in the analysis is then divided into this figure to arrive at the percentage of variance explained by that factor, i.e., V/N, WHERE V IS THE VARIANCE EXPLAINED BY THE FACTOR DIMENSION AND N IS THE NUMBER OF VARIABLES IN THE ANALYSIS. The variance explained by each factor can be summed to determine the total variance explained in the factor analysis, that is, T = SUM V, WHERE T IS THE TOTAL VARIANCE EXPLAINED IN THE ANALYSIS AND V IS THE VARIANCE EXPLAINED BY EACH FACTOR DIMENSION. For example, if the variance explained totals to 80 per cent, this means that 80 per cent of the original information is contained within the factors but 20 per cent is not.

(10). The purpose of multiple regression is to predict the values on a single dependent variable from more than one predictor variable. To simplify the discussion, it will be assumed that all data is in the form of z-scores. If D is the dependent variable and Y is the variable of predicted values, the solution to a multiple regression problem minimizes the expression: SUMMATION (D-Y) SQUARED. Thus, the smaller of the square differences between the predicted values and the dependent variable, the better the prediction. The Y in this expression is computed by the equation: Y is the sum vector of PB WHERE Y = THE PREDICTED VALUES, B = THE REGRESSION COEFFICIENTS AND P = THE PREDICTORS. In other words, each predictor is weighted to minimize the expression (D-Y)SQUARED. The weights are found by:

$B_{1XN} = C_{1XN} \, R^{-1}_{NXN}$, WERE B = A ROW VECTOR OF REGRESSION COEFFICIENTS, C = A ROW VECTOR OF CORRELATIONS OF THE PREDICTORS WITH THE DEPENDENT VARIABLE AND R = AN INTERCORRELATION MATRIX OF THE PREDICTORS. It can be seen, then, that all that is necessary to produce the weights for a multiple regression is an intercorrelation matrix of the predictors and a vector of correlations of the predictors with the dependent variable. When only one variable, as in this study, is used on the dependent side, multiple regression and canonical correlation yield the same results.

(11). A canonical correlation analysis assigns weights to two sets of variables so that the scores generated from the two sets are maximally correlated. The canonical variate scores themselves, for one set, can be computated by the formula C = SW,

WHERE C IS AN N X 1 VECTOR OF CANONICAL VARIATE SCORES, S IS AN N X M MATRIX OF SUBJECTS' STANDARD SCORES ON THE ORIGINAL VARIABLES, AND W IS A M X 1 VECTOR OF CANONICAL WEIGHTS, WHERE N = SUBJECT AND M = VARIABLES.

This formula is given here to make clear the meaning of canonical variate scores. The actual calculation of the weights, of course, is the solution to the basic canonical problem, which is to maximally correlate two such sets of scores, one generated from one set of variables and the other generated from the other set of variables. When weights are calculated where this is the case, the canonical variate scores predict the original variables to the extent of their loadings, if the original variables are mutually orthogonal in each set. Like factor scores, a great deal of information can be summarized by properly computed canonical variate scores.

If correlated data are used, then the individual importance of the predictors is not clear by examination of canonical weights, for the same reasons as in the application of multiple regression. That is, the weights are assigned so that only unique variance is considered. If the variables are uncorrelated, however, weights will be equal to the correlation of the variables with the canonical variate scores.

Although only one set of weights is likely to produce exactly the same maximal correlation, nevertheless, different weighting schemes may produce more than one statistically significant canonical correlation. When additional correlations are produced through different weighting schemes, they are subjected to the restriction that the subjects' canonical variate scores must be orthogonal to all previously calculated canonical variate scores. Thus, if two significant canonical correlations are produced, the canonical variate scores in the second canonical correlation will have a zero correlation with the canonical variate scores of the first canonical correlation. If statistical significance is ignored, there can be as many canonical correlations as there are variables in the smallest set, and thus, as many sets of canonical variate scores as there are variables in the smallest set.

(12). The eigenvalues of a symmetric matrix S may be defined as, E = VSV' WHERE E IS A DIAGONAL MATRIX OF EIGENVALUES, AND V IS AN ORTHOGONAL MATRIX OF EIGENVECTORS. The computation of eigenvalues is frequently the first step in advanced statistical applications such as factor analysis.

The eigenvectors of matrix A are given by the expression, (A-E)V = 0, WHERE A IS A SQUARE MATRIX, E IS THE DIAGONAL MATRIX OF EIGENVALUES AND V IS A MATRIX COMPOSED OF EIGENVECTORS. That is, when the matrix E is subtracted from A, the eigenvector matrix is that matrix which, if premultiplied by A - E equals a vector of zeros. In this connection, using a matrix of zeros for V is viewed as trivial solution. Eigenvalues have considerable value in many kinds of applications. For example, the eigenvalues of a correlation matrix are scaled to produce the principal component's loadings matrix in factor analysis.

CREATING INDEXES FOR NATIONAL CONFLICT AND COOPERATION EXPORTATIONS (1966-1969) WITH AN EMPIRICAL APPLICATION

By: Jack E. Vincent
Professor of Political Science
Florida Atlantic University
Boca Raton, Florida 33432

CREATING INDEXES FOR NATIONAL CONFLICT AND COOPERATION EXPORTATIONS (1966-69) WITH AN EMPIRICAL APPLICATION.[1]

Introduction.

One important concern of international relation scholars centers around patterns of national conflict and cooperation. For example, many of McGowan and Shapiro's (1973) collection of propositions about international relations utilize these concepts.[2]

One problem, however, has been the lack of comparability across studies, (different n's, different data sources, different time periods, different variables). At least part of the problem seems to stem from what one might call a research focus on specific acts as opposed to general acts. Usually when one thinks of conflict and cooperation one, in fact, thinks of a general propensity over time, although such a general propensity can be obviously illustrated by specific acts of the type usually contained in data collections. In the WEIS (McClelland, 1972) collection, for example, many nations have been scored as either doing or not doing some cooperative or conflictual act, such as extending aid or issuing a threat. A problem in building generalizations from this collection, however, due to the specific focus, is that the majority of states tend to have 0 scores regardless of what category is picked. Such scores, if used in correlational analyses, then, are highly non-normal and most entries are 0. In recognition of this problem, the WEIS scholars have attempted to develop somewhat more general categories by grouping highly similar acts resulting in 12 classifications of conflict and 8 classifications of cooperation. These are:

Put table 1 about here., I 3

Such variables are still basically full of "holes" in the sense that 0 is the most frequently obtained observation. This occurs even if one sums over a substantial time period. To illustrate, we will examine U.S. conflict for the years 1966-1969.

Put table 2 about here., I 5 (101 Is Afghanistan, 201 is Albania and so forth; see nation order in table 3.)

It can be seen that even though the U.S. is one of the most active exporters of conflict in the international system, the matrix is still basically 0's. One way to obtain fewer 0 entries in a final measure of conflict or cooperation is to reduce the matrix to a vector by weighting each of the categories according to the magnitude of conflict or cooperation. To accomplish this, 30 university scholars and graduate students were asked to evaluate each category of conflict and cooperation on a scale ranging from 1-5, with 5 indicating the most intensity.[3]

When such weights are applied to the conflict data for the United States, the following results are obtained:

Put table 3 about here., I 6

If we examine the results for less active actors such as Czechoslovakia, we obtain:

Put table 4 about here., I 7

Thus, in spite of the fact that the three year period is being considered and 12 categories of conflict have been summed the vectors, in both cases, still have a large percentage of O's. Also, comparing table 3 with table 4, although it is clear the U.S. exported more conflict than Czechoslovakia, their exact relative standing is not very clear and one can well imagine attempting to compare 128 such vectors, one for each state, and attempting to arrive at conclusions. It was decided, therefore, to carry the summation process one step further. Since each act has been weighted, according to intensity, it would seem permissable to sum the entries in the vectors to arrive at a general propensity score, which can then be used to compare each state with every other state.

To obtain this final index, then, the following steps were followed: (1) Each state's scores were tabulated over the three-year period, 1966-69, for 12 conflict categories and 8 cooperation categories; (2) Each conflict and cooperation matrix was reduced to a conflict and cooperation vector by weighting each category in terms of an intensity score; (3) Each entry in each of the conflict and cooperation vectors was summed for each state. When all of the above steps are taken, the following indexes were created.

Put table 5 about here., I 8

Put table 6 about here., I 9

We are now in a position to generalize (in terms of WEIS data

1966-69) about conflict and cooperation exportation. The 25 most conflict exporting states are:

Put table 7 about here., I 10

The 25 most cooperation exporting states are:

Put table 8 about here., I 11

The 25 least conflict exporting states are:

Put table 9 about here., I 12

The least cooperation exporting states are:

Put table 10 about here., I 13

Since a number of states are similar in both lists in respect to having high conflict and high cooperation or low conflict and low cooperation, the question arises to whether there is a considerable correlation between the scores (conflict vs. cooperation). The answer is yes r =.68, $p < 001$. Thus, an important finding in this study is that, for the time period considered, conflict and cooperation, as general propensities, tend to co-vary.

Use of the scales.

There are several uses for the above scales. First there is the possibility of classification and description. Numerous questions can be answered in such terms. Consider the followng kinds of questions: Is Cambodia more conflictual than Laos in the time period considered? The answer is yes (286 vs. 111). Is Pakistan more conflictual than India? The answer is no (India's score equals 306, Pakistan's score equals 81). Is Brazil more conflictual than Mexico? The answer is yes (66 vs. 15).

Hundreds, perhaps thousands, of questions of this type, can be answered by examination of the tables. These scales can now serve to stimulate further research for studies focusing on conflict and cooperation, in the time period considered. To illustrate this, a discriminant function analysis will be performed, comparing the national attributes of the 25 most active exporters with the national attributes of the least active exporters. In order to do this, various attribute variables were selected for the discriminant analysis. Because of their large number, they were factor analyzed.

Constructing the attribute scales.

See Paper 1 discussion, Insert 1

Discriminant function analysis.

With the above steps completed, the subject's attribute factor scores were divided in the following way: 25 most active vs. 25 least active (conflict) and 25 most active vs. 25 least active (cooperation).

The purpose of discriminant function analysis, which follows, is to determine, when considering two different groups, scored on a common group variables (in this case their attributes), which of the variables best discriminates between the groups. This is done by giving each group member a discriminant function score, which is a function of the original variables weighted so that the mean of the discriminant function scores, for each group, is maximally different. Correlations of the original variables with the discriminant function scores reveals which variables are the best discriminators. For example, if economic development correlates .60 with the discriminant function scores of a particular analysis, say, conflict, this would mean that those with high conflict tend to be developed states and those with low conflict underdeveloped states.

A side product of discriminant function analysis is an f-test of the means, of the two groups considered, on the original variables. In the above example, if the mean of the high conflict states is compared with the mean of the low conflict states in respect to economic development. The mean of the former might be .35, indicating that the high conflict group is above the system average in respect to economic development, while the low conflict states might have a score of -.12, indicating that the low conflict states are below the system average in respect to development. Such an analysis is distinct from discriminant function analysis since the discriminant function analysis tests the significance of the difference of the means between the two groups, in respect to the discriminant function scores, while the f-test tests the significant of the means between the two groups on the original variables. In this connection, it should be clear that the discriminant function scores are a composite index utilizing all of the variables. The discriminant results are given in the following table.

Put table 12 about here., I 14

Focusing on the centroid analysis first (the centroid is the mean of the groups discriminant function scores), it can be seen that the two groups are significantly different (p is less than .0000) and that the mean of the high conflict group is 1.19 while the mean of the low conflict group is -1.03. The variables with the highest correlation with the discriminant function scores are power base (correlation = .76, high power is associated with high conflict, mean = .78, and low power with low conflict, mean = -.83); non-competitive political system (correlation = .36, non-competitive political system is associated with high conflict, mean = .48, and competitive political system is associated with low conflict, mean = -.25); little domestic violence (correlation = -.52, much domestic violence is associated with high conflict, mean = -.31, and little domestic violence is associated with low conflict, mean = .69); few military personnel per capita (correlation = -.35, many military personnel is associated with high conflict, mean = -.76, fewer military personnel is associated with low conflict, mean = .02); little ethno-linguistic fractionalization (correlation = .34, little ethno-linguistic fractionalization is associated with high conflict, mean = .36, and much ethnolinguistic fractionalization is associated with low conflict, mean = -.31). All individual mean differences are significant at the .025 level or less.

We may now examine the actual discriminant function scores that the above analysis generated.

Put table 13 about here., I 15

Usually, in a discriminant function analysis, mis-classification analysis is an important aspect of the investigation. This would occur, in this case, if some of the high exporters received scores or some of the low exporters received + scores. It can be seen, however, that the two groups are completely separated in this analysis, in +, - terms. It should be recognized, however, that the discriminant function score is computed from all of the variables and so it is possible that some of the states do not possess the expected characteristics (for example, the U.S., in fact, stands low on non-competitive political system, ie., has a competitive system). In general, however, the above stated characteristics are those that separate the two groups and, as can be seen, the most salient discriminator is power base.

Table 14 gives the results for cooperation.

Put table 14 about here., I 16

The centroid in the case of high cooperation is 1.2 and for low cooperation is -.98. Again, the difference in means is significant at the .0000 level or less. The variables with the highest correlation with the discriminant function scores are: power base (correlation = .88, high power is associated with high cooperation, mean = 1.1, and low power is associated with low cooperation, mean = -.97); small Christian community (correlation = .31, small Christian community is associated with high cooperation, mean = .14, and large Christian community is associated with low cooperation, mean = -.41); little domestic violence (correlation = -.35, much domestic violence is associated with high cooperation, mean= -.32, and little domestic violence is associated with low cooperation, mean = .34). All mean differences are significant at the .04 level or less.

It can be seen that two of the discriminators that were important for conflict, power base and little domestic violence, remain important for cooperation. However, a new predictor, small Christian community, is elevated to importance for cooperation. Also, non-competitive political system, few military personnel per capita and little ethno-linguistic fractionalization drop out as important discriminators. With the exception of power base and little domestic violence, then, there is not a strong correspondence between the discriminators for conflict and cooperation, when the 25 most active nations are compared with the 25 least active nations. This occurs inspite of the strong correlation of the conflict and cooperation vectors. On the other hand, the most significant discriminator, power base is related in the same way in both cases, ie., high power is associated with high exportation whether one is considering conflict or cooperation.

Again, it may be of interest to examine the actual discriminant function scores.

Put table 15 about here., I 17

Again, perfect boundaries exist between the two groups in +, - terms. Returning to McGowan and Shapiro's (1973: 79-98) most relevant propositions, referred to at the begining of the paper, we may conclude that the following propositions were not supported by this data (when the basis of comparison is the 25 most active verses the 25 least active exporters, measured by WEIS 1966-69 data): Proposition 29 "there is little or no relationship between various national attributes, taken together, and a state's foreign conflict and cooperation behavior." Proposition 15 "there is little or no relationship between domestic conflict and foreign conflict at one point in time." Proposition 26 "there is no correlation between the degree of democracy or autocracy and the violent foreign conflict behavior of a state." That is, significant relationships do appear for these variables in this study.[4] On the other hand, Proposition 27 appears supported. "There is a positive relationship between the military power of a state and its foreign conflict behavior." In fact, power base appears to be the prime discriminator between the groups for both conflict and cooperation. Power base seems to be a crucial "activity factor" for conflict-cooperation, at least on this data set.

Summary.

The purpose of this study was to create indexes for conflict and cooperation to facilitate the work of scholars who wish to study such phenomena, as a a general propensity, in the years 1966-69. The indexes were created by summing all acts in the WEIS data collection 1966-69, for each category of conflict and cooperation, weighting each category according to its intensity, summing the categories to create conflict and cooperation vectors, and, then, summing the entries within these vectors to create the final general conflict and cooperation scores. This allowed the classification of natonal actors in terms of their exportations of conflict and cooperation. The 25 most active and least active nations, in this regard, were presented. One finding was that conflict and cooperation scores tend to co-vary (.68). The various uses to which the scales may be put was illustrated by answering certain hypothetical questions about state conflict and cooperation differences and then exploring, through discriminant function analysis, the relatiomship between national attributes and conflict and cooperation exportations for the 25 most and 25 least active exporters. Key discriminating factors, such as power base, were identified in each case.

Although beyond the resources of this study, future research designs might trace power shifts and correlate such shifts with conflict-cooperation shifts to probe further the possibility that conflict control, in part, might result from power base management. The fact that conflict co-varies with cooperation and both are strongly related to power base, however, suggests that suppression of one (if such conflict control is feasible and attemted) may also suppress the other. It is also possible that large power base states act as "suppressors" in the system for small power base states and, if the power base of the more powerful states were reduced, this might act as a catalyst for higher exportations at lower power base levels.

What this study has establisted, however, in terms of very significant p levels, is that for the time period considered, a real differrence appears to exist between the two most extreme conflict-cooperation (WEIS data) exporting groups. It would seem that any general conflict management schemes would want to take these findings in to account, or, at least, probe further possible relationships, including the possible impact of the other discriminators that may be significantly related.

Notes

(1). The assistance of Jim Slitor, Wes Kranitz and Carol Jones was greatly appreciated.

(2). See, for example, Propositon 29, "There is little or no relationship between various national attributes, taken together, and a state's foreign conflict and cooperation behavior"(p.98). Propositon 15, "There is little or no relationship between domestic conflict and foreign conflict at one point in time"(p.79). Propositon 26, "There is no correlation between the degree of democracy or autocracy and the violent foreign conflict behavior of a state"(p.9). Propositon 27, "There is a positive relationship between the military power of a state and its foreign conflict behavior"(p.95). and Propositiion 28 "A nation's length of independence is not related to its foreign conflict behavior"(p.97).

(3). The average standard error for the judges was .20. Thus, repeated samples should fall into limits of + or .40 around the means reported above, 95% of the time, if repeated samples are taken.

(4). Many of these propositions were generated by studies employing a less extensive data base than was attepted here.

COMPARING VARIOUS ATTRIBUTE BASED THEORIES ON SELECTED DIMENSIONS, IN TERMS OF EMPIRICAL RESULTS

By: Jack E. Vincent

Professor of Political Science

Florida Atlantic University

Boca Raton, Florida 33432

COMPARING VARIOUS ATTRIBUTE-DISTANCE BASED THEORIES, ON SELECTED DIMENSIONS, IN TERMS OF EMPIRICAL RESULTS[1]

Introduction.

Since Rummel first elaborated social field theory, considerable effort has been made to test and further develop attribute-distance based models.[2] So far, the results have been inconclusive.[3] This stems in part from the enormous effort that must be made to test such models for all states since, under the rules by which the models have been developed, each states exportations of behavior are treated separately.[4] Hence, for the entire international relations system, some 130 correlations runs are required for any one application. In view of this, Rummel in his tests has used a sample of 14 dyadic subsets of 13 observations each. That, is Rummel has dealt with 182 dyadic relations (total) per variable in his applications, with the exception of a few major states, and performed 14 correlation analyses (14 dyadic sets of 13 observations each) in his tests. In contrast, this paper treats 16,256 dyadic relations per variable and computes 256 correlational analyses for each theory tested (128 dyadic sets of 127 observations each for both conflict and cooperation).

Before considering findings, it might be wise to go over the basic formulae and some of the major features of attribute based theories, so far developed, and expectations connected with the theories. The theories may be summarized as follows:

Attribute theory.

Attribute theory conceptualizes two collections of variables, a-space variables relating to attributes, and b-space variables relating to behavior. It states that a-space variables, expressed as factor scores[5], should correlate highly with b-space variables.

In formal terms, attribute theory has both a formula and "axioms".

ATTRIBUTE THEORY, FORMULA

A=BW WHERE A=NATION BY BEHAVIOR VECTOR, B=NATION BY FACTOR SCORE MATRIX OF A-SPACE AND W=A LEAST SQUARES SOLUTION OF VECTOR PARAMETER WEIGHTS.

The axioms of attribute theory:

1. International relations is a field consisting of all of the attributes and interactions of nations and their complex interrelationships. 2. The international field can be analytically divided into attribute, a, behavior, b, spaces in which attributes and interactions are projected, respectively, as

vectors. 3. The attribute and behavioral spaces are generated by a finite set of linearly independent dimensions. 4. Nations are located as vectors in attribute and behavior space. 5. The vectors in a-space are forces determining the location of nations in b-space 6. B-space is a subspace of a-space.[6]

Attribute theory, in application, can be conviently summarized through the following figure:

Put figure 1 about here., I 18

The term, monadic, refers to the subjects of study, i.e., individual nations. Thus, when individual nations, such as the United States, are scored on the factor dimensions of a factor analysis of attribute variables, such scores should account for, in correlational terms, the scores generated from an analysis of behaviorial variables.

Various applications have shown that these procedures indeed do yield strong correlational fit, at least on some kinds of data.[7]

This formulation, in a disguised form, can frequently be found in the traditional literature of international relations. Whenever it is argued that one kind of state tends to do one thing and another kind of state another, this is a verbal expression of attribute theory. That is, when traditional literature explains behavior in terms of such factors as differences in economic development, differences in political systems, differences in relationships with the United States, etc., it is actually operating (perhaps unknowingly) within this framework. Traditional approaches, however, generally do not test such assertions in the rigorous way that attribute theory demands. Traditional theoretical statements are usually offered as propositions that are supposed to be true but are actually untested in any kind of precise sense.

Although attribute theory has been of considerable value, once mathematized and concretized, in the sense of specifying fairly exactly the relationships that do exist between attributes and behavior, its very breadth tends to reduce its usefulness. In applications of the theory, all states are treated simultaneously and thus any one state tends to be lost in the broad general picture, as when generating such statements as "developed nations tend to be negative, and underdeveloped positive, in their orientations toward the United Nations."

The remaining theories, through a dyadic approach, facilitate greater understanding of individual nations within the international relations system and, through special techniques, such as applying attribute theory to dyadic results, still allow broad generalizations concerning dyadic behavior.

The first dyadic theory to be discussed will be social field theory.

Social field theory.

Social field theory has as its formula:

SOCIAL FIELD THEORY, FORMULA [8]

S=TW, MODEL 2, WHERE S=DYAD BY BEHAVIOR VECTOR, T=DYAD BY ALGEBRAIC DISTANCE MATRIX OF FACTOR SCORES OF A-SPACE AND W=A LEAST SQUARES SOLUTION OF VECTOR PARAMETER WEIGHTS.

The axioms of social field theory:

1. International relations is a field consisting of all the attributes and interactions of nations and their complex interrelationships. 2. The international relations field can be analytically divided into attribute, a, and behavior, b, spaces into which attributes and interactions are projected, respectively, as vectors. 3. The attribute and behavioral spaces are generated by a finite set of linearly independent dimensions. 4. Nations are located as vectors in attribute space and coupled into dyads in behavior space. 5. The distance vectors in a-space that connect nations are social forces determining location of dyads in b-space. 6. The direction and velocity of movement over time of a dyad in b-space is along the resolution vector of the forces, d. 7. B-space is a subspace of a-space (Rummel, 1969,a: 16).

Again, a diagram may prove useful.

Put figure 2 about here.

It can be seen that in broad outlines social field theory is similar to attribute theory. The primary difference concerns the subjects of study, dyads instead of monads, and the use of distances instead of factor scores (in a-space).

The term, dyad, refers to two nations linked in some way. In b-space, for example, the protests of the United States toward Great Britain would be one value in a distribution of scores for the variable, protests. Another value might be the protests of the United States toward Russia, and so forth. In other other words, a numeric value in b-space represents the behavior of one actor toward another.

In a-space the dyadic value represents the distance between two monadic subjects in respect to their factor scores on some dimension, such as economic development. For example, the distance between the United States and Russia might be +1.0. This would indicate that the United States is more developed than Russia by one unit. That is, if the U.S. development score were +3.0 and Russia's development score were +2.0, the difference between them, 3.0 - 2.0, would equal 1.0. On the other hand, if a state were more developed than the United States, say, with a score of 4.0, the value would become 3.0 - 4.0 = -1.0, indicating that the United States was one unit of development below the state in question.

After the dyadic distances are computed in a-space, on the dimensions of a-space, they are correlated with b-space, using dyads as subjects.

The term, dyadic set, is used to describe a collection of dyadic values in either space. For example, all of the U.S. distances to other states constitutes the U.S. dyadic set in a-space, while all of the U.S. dyadic scores in b-space constitute the U.S. dyadic set of that space. It should be be obvious that there are as many dyadic sets in each space as there are nations treated in the analysis, i.e., a U.S.S.R. dyadic set, a French dyadic set, a Chinese dyadic set, etc.

If all dyadic sets are treated simultaneously in the correlational analyses, such an application is referred to as social field theory, model 1. Since the parameter weights generated through such an analysis (that is, the weights placed on the predictor variables of a-space in an analysis using multiple regression or canonical correlation are a linear function of the weights generated in the same space in attribute theory, using the same data and methods, model 1 is seldom employed.

Model 2 treats each dyadic set taken from each space separately. For example, there is a U.S. dyadic set analysis, a U.S.S.R. dyadic set analysis, a Chinese dyadic set analysis, etc. Through such procedures, parameter weights are allowed to vary from set to set, in contrast to model 1, where parameter weights are generated across all dyadic sets.

Social field theory, as elaborated by Rummel, does not go beyond this point. With the appliction of these procedures, then, each nation will have its own unique predictive equation. Vincent (1973,a), however, has argued that sign models should be employed to generate predictive equations cutting across dyadic sets. This will be more fully developed in the treatment of distance theory

To summarize, social field theory argues that dyadic algebraic distances, computed from the factor scores of a-space, should explain in correlational terms the behavior scores of b-space.

Status-field theory.

Status-field theory, formula.

(Same as for social field theory.)

Status-field theory is actually an amendment to social field theory. It attempts to incorporate status notions, such as those developed by Galtung, to social field theory, by making predictions about likely cooperation and conflict flows (and other matters). Basically, the idea is that nations, as actors with status, tend to relate to each other, at least in part, in status terms (defined by nation location on the factors of economic development and power).[9] Three theorems xave been explored in this regard -- the cooperational theorem, the developed conflict theorem, and the underdeveloped conflict theorem.[10]

Predictions in respect to conflict flows are made clear by the following figure.

Put Figure 3 about here., I 20

In the case of the cooperation theorem, if i is the nation of concern (the nation that is exporting the cooperation) then i's behavior is predicted to vary, depending on whether the j which receives the behavior is above or below i, in respect to status. Rummel has identified economic development and power as the status dimensions. The cooperation theorem argues that on both dimensions, if j is above i, i will export high cooperation, whereas, if j is below i, i will export low cooperation. The basis of Rummel's predictions in this regard are fully treated in "A Status-Field Theory of International Relations" and will not be repeated here.

The conflict theorems are somewhat more complicated, because predictions vary depending on whether i is a developed or underdeveloped actor and whether development or power is considered. In the case of developed i's, it is predicted that i will export low conflict to j's above him, but high conflict to j's that are below him, in respect to development. On the power dimension, the situation is reversed; i is predicted to export high conflict to j's above him and low conflict to j's below him.

The underdeveloped conflict theorem is a mirror image of developed conflict theorem. Underdeveloped i's are expected to export high conflict to j's above them and low conflict to j's below them, in respect to development, but low conflict to j's above them and high conflict to j's below them in respect to power.

Relative status-field theory.

Relative status-field theory, formula[11]

E=FW WHERE E=PARTITIONED DYAD BY BEHAVIOR VECTOR (EITHER TT, UT, TU, UU) F=PARTIONED DYAD BY FACTOR SCORE MATRIX OF A-SPACE AND W=A LEAST SQUARES SOLUTION OF VECTOR PARAMETER WEIGHTS.

Relative status-field theory presents a break with the status-field theory approach to the problem of assessing the impact of status on conflict and cooperation behavior. First, and most important, it calls for the partitioning of dyadic sets and it argues that status relationships ought to be treated in relative terms. In status-field theory, a nation is considered to have high status if it scores high on the economic development and power dimensions.[12] In contrast, in relative status-field theory, it is the relative location of an actor, not the absolute position, that defines status position. Using the notation of t = topdog (high status) and u = underdog (low status), the theory requires that all status configurations, tt (topdog in respect to economic development and power), tu (topdog in respect to economic development and underdog in respect to power), ut (underdog in respect to economic development and topdog in respect to power), and uu (underdog in respect to economic development and power) -be analyzed separately for each dyadic set. For example, in treating the French dyadic set, there is a tt run (all cases where France is topdog in respect to both economic development and power) a tu run (all cases where France is a topdog in economic development but underdog in respect to power) and so forth (for the ut and uu runs). In contrast, status-field theory treats all dyadic distances simultaneously within a dyadic set. In other words, status-field theory does not partition a dyadic set according to the tt, tu, etc., configurations.

When correlational runs are completed in relative status-field theory, across all partitioned dyadic sets, it is argued that the contribution of economic development and power can be assessed by comparing the results against four theoretical models. These are:

Put Figure 4 about here., I 21

The first model indicates that closeness in respect to economic development and power contributes to conflict. In other words, if this model is correct, the United States and Great Britain should experience more conflict (being closer on these dimensions) than the U.S. and Chad, in terms of U.S. exportation of conflict. The second model assumes that distance in respect to economic development and power contributes to conflict. If this model is correct, using the above example, the United States should export more conflict to Chad than it does to Great Britain. The other models can be interpreted in a similar fashion, only closeness on one dimension and farness on the other is assumed to be related to the conflict exportations. For example, considering model 3, if it is correct, the United States is expected to export more conflict to Kuwait (close to the U.S. in respect to economic development, but far from the U.S. in respect to power) than to India (far from the United States in respect to economic development, but fairly close in respect to power, as defined by the power dimension). Under model 4, on the other hand, the United States is predicted to export more conflict to India than to Kuwait.

Each of these models can be converted into equations which take into account the partitioning of the dyadic sets. For example, in the case of model 1, the equations are:

Put Figure 5 about here., I 22

The above equations indicate parameter signs if model 1 is correct. In the tt-uu run, for example, where i is topdog in respect to economic development and power relative to j's that are underdogs on these dimensions, the sign should be negative in both cases, with A = PARAMETER WEIGHT, E = ECONOMIC DEVELOPMENT, AND P = POWER. On the uu-tt run, however, the sign should be positive if the model is correct. The reasons for these sign predictors for model 1 are made clear from the following discusion.

Sign predictions for relative status-field theory can best be understood if we begin with the nature of the distance measure in status-field theory. It should be apparent from the basic distance formula (algebraic substraction) that when distance scores are computed, j's above i receive negative scores (indicating i is below those j's) and j's below i receive positive scores (indicating i is above those j's). If such a measure is highly correlated with the standardized conflict measure and the correlation is positive this means that the j's above i will have little conflict exportation from i (minuses go with minuses) and j's below i receive much conflict exportation from i (pluses go with pluses). If the correlation is negative, the opposite is, of course, true; above j's will be predicted to receive much conflict from i (minuses go with pluses) and j's below i should receive little conflict exportation from i (pluses go with minuses).

Applications of relative status-field theory can be understood in much the same terms. For example, if we were dealing with a u run (a partition where i is an underdog) we can think of the correlation in the following terms:

Put Figure 6 about here., I 23

A positive correlation implies that those close to i will receive much conflict from i and those distant from i (with large negative scores) will receive little conflict from i. At first this may seem puzzling. Such a prediction can be understood if it is seen that from a correlational perspective, little negative numbers (after standardization) become large positive numbers, while large negative numbers will remain large and negative. Thus, from a correlational point of view, when the correlation is positive, large negatives go with large negatives, and large positives go with large positives. This is why it is asserted that j's close to i will be predicted to have much conflict and j's distant from i (large negative numbers) will be predicted to have little conflict. In the case of a negative correlation the opposite is predicted, j's far from i should receive much conflict from i and j's close to i, little conflict. It can now be seen why in model 1, u runs are assigned a positive parameter weight. This is another way of saying that conflict is expected to increase as j approaches i in distance terms.

In the case of the t run, where i is topdog to the j's, the correlational relationship may be depicted as:

Put Figure 7 about here., I 24

A positive correlation implies j's far from i will receive the most conflict, while j's close to i the least conflict. Again, it must be understood that the small positive numbers become large negative numbers after standardization. Such numbers, indicating that the j's are close to i, will be associated with small conflict scores, indicating little conflict under a situation of positive correlation. Large positive j's, on the other hand will remain large and positive and thus will be associated with the scores indicating much conflict. In the case of a negative correlation the opposite, of course, is true; j's close to i will be predicted to have much conflict and j's far from i, little conflict.

It should now be easy to see why, in model 1, negative signs are attached to t runs. (This is another way of saying that j's close to i will be predicted to have much conflict).

If the sign configurations are clear for model 1, exactly the same logic, of course, applies to the other three models. Each has four equations, with sign affixed consistent with the model's assumptions.

Relative status-field theory asserts that through the appliction of these procedures, the contributions of economic development and power to conflict and cooperation can be revealed across dyadic sets. Here it stands distinct from social field and status-field theories, which seem to limit their perspective to individual dyadic sets, each with a separate predictive formulation. It is true that each partition of a dyadic set receives a separate predictive formulation in relative status-field theory. However, the purpose is to establish general models, cutting across the dyadic sets, by comparing empirical results with the sign models, such as given in model 1. This is accomplished by assigning a parameter weight of 1 to each equation and determining through the city block technique that model which deviates least from observed results. For example, it is clear through simple inspection that the result of (-.7e) + (-.8p) in a tt run (say, for France) comes closer than (-.7e) + (+.8p) to meeting model 1 (-ae) + (-ap). (-.7e) + (+.8p), however, comes closer to model 3 (-ae) + (+ap), indicating that closeness in respect to economic development and farness in respect to power predicts conflict, than (-.7e) + (-.8p).

Each model, then, through these techniques can be compared across the dyadic sets and various categories of analysis, such as African, European, etc., can be used to see if the models vary between such categories.

To summarize, relative status-field theory works with relative position on economic development and power to allow four different analyses of each dyadic set, i.e., tt, tu, ut, and uu runs. Parameter weights are compared with the four models of conflict across dyadic sets to determine the contributions of economic development and power (the status dimensions) to conflict and cooperation.

Distance theory.

3.DISTANCE THEORY, FORMULA[13],

C=DW WHERE C=DYAD BY BEHAVIOR VECTOR, D=DYAD BY FACTOR SCORES MATRIX OF D-SPACE AND W=A LEAST SQUARES SOLUTION OF VECTOR PARAMETER WEIGHTS.

Basic assumptions of distance theory, model 2

1. The international relations system can be described for predictive purposes as a collection of variables. 2. The

collection of variables can be divided into two infinite subsets: One, a-space, relates to the attributes of nations, and the other, b-space, relates to the dyadic behavior (i to j). 3. The distance of one nation to another on each of the variables of a-space can be ascertained by computing the absolute difference of their z-scores /(i-j)/ to create d-space. 4. An approximate basis of distance space (d-space) and b-space can be computed by factor analyzing, separately, a large sample of variables in each space. 5. Collectively, the factor scores of d-space can account for a significant portion of the variance of the dyadic factor scores of b-space. (Vincent, 1976).

Distance theory presents an alternative approach to the problem of assessing how attribute distances explains behavior. As indicated above, social field theory works with a signed measure. Examination of figure 8, below, shows that a j no distance from i, using Rummel's measure, is predicted, under the condition of positive perfect fit, to have average conflict with i while the j most deviant, above i, is predicted to have the least conflict with i and the j most deviant below i, the most conflict (that is, when +'s go with +'s and -'s go with -'s).

Put figure 8 about here., I 25

If distance is a force for conflict and/or cooperation, this may not be well captured using such a measure. Nations no different from i will be predicted (assuming postive fit) to have average conflict, as long as some actors are above i and other actors are below i. The question can be asked, "why should an actor no different from another be predicted to have average conflict if distance is supposed to be a cause of conflict and/or cooperation?"

An absolute measure of distance provides a scale that allows distance to contribute either one way or the other to conflict or cooperation. Using the formula /i-j/ to compute the distances, we get, in contrast to figure 8:

Put figure 9 about here., I 26

In terms of the above figure, it can be seen, if the parameter weight is positive, we expect little conflict for j's like i, and much conflict for j's distant from i, while, if the sign is negative, we expect much conflict for j's close to i and little conflict for j's distant from i. In other words, the role of distance (as a general non-directional concept) is captured by this measure. Positive correlations with the conflict scale indicate "the more distance the more conflict," while negative correlations indicate "the less distance the more conflict." The reversal of conflict expectations, depending on whether j is above or below i, is eliminated with this measure and the possibly counter-intuitive notion that no distance should predict average conflict and/or cooperation is eliminated. With the absolute measure, a j no distance from i will be predicted to have either the most or the least conflict or cooperation, but wY_average conflict or cooperation.

Figure 10 depicts the basic model of distance theory.

Put figure 10 about here., I 27

It can be seen that the dyadic factor scores of d-space are different from the distances of social field theory. Social field theory computes algebraic distances on a-space factor dimensions while distance theory creates factor dimensions out of absolute distances, computed from original variables. The predictors of social field theory are signed distances, while the predictors of distance theory are dyadic factor scores, indicating location in d-space.

To illustrate, assume that per capita gnp and radios per 1000 population loaded positively and heavily on a dimension called economic development distance. This would indicate that dyads with high factor scores tend to have large absolute distances on these variables and dyads with small factor scores, little absolute distance on these variables. If the parameter weight on economic development distance was positive in explaining some conflict dimension, say, threats, this would indicate that the more economic development distance between dyadic partners, the more likely i exports threats to j, and, the less distance between dyadic partners in respect to their economic development distance, the less likely i exports threats to j. A similar interpretation would pertain to all of the d- and b-space variables.

After all of the dyadic sets have been treated, a sign model is employed. This time it is utilized across all of the d-space dimensions to determine the general sign model for the international relations system or any of its subsystems such as Africa, Europe, etc. Procedures are similar to those employed in relative status-field theory.

If some classification is employed, such as Europe, exactly the same procedures are utilized, but only on the dyadic sets included within that classification.

Generalizing sign interpretations.

The simplest way to understand all of these dyadic equations is to consider what is expected when nation i exports to nation j, given various parameter sign patterns for each case. In these terms, we may state:

Put Figure 11 about here., I 28

The above then can be considered a guide to interpretation when a + or a- sign in fact appears in an analysis, using the theoretical models. We can now examine previous findings.[14] In terms of this framework.

Previous findings.

The following presents findings (Vincent et. al., 1971b) based on a 10 dyadic sample set, using DON data.

Put Figure 12 about here., I 29

For example, in the case of distance theory, those most distant from i on power base distance were found to receive the most conflict from i while, from the perspective of social field theory, j's highest above i on power base were found to receive the most conflict.

All of these findings had to be stated tentatively because there is no way of knowing, based on a small sample, (10 dyadic sets) whether they held for the universe of states. The purpose of this paper is to (1) test the above models on conflict and cooperation flows for virtually the universe of states (128 states), (2) establish a sign model for each theory from the empirical results, and (3) compare results with the previous tests. The foundations for these tests, that is, the factor analytic results for a and d-spaces and the WEIS data manipulations may be found in the Appendix.

Comparing theories, a broad overview.

Before looking at model results, it might be wise to compare the theories on a number of matters to establish firmly the foundation for the conclusions that follow. In this connection, it is convenient to think of each analysis as a distinct analytical category. Thus, we have 12 categories: 1. Distance theory, conflict 2. Distance theory, cooperation 3. Social field theory, conflict 4. Social field theory, cooperation 5. Relative status-field theory, tt, conflict 6. Relative status-field theory, tt, cooperation 7. Relative status-field theory, ut, conflict 8. Relative status-field theory, ut, cooperation 9. Relative status-field theory, tu, conflict 10. Relative status-field theory, tu, cooperation 11. Relative status-field theory, uu, conflict 12. Relative status-field theory, uu, cooperation.

Using these categories we can now rank order the theories in terms of a number of important matters.

The following compares the theories in such terms. Number of correlations refers to the number of dyadic sub-sets that were analyzed. In the case of distance theory and social field theory a subject was dropped if it did not export conflict or cooperation, although it might receive conflict or cooperation and be included in the analysis of other dyadic sets. The number of correlations are much smaller for relative status-field theory since the dyadic subsets were partitioned along lines as the theory requires. A partitioned set was not analyzed unless it included at least 30 dyads.

N of correlations refers to the actual number of dyads analyzed in the case of distance and social field theory and the average number in the case of relative status-field theory. For example, in the case of the tt conflict analyses, the n's for the canonical correlations averaged 57.

Range of correlations refers to the canonical correlation magnitudes, maximum and minimum, for the number of correlations attempted. For example, in respect to distance theory, conflict, of the 112 correlations attempted, the largest was .70 and the smallest .37.

Expected correlations refer to the expected average correlations when a large number of correlations are run using different v's and n's. This is this is based on the formula: V-I/N-I=SQUARE OF THE EXPECTED CORRELATION. (McNemar, 1968:203-13)

Number above expected correlation indicates the actual number of correlations which exceeded the expected value. For example, in the case of distance theory, cooperation, 102 of 116 correlations were above the expected value.

Percent above expected correlation is found by deviding entry 5 by entry 1. Thus, in the case of distance theory, conflict, 80 divided by 112=71.

Expected average square refers to the expected correlation squared, as computed from the above formula.

Actual average square refers to the actual results in average correlation squared terms.

Average square above expected square refers to the degree to which the average expected square was exceeded. For example, in the case of distance theory, conflict the average square was .05 above expected square. This is found by subtracting entry 7 from entry 8.

Total dyads considered refers to all of the dyads across all of the analyses, within a category, such as distance theory, conflict. It is found by multiplying entry 1 by entry 2. The number of dyads considered in the application of relative status-field theory falls off considerably, for reasons discussed above.

Column sums of squares of canonical correlations refers to the aggregate obtained when the canonical correlations are squared and then summed for a category. The figure obtained is the aggregate variance explained. For example, in the case of distance theory, conflict, the aggregate variance explained is 33.64.

Percent of total variance of theoretical maximum refers to the column sums of squares of the canonical correlations devided by the number of correlations. Since the maximum correlation is 1.0 and the square of 1.0 is equal to 1.0, the theoretical maximum, in variance explained terms, is equal to the number of correlations computed for a category, such as distance theory, conflict.

Put table 1 about here., I 33

These data firmly establish the importance of the theories from a statistical standpoint. Most of the theories exceed the expected correlational values by a substantial margin, are based on very large n's, and explain a substantial portion of the theoretical maximum variance that could be explained. Thus, it seems reasonable to look at the actual model weights generated for the theories.

Findings.

Table 2 presents the sign models for all the theories, using WEIS data.[15]

Put table 2 about here., I 34

Comparison with previous findings.

We may now compare these results, for the selected factors, with the previous findings, interpreting the signs according to Figure 11.

Put figure 13 about here., I 30

It can be seen that the agreement is substantial with the

previous pilot study. Only in respect to distance theory, conflict (power) and cooperation (economic development, power) and relative status-field theory (ut, economic development) is there disagreement. It should be understood in this respect that the previous pilot study only dealt with 10 sample dyadic sets, 67 variables to define a-and d-space and DON data to define conflict (cooperation data was taken from trade statistics and other sources). Thus, despite using a new data set to define a-and d-space (144 variables), WEIS data instead of DON (and other sources) data to define behavior and the use of 128 dyadic sets instead of 10, there is, in general terms, a strong degree of convergence, especially in the case of conflict. What, then, are the implications of these relationships? Again a diagram may prove useful.

Put Figure 14 about here., I 31

How are these results "policy relevant"? Obviously, the answer to that question depends on the paradigm from which the results are viewed. Can causal linkages be assumed? I see no harm in making such an assumption as long as it is clear that it is for the purpose of stimulating additional research and not to provide final and clear answers to immediate policy problems. In these terms we can summarize the possible policy prescriptions for each model as follows:

Put Figure 15 about here., I 32

Paradoxically, in each case, that which minimizes conflict also minimizes cooperation. If conflict reduction, assuming causal linkages, takes priority over cooperation maximization, however, these appear to be the proper policy prescriptions. In closing, it will be stated again that the purpose of these formulations at this time is more to stimulate relevant additional research, along these lines, than to suggest that these are, in any sense, final answers.

Summary.

The purpose of this research was to compare related but distinct attribute-distance based theories on identical behavioral data for comparative purposes. The theories tested were distance, social field, status-field and relative status-field theories. The behavioral data employed was WEIS data for the years 1966-69. Each theory was viewed as one possible way of establishing correlational linkages between attribute differences and behavior. The results showed a strong correspondence with the results for a small (10 dyadic sets) sample, on selected dimensions, using different data sources. Distance theory indicated that "differences", social field theory indicated that "j above i position" and relative status-field theory indicated that "distance for u's but closeness for t's" on these key dimensions may provide clues for possible conflict-cooperation control. If causal assuptions are made, reducing absolute distance (distance theory), reducing above j differences from i, power and economic development, (social field theory) and maximizing distance (t actor) and minimizing distance (u actor) may result in conflict reduction. In each case, however, if the casual assuption is valid, such policies may also reduce the cooperation from i to j.

NOTES

1. The assistance of Jim Slitor, Wes Kranitz and Carol Jones was greatly appreciated.

2. See the various DON research reports for background in respect to development of attribute, social field, and status-field theories,

3. This is asserted because of the relatively small number of nations treated in previous tests.

4. See Vincent (1973b) where the magnitude of the labor and numerous decisions involved in conceptualizing these theories, even for 10 dyadic sets, is well documented.

5. Subjects can be located on factor dimensions in a manner conceptually similar to the way that they are located on original variables.

6. Rummel does not provide axioms for attribute theory. These have been written by Vincent (1972a) to parallel as closely as possible the axioms of social field theory.

7. Vincent (1972a) has found that UN voting and UN delegate attitudes can be fairly well explained in terms of such a model.

8. Rummel has developed and worked primarily with this equation.

9. Rummel argues: "But why posit economic development and power as status dimensions? These are the only consistently delineated national dimensions invoking international consensus

about what is desirable. Other national dimensions, such as the aforemenioned ones comprising political orientation, religion, and culture, invoke no consensus about what is esteemed or desirable." (1971: 28).

10. An attempt was made to test those "theorems" (hypotheses might be a better term) which appear to be potentially most fruitful and easy to operationalize. An example of the opposite would be "Theorem 4, (mobility theorem): Nations desire upward mobility." In addition, certain corollaries seem to fall in this same category, such as "Corollary 5, (dissonance corollary): Status disequilibrium causes cognitive dissonance." (Rummel,1971)

11. Vincent (1976) has developed relative status-field theory as an alternative to status-field theory.

12. This is actually not made clear in the DON research reports. This interpretation was provided by Rummel, in a seminar setting, in answer to a student question.

13. The first elaboration of distance theory can be found in Vincent (1973a).

14. The factors focused on are those that explain the most variance in their respective factor analyses in the case of distance and social field theories and are the status dimensions in the remaining cases.

15. The last figure in each case, 53.00 for distance theory, conflict, is the sum of squares of the model entries. It can be viewed as a rough index to compare results in terms of general variance drift i.e. the fiqure is large if variance magnitude

tends to drift one way or the other, either + or -, across the dimensions for the the nations.

DISTANCE THEORY, RESULTS FOR CONFLICT, 1966-69.

By: Jack E. Vincent

Professor of Political Science

Florida Atlantic University

Boca Raton, Florida 33432

DISTANCE THEORY, RESULTS FOR CONFLICT, 1966-69.[1]

Introduction.

The purpose of this paper is to report on the testing of distance theory on WEIS conflict data for the years 1966-69.

Distance theory belongs to a famliy of theories. Each attempts to explain state behavior in terms of attributes or attribute distances.[2] Distance theory can be understood best by discussing its most direct predecessors, attribute and social field theories. Both will be treated briefly.

See Paper 3 discussion, Inserts 18,19,25,26,27,28

In technical terms, then, the purpose of the paper are to: 1. present the weights and signs for each state (128 in all) generated by applying distance theory to WEIS conflict data, 2. evaluate the weights and signs in terms of attribute theory (explained below), and 3. construct a general model, from the canonical analysis, for the state system as a whole.

To make the analysis meaningful it is first necessary to 1. present the major features of the a and d-space analyses and 2. discuss the WEIS conflict data manipulations.

Constructing a-space.

See Paper 1 discussion, Insert 1

Constructing d-space.

It is necessary, of course, to construct d-space to test distance theory. The d-space rotated loadings are presented in the following table. To illustrate, the loadings of total population on the 33 factors are given first. The 34th entry, .76, is the communality for total population. The explanatory power of the factors is given by the column sums of squares figures. It can be seen that the first factor explains 18.76 units of variance out of the possible 144 units of variance that could have been explained. Since Kaiser's (1958) rule of 1.0 cut off was utilized, all column sums the squares exceed 1.0

To simplify factor interpretation, loadings .49 or greater are grouped and sorted in terms of magnitude for each factor. In the case of the first factor, power base distance, total gross national product in millions of U.S. dollars loads .91, total educational expenditures in million of U.S. dollars loads .88 and so forth. Names, such as power based distance, of course, as in the case of a-space, are arbitrarily assigned.

Put table 2 about here., I 37

Considering the first dimension, knowing that absolute distances were computed on these variables and that all the variables positively correlate with the factor, we can make the fol~-7Ko interpretation. Dyads that are close (small /i-j/) in respect to their power base distance are grouped at the bottom of the dimension and dyads that are dissimilar in respect to their power base distance are grouped at the top of the dimension. The variable list indicates what the primary discriminators are, in respect to these factor score assignments. Distances, in respect to power base, then, are highly patterned. If we know a dyad's factor score on this dimension, we can predict, with varying degrees of confidence, distance in respect to 28 different variables. To put it another way, if a dyad has a high factor score on this dimension, it tends to be distance in respect to total gross national product, total educational expenditures, total energy consumption, etc. Conversely, if a dyad has a small factor score on this dimension, the partners tend to be close in respect to total gross national product, total educational expenditures, total energy consumption, etc. Knowledge of a dyad's factor score, then, immediately gives us information on likely location on a host of variables.

Considering the second dimension, it can be seen that almost all of these variables are per capita economic in nature. Again, the interpretation is relatively simple, since there are no negative loadings. All dyads with large factor scores tend to be distant in respect to these variables while dyads with small factor scores tend to be similar.

Considering the third dimension, since these are political variables and the loadings are positive, dyads with large factor scores tend to be dissimilar in respect to these variables, and those with small factor scores similar.

It should be apparent by now that to go through all 33 dimensions in this fashion is unnecessary.

Probably all that needs to be clarified now is how to make an interpretation when negative loadings occur, such as in the case of the sixth dimension. The reason the term, closeness, instead of distance is used is because of the negative signs are given to the heaviest loading variables. Since these loadings are correlations with the factor scores, it should be apparent that those with large factor scores will tend to be close (not have large distances) on the variables that are grouped, while those with small factor scores will tend to be distant on these variables. Thus, we may generalize, when loadings are positive we know that large factor scores indicate distance on the grouped variables, while, if the loadings are negative, such scores indicate closeness. When loadings are positive, small factor scores indicate closeness but when loadings are negative, small factor scores indicate distance. With this simple rule the implications of the factor scores and loadings should be clear.

The next step required to test distance theory is to score each dyad in respect to it's conflict and cooperation.

WEIS data manupulations.

See Paper 2 discussion, Inserts 3,8

The stage is now set for applying and interpreting distance theory results on the data. 128 Correlation runs were made using the d-space factor scores (matrix:16,256 X 33) and the WEIS dyadic vector (vector:16,256 X 1).

Findings: Canonical correlations[3].

The following analysis presents the canonical correlation results. Each country is listed with its canonical correlation in terms of descending magnitude. For example, Tanzania has the highest canonical correlation, .70. The states with zero canonical correlations, starting with Liberia, were countries which exported no conflict and hence could not be analyzed in the application. They may have received conflict, however, and where included in all analyses were that was the case and, thus, are listed for information purposes.

Put table 5 about here., I 38

Obviously, distance theory does not apply equally to all states. We may, however, use attribute theory to attempt to discern any patterns in these weights, that is, we can correlate the factor scores of a-space with the canonical correlation results. When this is done we obtain: economic development (.22), power base (.55), recent national independence (-.24), little domestic violence (-.54), large gnp growth rate (-.23), and little ethno-linguistic fractionalization (.26), R=.61, P=.006. Thus, the higher the economic development, power base and domestic violence of a state and the lower its gnp growth rate and the less the ethno-linguistic fractionalization, the higher its canonical correlation (using distance theory) tends to be. To put it another way, distance theory has the most relevance for states with such characteristics but less relevance for states with the opposite characteristics. In this connection, a crucial question concerns whether or not the theory is significant overall. Whenever many correlations are computed an average expected correlation can be computed in terms of n, the number of subjects, and v, the number of variables. We may then compare theortical expectations with actual results and draw a conclusion.

The following chart compares the theory on this and other important matters.

See Paper 3 discussion, Insert 33

It may be concluded that distance theory, overall, exceeds chance expectations. Also, the magnitudes of the correlations are related to certain state characteristics, as described above.

Findings: Canonical weights.

The following presents the results for the canonical correlation weights for distance theory, conflict. Although referred to as weights, in fact, these entries are correlations of the variables in question with the canonical variate scores generated in the canonical analysis. The term weights is used to avoid confusion with the output of canonical correlations themselves. For example, in the case of Albania the entry of .47, in the first column, indicates that power base distance is correlated .47 with the canonical variate scores generated in the analysis. In this case, we predict that those dyads that stand high on power base distance also stand high on the canonical variate scores. If the correlation is negative, as in the case of the fourth column, school enrollment distance, we predict that those dyads standing high on school enrolment distance tend to stand low on the canonical variate scores. All thirty-three entries can be interpreted in this way.

The last entry, the thirty-fourth, which is 1.37 in the case of Albania, indicates the aggregate variance for all thirty-three factors. In this way, states can be compared across ananxses. If the number is large, the correlations tend to be large while, of course, if the number is small they tend to be small. In cases like Afghanistan, where nothing but zeros have been entered, no analysis was performed because Afghanistan did not export conflict, in the time period considered, even though it may have received conflict from other states and, thus, is listed.

The entries under column sums of squares indicate the importance of the factors in aggregate variance terms. For example, in such terms, power base distance tended to be almost twice as important as political distance, 9.01 vs. 4.54.

Selected weights were then sorted in terms of descending magnitude for three factors. In the case of the first factor, power base distance, all states with positive weights, that is, from Kenya down through Burma tended to export conflict to countries that are distant from them in respect to power base distance. Countries with negative weights, that is, from Spain through the United Kingdom tended to export conflict to states that are close to them in respect to power base distance. The same kind of interpretation pertains to the economic development distance and political distance factors.

Put table 7 about here., I 40

The following presents the highest and lowest scores for power base distance, economic development distance, and political distance.

Put table 8 about here., I 41

Again the question arises, are these patterns describable in terms of attribute theory? Space does not permit analyzing all the dimensions in these terms but an analysis can be presented for the three selected factors.

The following presents the results of correlating a-space factor scores with + or - weights generated from canonical correlations used in testing the theories. For example, if the positive weights of the factor of power are under consideration, and, economic development correlates .50 with the power weights, we can conclude that, in respect to those that have positive weights on power, the higher the economic development of the nation the more likely it will have a large weight. The purpose of such an analysis is to see whether the magnitudes of the weights generated from the various theories are explainable in terms of attribute theory.

Put table 9 about here., I 42

Using the factor numbers, given below, 1=economic development etc., The results may be summarized as follows:

Put figure 7 about here., I 35

Thus, like the canonical correlations themselves, the weights generated on the factor dimensions of d-space appear predictable in terms of attribute theory.

Another approach is to examine the information in terms of an f-test of mean differences.

The significant discriminant f-test means, .05 level, of negative vs. postive weight subjects are given in table 10. Considering the first case, power base distance, the selected factors were economic development (1) power base (2) and little domestic violence (9). The f-ratio for economic development was 9.7895 and the probability .0025. The group means on this factor were .3379 (-weight subjects) and -.2261 (+ weight subjects).

Put table 10 about here,I 43

Again, we may summarize the key findings through a figure:

Put figure 8 about here., I 36

This further substantiates the above finding that the canonical patterns are predictable in terms of attributes.

Findings: General model

Although a model for, and the relevance of, distance theory for each state has been generated by presentation of the weights and canonical correlations given above, a systems model has not yet been discussed or presented. Following the methods discussed

4
above, we obtain for the "world":

Put table 11 about here., I 44

We can now list the factors and indicate whether distance or closeness contributes to conflict considering the world system as a whole.

Put table 12 about here., I 45

It may be concluded that assertions about distance or closeness, as predictors of conflict for the world, must be cast in factor

Conclusions

From the above investigation the following appears established: 1. State location on distance clusters (factors of d-space) are related to conflict exportation (as measured by WEIS data). 2. These relationships, overall, tend to exceed chance expectations (table 6). 3. The relevance of the theory for each state varies (table 5) but the magnitudes of the correlations are predictable, in part, from attributes (table 5, discussion). 4. Parameter weights for each state can be established on the variable clusters (table 7) and the magnitudes are related to attributes (table 9, for selected factors). In this connection, + weight nations tend to be different from - weight nations (table 10, for selected factors). 5. From the individual parameter weights, a general world model can be developed (table 11) and the implications of distance and closeness for conflict exportations can be established (table 12).

If distance is viewed as a possible cause of conflict, policy prescriptions might assert that to narrow state differences in respect to factors where distance predicts conflict (table 12, top part) and to enlarge state differences in respect to factors where closeness predicts conflict (table 12, lower part) would be proper. However, these findings are a starting point rather than an ending as far as policy presciptions are concerned. Will these relationships hold up in new time periods on new data sets? Can the concept of cause, as oppossed to correlation, be clearly delineated in the social sciences so that prescriptions can be soundly based on the former (assuming cause, itself, is a viable concept)? Clearly, boldly stated prescriptions are not in order at this time. On the other hand, correlational patterns have strongly emerged in this study and may be relevant to conflict management in the I.R. system. For example, changes in power base differences, economic developement differences, political differences, etc., do not appear beyond the ability of man to initiate. It might be noted, in closing, that in the case of these three "classic" concepts "power, economics and politics" differences (rather than closeness), for the world system as a whole, predict conflict.[5]

Notes

(1). The assistance of Jim Slitor, Wes Kranitz and Carol Jones was greatly appreciated.

(2). Distance has been measured in two ways in the theories. Absolute distance is a measure of the distance between two nations on a variable based on the formula: D = /i-j/. For example, if nation i = +5 and nation j = +2, the distance between them is +3. However, if i = +2 and j = +5, the distance between them remains +3. This measure, then, measures distance, regardless of direction, and all distance will have a positive sign. This metric finds its use in distance theory.

Algebraic distance is a measure of the distance between two nations on a variable, based on the formula: D = i-j. For example, if nation i = +5 and nation j = +2, the distance between them is +3. But, if i = +2 and j = +5, the distance is -3. This metric, then, measures whether i is above or below j. If i is above j, the distance value will have a + sign. If i is below j, the distance will have a - sign. This measure of distance is used in social field and status-field theories.

(3). Because only one dependant variable was used, these are the equivalent of a multiple regression analysis with the canonical correlations equal to R.

(4). Summing the squares of the parameter weights, but

retaining the original parameter weight signs, across states, will the same sign results as the city block method, and because of the simplicity of procedure and interpretation it is the method used.

(5). The model for any particular state, of course, may be found by reference to Table 7. A later paper will explore the models that were developed for some 30 plus major international groupings, such as NATO and the Warsaw Pact, by applying the above described model building techniques.

A STANDARDIZED APPROACH TO INTERNATIONAL RELATIONS ATTRIBUTE DATA

By: Jack E. Vincent

Professor of Political Science

Florida Atlantic University

Boca Raton, Florida 33432

A STANDARDIZED APPROACH TO INTERNATIONAL RELATIONS ATTRIBUTE DATA, WITH AN EXAMPLE OF USAGE

Introduction.

Scholars frequently wish to know the relative position of one state to another and to the entire collection of states respect to their attributes such as literacy rate, energy consumption, and per capita gnp. Surprisingly, no large scale attribute data bank presently exists in the literature which conviently and quickly answers such questions. It is the purpose of this paper to generate such a bank for selected attribute data describing the attributes of states in the mid-1960's.

Assuming that the data is available, how does one construct a data set which answers the above questions? The answer is quite simple, yet, the statistical technique which can produce such answers is virtually ignored at least in the type of application attempted here. Virtually every introductory text book on statistics fully describes the advantages of a z-score analysis, but, as already pointed out, one can look in vain for a single attribute collection that gives the answers a z-score analysis provides.

Z-scores show the location of subjects in respect to their deviation from the mean of a distribution. The z-score is computed by the formula: Z = X - M/S.D., WHERE Z = THE Z-SCORE VALUE FOR AN INDIVIDUAL SUBJECT, X = THAT SUBJECT'S RAW SCORE, M = THE MEAN OF THE DISTRIBUTION AND S.D. = THE STANDARD DEVIATION OF THE DISTRIBUTION.

When a distribution is normally distributed, 68% of the z-scores will lay approximately + or - 1.0 from the mean, 95% + or - 2.0 from the mean and 99% + or - 3.0 from the mean, with the mean equal to 0. For example, in a normal distribution, an individual with a z-score of 2.0 is above (approximately) 47.7% of those cases above the mean and an individual with a z-score of -2.0 is below (approximately) 47.7% of those cases below the mean. Therefore, a total of approximately 95% of the cases lie between +2.0 and -2.0 in a normal distribution.

Z-scores can be used to compare individuals both within and across distributions. For example, if Brazil scores 1.0 on one distribution, say, on literacy rate, and 2.0 on another distribution, say, total value of exports to the world, we would know that, compared to all other states, Brazil stands higher in respect to her exports than in respect to her literacy rate. Such comparative standings would not be obvious by examination of her raw scores on these variables.

This more or less classic approach to z-score interpretation will be altered slightly in this application, since IR data is seldom completely normal. One way to assure that the mean of a collection of scores truly assumes a central position, so the mean and median are very close, is to perform a rank transformation on data. Thus a number sequence such as 1 2 5 becomes 1 2 3 under a rank transformation. Strongly deviant cases, thev(are prevented from pulling the mean away from the median. Once the data is so transformed, however, the range of the z-scores is restricted to basically + or - 1.72. Thus, instead of a range, basically, of + or - 3.0, under conditions of normality, the range of the data bank generated here will be, basically, +1.72 to - 1.72.

The advantage of the rank transformation is, as indicated above, that the mean and median will now basically agree so that there will be as many cases above the mean as below the mean, considering that, in z-score analysis, the mean always assumes the value of 0. Through a rank transformation we can look at any variable and know, if a state's score equals 0, it is truly in a central position in respect to the distribution. We can also interpret any + score as being above the mean, where the mean is interpreted in terms of a true central tendency, and, any - score is indicating a position below that central tendency. Further, we can view scores approaching + or - 1.72 as indicating a standing very high in the distribution, in rank score terms. We can also compare the relative standing of states across the distributions. Thus, if the state stands + 1.0 on one distribution and + 1.5 on another, its relative rank standing is higher in the second distribution than in the first. Finally, if a second state has a score,of say, .05 on either distribution, then, we know that its rank standing is lower than the first state.

The attribute variables were taken, for the most part, from the Cross-Polity Time Series and the World Handbook of Political and Social Indicators (Taylor and Hudson, 1971). The exact variable list will be given shortly. Variables were selected on the following grounds: first, they had to clearly pertain to the attributes of states. Therefore, any variable with with a behavioral connotation was dropped.

Second, the information (total collection used) was required to be 90% complete. Where information was missing, or ambiguous, regression estimates were used. The regression estimate routine employed searches the entire collection of variables to find that variable on which the subject has information most closely related to the variable on which the information is missing. Simple regression is then used to estimate the missing value.

Once these decisions were made, the variable list was generated. It will now be presented.

Put table 1 about here., I 46

The meaning of most variables should be clear from the above titles. Precise definitions, of course, can be obtained, in all cases, from the original sources.

Computation of z-scores.

The z-score computation was then performed on the variables in question giving the following results.

Put table 2 about here., I 47

The above data bank answers thousands, perhaps hundreds of thousands of questions about the rank position of states on the variables during the time period considered. To demonstrate the power of the technique employed, ten hypothetical questions will be posed and then answered by reference to the data bank.

(1.) Is South Vietnam close to the system average in respect to her total population? Answer: No, she is distinctly above it (.85). (2.) Does Paraguay stand above Venezuala in respect to total working age population? Answer: Yes (1.31 vs. -.91). (3.) Are both Uraguay and Venezuala above the average for the IR system in this respect? Answer: No, Uraguay is above the average and Venezuala below the average. (4.) Is Kenya distinctly below the IR system average in reto radios per 1,000 population? Answer: Yes (-.83). (5.) Who had more deaths from domestic violence during 1963-67, Uganda or Tanzania? Answer: Uganda had more deaths from domestic violence (1.47 vs. 20). (6.) Who has the higher university enrollment per capita, the United Kingdom or Japan? Answer: Japan has the higher enrollment per capita (1.42 for Japan, 1.12 for the United Kingdom). (7.) Who has a greater total energy production in the years considered, Hungary or Poland? Answer: Poland did (1.07 vs. 1.50). (8.) Who has greater railroad mileage -- Mexico or Brazil? Answer: Brazil (1.37 vs. 1.45). (9.) Who has more total passenger cars, the United Kingdom, France or West Germany? Answer: France had the most (1.69), the United Kingdom was second most (1.66) and West Germany the least (1.64). (10.) Does the density of the Netherlands exceed that of Japan? Answer: Yes (1.64 vs. 1.50).

The value of this data bank, as a quick and easy reference to such questions, should now be apparent. Further, the presentation here is now conviently organized for correlation studies that might use such data, say, to predict the behavior of states.
To illustrate this, an analysis will be performed on WEIS conflict and cooperation data obtained for basically the same time period as the attribute data.

Weis data collection.

See Paper 2 discussion, Inserts 3,8,9

Correlation analysis.

The z-scores were then correlated with the conflict and cooperation scores. The results are given in the following table.

Put table 5 about here., I 48

These data suggest that the major conflict exporters tend to have large military forces, large expenses for such forces, be urban, have large educational expenses etc. The stronger correlations for such non-political variables stands in contrast to the weaker correlations for most political variables, such as legislative effectiveness. In general, bigness on such non-political variables is associated with conflict. It will be interesting to compare these outcomes with those for cooperation.

Put table 6 about here., I 49

It can be seen that there is a strong similarity with the results obtained in the conflict analysis. Again, military force expenditures, total school expenditures etc. are the best predictors and stand in contrast to the predictive relevance of political variables, such as the press freedom index. These results suggest a somewhat pessimistic interpretation. If there are causal linkages between such attribute variables and conflict and cooperation exportations and if attribute manipulation can effect changes in such exportation patterns, then, basically, manipulations that effect conflict are likely to effect cooperation. If conflict can be 'suppressed' so, apparently, will be cooperation. Also, it would seem that most states would like to achieve high scores on the variables with the strongest relationships. That is, they wish to 'modernize' and possess the attributes that define 'bigness'. Again, if the causal assumption is made, to achieve such aspirations may have the effect of increasing conflict in the international system.

Conclusion.

The purpose of this study was to establish a data bank for quick easy reference for IR scholars on a large number of attribute variables measured for states in the mid-1960's. Each score in the bank locates a state in respect to the system average in rank score terms. Specific questions relating to the relative position of a state to the system average (always equals 0) and to other states can be easily determined by reference to the bank. Also such data can be used for additional studies, such as those that attempt to relate attributes to national behavior. A study was undertaken in this regard which generated the correlational relationships between the attributes and WEIS based conflict and cooperation indexes. In general, the same variables were the best predictors in both cases. Political variables did not fare well compared to variables such as expenditures on military forces, total school enrollment, total physicians, in short, indexes which seem to define large and/or modern states. Many of these characteristics appear to those considered 'desirable' by many statesmen, a fact that will have to be taken if conflict management is attempted throught attribute manipulation, assuming such manipulation is considered desirable and possible, and, a causal assumption is either demonstated or assumed.

DISTANCE THEORY: A COMPARISON OF VARIOUS REGIONAL GROUPINGS ON 1966-69 CONFLICT DATA

By: Jack E. Vincent

Professor of Political Science

Florida Atlantic University

Boca Raton, Florida 33432

DISTANCE THEORY: A COMPARISON OF VARIOUS REGIONAL GROUPINGS ON 1966-69 CONFLICT DATA[1]

Introduction.

The purpose of this article is to report on the testing of distance theory on WEIS conflict data for the years 1966-69 considering selected regional groupings, such as Africa, Latin America etc. That is, we wish to know whether empirical results vary across such groupings and what significance, if any, this may have for possible conflict control.

The work reported here is part of a larger project which focuses on WEIS conflict and cooperation data for the mid 1960's using the frameworks of attribute, social field, status-field, relative status-field, distance and deviance theories, as guidelines for operational procedures. Since each of these theories are developed elsewhere, they will not be treated fully here (Rummel, 1969,a,b, 1971, Vincent, 1972, 1973,a,b, 1974, 1975, 1976). They can, however, be summarized in the following way.

Put Chart 1 here., I 57

From the above, the basic correlational design of each theory can easily be determined. For example, in using attribute theory, an investigator correlates the a-space factor scores of nations with their total behavior scores to determine the degree of association. In social field theory, dyadic a-space distances are correlated with measures of dyadic behavior and so forth.

Special terms in the above chart can be described as follows. A-space factor scores are derived from a factor analysis of national attribute variables. A-space distances are computed by the formula i-j=d where i is the nation of concern, j the other nation and d the distance. Partitioned a-space distances are generated by dividing the a-space distance matrix into four separate matrices, a tt matrix where i is topdog in economic development and power relative to all other j's in the matrix, a tu matrix where i is topdog in economic development and underdog in power relative to all other j's in the matrix, a ut matrix where i is underdog in economic development and topdog in power relative to all other j's in the matrix, and a uu matrix where i is underdog in economic development and power relative to all other j's in the matrix. D-space factor scores are dyadic factor scores generated by factor analyzing distances computed on nation attributes by the formula /i-j/=p where i is the nation of concern, j the other nation, and p the absolute distance between them. Means of d-space factor scores are computed by averaging the dyadic factor scores of a particular dyadic set, such as the U.S. set. Total behavior refers to the sum of all behavior (such as confict behavior) exported to all the other actors in the system. Dyadic behavior refers to the behavioral exportations of a dyadic set, such as the U.S. set, i.e., the U.S. exports to the U.S.S.R., to China, to France, etc. Partitioned dyadic behavior refers to exports of i to j's that are either tt, ut, tu, or uu, relative to i, in respect to economic development and power.

In general, the project attempts to determine the relationship of national attributes and attribute distances to national behavior.

The following list gives many of the main project steps.

Put List 1 here., I 58

List 2 gives some selected illustrative findings on the above steps.

Put List 2 here., I 59

Hopefully, the project may eventually suggest crucial or pivotal variables that will assist in controlling conflict in the international relation system. The purpose here is to report on major findings connected with distance theory, conflict for project steps 29 and 30.

An easy way to approach distance theory is to think in terms of "expectations" when either + or signs are observed, on factor dimensions in empirical applications. These may be summarized as:

See Paper 3 discussion, Insert 28

Before presenting the world model for distance theory, it seems proper to represent the highlights of the factor analysis of d-space so that the weights generated for the model will have concrete meaning.

Constructing d-space.

See Paper 4 discussion, Insert 37

The next step was to select the behavioral variables.

WEIS data manupulations.

See Paper 2 discussion, Inserts 3,8

When these steps were completed, distance theory was applied to the 16,256 (dyads) by 1 (conflict vector) scores for each states' dyadic set generating 128 correlations. The world model was obtained by applying the methods described above and is presented in the following table.

Put Table 4 about here., I 52

We may now interpret such weights according to figure 1.

Put List 3 about here., I 50

It may be concluded that assertions about distance or closeness, as predictors of conflict for the world, must be cast in factor specific terms.

The purpose of this paper is to compare this model with the results generated by analyzing a number of groups using the same techniques.

The groups chosen and their members were:

Put Table 5 about here., I 53

The model building technique described above was then applied to each group and the following table presents a sort listing of the results on selected factors.

Put Table 6 about here., I 54

Considering power base distance first, it is apparent that there are strong regional differences. For the world as a whole, distance in respect to power base (a + sign) predicts high conflict exportations. That is, states, when all states are considered, tend to export the most conflict to those states distant from them in respect to power base. This world model holds for groupings such as Third World, Africa, Commonwealth, Latin America, Asia and Arab League. The sign model reverses, however, as groupings tend to be European or have European members. Thus, members of groupings such as CENTO, Eastern Europe, COMECON, Warsaw Pact, SEATO, Council Of Europe and NATO tend to export the most conflict to states close to them in respect to power base.

Virtually an identical pattern holds for economic development distance. The African, Latin American and Asian groups tend to follow the world pattern (export to those distant) while the European groups and groups with some or many European members tend to export the most conflict to those close to them in respect to economic development.

Considering political distance, however, a new outcome is apparent. Eastern European groupings, such as COMECON, now conform to the world model (those distant receive the most conflict) and the same is true of Europe, as a whole, and some within Europe groups, such as the Coal And Steel Community, although the magnitude of some of the weights is small. In the main, however, most of the groups conform to the world model. The most notable exceptions are NATO and the French Community which have the largest negative signs.

Militarism presents a still different pattern. Latin american groups, such as LAFTA and OAS deviate most from the world model (a - sign) followed by certain African and Asian groups (such as OAU and the Arab League). The conformers in this case (that is, export most to those closest in respect to militarism) are, for the most part, Europe and European related groups, such as Warsaw Pact and NATO.

One way to make such patterns more explicit across all the d-space factors is to work within the framework of attribute theory. That is, if a-space is constructed, and the groups' mean factor scores are computed on the a-space dimensions, these mean factor scores can be used to more precisely define the relationship between group attributes and the group model scores.

The construction of a-space.

See Paper 1 discussion, Insert 1

Group means were then computed on the a-space dimensions and the resulting scores correlated with the group models.[2] The following matrix gives this information

Put Table 8 about here., I 56

For space reasons, we will primarily limit attention to the a-space factors of economic development, power base and non-competitive political system. A-space factors represent the columms of the matrix while the model signs are represented by the rows. Thus, considering the first row and columm, we can see that economic development (the first a-space factor) correlated -.79

with the signs on power base distance (the sign obtained on the first d-space factor). This means that the higher the mean economic development of the groups the more likely the group members will have a negative model sign. This is easily confirmed by inspection of Table 6. Groups such as OAU and OAS have positive signs (export to those distant) while groups such as NATO and and the Warsaw Pact have negative signs (export to those close). The following list fully interprets (correlations 50% or higher) the three a-space factors chosen.

Put List 4 about here., I 51

Thus, groups whose members have high mean economic development have members who tend to export the highest levels of conflict to j's that are close to them on power base, economic development, militarism, energy production, mail exchanges and infant mortality but distant in respect to per cent urban population and crude death rate. If a group posesses high development its members tend to export conflict to states that are close on most of the factors involved. Of particular interest is the fact that on the largest d-space factors, such as power base and economic development, a purely "closeness" exportation pattern is evident. Also, the association between a-space economic development and d-space political distance is only -.12 and, thus, is not deemed strong enough to include in List 4. It may be concluded that conflict exportations relating to power, economics, militarism and energy production take presidence over "politics" as predictable, from the perspective of this analysis.

Considering a-space power base, groups that have members with high mean power are groups that tend to have members which export conflict to those close to them in respect to power base, economic development, energy production, population size and infant mortality but distant from them in repect to internal security forces, per cent urban population and crude death rate. On the key d-space dimensions, of power base distace and economic development distance, the analysis, for a-space power base, indicates closeness predicts conflict. It also does so for the majority of the d-space dimensions listed.

It can be seen that closeness again wins over distance, as a predictor of conflict, by a narrow margin, for group members which tend to have non-competitive political systems.

Over the whole list, closeness predicts conflict more often than distance, by a margin of two to one.

Similar kinds of analyses, of course, can be made for the remaining a-space factors and model signs.

Clearly there are discernable differences between groups related to attributes that help illuminate the total world picture. These findings may have important implications for possible conflict control. The possible effects of distance change on one regional grouping may not be the same for one as for another. Considering one of our primary factors, power, groups such as NATO and the

Warsaw Pact may tend to react one way, if power distances change, and are linked to behavior (only an assumption at this point),[3] while groups such as OAU and OAS may act in the opposite direction. The concept of "region" and the possibility of regional oriented policies is clearly strengthened by these findings, to the extent attribute-attribute distance management is deemed relevant and possible.

Summary.

The purpose of this effort was to apply distance theory to several regional groupings in the world and compare the results with the world model. To do this, a-space and d-space were constructed and the model results for the groups determined. On factors, such as power base, regional differences were clearly apparent. Clarification of such differences was facilitated by relating a-space factor scores to the models. A portion of the matrix was interpreted in this regard. For example, it was found that groups with high mean economic development have members who tend to export high conflict to J's that are close to them in respect to power base. It was concluded that possible conflict management, based on attribute-attribute difference considerations, may have take in to account the potential reversal of consequences, depending on the region considered.

Notes

(1). The assistance of Jim Slitor, Wes Kranitz and Carol Jones was greatly appreciated.

(2). No tests of significance are possible with these correlations because some groups are sub-groups of others . However, the correlations can be interpreted in a purely descriptive sense.

(3). That is, if causal linkages are assumed, and distance is related is related to conflict for a group, reducing "distance", then, would become a policy objective. Similarly, policies might be developed where closeness appears to stimulate conflict exportations. Policies of this type, if causal linkages can be established, would have to be tailored in terms of where most conflict originates in the system. Also, even if linkages are clearly demonstrated, conflict control may have to give way to other policy objectives that may also be related to attribute distances.

Relative Status-field Theory, Results for Conflict, tt Behavior, 1966-69

By: Jack E. Vincent
Professor of Political Science
Florida Atlantic University
Boca Raton, Florida 33432

Relative Status-field Theory, Results for Conflict, tt Behavior, 1966-69

Introduction

The purpose of this paper is to report on the testing of relative status-field theory on WEIS conflict data for the years 1966-69 for international topdogs in economic development and power.

That is, the research focuses on the conflict exportations of developed and powerful nations, relative to the development and power of the nations receiving the behavior. Other reports will treat other classifications, such as underdeveloped powerful nations etc.

The work reported here is part of a larger project which focuses on WEIS conflict and cooperation data for the mid 1960's using the frameworks of attribute, social field, status-field, relative status-field, distance and deviance theories, as guidelines for operational procedures. Since each of these theories are developed elsewhere, they will not be treated fully here (Rummel, 1969,a,b, 1971, Vincent, 1972, 1973,a,b, 1974, 1975, 1976). They can, however, be summarized in the following way.

See Paper 6 discussion, Inserts 57,58,59

Hopefully, the project may eventually suggest crucial or pivotal variables that will assist in understanding conflict and cooperation flows in the international relation system. The purpose here is to report on major findings connected with relative status-field theory, conflict for project steps 13 and 14.

To facilitate further understanding, it is necessary to treat briefly some background concerning status-field and relative status-field theories.

See Paper 3 discussion, Inserts 20,21,22,25,23,24,

To summarize, relative status-field theory works with relative position on economic development and power to allow four different analyses of each dyadic set, i.e., tt, tu, ut, and uu runs. Parameter weights are compared with the four models of conflict across dyadic sets to determine the contributions of economic development and power (the status dimensions) to conflict and cooperation. Because of the complexity of the analysis, however, only tt actors will be analyzed here. The results for the other status combinations will be found in later papers.

In technical terms, then, the purpose of the paper are to: (1) present the weights and signs for each state (where possible) generated by applying relative status-field theory to WEIS conflict data, (2) evaluate the weights and signs in terms of attribute theory (explained below), and (3) construct a general model, from the canonical analysis, for the state system as a whole for tt behavior.

The make the analysis meaningful it is first necessary to (1) present the major features of an a-space analysis and (2) discuss features of the WEIS conflict data collection.

Constructing a-space.

See Paper 1 discussion, Insert 1

The next step required to test relative status-field theory is to score each dyad in respect to it's conflict.

WEIS data manupulations.

See Paper 2 discussion, Inserts 3,8

The stage is now set for applying and interpreting relative status-field theory results on the data. 38 correlation runs were made using the partitioned distance matrices (tt sets) computed from the a-space factor scores (total distance matrix = 16,256 x 22) and the matching WEIS tt dyadic vector (total behavior vector = 16,256 x 1).

Findings: Canonical correlations

The following analysis presents the canonical correlation results. Each country is listed with its canonical correlation in terms of desending magnitude. For example, Ecuador has the highest canonical corelation, .96. All other states, not on the list, exported little or no conflict, or, less than 30 cases were selected to form the tt set and, therefore, such sets were not analyzed.

Put Table 4 about here., I 60

Obviously, relative status-field theory, where a tt analysis was possible, does not apply equally to all states. We may, however, use attribute theory to attempt to discern any patterns in these correlations. That is, we can correlate the factor scores of a-space with the canonical correlation results. It should be clear that we are attempting to determine if the magnitudes of the correlations are related to national attributes and that the correlations, through these methods, are not statistically dependent on the attributes, ie., any tt state has the potential to have a high or low magnitude). When this is done we obtain: economic development (.64), power base (.53) and little ethno-linguistic fractionalization (.22), R=.73, P=.0000. Thus, the higher the economic development, power base and the less the ethno-linguistic fractionalization of a state, the higher its canonical correlation tends to be. To put it another way, relative status-field theory (tt analysis) has the most relevant for states with such characteristics but less relevance for states with the opposite characteristics. In this connection, a crucial question concerns whether or not the theory is significant overall. Whenever many correlations are computed an average expected correlation can be computed in terms of n, the number of subjects, and v, the number of variables. We may then compare theoretical expectations with actual results and draw a conclusion.

See Paper 3 discussion, Insert 33

It may be concluded that relative status-field theory, overall, exceeds chance expectations. Also, the magnitudes of the correlations are related to certain state characteristics, as described above.

Findings: Canonical weights

The following presents the results for the canonical correlation weights. These entries are correlations of the variables in question with the canonical variate scores generated in the canonical analysis. The term weights is used to avoid confusion with the output of canonical correlations. For example, in the case of Algeria, the entry of -.35, in the second column, indicates that power base is correlated -.37 with the canonical variate scores generated in the analysis. In this case, we predict that those dyads that stand low on power base distance stand high on the canonical variate scores. If the correlation is positive, as in the case of the eleventh column, few military personnel per capita (.36), we predict that those dyads standing high on this factor will tend to stand high on the canonical variate scores. All twenty-two entries can be interpreted in this way.

The last entry, the twenty-third, .88 in the case of Algeria, indicates the aggregate variance for all twenty-two factors. In this way, states can be compared across analyses. If the number is large, the correlations tend to be large while, of course, if the number is small they tend to be small.

The entries under column sums of squares indicate the importance of the factors in aggregate variance terms. For example, in such terms, power base tended to be almost twice as important as political instability, 3.00 vs 1.67.

Put Table 6 about here., I 61

Selected weights will now be sorted in terms of descending magnitude for three factors. In the case of the first factor, economic development, all states with positive weights, that is, from Ecuador down through Algeria tended to export conflict to countries that are distant below them in respect to economic development. Countries with negative weights, that is, from Denmark through Czechoslovakia tended to export conflict to states that are close below them in respect to economic development. The same kind of interpretation pertains to the power base and non-competitive political system factors, adjusting for the fact that j can can be above or below i on non-competitive political system.

Put Table 7 about here., I 62

Are these patterns describable in terms of attribute theory? Space does not permit analyzing all the dimensions in these terms but an analysis can be presented for the three selected factors.

The following presents the results of correlating a-space factor scores with + or - weights generated from canonical correlations used in testing the theories. For example, if the positive weights of the factor of power are under consideration, and, economic development correlates .50 with the power weights, we can conclude that, in respect to those that have positive weights on power, the higher the economic development of the nation the more likely it will have a large weight. The purpose of such an analysis is to see whether the magnitudes of the weights generated from the various theories are explainable in terms of attribute theory. Again, it should be clear that there is no necessary relationship between the attributes and the outcome of a + or - sign for tt states and, thus, such an analysis is possible.

Put Table 8 about here., I 63

Using the factor numbers, given below, 1=economic development etc., the results may be summarized as follows:

Put Figure 7 about here., I 64

Thus, like the canonical correlations themselves, the weights generated on the factor dimensions of d-space are partially predictable in terms of attribute theory.

Another approach is to examine the information in terms of an f-test of mean differences.

The significant f-test results, .05 level, means of negative vs. postive weight subjects are given in Table 9. Considering the first case, economic development, the selected factor was large gnp growth rate (12). The f-ratio was 6.8715 and the probability .0125. The group means on this factor were .1749 (- weight subjects) and -.8143 (+ weight subjects).

Put Table 9 about here., I 65

Again, we may summarize the findings:

Put Figure 8 about here., I 66

This further substantiates the above finding that the canonical patterns are predictable in terms of attributes.

Findings: General model

Following the methods discussed elsewhere, we obtain for the "world":

Put Table 10 about here., I 52

We can now list the factors and indicate whether distance or closeness contributes to conflict considering the world system as a whole. In this connection we must follow social field theory rules for interpreting signs on dimensions other than economic development and power since such dimensions were not partitioned on tt, ut etc. lines.

The social field theory rules are:

See Paper 3 discussion, Insert 28

On the status dimensions, then, the code "distant" or "close" will be used while on the remaining dimensions the code "far above" or "far below" be used. That is, these codes identify the characteristics of j's (in distance terms) receiving the most conflict from tt i's in the world system.

Put Table 11 about here., I 67

It follows that assertions about distance as a predictor of conflict for tt actors, is factor specific. Returning to our models for relative status-field theory, however, we see that the conditions for model 1 are met. Topdogs in the system, on economic development and power, tend to export conflict to j's closest to them on these dimensions.

Summary

From the above investigation the following appears established for tt actors: (1) state distances in a-space are related to conflict exportation (as measured by WEIS data), (2) these relationships, overall, tend to exceed chance expectations (table 5), (3) the relevance of the theory for each state varies (table 4) but the magnitudes of the correlations are predictable, in part, from attributes (table 4, discussion), (4) parameter weights for each state can be established on the the distances of a-space (table 6) and the magnitudes are related to attributes (table 8, for selected factors). In this connection, + weight nations tend to be different from - weight nations (table 9, for selected factors), and, (5) from the individual parameter weights, a general world model can be developed (table 10) and the implications of distance for conflict exportations can be established (table 11).

Topdogs on economic development and power tend to export conflict to those close to them on these dimensions.

DISTANCE THEORY, RESULTS FOR CONFLICT, 1966-69, AN INVENTORY OF FINDINGS

By: Jack E. Vincent

Professor of Political Science

Florida Atlantic University

Boca Raton, Florida 33432

DISTANCE THEORY: AN INVENTORY OF SIGNIFICANT FINDINGS FOR CONFLICT

In "Some Empirical Findings On Nations..." Rummel (1969,e) presented, in summary form, the major findings of the DON project and, in particular, those for social field theory.

The purpose here is similar. A summary will be given of the results for distance theory (Vincent,1973,a), using WEIS conflict data.

Distance theory has its roots in social field theory which, in turn, was stimulated primarily by the work of Quincey Wright. Wright (1955) argued that states can be located in "fields", consisting, basically, of each states' relative position on attribute variables, and that such variables can be evaluated in terms of their possible contributions to peace and war.

> The analytical approach to the study of international relations ... implies that each international organization, national goverment, association, individual, or other "system of action", or "decision maker" may be located in a multidimensional field ...A dozen factors are postulated and relations among them suggested ... in the hope that eventually

> measurement of these factors may permit ... correlations to determine the degree of their sufficiency, redundancy, and applicability. (Wright,1955:543-546)

Following this basic framework Wright created three capability and three value fields and predicted likely outcomes for various attribute locations for states in these fields. The assigned locations, however, were in many cases subjective. Also the predicted likely outcomes, such as a state "satisfaction", due to a particular location on the attribute variables in a field, were not operationaly defined.

Rummel first provided a way of operationalizing a version of Wright's ideas in a mathematical form, along with axioms, and called it social field theory. It may be summarized as follows:

See Paper 3 discussion, Insert 19

Rummel's efforts, viewed as a new invention, of course, have engendered considerable debate, discussion and criticism (Hilton, 1970; Vincent, 1972,b, 1975; Phillips, 1974; Zinnes, 1976). Although the dust has not yet settled, concerning social field theory, it may be possible to accept Phillips judgement on it as theory. Phillips (1974) relies upon Karl Popper to make his case:

1. We may look at the internal consistency of the state-

ments. Contradictions are not acceptable.

2. We may investigate the logical form of the statements to determine whether they are empirical or tautologous.

3. We may compare the theory with other theories to see if it is in some sense an advance over current theories.

4. We may test the theory by way of empirical application of the conclusions that can be derived.

(Phillips, 1974: 168)

Examining social field theory in such terms, Phillips concludes:

When evaluating the field theory by the four criteria ...it appears to contain empirical assertions that are not tautologies, to be internally consistent, and to lack empirical falsification. In comparison with other theories it would appear to emphasize a new point: That it is the differences and similarities between nations which are the forces leading to conflict and cooperation. One could certainly argue that the shift from thinking about national attributes as absolute concepts to considering them as relational forces, is a potential theoretical advance in the sense that it is a new mode of thinking. (Phillips, 1974: 172)

In his final concluding comments, Phillips states, "...This article has attempted to show that theory certainly does exist. It is time that we turn from the debate as to whether theory exists to the critical assessment of utilities of the present theories." (Phillips, 1974: 188) Obviously, I agree with Phillips, concerning the theoretical value of such frameworks.

Distance theory emerged, in part, from a criticism of some of the mathematical implications of Rummel's way of measuring distance (Vincent, 1972,b). To measure distance between nations, Rummel first computes factor scores for the nations on the factor dimensions of a-space (attribute space). Distance is then defined by algebraic subtraction of the factor scores. For any particular nation, it is possible to determine whether another nation is above (expressed as a negative distance) or below (expressed as a positive distance) as well as determine the "magnitude" of the distance. However, this particular way of measuring distance has certain implications, for correlational analysis, that may not, at first glance, be obvious. If such a measure of distance is correlated with a behavioral measure, say in respect to conflict, and the correlation is positive, we would obtain the following results:

See Paper 3 discussion, Inserts 25,26,27

Basically, then, distance theory is a dissimilarity model rather than a directed dissimilarity model, as in the case of social field theory. In distance theory every deviation of actor "J," in respect to his attributes, from actor "i" contributes to the absolute distance between them. The location of every actor to every other actor, in this absolute sense, is then summarized, in d-space, through the calculation of dyadic factor scores derived from the factor analysis of absolute distances. Thus, the purpose of distance theory is to provide a set of guidelines for determining the relationship of absolute attribute distance between states to international behavior. The basic formula and assumptions may be summarized as:

See Paper 3 discussion, Insert 27

When testing distance theory on a single index, as in the case of the application given here, the canonical model normally used in testing (that is, used in the case of several behavioral vectors), if applied, reduces mathematically to the multiple regression model. Thus, when using a single behavioral index, instead of several canonical correlations to interpret, for each dyadic sub-set, only one set of parameter weights are evaluated for each dyadic subset.

The decision to use a single index is related to the nature of the WEIS (McClelland,1972) data used to represent international behavior. Because many variables in the WEIS collection are badly skewed, that is, many states received a score of zero, non-zero data points can be reduced by aggregating across the WEIS categories. For this project, it was done for a three year period (1966-1969) for the following categories:

See Paper 2 discussion, Insert 3,8

The above decision to use the WEIS data bank my raise some eyebrows because of the concern that has developed about the collection regarding possible "American bias," as a consequence of using the New York Times as a data source. It has been shown that other data sources do vary from the New York Times in news coverage (Azar, 1975,b). Is it, then, worthwhile to use such a source? Perhaps McClelland himself provided the best answer to this type of question.

> We should expect some mistakes, some distortion, and some erroneous selection in the context of the international news. Some items will report events that never happen. Others will be products of governmental manipulation and deception and will have made their appearance on the record because they were "planted" there. How bad these defects are can be estimated only in very general terms. Several points can be made in support of the general reliability of the news:
> 1) There is no doubt that the volume, detail, and accuracy of international news reporting have greatly increased over the past half century...
> 2) The professionalization of journalism and the maturing

of newsgathering organizations are important forces in increasing the effort toward accuracy.

3) Mulitiple sources and channels of information provide some safeguard against the systematic falsifications of reports. The sovereignty of states and the diversity of national interests contribute some beneficial effects, globally, against news management.

4) The real source of large numbers of international news stories is the government agency. The news media are essentially, pipelines between the regime and the public. One of the oldest maxims of statecraft, stated by Machiavelli among others, is that it does not pay to lie to often.

5) "Hard news" has a more straightforward status than the news that is explanatory, interpretive, speculative, or predictive...(Note that the latter type of data are not included in the WEIS collection.)

6) Although the public record of international events is defective by any strict standard, it serves well enough for many kinds of analysis. It is to be argued that public reporting can be used more effectively for statistical evaluations than for the purposes of historical reconstruction - its most common use. It is unlikely that a few erroneous reports will make a big difference in an aggregate of several hundred items. (McClelland, 1968: 43 -48)

Even if the WEIS collection has an "American bias," it can be reasonably assumed that the research procedures used, if applied to other data sets, would yield findings that would correlate well with those generated here, although it is beyond the present resources of this researcher to demonstrate that this is the case at this time. The principal problem in this regard is that other major data sets such CREON (33 actor-states) and COPDAB (55 actor-states) have n's that are much smaller than the n employed in this project so that exact comparison, at this point in time, for the 128 states used in this study, is not possible.

It is admitted that the WEIS data is, in fact, somewhat distorted, but not so much so that the correlations generated through the analyses that follow would have reversed signs if the data bank, in fact, were not distorted. Thus, it is admitted the project is looking at the world through mirrors that are somewhat contorted, like those in a fun house. Non-distorted data can be symbolized by "true mirrors" while the WEIS (possible) distortion of the real world can be depicted as like a "fun house mirror." It is assumed that distortion is not so pronounced that the "reflection" is unrecognizable. In short, we would expect a highly similar set of correlations to be generated, if the research methods employed in this project, were applied to a completely unbiased data set, (which has not yet been constructed or demonstrated to exist).

In presenting the findings it is not going to be possible to present all of the intermediate steps since, even a few of them would consume virtually all available space. It is possible however, to treat briefly the construction of a- and d-space.

A-space is generated by factor analyzing attribute variables and locating the states on factor dimensions, which emerge, through the calculation of factor scores. These scores become useful in interpreting the parameter weights that develop in applying distance theory. The factors generated from analyzing 144 attribute variables were:

See Paper 1 discussion, Insert 1

D-space construction utilizes the same 144 variables but factor analyzes a matrix of absolute distances computed on the original variables to locate dyads rather than individual nations in the space. The factors generated were:

See Paper 4 discussion, Insert 37

In testing distance theory the major purpose is to correlate d-space factor scores with the WEIS conflict vector. This means that 128 separate correlations must be computed, since 128 states (and hence 128 dyadic subsets) were used. The effort here is to go beyond simply ascertaining various state models. Each model, of course, tends to be different. For example, the United States has a weight of -.32, the U.S.S.R., -.49 and Kenya, .53, on the factor of power base.

Such results indicate that some states have large positive

weights, some states moderate or weak positive weights, some states weak or moderate negative weights and some states large negative weights. Our major purpose, in this paper, is to bring some order out of what appears, at first glance, to be chaos. This will be accomplished by special modes of additional analysis.

The first mode will be to perform a discriminant function analysis on the positive versus the negative weight subjects, for each of the factors of d-space using the factors of a-space as discriminators. The second will be to correlate the factor scores of a-space with the magnitude of the weights.

A brief statement on discriminant function analysis (Hadley,1961) seems to be in order.

See Paper 2 discussion, Insert 14

Each of the findings, which follows, is based on a significance level of .05 or less, and compares the characteristics of those with - versus + weights that developed when discriminant function analysis (using a-space factors as the discriminators) was applied to the model weights generated on the d-space dimensions.

Positive weights will be treated first. From the above discussion of distance theory, it is apparent that a positive weight on a d-space distance dimension indicates that "i" is exporting conflict to those distant from him, on the dimension considered, while a negative weight indicates that those close to i receive the conflict. On a closeness dimension however, the relationship is reversed. A positive weight indicates that those J's that are close to i will receive the conflict, while a negative weight indicates that those that are distant from i tend to receive the conflict. In presenting the results of the positive weight analysis, then, whenever the phrase is observed "J's distant" we know that we are dealing with a "distance dimension" while the phrase "J's close" indicates that we are dealing with a "closeness dimension." In general we are attempting to determine the a-space characteristics of those nations which received positive weights across the dimensions of d-space (in applying distance theory).

The analysis generated the following inventory of findings.

(See: Appendix A, List 1)., I 73

Thus, those that export conflict to those distant from them on power base tend to be underdeveloped and small and have much domestic violence. The positive weight nation's mean scores on the a-space factors are -.2261 on economic development, -.4451 for power and -.3186 for little domestic violence.

Performing the same analysis for negative weight nations, we find:

(See: Appendix A, List 2)., I 74

It can be seen that those that export conflict to those close to them in respect to economic development tend to be developed, powerful and have little domestic violence.

As noted above, however, the tendency to export conflict varies, in the sense that not all of the positive weight nations have the same weight magnitudes. Is there a pattern to such fluctuations? In this case the question can be answered by computing the correlation between the a-space factors and the magnitude of the weights. For positive weight subjects we find:

(See: Appendix A, List 3)., I 75

The term "most likely" is used in the above statements because this analysis indicates the attributes characteristics of those with the largest weights. Thus, in respect to power base, those "most likely" to export conflict distant from them tend to have the characteristics of few military personnel per capita.

For the negative weight subjects we find:

(See: Appendix A, List 4).,I 76

Each of these findings may be viewed as having potential policy relevance. For example, examining the first set of findings in Lists 1 and 2, we would expect, making a causal assumption, that if a nation were to shift from high development to low development and from high power base to low power base and move from a situation of little domestic to much domestic violence, then, it should tend tend to shift from a - type exporter on power base (indicating high exportation to those close on power base) to a + type exporter (indicating high exportation to those distant on power base). In addition as long as a nation remained a - type exporter, we would also expect that decreases in the magnitude of economic development, power base and energy production would tend to reduce the magnitude of the - weight on power base (as suggested by the correlational analysis for negative weights, given in List 4). Obviously space does not permit a restatement of each inventory finding in such terms, but each can be so interpreted, if one is prepared to make a causal assumption, recognizing that some attributes are, in fact, not likely to change.

It is also possible to analyse the relative power and direction of the a-space discriminators across the d-space dimensions. This can be done by indicating the frequencies, of significant discrimination for each a-space factor, and whether high scores (h in the table below = same as factor name) or low scores (l in the table below = opposite of factor name) indicate likely conflict exportation.

Analyzing the situation of closeness first (when i's export to j's close to them in respect to their attributes) we obtain:

Table 7., I 70

The major discriminators, then, tend to be economic development population growth rate, domestic violence, health expenditures, energy production and executive adjustments. For example, economic development discriminated 9 times (9 h's and l's), with every h indicating high development predicting high conflict exportation (in the case of closeness to i's attributes) and every l indicating low development predicting high exportation. To illustrate, using the Inventory (List 2), we see that high economic development predicted high conflict exportation in respect to closeness on economic developmentand power base but low economic development predicted high exportation in respect to closeness on religion etc. Thus, high development does not predict high conflict in the case of closeness for all attributes but only for the five d-space factors identified above in the Inventory, such as power base. Low development predicted high conflict, in the case of closeness, in the remaining cases.

It is interesting to note that the largest "pure" (one direction only) discriminator is power. High power base, in each case, predicts high conflict exportation, in the case of closeness on the five attribute dimensions where a significant discrimination occured.

The distance (as oppossed to closeness) findings, of course, do not have to be analyzed, in such terms, since such an analysis will produce mirror image results of those generated for the closeness data.

It will now be interesting to subject the correlational data to the same type of anaylsis.

For the closeness data we obtain:

Table 8., I 71

For the distance data we obtain:

Table 9., I 72

Considerable differences are apparent between the closeness and distance analyses. For states that export high conflict to those close to them in respect to their own attributes, high economic development and high power are the best predictors. There are only two cases where low development or low power are linked with large parameter weights. In contrast, considering states which tend to export high conflict to those distant from them, in respect to their attributes, we find that few military personnel per capita is the the most consistant predictor. Those most likely to export to those distant from them, in respect to the attribute dimensions of d-space, tend to have few military personnel per capita.

These data suggest, then, that changes in economic development and power base may have the most impact for those most likely to export conflict to those close to their own attributes, while few military personnel per capita appears to be of particular relevance to states that tend to export conflict to those distant from their attributes.

We must conclude that the tendency to export conflict is not a random event relative to attribute distance. Not only is the tendency to have negative or positive weights on the d-space distance dimensions related to attributes, but so are the magnitude of such weights. The primary discriminators for positive versus negative weights are economic development, population growth rate, domestic violence, health expendituress, energy production and executive adjustments, with power base emerging as the "purist" discriminator. The primary and purist dicriminators for the magnitude of the weights in d-space were economic development and power for closeness and few military personnel per capita for distance.

Thus, it is possible that attributes are related to conflict exportations. Further, suppression of conflict may, in part, result from attribute manipulation. At first glance, such a statement, without fully appreciating the implications of the above analysis, may sound strained and, yet, the major purpose of many foreign policy decisions is, in fact, a form of attribute manipulation. It should be clear that policies that concern exportation of arms, land area, birth control, education, etc., all fall within the realm of attribute manipulation within the purview of distance theory. If the arguments of Phillips (1974) are accepted, concerning the theoretical nature of this type of framework and those of McClelland (1968) accepted, concerning the potential usefullness of the WEIS data set for broad scale hypothesis testing, then the opinion held by some that dyadic-attribute type research holds little promise needs to be revised.

A single study of this type, of course, is not conclusive. Various attribute related models need to be explored and cross-time perspectives may prove to be particularly profitable. In view of these findings, however, such research needs to be encouraged and stimulated, given the long range potential payoffs, instead of ignored or discouraged which, at times, has been the case.

PATTERNS OF CONFLICT: DISTANCE THEORY

By: Jack E. Vincent

Professor of Political Science

Florida Atlantic University

Boca Raton, Florida 33432

PATTERNS OF CONFLICT: RESULTS FOR DISTANCE THEORY

See Paper 8 introductory discussion

Our purpose here is to evaluate distance theory results for conflict using two further modes of analysis.

The first mode will be to perform a factor analysis on the weights of the nations across the d-space dimensions. The second will be to correlate the factor scores of a-space with the factor scores generated from the analysis of the weights.

These modes of analysis will show how conflict export patterns cluster, how nations are, in fact, located on such clusters and reveal characteristics of + vs. - weight nations.

The results follow:

(See Appendix A)., I 77

From the Appendix it can be seen that, in applying distance theory to conflict data, the resulting distance theory weights of nation states tend to cluster. When each state is located on each factor cluster, the factor scores indicates the degree to which each state approximates the behavior indicated.

For example, on the first cluster, grouping energy production, power base and economic development, Ghana, Kenya and Guyana best fit the pattern of exporting to those distant on these variables. East Germany, Poland, West Germany and Canada, however, best fit the pattern of exporting to states close to them on these variables. The anaylsis of characteristics (correlating a-space with the factor score resuLts) indicates that states with low economic development, small power base and low energy production tend to fit the + model (export to those distant) while states with high economic development, large power base and high energy production tend to fit the - model (export to those close).

These results may suggest causal linkages relating to the clusters. That is, as states move from a situation of low economic development, small power base and low energy production to a situation of high economic development, large power base and high energy production, there may be a tendency for such states to move from a pattern of exporting to those distant, on the variable cluster indicated, to a pattern of exporting to those close.

It is not necessary to treat each set of findings in this way since each can be evaluated in the same terms. Each gives a description of a variable cluster, a sort listing of the states in terms of their tendency to approximate the variable cluster model, and, from the characteristics analysis, a suggestion as to possible causal linkages between export patterns and national attributes.

The Appendix also allows other hypothesis testing and research uses. For example, pairs of nations can be traced throughout the analysis to see if they tend to fit the same profile. To illustrate, in tracing the patterns for the U.S. and U.S.S.R., it is found that they follow the same pattern for 11 out of the total of 13 variable clusters, with opposite signed factor scores found only on two clusters. From this, it can be concluded that the U.S. and the U.S.S.R. tend to "look alike" in their behavioral patterns, as measured by the WEIS data, in terms of attribute-distance predictions.

Summary

Exportation of conflict is not random, in the I.R. system, in respect to attributes and attribute distances. Patterned behavior can be established by factor analyzing the weights generated by applying distance theory to WEIS data. Thirteen clusters developed out of the 33 weight variables and were presented in Appendix. States were located on the cluters by computing factor scores, which show the degree to which each state approximates the "model" suggested by the cluster. Correlation of a-space factor scores with such scores may suggest the possible casual linkages between attributes and location on the variable clusters. The results also lend themselves to other descriptive and hypothesis testing purposes. For example, a trace of the U.S. And U.S.S.R. scores showed them agreeing on 11 out of the total of 13 clusters.

Bibliography

Adelman, Irma, And Morris, Cynthia Taft. Society, Politics, And Economic Development: A Quantitative Approach. Baltimore: John Hopkins Press, 1967.

Azar, E. E., Cohen, S.H., And McCormick, J. The Problem Of Source Coverage In The Use Of International Events Data, International Studies Quarterly, 1972, 16, pp. 373-388.

Azar, E.E., And Sloan, T.J. Dimensions Of Interaction: A Source Book For The Study Of The Behavior Of 31 Nations From 1948 Through 1973. University Of Pittsburgh Center For International Studies, Pittsburgh, Pennsylvania, 1975a.

Azar, E.E. Ten Issues In Events Research, E. Azar And J. Ben-Dak, Eds. Theory And Practice Of Events Research. New York, New York: Gordon And Breach, 1975b, pp. 1-17.

Banks, Arthur S., And Textor, Robert. A Cross-Polity Survey. Cambridge, Massachusetts: Mit Press, 1963.

Banks, Arthur S., And Gregg, Phillip. Grouping Political Systems: Q Factor Analysis Of A Cross-Polity Survey, American Behavioral Scientist, 1965, 3, pp. 3-5.

Banks, Arthur S. Cross-Polity Time Series. Cambridge, Massachusetts: Mit Press, 1971.

Burgess, Philip M. And Munton, Donald. An Inventory Of Archived And Fugitive International Relations Data. Behavioral Science Laboratory, Department Of Political Science, Ohio State University, Mershon Centre, Columbus, Ohio.

Calhoun, Herbert L. Exploratory Applications To Scaled Event Date, Paper Read At The 13th Annual Meeting Of The International Studies Association, Dallas, March 1972.

Cattell, Raymond B. The Basis Of Recognition And Interpretation Of Factors, Educational And Psychological Measurement, 1962, 22, pp. 667-695.

Cattell, Raymond B. The Meaning And Strategic Use Of Factor Anaylsis, In Raymond B. Cattell, Ed., Handbook Of Multivariate Experimental Psychology. Chicago: Rand Mcnally, 1966.

Collins, John. Factor Analysis And The Grouping Of Events Data: Problems And Possible Solutions. St. Louis, Missouri: University Of Missouri, 1969, pp. 121-128.

Doran, C. F., Pendley, R.E., And Antunes, G.E. A Test Of Cross-National Event Reliability: Global Versus Regional Data Sources, International Studies Quarterly, 1973, 17, pp. 175-203.

East, M.A. And Gregg, P.M. Factors Influencing Cooperation And Conflict In The International System, International Studies Quarterly, 1967, 11, pp. 244-269.

Goodman, R., Hart, J., And Rosecrance, R. Testing International Theory: Methods And Data In A Situational Analysis Of International Politics, Situational Analysis Project, Paper Number 2, Mimeo, 1972.

Gregg, Phillip M. And Banks, Arthur S. Dimensions Of Political Systems: Factor

Analysis Of A Cross Polity Survey, American Political Science Review, 1965, 59, pp. 602-614.

Hadley, G. Linear Algebra. Reading, Massachusetts: Addison-Westley, 1961.

Harman, Harry H. Modern Factor Analysis. Chicago: University Of Chicago Press, 1960.

Hilton, Gordon. A Review Of The Dimensionality Of Nations Project, Richardson Institute For Conflict And Peace Research, Mimeo, 1971.

Hoggard, G. An Analysis Of The Real Data, E. Azar And J. Ben-Dak, Eds., Theory And Practice Of Events Research. New York: Gordon And Breach, 1975, pp. 19-27.

Horst, Paul. Generalized Canonical Correlations And Their Applications To Experimental Data. Seattle: University Of Washington, Mimeo, 1961a.

Horst, Paul. Relations Among M Sets Of Measures, Psychometrika, 1961b, 26, pp. 129-149.

Hotelling, Harold. Relations Between Two Sets Of Variates, Biometrika, 1936, 28, pp. 321-377.

Hotelling, Harold. The Most Predictable Criterion, Journal Of Educational Psychology, 1953, 26, pp. 139-142.

Kaiser, Henry F. The Varimax Criterion For Analytical Rotation In Factor Analysis, Psychometrika, 1958, 23, pp. 187-200.

Kegley, Charles W., Jr. A Circumplex Model Of International Interactions, Institute Of International Studies, University Of North Carolina, 1976a.

Kegley, C. And Skinner, R.A. The Case-for-Analysis Problem In The Comparative Study Of Foreign Policy, J.N. Rosenau, Ed., In Search Of Global Patterns. New York: Free Press, 1976b.

Lewin, Kurt. Field Theory In Social Science. Dorwin Cartwright, Ed. New York: Hammer Torch Books, 1964.

McClelland, C. International Interaction Analysis: Basic Research And Some Practical Applications, WEIS Technical Report No. 2, University Of Souther California, Los Angeles, 1968.

McClelland, C. World Event Interaction Survey. ICPR Edition, University Of Southern California, Los Angeles, 1972.

McGowan, P.J. And Shapiro, H.B. The Comparative Study Of Foreign Policy. Beverly Hills, California: Sage Publications, 1973.

McNemar, Q. Psychological Statistics, New York: John Wiley and Sons, Inc., 1968.

Newcombe, Alan And Wert, James. An Internation Tensiometer For The Prediction Of War. Canadian Peace Research Institute, Oakville, Ontario, Canada, 1972.

Park, Tong Whan. Asian Conflict In Systematic Perspective: Application Of Field Theory (1955 And 1963), Research Report No. 35, The Dimensionality Of Nations Project, University Of Hawaii, 1969.

Park, Tong Whan. The Role Of Distance In International Relations: A New Look At The Social Field Theory, Paper, Presented To The International Studies Association, New Orleans, 1970.

Phillips, Warren R. A Mathematical Theory Of Conflict Dynamics, Research Report No. 39, The Dimensionality Of Nations Project, University Of Hawaii, 1970.

Phillips, Warren R. Where Have All The Theories Gone? World Politics, 1974, 26, pp. 156-188.

Popper, Karl. The Logic Of Scientific Discovery. New York: Basic Books, 1959.

Rummel, R.J. Field Theory And Attribute Theories Of Nationa Behavior: Some Mathematical Interrelationships, Research Report No. 31, The Dimensionality Of Nations Project, University Of Hawaii, 1969a.

Rummel, R.J. Field Theory And Indicators Of International Behavior, Research Report No. 29, The Dimensionality Of Nations Project, University Of Hawaii, 1969b.

Rummel, R.J. Forcasting International Relations: A Proposed Investigation Of 3-Mode Factor Analysis, Technological Forecasting, 1969c, 1, pp. 197-216.

Rummel, R.J. Indicators Of Cross National And International Patterns, American Political Science Review, 1969d, 63, pp. 127-147.

Rummel, R.J. Some Empirical Findings On Nations And Their Behvaior, World Politics, 1969,e, 21, pp. 226-241.

Rummel, R.J. Applied Factor Analysis. Evanston, Illinois: Northwestern University Press, 1970a.

Russett, Bruce M., et al. World Handbook Of Political And Social Indicators. New Haven, Connecticut: Yale University Press, 1964.

Russett, Bruce M. International Regions And The International System. Chicago: Rand Mcnally, 1967.

Salmore, S.A. And Hermann, C.F. The Effect Of Size, Development, And Accountability On Foreign Policy, Peace Research Papers, 1969, 14, pp. 15-30.

Sawyer, Jack. Dimensions Of Nations: Size, Wealth And Politics, The American Journal Of Sociology, 1967, 73, pp. 145-172.

Sigler, J. Reliability Problems In The Measurement Of International Events In The Elite Press, V. Davis, Ed., Application Of Events Data Analysis: Cases, Issues, And Programmes In International Interaction. Beverly Hills, California: Sage Publications, 1972.

Sloan, Thomas. The Development Of Cooperation And Conflict Interaction Scales: An Advance In The Measurement And Analysis Of Events Data, Studies Of Conflict And Peace, Department Of Political Science, University Of North Carolina, Chapel Hill.

Tanter, Raymond. Dimensions Of Conflict Behavior Within And Between Nations, 1958-60, Journal Of Conflict Resolution, 1966, 10, pp. 41-64.

Taylor, Charles L. And Hudson, Michael C. World Handbook Of Political And Social Indicators. First ICPR Edition. Ann Arbor, Michigan, 1971.

Vincent, Jack E. Factor Analysis In International Relations: Interpretation, Problem Areas And An Application. Gainesville, Florida: University Of Florida Press, 1971a.

Vincent, Jack E. Generating Some Empirically Based Indices For International Alliance And Regional Systems Operating In The Early 1960S, (with Joseph Falardeau, Edward Schwerin, Barry!Boseman, And Robert Jednak). International Studies Quarterly, 1971b, 15, pp. 465-525.

Vincent, Jack E. Predicting Voting Patterns In The General Assembly, American Political Science Review, 1971c, 65, pp. 471-498.

Vincent, Jack E. Scaling The Universe Of States On Certain Useful Multivariate Dimensions, Journal Of Social Psychology, 1971d, 85, pp. 261-283.

Vincent, Jack E. An Application Of Attribute Theory To General Assembly Voting Patterns And Some Implications, International Organization, 1972a, 26, pp. 551-582.

Vincent, Jack E. Comments On Social Field Theory, Research Report No. 58, The Dimensionality Of Nations Project, University Of Hawaii, 1972b.

Vincent, Jack E. Distance Theory, Florida Atlantic University, Mimeo, 1973a.

Vincent, Jack E. Empirical Tests Of Attributes, Social Field And Status-Field Theories On International Relations Data, (with Roger Baker, Susan Gagnon, Keith Hamm, And Scott Reilly). International Studies Quarterly, 1973b, 17, pp. 405-443.

Vincent, Jack E. A Critique Of Social Field Theory And Some Suggestions For Further Elaborations, Political Methodology, 1975, 2, pp. 151-188.

Vincent, Jack E. Explorations In D-space: An Application Of Deviance Theory, Comparative Political Studies, 1976, 9, pp. 107-135.

Vincent Jack E. Analyzing International Conflict And Cooperation Flows: An Application Of Attribute Theory, Social Science Quarterly, 1977, 58, pp. 111-120.

Wright, Quincy. A Study Of International Relations. New York: Appleton-Century-Crofts, 1955.

Young, Robert A. A Classification Of Nations According To Foreign Policy Output, Paper, Read At The 66th Annual Meeting Of The American Political Science Association, Los Angeles, September 1970.

Zinnes, Dina A. Contemporary Research In International Relations: A Perspective And A Critical Appraisal. New York: The Free Press, 1976.

SPECIAL ATTACHMENT

ATTRIBUTES AND NATIONAL BEHAVIOR: MODERN INTERNATIONAL RELATIONS MONOGRAPH SERIES: PART 2

BY

Jack E. Vincent, Ph.D.
Professor of Political Science
Florida Atlantic University
Boca Raton, Florida 33432

ATTRIBUTES AND NATIONAL BEHAVIOR, PART 2

Part 2 consists of 42 monographs of a large scale project testing several attribute, attribute distance based theories. Each research monograph is numbered and given a sub-title, listed below. Each focuses upon some aspect of a large scale research effort correlating national attributes to international behavior. All monographs can be printed from tape by computer.

Tape specs are: 9 track, 800 BPI, EBCDIC, 132 character records, 2400 feet.

INDEX

1. GENERATING A-SPACE FOR THE MID-1960'S: WITH AN EXAMPLE OF POSSIBLE USAGE

Nations are located on 22 factor dimensions generated from a factor analysis of 144 attribute variables. Factor scores are provided. The various uses of a-space are discussed and demonstrated.

2. CREATING INDEXES FOR NATIONAL CONFLICT AND COOPERATION EXPORTATIONS (1966-1969) WITH AN EMPIRICAL APPLICATION

One hundred and twenty-eight states are located on vectors of conflict and cooperation built from the WEIS data bank. Various uses for these vectors are illustrated and discussed.

3. COMPARING VARIOUS ATTRIBUTE BASED THEORIES ON SELECTED DIMENSIONS, IN TERMS OF EMPIRICAL RESULTS

World models for social field theory, distance theory, and relative status-field theory are presented and compared and discussed. Policy prescriptions based on each model are then presented.

4. DISTANCE THEORY, RESULTS FOR CONFLICT, 1966-69.

Distance theory is tested on WEIS 1966-69 data for over 16,000 dyadic relationships. A model for each nation in the system is generated and compared to a world model.

5. A STANDARDIZED APPROACH TO INTERNATIONAL RELATIONS ATTRIBUTE DATA

One hundred and forty-four attribute variables are standardized for 128 states. The various uses to which such data can be put are demonstrated and the value of utilizing z-scores discussed.

6 DISTANCE THEORY: A COMPARISON OF VARIOUS REGIONAL GROUPINGS ON 1966-69 CONFLICT DATA

Over 30 regional groupings such as NATO and OAS are analyzed in terms of distance theory. A model is generated for each region which describes typical conflict flows and comparisons are made.

7. DISTANCE THEORY, A COMPARISON OF VARIOUS REGIONAL GROUPINGS ON 1966-69 COOPERATION DATA

This has the same purpose as the sixth monograph, but applies the distance theory framework to cooperation data.

9. DISTANCE THEORY, RESULTS FOR COOPERATION, 1966-69

This has the same objectives as the fourth monograph, but uses cooperation rather than conflict data.

10. RELATIVE STATUS-FIELD THEORY, RESULTS FOR CONFLICT, TT BEHAVIOR, 1966-69

11. RELATIVE STATUS-FIELD THEORY, RESULTS FOR COOPERATION, TT BEHAVIOR, 1966-69

12. RELATIVE STATUS-FIELD THEORY, RESULTS FOR CONFLICT, TU BEHAVIOR, 1966-69

13. RELATIVE STATUS-FIELD THEORY, RESULTS FOR COOPERATION, TU BEHAVIOR, 1966-69

14. RELATIVE STATUS-FIELD THEORY, RESULTS FOR CONFLICT, UT BEHAVIOR, 1966-69

15. RELATIVE STATUS-FIELD THEORY, RESULTS FOR COOPERATION, UT BEHAVIOR, 1966-69

16. RELATIVE STATUS-FIELD THEORY, RESULTS FOR CONFLICT, UU

BEHAVIOR, 1966-69

17. RELATIVE STATUS-FIELD THEORY, RESULTS FOR COOPERATION, UU BEHAVIOR, 1966-69

The above monographs concern relative status-field theory and its application to conflict or cooperation data for the time period indicated. A model for each state is generated whenever a tt, tu, ut, or uu analysis is possible. Generally speaking, this means that approximately 30 states are given a model in any one of the above applications. Implications for policymaking are generated from world models constructed out of such empirical results. All layouts are standardized.

19. STATISTICAL CONCEPTS FOR STUDENTS OF INTERNATIONAL RELATIONS

This provides an introduction to virtually all of the methodology utilized in connection with the generation of the research supplements. Topics treated include factor analysis, discriminant function analysis, path analysis, and matrix algebra.

26. PROJECT PROGRAMS

All significant project programs are given, many with innovative design (operation on Univac 1108, 256 k exec-8 operating system, level 33 R2). All basic commands are defined in a thorough introduction to the supplement. Local programmers should be able to adjust the programs for use on their own system.

27. DISTANCE THEORY, RESULTS FOR CONFLICT, 1966-69, AN INVENTORY OF FINDINGS

28. DISTANCE THEORY, RESULTS FOR COOPERATION, 1966-69, AN INVENTORY OF FINDINGS

29. SOCIAL FIELD THEORY, RESULTS FOR CONFLICT, 1966-69, AN INVENTORY OF FINDINGS

30. SOCIAL FIELD THEORY, RESULTS FOR COOPERATION, 1966-69, AN INVENTORY OF FINDINGS

31. RELATIVE STATUS-FIELD THEORY, RESULTS FOR CONFLICT, TT ACTORS, 1966-1969, AN INVENTORY OF FINDINGS

32. RELATIVE STATUS-FIELD THEORY, RESULTS FOR COOPERATION, TT ACTORS, 1966-1969, AN INVENTORY OF FINDINGS

33. RELATIVE STATUS-FIELD THEORY, RESULTS FOR CONFLICT, TU ACTORS, 1966-1969, AN INVENTORY OF FINDINGS

34. RELATIVE STATUS-FIELD THEORY, RESULTS FOR COOPERATION, TU ACTORS, 1966-1969, AN INVENTORY OF FINDINGS

35. RELATIVE STATUS-FIELD THEORY, RESULTS FOR CONFLICT, UT ACTORS, 1966-1969, AN INVENTORY OF FINDINGS

36. RELATIVE STATUS-FIELD THEORY, RESULTS FOR COOPERATION, UT ACTORS, 1966-1969, AN INVENTORY OF FINDINGS

37. RELATIVE STATUS-FIELD THEORY, RESULTS FOR CONFLICT, UU ACTORS, 1966-1969, AN INVENTORY OF FINDINGS

38. RELATIVE STATUS-FIELD THEORY, RESULTS FOR COOPERATION, UU ACTORS, 1966-1969, AN INVENTORY OF FINDINGS

The above monographs apply discriminant function analysis to nations exhibiting positive vs. negative weights, across all of the dimensions of a- and d-space, for each of the theories. Thus, the attribute characteristics of nations exporting a particular way, say to those close below them on economic development, are identified and compared with the characteristics of those exporting differently.

39. PATTERNS OF CONFLICT: DISTANCE THEORY

40. PATTERNS OF COOPERATION: DISTANCE THEORY

41. PATTERNS OF CONFLICT: SOCIAL FIELD THEORY

42. PATTERNS OF COOPERATION: SOCIAL FIELD THEORY

43. PATTERNS OF CONFLICT: RELATIVE STATUS-FIELD THEORY, TT ACTORS

44. PATTERNS OF COOPERATION: RELATIVE STATUS-FIELD THEORY, TT ACTORS

45. PATTERNS OF CONFLICT: RELATIVE STATUS-FIELD THEORY, TU ACTORS

46. PATTERNS OF COOPERATION: RELATIVE STATUS-FIELD THEORY, TU ACTORS

47. PATTERNS OF CONFLICT: RELATIVE STATUS-FIELD THEORY, UT ACTORS

48. PATTERNS OF COOPERATION: RELATIVE STATUS-FIELD THEORY, UT ACTORS

49. PATTERNS OF CONFLICT: RELATIVE STATUS-FIELD THEORY, UU ACTORS

50. PATTERNS OF COOPERATION: RELATIVE STATUS-FIELD THEORY, UU ACTORS

The above monographs apply second stage factor analysis to the parameter weights for all the theories. Such analyses determine whether behavioral tendencies tend to cluster. That is, to illustrate, if a nation tends to export conflict to other nations close below it in respect to economic development, does it also tend to do so in respect to power base? All nations are rank sorted in terms of the variable clusters that develop so that it is possible to determine whether any two nations, or, any group of nations, share the same "export profiles."

Note: All monographs on tape are set up to print on a Univac document processor. Special programs to assist in printing on a Decwriter II for upper and lower case, double space, length adjusted for the Decwriter and with footnote capability, are contained in Monograph 26. Tables or figures that go beyond 80 columns may be folded if the document processor is used. If this is undesirable, they can be printed by other standard print commands, such as an editor program, which can print, without folding, to 132 columns. Also, document commands are invisible in the copy only if the document processor is used. If other print commands are used, the document commands will be visible, i.e., will appear as "double", "space", etc. and are left justified. If they are not needed, they can be ignored or edited out. All monographs are in mixed upper and lower case, except Monographs 19 and 26, which are in upper case only.

COMMON APPENDIX

INSERT 1

A-SPACE ROTATED LOADINGS

001 TOTAL POPULATION					-.23	.93	-.01	.06	.03	-.00
					-.00	-.08	-.08	-.05	-.01	.01
					-.04	-.03	-.02	.04	-.00	-.03
					-.07	-.02	-.02	.02	.95	
002 POPULATION GROWTH RATE, 1960-65					-.28	-.18	.07	-.04	-.83	.0
					.03	.01	.01	.11	.00	.19
					.09	.05	-.03	-.04	.05	.02
					-.03	-.02	.04	.01	.88	
003 POPULATION GROWTH RATE, 1950-65					-.20	-.17	.10	-.01	-.82	.0
					.02	.01	-.04	.09	.03	.14
					.05	.15	-.07	-.06	.06	.06
					-.04	-.02	-.02	.02	.83	
004 TOTAL AREA					-.28	.47	.02	.08	-.04	.72
					.14	-.06	-.13	.08	.10	-.12
					-.01	-.01	.01	.14	.03	-.04
					.02	-.00	-.05	-.04	.92	
005 DENSITY(PEOPLE PER SQUARE KILOMETER)					.12	.27	.00	-.08	.07	-.87
					-.05	.09	.06	-.09	-.06	.06
					.13	-.06	.01	-.05	-.05	.02
					.02	.02	.08	-.02	.92	
**********************************										
COLUMN SUM OF SQUARES	31.17	30.98	5.98	7.94	4.44	4.09	3.61	3.64	3.59	2.34
	3.64	2.21	2.05	3.06	2.16	2.00	1.62	1.62	1.51	1.58
	1.84	1.57								

01 ECONOMIC DEVELOPMENT

085 NATIONAL GOVERNMENT REVENUE PER CAPITA	.92
087 NATIONAL GOVERNMENT EXPENDITURE PER CAPITA	.91
095 IMPORTS PER CAPITA	.91
031 GNP PER CAPITA (IN U.S. DOLLARS)	.90
058 EDUCATION EXPENDITURE PER CAPITA (IN MILLION U.S. DOLLARS)	.89
115 TOTAL HIGHWAY VEHICLES PER CAPITA	.89
111 PASSENGER CARS PER CAPITA	.88
116 GROSS DOMESTIC PRODUCT PER CAPITA	.88
097 EXPORTS PER CAPITA	.87
093 TELEPHONES PER CAPITA	.87
113 COMMERCIAL VEHICLES PER CAPITA	.86
015 RADIOS PER 1,000 POPULATION	.86
120 ENERGY CONSUMPTION IN KILOGRAS PER CAPITA	.85
016 TELEVISIONS PER 1,000 POPULATION	.80
017 CINEMA ATTENDANCE PER CAPITA, 1960	.78
061 HEALTH EXPENDITURE PER CAPITA	.77
049 PHYSICIANS PER ONE MILLION POPULATION, 1965	.76
091 ALL MAIL PER CAPITA	.76
020 ADJUSTED SCHOOL ENROLLMENT RATIO	.74
019 UNADJUSTED SCHOOL ENROLLMENT RATIO	.73
043 PERCENTAGE OF GROSS DOMESTIC PRODUCT ORIGINATING IN INDUSTRY	.72

Variable	Loading
014 NEWSPAPERS PER 1,000 POPULATION	.72
013 CONCENTRATION OF POPULATION IN CITIES	.71
018 LITERACY RATES	.70
122 BOOK PRODUCTION BY TITLES PER MILLION POPULATION	.70
055 DEFENSE EXPENDITURE PER CAPITA (IN U.S. DOLLARS)	.69
044 GROSS DOMESTIC FIXED CAPITAL FORMATION, % OF GNP	.65
083 PER CAPITA POPULATION IN CITIES OF 50,000+	.65
047 PROTEINS PER CAPITA PER DIEM, 1960	.63
106 UNIVERSITY ENROLLMENT PER CAPITA	.61
046 CALORIES PER CAPITA PER DIEM, 1960	.61
102 SECONDARY SCHOOL ENROLLMENT PER CAPITA	.59
108 TOTAL SCHOOL ENROLLMENT PER CAPITA	.57
081 PER CAPITA POPULATION IN CITIES OF 100,000+	.57
118 ENERGY PRODUCTION IN KILOGRAMS PER CAPITA	.55
104 PRIMARY AND SECONDARY ENROLLMENT PER CAPITA	.55
012 ADULT POPULATION	.54
092 TOTAL TELEPHONES	.53
084 NATIONAL GOVERNMENT REVENUE	.52
008 CRUDE BIRTH RATES, 1960	-.55
069 BEGINNING YEAR OF MODERNIZATION	-.55
042 PERCENTAGE OF GROSS DOMESTIC PRODUCT ORIGINATING IN AGRICULTURE	-.59

02 POWER BASE

Variable	Loading
099 TOTAL PRIMARY SCHOLL ENROLLMENT	.94
107 TOTAL SCHOOL ENROLLMENT	.93
001 TOTAL POPULATION	.93
080 POPULATION IN CITIES OF 100,000+	.92
030 TOTAL GNP (IN MILLIONS U.S. DOLLARS)	.91
101 TOTAL SECONDARY SCHOOL ENROLLMENT	.90
082 POPULATION IN CITIES OF 50,000+	.89
088 RAILROAD MILEAGE	.88
109 RAIL PASSENGER KILOMETERS	.88
057 TOTAL EDUCATION EXPENDITURE (IN MILLION U.S. DOLLARS)	.87
105 TOTAL UNIVERSITY ENROLLMENT	.85
119 TOTAL ENERGY CONSUMPTION IN METRIC TONS OF COAL EQUIVALENT	.84
066 TOTAL INTERNAL SECURITY FORCES (IN UNITS)	.84
103 TOTAL PRIMARY AND SECONDARY ENROLLMENT	.84
036 TOTAL TRADE, 1960 (IN MILLIONS U.S. DOLLARS)	.82
048 TOTAL NUMBER OF PHYSICIANS	.81
094 TOTAL IMPORTS	.80
098 PROPORTION OF TOTAL WORLD TRADE	.80
060 TOTAL HEALTH EXPENDITURE (IN MILLIONS U.S. DOLLARS)	.80
041 PERCENTAGE CONTRIBUTION TO WORLD TOTAL OF SCIENTIFIC AUTHORS	.79
096 TOTAL EXPORTS	.79
086 NATIONAL GOVERNMENT EXPENDITURE	.78
112 TOTAL COMMERCIAL VEHICLES	.78
050 TOTAL MILITARY MANPOWER	.77
114 TOTAL HIGHWAY VEHICLES	.77
121 BOOK PRODUCTION BY TITLES	.76
092 TOTAL TELEPHONES	.74
084 NATIONAL GOVERNMENT REVENUE	.74
110 TOTAL PASSENGER CARS	.74
040 TOTAL SCIENTIFIC AND TECHNICAL SERIALS PUBLISHED	.72
090 ALL MAIL	.66
054 TOTAL DEFENSE EXPENDITURE (IN MILLIONS U.S. DOLLARS)	.63
027 NUMBER OF SEPARATE CHRISTIAN CHURCHES	.60
006 TOTAL AGRICULTURAL AREA	.57
089 RAILROAD MILEAGE PER SQUARE MILE	.57
144 MEAN RELAXATIONS OF GOV. RETRICTIONS ON POL. ACTIVITY, 1963-1967	.52
139 MEAN NUMBER OF REGIME-SUPPORT DEMONSTRATIONS DURING 1963-1967	.51
117 TOTAL ENERGY PRODUCTION IN METRIC TONS COAL EQUIVALENT	.51
125 SIZE OF LEGISLATURE (LOWER HOUSE)	.51
037 TOTAL TRADE,% OF GNP, 1960	-.51

Variable	Loading
071 DATE OF INSTITUTIONAL FORMATION(HUDSON)	-.53

03 POLITICAL INSTABILITY

Variable	Loading
142 MEAN UNSUCCESSFUL IRREGULAR POWER TRANSFERS, 1963-1967	.83
074 MILITARY REGIME	.81
137 MEAN NUMBER OF POLITICAL ASSASSINATIONS DURING 1963-1967	.77
075 MEAN NUMBER OF MAJOR CONSTITUTIONAL CHANGES, 1962-1966	.75
136 MEAN NUMBER OF IRREGULAR POWER TRANSFERS DURING 1963-1967	.73
143 MEAN NUMBER OF POLITICAL EXECUTIONS DURING 1963-1967	.73

04 NON-COMPETITIVE POLITICAL SYSTEM

Variable	Loading
078 LEGISLATIVE SELECTION	-.50
063 POLITICAL PARTY FRACTIONALIZATION BASED ON NUMBER OF SEATS, 1964	-.70
065 PRESS FREEDOM INDEX	-.71
064 ELECTORAL IRREGULARITY SCORE	-.76
126 SIZE OF LEGISLATURE/NUMBER OF SEATS HELD BY LARGEST PARTY	-.80
077 LEGISLATIVE EFFECTIVENESS	-.83
127 COMPETITIVENESS OF NOMINATING PROCESS	-.86
128 PARTY LEGITIMACY	-.87
129 AGGREGATE COMPETITION INDEX	-.88

05 SMALL POPULATION GROWTH RATE

Variable	Loading
011 WORKING AGE POPULATION	.66
012 ADULT POPULATION	.60
003 POPULATION GROWTH RATE, 1950-65	-.82
002 POPULATION GROWTH RATE, 1960-65	-.83

06 SMALL POPULATION DENSITY

Variable	Loading
004 TOTAL AREA	.72
006 TOTAL AGRICULTURAL AREA	.68
053 MILITARY MANPOWER PER AREA	-.59
007 PEOPLE PER SQUARE KILOMETER OF AGRICULTURAL LAND AREA	-.87
005 DENSITY(PEOPLE PER SQUARE KILOMETER)	-.87

07 SMALL CHRISTIAN COMMUNITY

Variable	Loading
024 MOSLEM, % OF THE TOTAL POP.	.73
023 CHRISTIAN COMMUNITY, % OF THE TOTAL POP.	-.66
026 CATHOLIC, % OF THE TOTAL POP.	-.77

08 RECENT NATIONAL INDEPENDENCE

Variable	Loading
072 DATE OF INDEPENDENT IDENTIFICATION(RUSTOW)	.74
070 DATE OF INDEPENDENCE(BANKS)	.72
071 DATE OF INSTITUTIONAL FORMATION(HUDSON)	.67

09 LITTLE DOMESTIC VIOLENCE

135 MEAN NUMBER OF EXECUTIVE ADJUSTMENTS DURING 1963-1967	-.52
130 MEAN NUMBER OF PROTEST DEMONSTRATIONS DURING 1963-1967	-.60
132 MEAN NUMBER OF ARMED ATTACKS DURING 1963-1967	-.63
131 MEAN NUMBER OF RIOTS DURING 1963-1967	-.74
10 LARGE GNP GROWTH RATE AT FIXED PRICES	
033 GNP PER CAPITA AT FIXED PRICES (GROWTH RATES)	.74
032 GNP AT FIXED PRICES FOR CALCULATING GROWTH RATES	.73
11 FEW MILITARY PERSONNEL PER CAPITA	
050 TOTAL MILITARY MANPOWER	-.49
056 DEFENSE EXPENDITURE, % OF GNP	-.61
051 MILITARY MANPOWER PER ONE THOUSAND POPULATION	-.70
052 MILITARY MANPOWER PER ONE THOUSAND WORKING AGED POPULATION	-.78
12 LARGE GNP GROWTH RATE	
034 TOTAL GNP GROWTH RATES, ANNUAL AVERAGES, 1960-1965	.73
035 TOTAL GNP PER CAPITA GROWTH RATES, ANNUAL AVERAGES, 1960-1965	.59
13 SMALL HEALTH EXPENDITURE AS PERCENT OF GNP	
062 TOTAL HEALTH EXPENDITURE AS A PERCENTAGE OF GNP	-.84
14 HIGH PER CAPITA SCHOOL ENROLLMENT	
100 PRIMARY SCHOOL ENROLLMENT PER CAPITA	.70
104 PRIMARY AND SECONDARY ENROLLMENT PER CAPITA	.69
108 TOTAL SCHOOL ENROLLMENT PER CAPITA	.69
15 HIGH PER CAPITA INTERNAL SECURITY FORCE	
067 INTERNAL SECURITY FORCES PER ONE THOUSAND WORKING AGE POP.	.79
068 INTERNAL SECURITY FORCES PER ONE MILLION POPULATION	.74
16 HIGH ENERGY PRODUCTION	
117 TOTAL ENERGY PRODUCTION IN METRIC TONS COAL EQUIVALENT	.67
118 ENERGY PRODUCTION IN KILOGRAMS PER CAPITA	.66
17 MANY ELECTIONS	
079 MEAN NUMBER OF LEGISLATIVE ELECTIONS, 1962-1966	.79
18 HIGH RATIO OF BLACK MARKET TO OFFICIAL EXCHANGE	

124 RATIO OF BLACK MARKET TO OFFICIAL EXCHANGE RATE	-.69
19 FEW EXECUTIVE ADJUSTMENTS	
20 LOW CRUDE DEATH RATE	
009 CRUDE DEATH RATES, 1960	-.72
21 LITTLE ETHNO-LINGUISTIC FRACTIONALIZATION	
022 LINGUISTIC FRACTIONALIZATION, MULLER SCALE	-.71
021 ETHNO-LINGUISTIC FRACTIONALIZATION	-.74
22 NEW CURRENCY	
123 AGE OF CURRENCY IN MONTHS	-.82

INSERT 2

A-SPACE FACTOR SCORES

1	AFGHANISTAN	-.97	-.29	-2.85	.46	-1.85	-.16	-.89	.71	-.12	-.53
		-2.84	3.33	-3.32	-2.76	.57	-1.91	-.95	-.75	.24	-.48
		-2.27	1.51								
2	ALBANIA	.47	-.88	-1.96	1.61	-.54	-.84	1.20	-.67	1.12	-1.60
		-.77	.81	.42	1.60	.32	.38	.52	.67	1.68	-.50
		.68	-.04								
3	ALGERIA	.37	.44	.61	2.10	-.07	1.33	.16	1.53	-.80	-.02
		-.01	-1.82	1.92	-.60	1.13	.39	1.12	-.99	-1.17	1.11
		-.51	.59								
4	ARGENTINA	.66	.88	-.09	.12	.65	1.52	-1.27	-.79	-1.29	-1.22
		-.34	-1.23	1.80	-.17	-1.81	.51	.34	.25	-.70	-.07
		-.47	2.14								
5	AUSTRALIA	1.47	.94	-1.59	-.53	-.19	2.37	.14	-.00	-.00	.72
		-.03	-.43	.25	.29	-.01	-.34	-.06	.04	.58	-1.06
		.68	-.42								

****

01 ECONOMIC DEVELOPMENT

116	KUWAIT	2.26
46	ICELAND	1.90
64	LUXEMBOURG	1.84
73	NEW ZEALAND	1.81
5	AUSTRALIA	1.47
119	MALTA	1.42
99	TRINIDAD	1.40
77	NORWAY	1.40
26	CYPRUS	1.38

15	CANADA	1.31
27	CZECHOSLOVAKIA	1.29
7	BELGIUM	1.26
52	ISRAEL	1.25
94	SWEDEN	1.24
51	IRELAND	1.23
109	VENEZUELA	1.18
6	AUSTRIA	1.16
123	W. SAMOA	1.14
34	FINLAND	1.11
10	BULGARIA	1.10
95	SWITZERLAND	1.10
106	UNITED STATES	1.08
37	EAST GERMANY	1.05
45	HUNGARY	1.04
63	LIBYA	1.03
25	CUBA	1.02
72	NETHERLANDS	1.00
105	UNITED KINGDOM	.98
29	DENMARK	.97
50	IRAQ	.97
127	MALDIVE ISLANDS	.96
35	FRANCE	.95
108	URUGUAY	.89
79	PANAMA	.86
126	MALAYSIA	.80
124	SINGAPORE	.78
38	WEST GERMANY	.77
103	U.S.S.R	.73
83	POLAND	.70
61	LEBANON	.69
4	ARGENTINA	.66
55	JAMAICA	.60
92	SPAIN	.56
69	MONGOLIA	.54
2	ALBANIA	.47
91	SOUTH AFRICA	.46
53	ITALY	.44
24	COSTA RICA	.44
40	GREECE	.43
85	ROMANIA	.40
3	ALGERIA	.37
36	GABON	.35
113	YUGOSLAVIA	.34
19	CHILE	.34
56	JAPAN	.32
96	SYRIA	.29
84	PORTUGAL	.28
121	ZAMBIA	.28
57	JORDAN	.23
87	SAUDI ARABIA	.22
22	CONGO (BRA)	.20
31	ECUADOR	.13
41	GUATEMALA	.13
125	GUYANA	.08
30	DOMINICAN REPUBLIC	.04
74	NICARAGUA	-.03
88	SENEGAL	-.03
81	PERU	-.04
68	MEXICO	-.06
54	IVORY COAST	-.08
49	IRAN	-.13
32	EL SALVADOR	-.15
39	GHANA	-.16
100	TUNISIA	-.22
70	MOROCCO	-.24

62	LIBERIA	-.30
8	BOLIVIA	-.32
9	BRAZIL	-.35
104	U.A.R.	-.42
117	LESOTHO	-.51
80	PARAGUAY	-.51
44	HONDURAS	-.52
114	BOTSWANA	-.53
67	MAURITANIA	-.53
21	COLOMBIA	-.55
58	NORTH KOREA	-.55
128	BARBADOS	-.58
112	YEMEN	-.60
111	SOUTH VIETNAM	-.63
110	NORTH VIETNAM	-.71
115	GAMBIA	-.73
89	SIERRA LEONE	-.74
16	CENTRAL AFRICAN REP	-.77
86	RWANDA	-.79
42	GUINEA	-.80
101	TURKEY	-.83
28	DAHOMEY	-.87
17	CEYLON	-.94
98	TOGO	-.95
13	CAMBODIA	-.95
71	NEPAL	-.96
1	AFGHANISTAN	-.97
23	CONGO (LEO)	-.97
14	CAMEROUN	-.97
93	SUDAN	-1.02
102	UGANDA	-1.02
97	THAILAND	-1.06
122	KENYA	-1.07
65	MALAGASY REP	-1.15
75	NIGER	-1.16
82	PHILIPPINES	-1.19
11	BURMA	-1.27
120	TANZANIA	-1.29
59	SOUTH KOREA	-1.31
20	CHINA, PR	-1.34
118	MALAWI	-1.34
107	UPPER VOLTA	-1.36
18	CHAD	-1.39
12	BURUNDI	-1.39
90	SOMALIA	-1.41
66	MALI	-1.48
60	LAOS	-1.49
43	HAITI	-1.72
48	INDONESIA	-1.78
33	ETHIOPIA	-1.83
76	NIGERIA	-2.00
78	PAKISTAN	-2.01
47	INDIA	-2.02

02 POWER BASE

47	INDIA	2.32
20	CHINA, PR	2.06
103	U.S.S.R	1.85
9	BRAZIL	1.77
78	PAKISTAN	1.74
56	JAPAN	1.71
68	MEXICO	1.57
106	UNITED STATES	1.55

35	FRANCE	1.52
38	WEST GERMANY	1.49
83	POLAND	1.49
105	UNITED KINGDOM	1.42
53	ITALY	1.38
92	SPAIN	1.35
48	INDONESIA	1.32
91	SOUTH AFRICA	1.29
101	TURKEY	1.26
82	PHILIPPINES	1.25
104	U.A.R.	1.23
37	EAST GERMANY	1.20
76	NIGERIA	1.19
113	YUGOSLAVIA	1.17
85	ROMANIA	1.15
97	THAILAND	1.14
15	CANADA	1.11
27	CZECHOSLOVAKIA	1.10
49	IRAN	1.01
5	AUSTRALIA	.94
4	ARGENTINA	.88
59	SOUTH KOREA	.87
72	NETHERLANDS	.84
45	HUNGARY	.77
11	BURMA	.74
21	COLOMBIA	.73
10	BULGARIA	.62
128	BARBADOS	.62
94	SWEDEN	.61
70	MOROCCO	.55
125	GUYANA	.55
58	NORTH KOREA	.54
7	BELGIUM	.53
23	CONGO (LEO)	.51
17	CEYLON	.49
6	AUSTRIA	.48
95	SWITZERLAND	.46
109	VENEZUELA	.45
81	PERU	.44
3	ALGERIA	.44
19	CHILE	.42
29	DENMARK	.41
84	PORTUGAL	.39
25	CUBA	.36
34	FINLAND	.27
122	KENYA	.26
50	IRAQ	.24
39	GHANA	.23
110	NORTH VIETNAM	.17
33	ETHIOPIA	.16
40	GREECE	.13
111	SOUTH VIETNAM	.13
87	SAUDI ARABIA	.12
77	NORWAY	.03
93	SUDAN	-.01
73	NEW ZEALAND	-.02
120	TANZANIA	-.02
65	MALAGASY REP	-.11
100	TUNISIA	-.14
96	SYRIA	-.16
41	GUATEMALA	-.18
123	W. SAMOA	-.18
31	ECUADOR	-.27
1	AFGHANISTAN	-.29
51	IRELAND	-.30
52	ISRAEL	-.30

121	ZAMBIA	-.32
54	IVORY COAST	-.35
102	UGANDA	-.36
71	NEPAL	-.40
14	CAMEROUN	-.41
13	CAMBODIA	-.44
108	URUGUAY	-.49
8	BOLIVIA	-.50
32	EL SALVADOR	-.61
61	LEBANON	-.64
126	MALAYSIA	-.65
88	SENEGAL	-.68
66	MALI	-.69
30	DOMINICAN REPUBLIC	-.71
42	GUINEA	-.72
63	LIBYA	-.78
55	JAMAICA	-.78
24	COSTA RICA	-.81
44	HONDURAS	-.81
118	MALAWI	-.87
2	ALBANIA	-.88
69	MONGOLIA	-.88
114	BOTSWANA	-.89
99	TRINIDAD	-.91
86	RWANDA	-.91
43	HAITI	-.91
124	SINGAPORE	-.95
80	PARAGUAY	-.96
89	SIERRA LEONE	-.96
112	YEMEN	-1.01
18	CHAD	-1.02
74	NICARAGUA	-1.04
28	DAHOMEY	-1.06
90	SOMALIA	-1.07
107	UPPER VOLTA	-1.08
57	JORDAN	-1.09
75	NIGER	-1.10
117	LESOTHO	-1.17
115	GAMBIA	-1.18
79	PANAMA	-1.19
127	MALDIVE ISLANDS	-1.22
16	CENTRAL AFRICAN REP	-1.24
116	KUWAIT	-1.28
98	TOGO	-1.28
12	BURUNDI	-1.29
67	MAURITANIA	-1.39
62	LIBERIA	-1.42
60	LAOS	-1.47
64	LUXEMBOURG	-1.47
22	CONGO (BRA)	-1.50
119	MALTA	-1.71
46	ICELAND	-1.76
26	CYPRUS	-1.81
36	GABON	-1.94

04 NON-COMPETITIVE POLITICAL SYSTEM

25	CUBA	2.61
3	ALGERIA	2.10
27	CZECHOSLOVAKIA	2.09
10	BULGARIA	1.93
37	EAST GERMANY	1.77

50	IRAQ	1.73
45	HUNGARY	1.72
2	ALBANIA	1.61
8	BOLIVIA	1.53
92	SPAIN	1.49
22	CONGO (BRA)	1.46
30	DOMINICAN REPUBLIC	1.43
83	POLAND	1.42
85	ROMANIA	1.34
9	BRAZIL	1.33
11	BURMA	1.32
28	DAHOMEY	1.30
41	GUATEMALA	1.28
87	SAUDI ARABIA	1.21
20	CHINA, PR	1.20
84	PORTUGAL	1.20
96	SYRIA	1.18
31	ECUADOR	1.17
69	MONGOLIA	1.15
23	CONGO (LEO)	1.13
58	NORTH KOREA	1.11
111	SOUTH VIETNAM	1.06
103	U.S.S.R	1.03
63	LIBYA	.99
39	GHANA	.89
54	IVORY COAST	.87
36	GABON	.78
67	MAURITANIA	.77
70	MOROCCO	.75
18	CHAD	.72
43	HAITI	.72
16	CENTRAL AFRICAN REP	.70
13	CAMBODIA	.61
97	THAILAND	.56
14	CAMEROUN	.55
71	NEPAL	.54
88	SENEGAL	.53
57	JORDAN	.52
42	GUINEA	.50
104	U.A.R.	.47
107	UPPER VOLTA	.47
1	AFGHANISTAN	.46
116	KUWAIT	.39
113	YUGOSLAVIA	.38
112	YEMEN	.38
86	RWANDA	.36
62	LIBERIA	.32
75	NIGER	.24
110	NORTH VIETNAM	.19
4	ARGENTINA	.12
33	ETHIOPIA	.07
66	MALI	.04
98	TOGO	.03
121	ZAMBIA	-.01
100	TUNISIA	-.07
48	INDONESIA	-.09
89	SIERRA LEONE	-.11
49	IRAN	-.23
99	TRINIDAD	-.24
126	MALAYSIA	-.25
59	SOUTH KOREA	-.28
74	NICARAGUA	-.31
123	W. SAMOA	-.32
55	JAMAICA	-.33
6	AUSTRIA	-.38
68	MEXICO	-.39

119	MALTA	-.43
93	SUDAN	-.45
91	SOUTH AFRICA	-.45
38	WEST GERMANY	-.51
7	BELGIUM	-.52
5	AUSTRALIA	-.53
128	BARBADOS	-.54
15	CANADA	-.55
26	CYPRUS	-.55
32	EL SALVADOR	-.56
118	MALAWI	-.63
12	BURUNDI	-.63
44	HONDURAS	-.63
64	LUXEMBOURG	-.69
65	MALAGASY REP	-.70
73	NEW ZEALAND	-.71
21	COLOMBIA	-.73
35	FRANCE	-.74
80	PARAGUAY	-.74
102	UGANDA	-.83
109	VENEZUELA	-.83
51	IRELAND	-.84
79	PANAMA	-.85
19	CHILE	-.87
76	NIGERIA	-.88
40	GREECE	-.89
29	DENMARK	-.89
127	MALDIVE ISLANDS	-.92
61	LEBANON	-.93
120	TANZANIA	-.94
122	KENYA	-.96
53	ITALY	-.96
114	BOTSWANA	-.96
117	LESOTHO	-.99
52	ISRAEL	-1.00
56	JAPAN	-1.02
24	COSTA RICA	-1.03
72	NETHERLANDS	-1.06
46	ICELAND	-1.06
77	NORWAY	-1.07
90	SOMALIA	-1.08
34	FINLAND	-1.08
94	SWEDEN	-1.08
60	LAOS	-1.10
78	PAKISTAN	-1.11
125	GUYANA	-1.13
124	SINGAPORE	-1.13
105	UNITED KINGDOM	-1.20
106	UNITED STATES	-1.21
115	GAMBIA	-1.21
17	CEYLON	-1.26
95	SWITZERLAND	-1.31
101	TURKEY	-1.50
81	PERU	-1.52
82	PHILIPPINES	-1.56
47	INDIA	-1.63
108	URUGUAY	-1.63

WEIS CONFLICT AND COOPERATION CLASSIFICATIONS

CONFLICT

1. REJECT	2.6
2. ACCUSE	2.9
3. PROTEST	2.4
4. DENY	2.2
5. DEMAND	3.4
6. WARN	3.3
7. THREATEN	3.9
8. DEMONSTRATE	3.0
9. REDUCE RELATIONSHIP	3.5
10. EXPEL	3.8
11. SEIZE	4.5
12. FORCE	4.7

COOPERATION

1. YIELD	3.5
2. APPROVE	2.9
3. PROMISE	3.0
4. GRANT	3.3
5. REWARD	4.5
6. AGREE	3.0
7. REQUEST	2.7
8. PROPOSE	2.8

(THE NUMBERS BESIDE THE VARIABLE NAMES ARE THE ADDITIVE WEIGHTS EXPLAINED BELOW)

INSERT 4

CORRELATIONS OF A-SPACE FACTOR SCORES WITH WEIS DATA, RANK SORTED

02 POWER BASE	.54
14 HIGH PER CAPITA SCHOOL ENROLLMENT	.26
07 SMALL CHRISTIAN COMMUNITY	.24
16 HIGH ENERGY PRODUCTION	.24
01 ECONOMIC DEVELOPMENT	.12
21 LITTLE ETHNO-LINGUISTIC FRACTIONALIZATION	.12
04 NON-COMPETITIVE POLITICAL SYSTEM	.10
08 RECENT NATIONAL INDEPENDENCE	.09
18 HIGH RATIO OF BLACK MARKET TO OFFICIAL EXCHANGE	.08
12 LARGE GNP GROWTH RATE	.07
03 POLITICAL INSTABILITY	.07
06 SMALL POPULATION DENSITY	.00
17 MANY ELECTIONS	-.02
15 HIGH PER CAPITA INTERNAL SECURITY FORCE	-.03
20 LOW CRUDE DEATH RATE	-.04
05 SMALL POPULATION GROWTH RATE	-.10
22 NEW CURRENCY	-.14
10 LARGE GNP GROWTH RATE AT FIXED PRICES	-.15
13 SMALL HEALTH EXPENDITURE AS PERCENT OF GNP	-.17
19 FEW EXECUTIVE ADJUSTMENTS	-.22
09 LITTLE DOMESTIC VIOLENCE	-.25
11 FEW MILITARY PERSONNEL PER CAPITA	-.52

INSERT 5

U.S. CONFLICT MATRIX, 1966-69

**	101	0	0	0	0	0	0	0	0	0	0	0	0
**	201	0	0	0	0	0	0	0	0	0	0	0	0
**	301	0	0	1	0	0	0	0	0	0	0	0	0
**	401	0	2	0	0	0	0	0	0	1	0	0	0
**	501	0	0	0	0	0	0	0	0	0	0	0	0
**	601	0	0	0	0	0	0	0	0	0	0	0	0
**	701	0	0	0	0	0	0	0	0	0	0	0	0
**	801	1	0	0	0	0	0	0	0	1	0	0	0

****

INSERT 6

U.S. CONFLICT VECTOR

1	AFGHANISTAN	.00
2	ALBANIA	.00
3	ALGERIA	2.40
4	ARGENTINA	9.30
5	AUSTRALIA	.00
6	AUSTRIA	.00
7	BELGIUM	.00
8	BOLIVIA	6.10
9	BRAZIL	3.50
10	BULGARIA	11.20
11	BURMA	.00
12	BURUNDI	6.20
13	CAMBODIA	24.80
14	CAMEROUN	.00
15	CANADA	14.70

****

INSERT 7

CZECHOSLOVAKIA CONFLICT VECTOR

.0000
.0000
.0000
.0000
.0000
.0000
.0000
.0000
.0000
2.2000
****

INSERT 8

GENERAL CONFLICT SCORE

1	AFGHANISTAN	.00
2	ALBANIA	70.00
3	ALGERIA	159.00
4	ARGENTINA	61.50
5	AUSTRALIA	41.90
6	AUSTRIA	11.00
7	BELGIUM	70.10
8	BOLIVIA	13.30
9	BRAZIL	66.40
10	BULGARIA	54.80
11	BURMA	12.80
12	BURUNDI	3.80
13	CAMBODIA	286.80
14	CAMEROUN	.00
15	CANADA	94.60
16	CENTRAL AFRICAN REP	14.30
17	CEYLON	12.80
18	CHAD	14.40
19	CHILE	49.00
20	CHINA, PR	1728.60
21	COLOMBIA	31.70
22	CONGO (BRA)	21.00
23	CONGO (LEO)	76.60
24	COSTA RICA	15.00
25	CUBA	190.60
26	CYPRUS	14.90
27	CZECHOSLOVAKIA	258.30
28	DAHOMEY	3.50
29	DENMARK	26.50
30	DOMINICAN REPUBLIC	15.30
31	ECUADOR	40.50
32	EL SALVADOR	66.00
33	ETHIOPIA	13.20
34	FINLAND	2.60
35	FRANCE	310.30
36	GABON	6.70
37	EAST GERMANY	297.60
38	WEST GERMANY	273.20
39	GHANA	69.50
40	GREECE	110.50
41	GUATEMALA	12.00
42	GUINEA	25.70
43	HAITI	11.90
44	HONDURAS	59.60
45	HUNGARY	80.40
46	ICELAND	.00
47	INDIA	306.90
48	INDONESIA	105.60
49	IRAN	17.30
50	IRAQ	132.80
51	IRELAND	33.30
52	ISRAEL	2076.60
53	ITALY	99.10
54	IVORY COAST	14.90
55	JAMAICA	2.90
56	JAPAN	116.10
57	JORDAN	788.40
58	NORTH KOREA	444.50
59	SOUTH KOREA	331.50
60	LAOS	111.60

61	LEBANON	109.50
62	LIBERIA	.00
63	LIBYA	8.20
64	LUXEMBOURG	.00
65	MALAGASY REP	.00
66	MALI	.00
67	MAURITANIA	6.90
68	MEXICO	15.70
69	MONGOLIA	52.40
70	MOROCCO	11.10
71	NEPAL	16.20
72	NETHERLANDS	76.60
73	NEW ZEALAND	17.60
74	NICARAGUA	10.50
75	NIGER	.00
76	NIGERIA	69.30
77	NORWAY	20.80
78	PAKISTAN	81.20
79	PANAMA	19.90
80	PARAGUAY	2.20
81	PERU	71.30
82	PHILIPPINES	61.60
83	POLAND	221.70
84	PORTUGAL	53.60
85	ROMANIA	63.60
86	RWANDA	.00
87	SAUDI ARABIA	50.50
88	SENEGAL	.00
89	SIERRA LEONE	6.30
90	SOMALIA	22.10
91	SOUTH AFRICA	68.50
92	SPAIN	134.50
93	SUDAN	48.30
94	SWEDEN	31.60
95	SWITZERLAND	13.50
96	SYRIA	442.60
97	THAILAND	54.00
98	TOGO	4.50
99	TRINIDAD	2.90
100	TUNISIA	36.80
101	TURKEY	90.70
102	UGANDA	18.80
103	U.S.S.R	2010.20
104	U.A.R.	1187.10
105	UNITED KINGDOM	453.80
106	UNITED STATES	1747.60
107	UPPER VOLTA	.00
108	URUGUAY	35.60
109	VENEZUELA	33.30
110	NORTH VIETNAM	983.50
111	SOUTH VIETNAM	164.40
112	YEMEN	66.60
113	YUGOSLAVIA	98.40
114	BOTSWANA	.00
115	GAMBIA	3.00
116	KUWAIT	32.80
117	LESOTHO	.00
118	MALAWI	15.10
119	MALTA	12.70
120	TANZANIA	35.80
121	ZAMBIA	82.70
122	KENYA	54.90
123	W. SAMOA	.00
124	SINGAPORE	17.50
125	GUYANA	15.50
126	MALAYSIA	53.00

127	MALDIVE ISLANDS	.00
128	BARBADOS	.00

INSERT 9

GENERAL COOPERATION SCORE

1	AFGHANISTAN	5.70
2	ALBANIA	31.30
3	ALGERIA	71.20
4	ARGENTINA	30.70
5	AUSTRALIA	165.20
6	AUSTRIA	33.10
7	BELGIUM	41.80
8	BOLIVIA	22.60
9	BRAZIL	48.60
10	BULGARIA	39.60
11	BURMA	8.90
12	BURUNDI	12.00
13	CAMBODIA	97.50
14	CAMEROUN	.00
15	CANADA	167.90
16	CENTRAL AFRICAN REP	9.10
17	CEYLON	29.60
18	CHAD	11.80
19	CHILE	20.30
20	CHINA, PR	426.20
21	COLOMBIA	29.90
22	CONGO (BRA)	2.90
23	CONGO (LEO)	62.90
24	COSTA RICA	8.70
25	CUBA	154.50
26	CYPRUS	15.10
27	CZECHOSLOVAKIA	221.90
28	DAHOMEY	.00
29	DENMARK	28.50
30	DOMINICAN REPUBLIC	17.40
31	ECUADOR	15.30
32	EL SALVADOR	3.10
33	ETHIOPIA	34.00
34	FINLAND	18.00
35	FRANCE	495.90
36	GABON	2.70
37	EAST GERMANY	206.20
38	WEST GERMANY	489.10
39	GHANA	66.90
40	GREECE	72.90
41	GUATEMALA	2.90
42	GUINEA	22.60
43	HAITI	2.80
44	HONDURAS	11.80
45	HUNGARY	47.60
46	ICELAND	.00
47	INDIA	198.00
48	INDONESIA	133.00
49	IRAN	58.30
50	IRAQ	108.70

51	IRELAND	10.00
52	ISRAEL	241.70
53	ITALY	119.80
54	IVORY COAST	6.20
55	JAMAICA	.00
56	JAPAN	209.30
57	JORDAN	140.00
58	NORTH KOREA	58.40
59	SOUTH KOREA	102.00
60	LAOS	24.20
61	LEBANON	27.20
62	LIBERIA	7.40
63	LIBYA	11.60
64	LUXEMBOURG	.00
65	MALAGASY REP	6.20
66	MALI	.00
67	MAURITANIA	5.60
68	MEXICO	46.30
69	MONGOLIA	8.60
70	MOROCCO	26.20
71	NEPAL	6.20
72	NETHERLANDS	38.90
73	NEW ZEALAND	46.00
74	NICARAGUA	2.90
75	NIGER	3.30
76	NIGERIA	36.40
77	NORWAY	24.70
78	PAKISTAN	142.00
79	PANAMA	8.70
80	PARAGUAY	.00
81	PERU	34.30
82	PHILIPPINES	145.20
83	POLAND	108.70
84	PORTUGAL	39.60
85	ROMANIA	134.50
86	RWANDA	5.80
87	SAUDI ARABIA	59.30
88	SENEGAL	5.70
89	SIERRA LEONE	8.40
90	SOMALIA	15.20
91	SOUTH AFRICA	34.60
92	SPAIN	124.00
93	SUDAN	32.80
94	SWEDEN	112.30
95	SWITZERLAND	38.90
96	SYRIA	132.80
97	THAILAND	79.30
98	TOGO	2.70
99	TRINIDAD	.00
100	TUNISIA	24.40
101	TURKEY	61.80
102	UGANDA	17.10
103	U.S.S.R	1467.00
104	U.A.R.	276.10
105	UNITED KINGDOM	612.60
106	UNITED STATES	3268.70
107	UPPER VOLTA	.00
108	URUGUAY	8.50
109	VENEZUELA	18.50
110	NORTH VIETNAM	304.30
111	SOUTH VIETNAM	210.30
112	YEMEN	24.20
113	YUGOSLAVIA	131.70
114	BOTSWANA	.00
115	GAMBIA	8.10
116	KUWAIT	38.10

117	LESOTHO	.00
118	MALAWI	5.60
119	MALTA	9.90
120	TANZANIA	41.40
121	ZAMBIA	37.60
122	KENYA	26.80
123	W. SAMOA	.00
124	SINGAPORE	37.50
125	GUYANA	31.20
126	MALAYSIA	88.90
127	MALDIVE ISLANDS	3.30
128	BARBADOS	8.70

INSERT 10

25 MOST CONFLICT EXPORTING STATES

52	ISRAEL	2076.60
103	U.S.S.R	2010.20
106	UNITED STATES	1747.60
20	CHINA, PR	1728.60
104	U.A.R.	1187.10
110	NORTH VIETNAM	983.50
57	JORDAN	788.40
105	UNITED KINGDOM	453.80
58	NORTH KOREA	444.50
96	SYRIA	442.60
59	SOUTH KOREA	331.50
35	FRANCE	310.30
47	INDIA	306.90
37	EAST GERMANY	297.60
13	CAMBODIA	286.80
38	WEST GERMANY	273.20
27	CZECHOSLOVAKIA	258.30
83	POLAND	221.70
25	CUBA	190.60
111	SOUTH VIETNAM	164.40
3	ALGERIA	159.00
92	SPAIN	134.50
50	IRAQ	132.80
56	JAPAN	116.10
60	LAOS	111.60

INSERT 11

25 MOST COOPERATION EXPORTING STATES

106	UNITED STATES	3268.70
103	U.S.S.R	1467.00
105	UNITED KINGDOM	612.60
35	FRANCE	495.90
38	WEST GERMANY	489.10
20	CHINA, PR	426.20
110	NORTH VIETNAM	304.30
104	U.A.R.	276.10
52	ISRAEL	241.70
27	CZECHOSLOVAKIA	221.90
111	SOUTH VIETNAM	210.30
56	JAPAN	209.30
37	EAST GERMANY	206.20
47	INDIA	198.00
15	CANADA	167.90

5	AUSTRALIA	165.20
25	CUBA	154.50
82	PHILIPPINES	145.20
78	PAKISTAN	142.00
57	JORDAN	140.00
85	ROMANIA	134.50
48	INDONESIA	133.00
96	SYRIA	132.80
113	YUGOSLAVIA	131.70
92	SPAIN	124.00

INSERT 12

25 LEAST CONFLICT EXPORTING STATES

89	SIERRA LEONE	6.30
98	TOGO	4.50
12	BURUNDI	3.80
28	DAHOMEY	3.50
115	GAMBIA	3.00
99	TRINIDAD	2.90
55	JAMAICA	2.90
34	FINLAND	2.60
80	PARAGUAY	2.20
88	SENEGAL	.00
114	BOTSWANA	.00
64	LUXEMBOURG	.00
86	RWANDA	.00
117	LESOTHO	.00
1	AFGHANISTAN	.00
14	CAMEROUN	.00
46	ICELAND	.00
62	LIBERIA	.00
66	MALI	.00
123	W. SAMOA	.00
75	NIGER	.00
107	UPPER VOLTA	.00
65	MALAGASY REP	.00
127	MALDIVE ISLANDS	.00
128	BARBADOS	.00

INSERT 13

25 LEAST COOPERATION EXPORTING STATES

1	AFGHANISTAN	5.70
88	SENEGAL	5.70
118	MALAWI	5.60
67	MAURITANIA	5.60
75	NIGER	3.30
127	MALDIVE ISLANDS	3.30
32	EL SALVADOR	3.10
22	CONGO (BRA)	2.90
74	NICARAGUA	2.90
41	GUATEMALA	2.90
43	HAITI	2.80
98	TOGO	2.70
36	GABON	2.70
117	LESOTHO	.00
114	BOTSWANA	.00
55	JAMAICA	.00
14	CAMEROUN	.00

66	MALI	.00
107	UPPER VOLTA	.00
123	W. SAMOA	.00
80	PARAGUAY	.00
99	TRINIDAD	.00
46	ICELAND	.00
64	LUXEMBOURG	.00
28	DAHOMEY	.00

INSERT 14

DISCRIMINANT FUNCTION RESULTS FOR CONFLICT

GROUP 1 25 SUBJECTS. HIGH CON.

GROUP 2 25 SUBJECTS. LOW CON.

PRINCIPAL AXIS ANALYSIS (ASYMMETRIC MATRIX).

TRACE = 8.8642

100.00 PCT. OF TRACE WAS EXTRACTED BY 1 ROOTS.

WILKS LAMBDA = .101

D.F. = 22. AND 27.

F-RATIO = 10.879 P = .0000

ROOT 1 100.00 PCT. VARIANCE

CHI-SQUARE = 86.979 D.F. = 22. P = .0000

CENTROID	1	2
	1.1906	-1.0296

COREL.	1	2	3	4	5	6	7	8	9	10
	.1917	.7605	-.0066	.3664	-.0361	-.0728	.2344	-.0762	-.5215	-.2639
COREL.	11	12	13	14	15	16	17	18	19	20
	-.3452	-.1583	-.0517	.1542	.0940	.0769	-.0473	-.0430	-.1797	.1224
COREL.	21	22								
	.3388	-.1051								

UNIVARIATE F-TESTS. DFB = 1. DFW = 48.

VARIABLE	F-RATIO	P	
1	1.6398	.2039	ECONOMIC DEVELOPMENT
2	51.9306	.0000	POWER BASE
3	.0019	.9644	POLITICAL INSTABILITY
4	6.5856	.0129	NON-COMPETITIVE POLITICAL SYSTEM

5	.0561	.8087	SMALL POPULATION GROWTH RATE
6	.2300	.6390	SMALL POPULATION DENSITY
7	2.4928	.1171	SMALL CHRISTIAN COMMUNITY
8	.2521	.6237	RECENT NATIONAL INDEPENDENCE
9	15.5246	.0005	LITTLE DOMESTIC VIOLENCE
10	3.2054	.0762	LARGE GNP GROWTH RATE AT FIXED PRICES
11	5.7548	.0193	FEW MILITARY PERSONNEL PER CAPITA
12	1.1062	.2985	LARGE GNP GROWTH RATE
13	.1154	.7350	SMALL HEALTH EXPENDITURE AS PERCENT OF GNP
14	1.0481	.3120	HIGH PER CAPITA SCHOOL ENROLLMENT
15	.3840	.5454	HIGH PER CAPITA INTERNAL SECURITY FORCE
16	.2567	.6206	HIGH ENERGY PRODUCTION
17	.0967	.7552	MANY ELECTIONS
18	.0798	.7755	HIGH RATIO OF BLACK MARKET TO OFFICIAL EXCHANGE
19	1.4341	.2352	FEW EXECUTIVE ADJUSTMENTS
20	.6548	.5721	LOW CRUDE DEATH RATE
21	5.5193	.0217	LITTLE ETHNO-LINGUISTIC FRACTIONALIZATION
22	.4809	.5017	NEW CURRENCY

G MEANS	HIGH	LOW	
1	.1254	-.2436	ECONOMIC DEVELOPMENT
2	.7835	-.8360	POWER BASE
3	.0477	.0605	POLITICAL INSTABILITY
4	.4755	-.2479	NON-COMPETITIVE POLITICAL SYSTEM
5	-.0522	.0081	SMALL POPULATION GROWTH RATE
6	-.2471	-.1087	SMALL POPULATION DENSITY
7	.1647	-.2132	SMALL CHRISTIAN COMMUNITY
8	.1825	.3068	RECENT NATIONAL INDEPENDENCE
9	-.3136	.6918	LITTLE DOMESTIC VIOLENCE
10	-.1433	.2467	LARGE GNP GROWTH RATE AT FIXED PRICES
11	-.7614	.0179	FEW MILITARY PERSONNEL PER CAPITA
12	-.0602	.2645	LARGE GNP GROWTH RATE
13	-.0597	.0389	SMALL HEALTH EXPENDITURE AS PERCENT OF GNP
14	.2540	-.0179	HIGH PER CAPITA SCHOOL ENROLLMENT

15	.1543	-.0332	HIGH PER CAPITA INTERNAL SECURITY FORCE
16	.3482	.2041	HIGH ENERGY PRODUCTION
17	-.1767	-.0779	MANY ELECTIONS
18	.0774	.1634	HIGH RATIO OF BLACK MARKET TO OFFICIAL EXCHANGE
19	-.2737	.0854	FEW EXECUTIVE ADJUSTMENTS
20	-.0985	-.3168	LOW CRUDE DEATH RATE
21	.3585	-.3059	LITTLE ETHNO-LINGUISTIC FRACTIONALIZATION
22	-.0649	.1285	NEW CURRENCY

INSERT 15

DISCRIMINANT FUNCTION SCORES FOR CONFLICT

25 MOST CONFLICT EXPORTING STATES

1DS 1	1.6264	ALGERIA
2DS 1	.5485	CAMBODIA
3DS 1	2.1417	CHINA, PR
4DS 1	.9946	CUBA
5DS 1	1.2165	CZECHOSLOVAKIA
6DS 1	1.0298	FRANCE
7DS 1	1.4042	EAST GERMANY
8DS 1	1.4101	WEST GERMANY
9DS 1	.7819	INDIA
10DS 1	.9186	IRAQ
11DS 1	.9048	ISRAEL
12DS 1	1.3309	JAPAN
13DS 1	1.7221	JORDAN
14DS 1	1.0492	NORTH KOREA
15DS 1	1.3633	SOUTH KOREA
16DS 1	.7217	LAOS
17DS 1	1.0642	POLAND
18DS 1	.8959	SPAIN
19DS 1	1.1996	SYRIA
20DS 1	1.4469	U.S.S.R
21DS 1	1.3395	U.A.R.
22DS 1	.9996	UNITED KINGDOM
23DS 1	1.2482	UNITED STATES
24DS 1	.7179	NORTH VIETNAM
25DS 1	1.6882	SOUTH VIETNAM

25 LEAST CONFLICT EXPORTING STATES

26DS 1	-.9006	AFGHANISTAN
27DS 1	-.9239	BURUNDI
28DS 1	-1.2062	CAMEROUN
29DS 1	-.9543	DAHOMEY
30DS 1	-.2711	FINLAND
31DS 1	-1.4373	ICELAND
32DS 1	-.9156	JAMAICA
33DS 1	-.9908	LIBERIA
34DS 1	-1.0651	LUXEMBOURG
35DS 1	-1.3575	MALAGASY REP
36DS 1	-.7597	MALI
37DS 1	-1.4163	NIGER
38DS 1	-.5618	PARAGUAY
39DS 1	-1.1557	RWANDA

```
40DS 1    -.4193    SENEGAL
41DS 1   -1.0797    SIERRA LEONE
42DS 1   -1.8828    TOGO
43DS 1   -1.5992    TRINIDAD
44DS 1   -1.4257    UPPER VOLTA
45DS 1   -1.1628    BOTSWANA
46DS 1   -1.0603    GAMBIA
47DS 1   -1.2130    LESOTHO
48DS 1    -.7290    W. SAMOA
49DS 1    -.9800    MALDIVE ISLANDS
50DS 1    -.2724    BARBADOS
```

INSERT 16

DISCRIMINANT FUNCTION RESULTS FOR COOPERATION

```
GROUP 1      25 SUBJECTS.     HIGH COOP..

GROUP 2      25 SUBJECTS.     LOW COOP.

PRINCIPAL AXIS ANALYSIS (ASYMMETRIC MATRIX).

TRACE =   11.8321

100.00 PCT. OF TRACE WAS EXTRACTED BY  1 ROOTS.

WILKS LAMBDA =       .078

D.F. =  22. AND    27.

F-RATIO =  14.521     P =  .0000

ROOT 1    100.00 PCT. VARIANCE

CHI-SQUARE =    96.974     D.F. =  22.     P =  .0000

CENTROID          1          2
             1.1644     -.9838

COREL.            1          2          3          4          5          6          7          8          9         10
              .1681      .8841     -.0347      .0681      .0657     -.0072      .3122      .0525     -.3539     -.0991

COREL.           11         12         13         14         15         16         17         18         19         20
             -.2525     -.0271     -.0942      .1469      .0249      .0357     -.0552      .1299     -.1391      .1463

COREL.           21         22
              .2075     -.0246

UNIVARIATE F-TESTS. DFB = 1. DFW =   48.

VARIABLE  F-RATIO      P

    1       1.2845    .2617     ECONOMIC DEVELOPMENT

    2     123.8387    .0000     POWER BASE

    3        .0535    .8130     POLITICAL INSTABILITY
```

4	.2063	.6562	NON-COMPETITIVE POLITICAL SYSTEM
5	.1920	.6672	SMALL POPULATION GROWTH RATE
6	.0023	.9607	SMALL POPULATION DENSITY
7	4.7416	.0324	SMALL CHRISTIAN COMMUNITY
8	.1224	.7280	RECENT NATIONAL INDEPENDENCE
9	6.2676	.0150	LITTLE DOMESTIC VIOLENCE
10	.4385	.5179	LARGE GNP GROWTH RATE AT FIXED PRICES
11	2.9979	.0861	FEW MILITARY PERSONNEL PER CAPITA
12	.0324	.8521	LARGE GNP GROWTH RATE
13	.3956	.5393	SMALL HEALTH EXPENDITURE AS PERCENT OF GNP
14	.9749	.6705	HIGH PER CAPITA SCHOOL ENROLLMENT
15	.0275	.8634	HIGH PER CAPITA INTERNAL SECURITY FORCE
16	.0564	.8083	HIGH ENERGY PRODUCTION
17	.1352	.7156	MANY ELECTIONS
18	.7587	.6078	HIGH RATIO OF BLACK MARKET TO OFFICIAL EXCHANGE
19	.8716	.6423	FEW EXECUTIVE ADJUSTMENTS
20	.9661	.6682	LOW CRUDE DEATH RATE
21	1.9838	.1620	LITTLE ETHNO-LINGUISTIC FRACTIONALIZATION
22	.0269	.8648	NEW CURRENCY

G MEANS	HIGH	LOW	
1	.1582	-.1846	ECONOMIC DEVELOPMENT
2	1.0636	-.9739	POWER BASE
3	.0095	.0763	POLITICAL INSTABILITY
4	.1667	.0354	NON-COMPETITIVE POLITICAL SYSTEM
5	.1295	.0013	SMALL POPULATION GROWTH RATE
6	-.0845	-.0705	SMALL POPULATION DENSITY
7	.1442	-.4052	SMALL CHRISTIAN COMMUNITY
8	.2226	.1354	RECENT NATIONAL INDEPENDENCE
9	-.3225	.3377	LITTLE DOMESTIC VIOLENCE
10	-.1054	.0565	LARGE GNP GROWTH RATE AT FIXED PRICES
11	-.4169	.0994	FEW MILITARY PERSONNEL PER CAPITA
12	.1324	.1890	LARGE GNP GROWTH RATE
13	-.1342	.0386	SMALL HEALTH EXPENDITURE AS PERCENT OF GNP

14	.2833	.0076	HIGH PER CAPITA SCHOOL ENROLLMENT
15	.0502	.0003	HIGH PER CAPITA INTERNAL SECURITY FORCE
16	.1512	.0;05	HIGH ENERGY PRODUCTION
17	-.1631	-.0575	MANY ELECTIONS
18	.0829	-.1950	HIGH RATIO OF BLACK MARKET TO OFFICIAL EXCHANGE
19	-.0568	.2004	FEW EXECUTIVE ADJUSTMENTS
20	-.0641	-.3426	LOW CRUDE DEATH RATE
21	.1343	-.2661	LITTLE ETHNO-LINGUISTIC FRACTIONALIZATION
22	-.1083	-.0642	NEW CURRENCY

INSERT 17

DISCRIMINANT FUNCTION SCORES FOR COOPERATION

25 MOST COOPERATION EXPORTING STATES

1DS 1	.9316	AUSTRALIA
2DS 1	1.2700	CANADA
3DS 1	1.6864	CHINA, PR
4DS 1	1.0290	CUBA
5DS 1	1.0850	CZECHOSLOVAKIA
6DS 1	1.0797	FRANCE
7DS 1	1.0429	EAST GERMANY
8DS 1	1.1667	WEST GERMANY
9DS 1	1.3763	INDIA
10DS 1	1.1542	INDONESIA
11DS 1	1.2633	ISRAEL
12DS 1	1.7702	JAPAN
13DS 1	.7822	JORDAN
14DS 1	.9630	PAKISTAN
15DS 1	.6332	PHILIPPINES
16DS 1	1.1453	ROMANIA
17DS 1	.9777	SPAIN
18DS 1	.9022	SYRIA
19DS 1	2.0077	U.S.S.R
20DS 1	1.3897	U.A.R.
21DS 1	1.2086	UNITED KINGDOM
22DS 1	1.5396	UNITED STATES
23DS 1	.6269	NORTH VIETNAM
24DS 1	1.3198	SOUTH VIETNAM
25DS 1	.7601	YUGOSLAVIA

25 LEAST COOPERATION EXPORTING STATES

26DS 1	-.8276	AFGHANISTAN
27DS 1	-.9083	CAMEROUN
28DS 1	-.4417	CONGO (BRA)
29DS 1	-1.2031	DAHOMEY
30DS 1	-.7233	EL SALVADOR
31DS 1	-1.3234	GABON
32DS 1	-1.0491	GUATEMALA
33DS 1	-.8913	HAITI
34DS 1	-1.5559	ICELAND
35DS 1	-.9243	JAMAICA

36DS	1	-1.1908	LUXEMBOURG
37DS	1	-1.0523	MALI
38DS	1	-.9735	MAURITANIA
39DS	1	-.9292	NICARAGUA
40DS	1	-1.5210	NIGER
41DS	1	-.4951	PARAGUAY
42DS	1	-.5898	SENEGAL
43DS	1	-1.1845	TOGO
44DS	1	-.9393	TRINIDAD
45DS	1	-1.0996	UPPER VOLTA
46DS	1	-1.2019	BOTSWANA
47DS	1	-1.0699	LESOTHO
48DS	1	-1.1858	MALAWI
49DS	1	-.4136	W. SAMOA
50DS	1	-.9016	MALDIVE ISLANDS

INSERT 18

Attribute theory

a-space		b-space
monadic factor scores	predict	monadic behavior scores

INSERT 19

Social field theory

a-space		b-space
dyadic algebraic distance computed from monadic factor scores	predict	dyadic behavior scores

INSERT 20

Status-field theory

cooperation theorem

j above i(high cooperation)

i(exports to)

j below i(low cooperaion)

(development and power dimensions)

---

developed conflict theorem

	j above i(low conflict)		j above i(high conflict)
i(exports to)		i(exports to)	
	j below i(high conflict)		j below i(low conflict)
(development)			(power)

---

undeveloped conflict theorem

	j above i(high conflict)		j above i(low conflict)
i(exports to)		i(exports to)	
	j below i(low conflict)		j below i(high conflict)
(development)			(power)

INSERT 21

Relative status field theory

model 1

economic development (close)

power (close)

model 2

economic development (far)

power (far)

model 3

economic development (close)

power (far)

model 4

economic development (far)

power (close)

INSERT 22

Model 1 of relative status field theory

tt ---> uu = (-ae) + (-ap)

uu ---> tt = (ae) + (ap)

ut ---> tu = (ae) + (-ap)

tu ---> ut = (-ae) + (ap)

INSERT 23

U run, rel. status-field theory, positive corr. case
case

-	j far above i	+	much conflict
	j average distance above i		average conflict
	j same as i	-	little conflict

INSERT 24

T run, rel. status-field theory, positive corr. case

j same as i	+ much conflict
j average distance	average conflict
+ j far below i	- little conflict

INSERT 25

Rummel's distance metric, positive correlation case

- j far above i	+ much conflict
j same as i	average conflict
+ j far below i	- little conflict

INSERT 26

Absolute distance metric, positive correlation case

+ j very distant from i	+ much conflict
j average distance from i	average conflict
j same as i	- little conflict

INSERT 27

Model of distance theory

d-space		b-space
dyadic factor scores of absolute distances on variables	predict	dyadic behavior scores

INSERT 28

Conflict and cooperation flows
given various sign configurations.

Distance theory, sign interpretation of conflict and cooperation flows when i exports to j.

I exports most to far j's on the factor and least to close j's when
+ sign on a farness factor or
- sign on a closeness factor.

I exports least to far j's on the factor and most to close j's when
- sign on a farness factor or
+ sign on a closeness factor.

Social field theory, sign interpretation of conflict and cooperation flows when i exports to j.

I exports most to j's far above i on the factor and least to j's far below i on the factor when
- sign on factor algebraic distances.

I exports least to j's far above i on the factor and most to j's far below i on the factor when
+ sign on factor algebraic distances.

Status field theory, predictions of conflict exportations for underdeveloped and developed states in respect to economic development and power distances.

For developed states, conflict exportations,
+ sign on economic development distances,
- sign on power distances.

For underdeveloped states, conflict exportations,
- sign on economic development distances,
+ sign on power distances.

For all states, cooperation exportations,
- Sign on economic development distances,
- sign on power distances.

Relative status field theory, predictions.

Model 1 predicts that j's that are close to i on economic development and power will receive more conflict from i than j's that are far from i on these dimensions.

Expected signs if this is the case:
If i is tt, - ed, - p.
If i is uu, + ed, + p.
If i is ut, + ed, - p.
If i is tu, - ed, + p.

Model 2 predicts that j's that are far from i on economic development and power will receive more conflict from i than j's that are close to i on these dimension.

Expected signs if this is the case:
If i is tt, + ed, + p.
If i is uu, - ed, - p.
If i is ut, - ed, + p.
If i is tu, + ed, - p.

Model 3 predicts that j's that are close to i on economic

development
and far from i on power will receive more conflict from i than j's
that are far on economic development and close on power.

Expected signs if this is the case:
If i is tt, − ed, + p.
If i is uu, + ed, − p.
If i is ut, + ed, + p.
If i is tu, − ed, − p.

Model 4 predicts that j's that are far from i on economic
development
and close to i on power will receive more conflict from i than j's
that
are close on economic development and far on power.

Expected signs if this is the case:
If i is tt, + ed, − p.
If i is uu, − ed, + p.
If i is ut, − ed, − p.
If i is tu, + ed, + p.

INSERT 29

Previous findings, implications of observed signs (those that receive high exportations on selected factors in terms of associations with conflict and cooperation, dist = distance, cl = close).
(Note: tt, ut etc. refers to the status of i and status-field theory is tested with social field theory since their is no difference between the "developed" and the "underdeveloped" models using this data.)

Distance theory, conflict, general model.

01 Power base distance, cl.
02 Economic development dist, dist.
03 Political distance, dist.

Distance theory, cooperation, general model.

01 Power base distance, cl.
02 Economic development distance, cl.
03 Political distance, dist.

Social field theory, conflict, general model.

01 Economic development, j's above
02 power base, j's above
03 non-competitive political system, j's above

social field theory, cooperation, general model.

01 Economic development, j's above
02 power base, j's above
03 non-competitive political system, j's above

relative status-field theory, tt, conflict, general model.

01 Economic development, cl.
02 Power base, cl.

Relative status-field theory, tt, cooperation, general model.

01 Economic development, cl.
02 Power base, cl.

Relative status-field theory, ut, conflict, general model.

01 Economic development, dist.
02 Power base, cl.

Relative status-field theory, ut, cooperation, general model.

01 Economic development, dist.
02 Power base, cl.

Relative status-field theory, tu, conflict, general model.

01 Economic development, cl.
02 Power base, dist.

RelxWKe status-field theory, tu, cooperation, general modet*

01 Economic development, cl.
02 Power base, dist.

Relative status-field theory, uu, conflict, general model.

01 Economic development, dist.
02 Power base, dist.

Relative status-field theory, uu, cooperation, general model.

01 Economic development, dist.
02 Power base, dist.

INSERT 30

Implication of signs on selected factors in terms of associations with conflict and cooperation. (Note: tt, ut etc. refers to the status of i and status-field theory is treated with social field theory since their is no difference between the "developed" and the "underdeveloped" models using this data).

Distance theory, conflict, general model.

01 Power base distance, dist.
02 Economic development dist, dist.
03 Political distance, dist.

Distance theory, cooperation, general model.

01 Power base distance, dist.
02 Economic development distance, dist.
03 Political distance, dist.

Social field theory, conflict, general model.

01 Economic development, j's above
02 power base, j's above
03 non-competitive political system, j's below

social field theory, cooperation, general model.

01 Economic development, j's above
02 power base, j's above
03 non-competitive political system, j's below

relative status-field theory, tt, conflict, general model.

01 Economic development, cl.
02 Power base, cl.

Relative status-field theory, tt, cooperation, general model.

01 Economic development, cl.
02 Power base, cl.

Relative status-field theory, ut, conflict, general model.

01 Economic development, cl.
02 Power base, cl.

Relative status-field theory, ut, cooperation, general model.

01 Economic development, cl.
02 Power base, cl.

Relative status-field theory, tu, conflict, general model.

01 Economic development, cl.
2 Power base, dist.

Relative status-field theory, tu, cooperation, general model.

01 Economic development, cl.
2 Power base, dist.

Relative status-field theory, uu, conflict, general model.

01 Economic development, dist.
2 Power base, dist.

Relative status-field theory, uu, cooperation, general model.

01 Economic development, dist.
2 Power base, dist.

INSERT 31

Implications of findings, on selected dimensions for behavioral exportations.

From the perspective of distance theory

j(dist., most behavior)
i exports to j(average distance, average behavior)
j(cl., least behavior)

From the perspective of social field theory

j(dist above, most behavior)
i exports to j(no dist., average behavior)
j(dist. below, least behavior)
(opposite for the dimension of non-competitive political system)

From the perspective of relative status-field theory

j(dist. above, most behavior)

j(slightly above, least behavior)

i exports to

j(slightly below, most behavior)

j(dist. below, least behavior)
(exempt from the rule ut nations on economic developement)

Model for ut nations, economic developement

on economic development

j(dist. above, least behavior)

j(slightly above, most behavior)

i exports to

j(slightly below, most behavior)

j(dist. below, least behavior)

(These generalizations pertain to the selected dimensions, power base, etc.) treated above.)

INSERT 32

Policy prescriptions.

From the perspective of distance theory.

Prescription: Reduce economic, power and political system differences between states (because i exports most to j's most different from i on these dimensions)

From the perspective of social field theory.

Prescription: Each i should attempt to reduce differences between his position and j's above him on the dimensions of economic development, power and below him on non-competitive political system.

From the perspective of relative status field theory.

Prescription: I's should attempt to maximize differences between themselves and j's immediately below them but minimize differences
between themselves and j's far above them in respect to economic development and power (exempt ut nations, economic development).

INSERT 33

Comparing theories

(tt,ut etc. Refers to the status of j)

1.No. of correlations

2.Distance theory, cooperation	116.00
4.Social field theory, cooperation	116.00
3.Social field theory, conflict	112.00
1.Distance theory, conflict	112.00
12.Relative status-field theory, uu,cooperation	44.00
6.Relative status-field theory, tt,cooperation	43.00
5.Relative status-field theory, tt,conflict	41.00
10.Relative status-field theory, tu,cooperation	39.00
11.Relative status-field theory, uu,conflict	38.00
8.Relative status-field theory, ut,cooperation	33.00
7.Relative status-field theory, ut,conflict	32.00
9.Relative status-field theory, tu,conflict	30.00

2.N of correlations

1.Distance theory, conflict	128.00
2.Distance theory, cooperation	128.00
3.Social field theory, conflict	128.00
4.Social field theory, cooperation	128.00
11.Relative status-field theory, uu,conflict	67.00
9.Relative status-field theory, tu,conflict	65.00
12.Relative status-field theory, uu,cooperation	64.00
6.Relative status-field theory, tt,cooperation	59.00
7.Relative status-field theory, ut,conflict	58.00
5.Relative status-field theory, tt,conflict	57.00
10.Relative status-field theory, tu,cooperation	55.00
8.Relative status-field theory, ut,cooperation	55.00

3.Range of correlations

7.Relative status-field theory, ut,conflict	97.76
6.Relative status-field theory, tt,cooperation	97.40
11.Relative status-field theory, uu,conflict	96.45
10.Relative status-field theory, tu,cooperation	96.42
8.Relative status-field theory, ut,cooperation	95.44
9.Relative status-field theory, tu,conflict	93.38
12.Relative status-field theory, uu,cooperation	92.38
5.Relative status-field theory, tt,conflict	90.44
2.Distance theory, cooperation	73.39
1.Distance theory, conflict	70.37
4.Social field theory, cooperation	68.28
3.Social field theory, conflict	63.32

4.Expected correlation

8.Relative status-field theory, ut,cooperation	.62
10.Relative status-field theory, tu,cooperation	.62
5.Relative status-field theory, tt,conflict	.61
7.Relative status-field theory, ut,conflict	.61
6.Relative status-field theory, tt,cooperation	.60
12.Relative status-field theory, uu,cooperation	.58
9.Relative status-field theory, tu,conflict	.57
11.Relative status-field theory, uu,conflict	.56

2.Distance theory, cooperation	.50
1.Distance theory, conflict	.50
4.Social field theory, cooperation	.41
3.Social field theory, conflict	.41

5.No. above expected correlation

2.Distance theory, cooperation	102.00
4.Social field theory, cooperation	98.00
3.Social field theory, conflict	85.00
1.Distance theory, conflict	80.00
11.Relative status-field theory, uu,conflict	29.00
12.Relative status-field theory, uu,cooperation	29.00
5.Relative status-field theory, tt,conflict	28.00
6.Relative status-field theory, tt,cooperation	28.00
9.Relative status-field theory, tu,conflict	24.00
10.Relative status-field theory, tu,cooperation	24.00
8.Relative status-field theory, ut,cooperation	21.00
7.Relative status-field theory, ut,conflict	16.00

6.% above expected correlation

2.Distance theory, cooperation	88.00
4.Social field theory, cooperation	84.00
9.Relative status-field theory, tu,conflict	80.00
3.Social field theory, conflict	76.00
11.Relative status-field theory, uu,conflict	76.00
1.Distance theory, conflict	71.00
5.Relative status-field theory, tt,conflict	68.00
12.Relative status-field theory, uu,cooperation	66.00
6.Relative status-field theory, tt,cooperation	65.00
8.Relative status-field theory, ut,cooperation	64.00
10.Relative status-field theory, tu,cooperation	62.00
7.Relative status-field theory, ut,conflict	50.00

7.Expected average square

8.Relative status-field theory, ut,cooperation	.38
10.Relative status-field theory, tu,cooperation	.38
5.Relative status-field theory, tt,conflict	.37
7.Relative status-field theory, ut,conflict	.37
6.Relative status-field theory, tt,cooperation	.36
12.Relative status-field theory, uu,cooperation	.33
9.Relative status-field theory, tu,conflict	.32
11.Relative status-field theory, uu,conflict	.31
2.Distance theory, cooperation	.25
1.Distance theory, conflict	.25
4.Social field theory, cooperation	.17
3.Social field theory, conflict	.17

8.Actual average square

8.Relative status-field theory, ut,cooperation	.52
7.Relative status-field theory, ut,conflict	.51
5.Relative status-field theory, tt,conflict	.48
6.Relative status-field theory, tt,cooperation	.48
10.Relative status-field theory, tu,cooperation	.46
12.Relative status-field theory, uu,cooperation	.46

11.Relative status-field theory, uu,conflict	.44
9.Relative status-field theory, tu,conflict	.42
2.Distance theory, cooperation	.33
1.Distance theory, conflict	.30
4.Social field theory, cooperation	.24
3.Social field theory, conflict	.21

9.Average square above expected square

7.Relative status-field theory, ut,conflict	.14
8.Relative status-field theory, ut,cooperation	.14
5.Relative status-field theory, tt,conflict	.13
11.Relative status-field theory, uu,conflict	.13
12.Relative status-field theory, uu,cooperation	.13
6.Relative status-field theory, tt,cooperation	.12
9.Relative status-field theory, tu,conflict	.10
2.Distance theory, cooperation	.08
10.Relative status-field theory, tu,cooperation	.08
4.Social field theory, cooperation	.07
1.Distance theory, conflict	.05
3.Social field theory, conflict	.04

10.Total dyads considered

2.Distance theory, cooperation	14848.00
4.Social field theory, cooperation	14848.00
3.Social field theory, conflict	14336.00
1.Distance theory, conflict	14336.00
12.Relative status-field theory, uu,cooperation	2816.00
11.Relative status-field theory, uu,conflict	2546.00
6.Relative status-field theory, tt,cooperation	2537.00
5.Relative status-field theory, tt,conflict	2337.00
10.Relative status-field theory, tu,cooperation	2145.00
7.Relative status-field theory, ut,conflict	1856.00
8.Relative status-field theory, ut,cooperation	1815.00
9.Relative status-field theory, tu,conflict	1650.00

11.Col. sums of squares of canonical correlations

2.Distance theory, cooperation	37.96
1.Distance theory, conflict	33.64
4.Social field theory, cooperation	27.65
3.Social field theory, conflict	23.86
6.Relative status-field theory, tt,cooperation	20.65
12.Relative status-field theory, uu,cooperation	20.03
5.Relative status-field theory, tt,conflict	19.86
10.Relative status-field theory, tu,cooperation	18.06
8.Relative status-field theory, ut,cooperation	17.11
11.Relative status-field theory, uu,conflict	16.91
7.Relative status-field theory, ut,conflict	16.49
9.Relative status-field theory, tu,conflict	12.67

12.% Of total variance of theoretical maximum

8.Relative status-field theory, ut,cooperation	52.00
7.Relative status-field theory, ut,conflict	51.00
5.Relative status-field theory, tt,conflict	48.00
6.Relative status-field theory, tt,cooperation	48.00

10.Relative status-field theory, tu,cooperation	46.00
12.Relative status-field theory, uu,cooperation	46.00
11.Relative status-field theory, uu,conflict	45.00
9.Relative status-field theory, tu,conflict	42.00
2.Distance theory, cooperation	33.00
3.Social field theory, conflict	31.00
1.Distance theory, conflict	30.00
4.Social field theory, cooperation	24.00

INSERT 34

14 MODELS GENERATED

(TT,UT,ETC. REFERS TO THE STATUS OF I).
(LOOK ELSEWHERE FOR THE RELEVANT FACTOR DIMENSIONS,
D-SPACE FOR DISTANCE THEORY AND A-SPACE FOR THE REMAINING
THEORIES. THAT IS, 1.26 IS THE MODEL SCORE FOR POWER BASE DISTANCE, DISTANCE THEORY, CONFLICT).

DISTANCE THEORY,CONFLICT,GENERAL MODEL

1. WORLD	1.26	.66	1.21	.18	-1.11	-.93	-.60	.22	-1.83	-1.58
	-1.74	.88	-2.73	2.53	-1.46	-.83	.01	-1.08	-2.05	-.69
	.16	-1.54	.99	-1.17	.94	-.62	.35	.22	-.59	-.15
	.42	2.33	1.61	53.00						

DISTANCE THEORY,COOPERATION,GENERAL MODEL

1. WORLD	.29	.23	1.16	.17	-1.10	-.84	-2.49	-.82	-2.24	-2.11
	-2.01	-.08	-4.22	2.46	-1.62	.23	.30	-1.23	-2.28	.73
	.26	-2.34	.84	-1.24	-.51	-.27	.97	1.37	-.13	-.52
	.04	1.56	1.72	74.28						

SOCIAL FIELD THEORY,CONFLICT,GENERAL MODEL

1. WORLD	-3.66	-16.42	-3.16	2.71	-1.58	-5.13	-.79	-.18	3.85	3.94
	7.30	1.70	2.67	-2.56	1.36	-5.43	.19	.68	1.22	3.75
	-1.57	9.89	577.63							

SOCIAL FIELD THEORY,COOPERATION,GENERAL MODEL

1. WORLD	-2.84	-20.37	-4.66	2.47	-1.32	-6.29	-.63	-.27	4.08	3.87
	7.81	2.32	2.23	-2.16	.55	-4.15	-.20	.18	.30	4.20
	-1.46	7.17	689.03							

RELATIVE STATUS-FIELD THEORY,UU,CONFLICT,GENERAL MODEL

1. WORLD	-.91	-3.61	-1.90	1.03	-.70	-2.22	-.15	.14	1.43	1.52
	2.82	1.21	1.42	-1.50	.55	-1.49	-.67	.16	.07	2.73
	-.21	3.84	67.29							

RELATIVE STATUS-FIELD THEORY,UU,COOPERATION,GENERAL MODEL

1. WORLD	-.81	-3.81	-2.09	1.41	-.51	-2.49	.05	-.09	1.51	1.35
	3.10	1.31	.72	-1.18	.20	-1.61	-.41	.49	.02	2.94
	-.34	4.17	74.52							

RELATIVE STATUS-FIELD THEORY,TU,CONFLICT,GENERAL MODEL

1. WORLD	-1.38	-2.02	-.88	.42	-.40	-1.51	-.54	-.00	.42	.83
	1.56	.55	1.03	-.49	.76	-1.75	.34	-.01	.53	1.10
	-.27	1.36	21.77							

RELATIVE STATUS-FIELD THEORY,TU,COOPERATION,GENERAL MODEL

1. WORLD	-1.68	-2.09	-1.34	-.23	-.61	-2.44	-.63	.16	.51	.70
	1.44	-.12	1.45	-.47	.72	-.49	-.13	-.45	.09	1.04
	-1.29	.58	25.04							

RELATIVE STATUS-FIELD THEORY,UT,CONFLICT,GENERAL MODEL

1. WORLD	.04	-2.87	.49	-.90	-.55	-.40	-.50	-.58	.78	.85
	1.73	-.78	-.08	-.37	.00	-.58	-.03	.06	-.23	-.92
	-.61	.65	17.48							

RELATIVE STATUS-FIELD THEORY,UT,COOPERATION,GENERAL MODEL

1. WORLD	.41	-4.41	-.39	-1.61	-.09	-.58	-.77	-.91	1.82	.66
	2.76	.06	-.15	-.08	.42	-.08	-.18	-.53	.31	-.28
	-.38	.19	36.37							

RELATIVE STATUS-FIELD THEORY,TT,CONFLICT,GENERAL MODEL

1. WORLD	-1.96	-2.64	-.45	-.99	-.94	.33	-.82	.08	2.03	.41
	1.57	-.99	-.05	-.11	-.94	.60	-.18	-.42	.67	-.35
	-1.03	.14	24.50							

RELATIVE STATUS-FIELD THEORY,TT,COOPERATION,GENERAL MODEL

1. WORLD	-1.46	-4.44	-1.19	-.70	1.03	1.36	-.53	.19	1.33	.81
	2.30	.49	.56	.15	-1.81	.18	-.68	.02	.24	-.60
	-.53	.71	40.30							

INSERT 35

CORRELATIONS, SUMMARY.

TYPE OF STATE WITH BIG + WEIGHT,
POWER BASE DISTANCE

(TENDS TO EXPORT CONFLICT TO THOSE DISTANT)

FEW MILITARY PERSONNEL PER CAPITA

TYPE OF STATE WITH BIG + WEIGHT,
ECONOMIC DEVELOPMENT DISTANCE

(TENDS TO EXPORT CONFLICT TO THOSE DISTANT)

UNDERDEVELOPED

LITTLE ETHNIC-LINGUISTIC FRACTIONALIZATION

TYPE OF STATE WITH BIG + WEIGHT,
POLITICAL DISTANCE

(TENDS TO EXPORT CONFLICT TO THOSE DISTANT)

NON-COMPETITIVE POLITICAL SYSTEM

FEW PER CAPITA SCHOOL ENROLLMENT

TYPE OF STATE WITH BIG - WEIGHT,
POWER BASE DISTANCE

(TENDS TO EXPORT MOST CONFLICT TO THOSE CLOSE)

DEVELOPED

BIG POWER BASE

HIGH ENERGY PRODUCTION

TYPE OF STATE WITH BIG - WEIGHT,
ECONOMIC DEVELOPMENT DISTANCE

(TENDS TO EXPORT MOST CONFLICT TO THOSE CLOSE)

DEVELOPED

HIGH CRUDE DEATH RATE

TYPE OF STATE WITH BIG - WEIGHT,
POLITICAL DISTANCE

(TENDS TO EXPORT MOST CONLICT TO THOSE CLOSE)

HIGH PER CAPITA SCHOOL ENROLLMENT

LOW ENERGY PRODUCTION

INSERT 36

F-TEST OF MEANS, SUMMARY

TYPE OF STATE WITH + WEIGHT,
POWER BASE DISTANCE

(TENDS TO EXPORT MOST CONFLICT TO THOSE DISTANT)

UNDERDEVELOPED

LOW POWER BASE

MUCH DOMESTIC VIOLENCE

TYPE OF STATE WITH - WEIGHT,
POWER BASE DISTANCE
(TENDS TO EXPORT MOST CONFLICT TO THOSE CLOSE)

DEVELOPED

HIGH POWER BASE

LITTLE DOMESTIC VIOLENCE

TYPE OF STATE WITH + WEIGHT,
ECONOMIC DEVELOPMENT DISTANCE

(TENDS TO EXPORT MOST CONFLICT TO THOSE DISTANT)

UNDERDEVELOPED

POLITICALLY UNSTABLE

LARGE POPULATION GROWTH RATE

MUCH DOMESTIC VIOLENCE

TYPE OF STATE WITH - WEIGHT,
ECONOMIC DEVELOPMENT DISTANCE

(TENDS TO EXPORT MOST CONFLICT TO THOSE CLOSE)

DEVELOPED

POLITICALLY STABLE

LITTLE POPULATION GROWTH RATE

LITTLE DOMESTIC VIOLENCE

TYPE OF STATE WITH + WEIGHT,
POLITICAL DISTANCE

(TENDS TO EXPORT MOST CONFLICT TO THOSE DISTANT)

NON-COMPETITIVE POLITICAL SYSTEM

MANY MILITARY PERSONNEL PER CAPITA

HIGH ENERGY PRODUCTION

TYPE OF STATE WITH - WEIGHT,
POLITICAL DISTANCE

(TENDS TO EXPORT MOST CONFLICT TO THOSE CLOSE)

COMPETITIVE POLITICAL SYSTEM

FEW MILITARY PERSONNEL PER CAPITA

LOW ENERGY PRODUCTION

INSERT 37

D-SPACE, ROTATED FACTOR LOADINGS

001 TOTAL POPULATION	.49	-.08	-.01	-.03	-.04
	-.14	-.08	.07	-.01	-.04
	.01	.59	-.01	.03	-.03
	-.03	-.02	-.06	.16	.04
	-.02	-.28	-.01	.03	-.04
	-.04	.02	-.04	.01	-.07
	-.00	.08	.05	.76	
002 POPULATION GROWTH RATE, 1960-65	.06	.10	.00	-.01	.0
	.01	-.01	-.02	.88	.01

						-.00	.01	.09	.04	.07
						-.06	.03	.01	.01	.02
						-.01	-.03	.04	.03	-.03
						-.04	.00	-.02	-.05	-.03
						.00	-.03	.02	.81	
003 POPULATION GROWTH RATE, 1950-65						.03	.08	.04	.01	-.0
						.02	.01	.01	.87	.03
						.01	.01	.04	.04	.02
						.00	-.00	.00	.03	.03
						-.00	-.03	.00	.06	-.03
						-.03	.02	-.02	-.03	-.08
						.00	-.02	.05	.78	

****

COLUMN SUM OF SQUARES	18.76	17.31	4.94	3.35	3.78	2.09	3.16	3.16	2.79	2.09
	1.90	4.14	2.21	1.80	1.86	1.43	1.54	1.78	1.59	1.60
	1.93	2.09	1.32	1.78	1.22	1.31	1.28	1.18	1.37	1.31
	1.24	1.26	1.58							

FACTORS, SORTED

01 POWER BASE DISTANCE

030 TOTAL GNP (IN MILLIONS U.S. DOLLARS)	.91
057 TOTAL EDUCATION EXPENDITURE (IN MILLION U.S. DOLLARS)	.88
119 TOTAL ENERGY CONSUMPTION IN METRIC TONS OF COAL EQUIVALENT	.86
098 PROPORTION OF TOTAL WORLD TRADE	.85
094 TOTAL IMPORTS	.85
036 TOTAL TRADE, 1960 (IN MILLIONS U.S. DOLLARS)	.83
114 TOTAL HIGHWAY VEHICLES	.82
096 TOTAL EXPORTS	.81
110 TOTAL PASSENGER CARS	.79
092 TOTAL TELEPHONES	.79
041 PERCENTAGE CONTRIBUTION TO WORLD TOTAL OF SCIENTIFIC AUTHORS	.78
086 NATIONAL GOVERNMENT EXPENDITURE	.78
084 NATIONAL GOVERNMENT REVENUE	.76
060 TOTAL HEALTH EXPENDITURE (IN MILLIONS U.S. DOLLARS)	.75
112 TOTAL COMMERCIAL VEHICLES	.75
109 RAIL PASSENGER KILOMETERS	.73
048 TOTAL NUMBER OF PHYSICIANS	.72
080 POPULATION IN CITIES OF 100,000+	.72
105 TOTAL UNIVERSITY ENROLLMENT	.72
082 POPULATION IN CITIES OF 50,000+	.71
088 RAILROAD MILEAGE	.70
101 TOTAL SECONDARY SCHOOL ENROLLMENT	.64
040 TOTAL SCIENTIFIC AND TECHNICAL SERIALS PUBLISHED	.62
107 TOTAL SCHOOL ENROLLMENT	.56
066 TOTAL INTERNAL SECURITY FORCES (IN UNITS)	.56
099 TOTAL PRIMARY SCHOOL ENROLLMENT	.55
121 BOOK PRODUCTION BY TITLES	.54
090 ALL MAIL	.54
001 TOTAL POPULATION	.49

02 ECONOMIC DEVELOPMENT DISTANCE

085 NATIONAL GOVERNMENT REVENUE PER CAPITA	.88

031 GNP PER CAPITA (IN U.S. DOLLARS)	.87
087 NATIONAL GOVERNMENT EXPENDITURE PER CAPITA	.87
115 TOTAL HIGHWAY VEHICLES PER CAPITA	.86
111 PASSENGER CARS PER CAPITA	.84
116 GROSS DOMESTIC PRODUCT PER CAPITA	.84
093 TELEPHONES PER CAPITA	.84
058 EDUCATION EXPENDITURE PER CAPITA (IN MILLION U.S. DOLLARS)	.83
095 IMPORTS PER CAPITA	.81
120 ENERGY CONSUMPTION IN KILOGRAMS PER CAPITA	.80
113 COMMERCIAL VEHICLES PER CAPITA	.80
097 EXPORTS PER CAPITA	.75
015 RADIOS PER 1,000 POPULATION	.75
091 ALL MAIL PER CAPITA	.69
016 TELEVISIONS PER 1,000 POPULATION	.68
049 PHYSICIANS PER ONE MILLION POPULATION, 1965	.65
017 CINEMA ATTENDANCE PER CAPITA, 1960	.64
014 NEWSPAPERS PER 1,000 POPULATION	.63
019 UNADJUSTED SCHOOL ENROLLMENT RATIO	.60
061 HEALTH EXPENDITURE PER CAPITA	.60
018 LITERACY RATES	.58
020 ADJUSTED SCHOOL ENROLLMENT RATIO	.58
043 PERCENTAGE OF GROSS DOMESTIC PRODUCT ORIGINATING IN INDUSTRY	.54
122 BOOK PRODUCTION BY TITLES PER MILLION POPULATION	.53
055 DEFENSE EXPENDITURE PER CAPITA (IN U.S. DOLLARS)	.50

03 POLITICAL DISTANCE

129 AGGREGATE COMPETITION INDEX	.87
128 PARTY LEGITIMACY	.84
127 COMPETITIVENESS OF NOMINATING PROCESS	.82
077 LEGISLATIVE EFFECTIVENESS	.80
126 SIZE OF LEGISLATURE/NUMBER OF SEATS HELD BY LARGEST PARTY	.78
064 ELECTORAL IRREGULARITY SCORE	.61
065 PRESS FREEDOM INDEX	.58
063 POLITICAL PARTY FRACTIONALIZATION BASED ON NUMBER OF SEATS, 1964	.55

04 SCHOOL ENROLLMENT DISTANCE

104 PRIMARY AND SECONDARY ENROLLMENT PER CAPITA	.92
108 TOTAL SCHOOL ENROLLMENT PER CAPITA	.90
100 PRIMARY SCHOOL ENROLLMENT PER CAPITA	.89

05 INTERNAL POLITICAL TURMOIL DISTANCE

142 MEAN UNSUCCESSFUL IRREGULAR POWER TRANSFERS, 1963-1967	.79
074 MILITARY REGIME	.76
136 MEAN NUMBER OF IRREGULAR POWER TRANSFERS DURING 1963-1967	.73
075 MEAN NUMBER OF MAJOR CONSTITUTIONAL CHANGES, 1962-1966	.67
137 MEAN NUMBER OF POLITICAL ASSASSINATIONS DURING 1963-1967	.67
143 MEAN NUMBER OF POLITICAL EXECUTIONS DURING 1963-1967	.63

06 INTERNAL VIOLENCE CLOSENESS

144 MEAN RELAXATIONS OF GOV. RETRICTIONS ON POL. ACTIVITY, 1963-1967	-.52
133 MEAN NUMBER OF DEATHS FROM DOMESTIC VIOLENCE DURING 1963-1967	-.71
132 MEAN NUMBER OF ARMED ATTACKS DURING 1963-1967	-.75

07 MILITARISM DISTANCE

052 MILITARY MANPOWER PER ONE THOUSAND WORKING AGED POPULATION	.88
051 MILITARY MANPOWER PER ONE THOUSAND POPULATION	.88
053 MILITARY MANPOWER PER AREA	.57
055 DEFENSE EXPENDITURE PER CAPITA (IN U.S. DOLLARS)	.52
050 TOTAL MILITARY MANPOWER	.52

08 DATE OF INDEPENDENCE DISTANCE

070 DATE OF INDEPENDENCE(BANKS)	.86
072 DATE OF INDEPENDENT IDENTIFICATION(RUSTOW)	.86
071 DATE OF INSTITUTIONAL FORMATION(HUDSON)	.86

09 POPULATION GROWTH RATE DISTANCE

002 POPULATION GROWTH RATE, 1960-65	.88
003 POPULATION GROWTH RATE, 1950-65	.87
011 WORKING AGE POPULATION	.60
012 ADULT POPULATION	.56

10 DENSITY DISTANCE

005 DENSITY(PEOPLE PER SQUARE KILOMETER)	.85
007 PEOPLE PER SQUARE KILOMETER OF AGRICULTURAL LAND AREA	.79
053 MILITARY MANPOWER PER AREA	.56

11 INTERNAL SECURITY FORCES DISTANCE

067 INTERNAL SECURITY FORCES PER ONE THOUSAND WORKING AGE POP.	.93
068 INTERNAL SECURITY FORCES PER ONE MILLION POPULATION	.92

12 POPULATION SIZE DISTANCE

107 TOTAL SCHOOL ENROLLMENT	.75
099 TOTAL PRIMARY SCHOOL ENROLLMENT	.75
103 TOTAL PRIMARY AND SECONDARY ENROLLMENT	.74
001 TOTAL POPULATION	.59
101 TOTAL SECONDARY SCHOOL ENROLLMENT	.58
050 TOTAL MILITARY MANPOWER	.52
080 POPULATION IN CITIES OF 100,000+	.50

13 RELIGIOUS DISTANCE

023 CHRISTIAN COMMUNITY, % OF THE TOTAL POP.	.79
026 CATHOLIC, % OF THE TOTAL POP.	.76
024 MOSLEM, % OF THE TOTAL POP.	.72

14 ENERGY PRODUCTION DISTANCE

118 ENERGY PRODUCTION IN KILOGRAMS PER CAPITA	.81

Variable	Value
117 TOTAL ENERGY PRODUCTION IN METRIC TONS COAL EQUIVALENT	.81
15 GNP GROWTH RATE DISTANCE	
035 TOTAL GNP PER CAPITA GROWTH RATES, ANNUAL AVERAGES, 1960-1965	.60
034 TOTAL GNP GROWTH RATES, ANNUAL AVERAGES, 1960-1965	.50
16 FIXED PRICES GNP GROWTH RATE CLOSENESS	
032 GNP AT FIXED PRICES FOR CALCULATING GROWTH RATES	-.70
033 GNP PER CAPITA AT FIXED PRICES (GROWTH RATES)	-.76
17 ETHNO-LINGUISTIC FRACTIONALIZATION CLOSENESS	
021 ETHNO-LINGUISTIC FRACTIONALIZATION	-.75
022 LINGUISTIC FRACTIONALIZATION, MULLER SCALE	-.78
18 PER CENT URBAN POPULATION DISTANCE	
081 PER CAPITA POPULATION IN CITIES OF 100, 000+	.69
083 PER CAPITA POPULATION IN CITIES OF 50, 000+	.66
19 ALL MAIL CLOSENESS	
20 POLITICAL PARTY FRACTIONALIZATION CLOSENESS	
065 PRESS FREEDOM INDEX	-.56
063 POLITICAL PARTY FRACTIONALIZATION BASED ON NUMBER OF SEATS, 1964	-.60
21 DOMESTIC TURMOIL DISTANCE	
130 MEAN NUMBER OF PROTEST DEMONSTRATIONS DURING 1963-1967	.65
140 MEAN NUMBER OF POLITICAL STRIKES DURING 1963-1967	.64
131 MEAN NUMBER OF RIOTS DURING 1963-1967	.58
22 TOTAL AREA CLOSENESS	
004 TOTAL AREA	-.82
006 TOTAL AGRICULTURAL AREA	-.84
23 PER CAPITA ENERGY CONSUMPTION GROWTH RATE DISTANCE	
029 ENERGY CONSUMPTION PER CAPITA GROWTH RATES	.67
025 PROTESTANT, % OF THE TOTAL POP.	.51
24 INFANT MORTALITY CLOSENESS	

010 INFANT MORTALITY RATES	-.60
25 AGE OF CURRENCY CLOSENESS	
123 AGE OF CURRENCY IN MONTHS	.63
124 RATIO OF BLACK MARKET TO OFFICIAL EXCHANGE RATE	.52
26 TOTAL HEALTH EXPENDITURE CLOSENESS	
062 TOTAL HEALTH EXPENDITURE AS A PERCENTAGE OF GROSS NATIONAL PRODUCT	-.81
27 CRUDE DEATH RATE CLOSENESS	
008 CRUDE BIRTH RATES, 1960	-.50
009 CRUDE DEATH RATES, 1960	-.78
28 REGULAR EXECUTIVE TRANSFERS CLOSENESS	
134 MEAN NUMBER OF REGULAR EXECUTIVE TRANSFERS DURING 1963-1967	-.61
29 PER CAPITA ECONOMIC ACTIVE MALE POPULATION DISTANCE	
30 CONCENTRATION OF EXPORT COMMODITIES CLOSENESS	
31 MEAN ELECTIONS DISTANCE	
138 MEAN NUMBER OF ELECTIONS DURING 1963-1967	.69
32 CONCENTRATION OF EXPORT RECEIVERS DISTANCE	
039 CONCENTRATION OF EXPORT RECEIVING COUNTRIES	.60
33 ORTHODOX COMMUNITY CLOSENESS	
028 ORTHODOX COMMUNITY, % OF THE TOTAL POP.	-.69

CANONICAL CORRELATIONS FOR 128 STATES

120	TANZANIA	.70
22	CONGO (BRA)	.68
3	ALGERIA	.66
72	NETHERLANDS	.66
122	KENYA	.65
20	CHINA, PR	.64
73	NEW ZEALAND	.63
116	KUWAIT	.63
5	AUSTRALIA	.63
10	BULGARIA	.63
30	DOMINICAN REPUBLIC	.63
76	NIGERIA	.63
41	GUATEMALA	.63
77	NORWAY	.63
108	URUGUAY	.62
9	BRAZIL	.62
6	AUSTRIA	.62
52	ISRAEL	.62
106	UNITED STATES	.62
94	SWEDEN	.61
111	SOUTH VIETNAM	.61
103	U.S.S.R	.61
27	CZECHOSLOVAKIA	.61
60	LAOS	.60
87	SAUDI ARABIA	.60
59	SOUTH KOREA	.60
29	DENMARK	.60
58	NORTH KOREA	.59
2	ALBANIA	.59
91	SOUTH AFRICA	.59
95	SWITZERLAND	.59
8	BOLIVIA	.59
47	INDIA	.58
15	CANADA	.58
125	GUYANA	.58
53	ITALY	.58
112	YEMEN	.58
50	IRAQ	.58
110	NORTH VIETNAM	.58
17	CEYLON	.58
105	UNITED KINGDOM	.57
40	GREECE	.57
48	INDONESIA	.57
21	COLOMBIA	.56
92	SPAIN	.56
28	DAHOMEY	.56
109	VENEZUELA	.56
61	LEBANON	.56
56	JAPAN	.55
36	GABON	.55
124	SINGAPORE	.55
31	ECUADOR	.55
57	JORDAN	.55
16	CENTRAL AFRICAN REP	.55
45	HUNGARY	.55
100	TUNISIA	.54
13	CAMBODIA	.54
74	NICARAGUA	.54
82	PHILIPPINES	.54
38	WEST GERMANY	.54
85	ROMANIA	.54
79	PANAMA	.53
97	THAILAND	.53

49	IRAN	.53
102	UGANDA	.53
35	FRANCE	.53
37	EAST GERMANY	.53
126	MALAYSIA	.53
39	GHANA	.53
24	COSTA RICA	.52
84	PORTUGAL	.52
25	CUBA	.52
80	PARAGUAY	.52
71	NEPAL	.52
11	BURMA	.52
63	LIBYA	.52
90	SOMALIA	.51
113	YUGOSLAVIA	.51
67	MAURITANIA	.51
44	HONDURAS	.51
7	BELGIUM	.50
43	HAITI	.50
96	SYRIA	.50
4	ARGENTINA	.50
119	MALTA	.49
81	PERU	.49
18	CHAD	.49
32	EL SALVADOR	.49
42	GUINEA	.48
12	BURUNDI	.48
23	CONGO (LEO)	.48
83	POLAND	.48
121	ZAMBIA	.48
101	TURKEY	.48
93	SUDAN	.47
115	GAMBIA	.47
69	MONGOLIA	.47
26	CYPRUS	.47
78	PAKISTAN	.47
51	IRELAND	.46
54	IVORY COAST	.46
68	MEXICO	.46
19	CHILE	.45
98	TOGO	.45
34	FINLAND	.45
89	SIERRA LEONE	.45
104	U.A.R.	.45
99	TRINIDAD	.44
55	JAMAICA	.44
118	MALAWI	.43
33	ETHIOPIA	.42
70	MOROCCO	.37
62	LIBERIA	.00
114	BOTSWANA	.00
86	RWANDA	.00
88	SENEGAL	.00
117	LESOTHO	.00
14	CAMEROUN	.00
107	UPPER VOLTA	.00
1	AFGHANISTAN	.00
46	ICELAND	.00
75	NIGER	.00
123	W. SAMOA	.00
64	LUXEMBOURG	.00
66	MALI	.00
65	MALAGASY REP	.00
127	MALDIVE ISLANDS	.00
128	BARBADOS	.00

INSERT 39

DISTANCE THEORY, SOME ANALYTICAL COMPARISONS

1.NO. OF CORRELATIONS 112
2.N OF CORRELATIONS 128
3.RANGE OF CORRELATIONS 70 TO 37
4.EXPECTED CORRELATION .50
5.NO. ABOVE EXPECTED CORRELATION 80.
6.% ABOVE EXPECTED CORRELATION 71.
7.EXPECTED AVERAGE SQUARE .25
8.ACTUAL AVERAGE SQUARE .30
9.AVERAGE SQUARE ABOVE EXPECTED SQUARE .05
10.TOTAL DYADS CONSIDERED 14336
11.COL. SUMS OF SQUARES OF CANONICAL CORRELATIONS 33.64
12.% OF TOTAL VARIANCE OF THEORETICAL MAXIMUM 30%

INSERT 40

CANONICAL WEIGHTS

1 AFGHANISTAN	.00	.00	.00	.00	.00	.00	.00	.00	.00	.00
	.00	.00	.00	.00	.00	.00	.00	.00	.00	.00
	.00	.00	.00	.00	.00	.00	.00	.00	.00	.00
	.00	.00	.00	.00						
2 ALBANIA	.47	-.07	-.07	-.30	.14	-.07	-.29	-.23	.08	-.08
	-.08	.14	.03	.06	.05	.31	-.07	.24	.22	.01
	.15	-.32	.08	-.13	-.07	-.11	-.20	.24	-.23	-.28
	.08	.44	.20	1.37						
3 ALGERIA	-.07	.34	.39	.10	-.10	.27	.17	.42	-.19	.19
	-.21	.19	-.11	-.18	.26	-.15	-.08	-.28	-.03	-.01
	-.22	.16	-.05	-.29	-.07	-.08	.22	-.17	.31	.10
	-.37	.20	-.21	1.52						
4 ARGENTINA	-.24	-.23	.44	.10	-.01	.32	.14	-.23	-.20	-.03
	.19	.01	-.24	-.07	.22	.06	-.03	-.27	.28	-.01
	-.13	.29	-.07	-.35	-.12	-.23	.12	.27	-.26	.12
	-.10	-.04	.27	1.38						

****

COLUMN SUM OF SQUARES	9.01	5.20	4.54	3.66	2.83	5.07	5.24	4.55	3.50	3.11
	3.14	5.56	3.37	6.50	2.84	3.71	2.34	4.86	4.28	3.14
	4.13	5.41	4.73	4.33	3.45	3.15	2.72	3.26	4.34	3.04
	3.68	6.60	4.57							

INSERT 41

TWENTY HIGHEST AND LOWEST WEIGHTS FOR SELECTED FACTORS

01 POWER BASE DISTANCE

No.	Country	Weight
122	KENYA	.53
2	ALBANIA	.47
99	TRINIDAD	.47
71	NEPAL	.45
100	TUNISIA	.44
55	JAMAICA	.41
120	TANZANIA	.41
121	ZAMBIA	.41
22	CONGO (BRA)	.40
108	URUGUAY	.40
112	YEMEN	.40
116	KUWAIT	.39
119	MALTA	.39
39	GHANA	.38
41	GUATEMALA	.38
43	HAITI	.38
110	NORTH VIETNAM	.37
124	SINGAPORE	.36
8	BOLIVIA	.35
11	BURMA	.34
92	SPAIN	-.27
10	BULGARIA	-.27
104	U.A.R.	-.28
6	AUSTRIA	-.29
113	YUGOSLAVIA	-.30
47	INDIA	-.30
37	EAST GERMANY	-.32
106	UNITED STATES	-.32
20	CHINA, PR	-.34
5	AUSTRALIA	-.34
56	JAPAN	-.35
27	CZECHOSLOVAKIA	-.38
72	NETHERLANDS	-.41
15	CANADA	-.43
53	ITALY	-.47
103	U.S.S.R	-.49
83	POLAND	-.51
35	FRANCE	-.53
38	WEST GERMANY	-.56
105	UNITED KINGDOM	-.59

02 ECONOMIC DEVELOPMENT DISTANCE

No.	Country	Weight
82	PHILIPPINES	.47
17	CEYLON	.37
101	TURKEY	.37
104	U.A.R.	.35
20	CHINA, PR	.34
3	ALGERIA	.34
43	HAITI	.32
70	MOROCCO	.32
89	SIERRA LEONE	.32

120	TANZANIA	.32
96	SYRIA	.30
110	NORTH VIETNAM	.30
115	GAMBIA	.30
93	SUDAN	.29
21	COLOMBIA	.28
67	MAURITANIA	.28
76	NIGERIA	.28
9	BRAZIL	.28
31	ECUADOR	.27
41	GUATEMALA	.27
53	ITALY	-.23
4	ARGENTINA	-.23
27	CZECHOSLOVAKIA	-.24
99	TRINIDAD	-.24
29	DENMARK	-.24
34	FINLAND	-.25
37	EAST GERMANY	-.25
109	VENEZUELA	-.26
108	URUGUAY	-.27
94	SWEDEN	-.27
16	CENTRAL AFRICAN REP	-.28
51	IRELAND	-.28
98	TOGO	-.29
5	AUSTRALIA	-.29
95	SWITZERLAND	-.30
15	CANADA	-.32
38	WEST GERMANY	-.32
18	CHAD	-.34
116	KUWAIT	-.38
35	FRANCE	-.41

03 POLITICAL DISTANCE

4	ARGENTINA	.44
92	SPAIN	.40
3	ALGERIA	.39
43	HAITI	.36
49	IRAN	.35
104	U.A.R.	.35
116	KUWAIT	.33
121	ZAMBIA	.33
50	IRAQ	.32
6	AUSTRIA	.32
71	NEPAL	.31
83	POLAND	.31
41	GUATEMALA	.30
12	BURUNDI	.28
67	MAURITANIA	.27
96	SYRIA	.26
31	ECUADOR	.25
45	HUNGARY	.25
48	INDONESIA	.25
57	JORDAN	.24
115	GAMBIA	-.17
18	CHAD	-.17
17	CEYLON	-.18
29	DENMARK	-.19
94	SWEDEN	-.19
11	BURMA	-.19
69	MONGOLIA	-.20
28	DAHOMEY	-.20
81	PERU	-.20
82	PHILIPPINES	-.20

51	IRELAND	-.25
125	GUYANA	-.26
44	HONDURAS	-.27
32	EL SALVADOR	-.30
101	TURKEY	-.30
16	CENTRAL AFRICAN REP	-.32
40	GREECE	-.32
39	GHANA	-.33
54	IVORY COAST	-.36
22	CONGO (BRA)	-.43

INSERT 42

A-SPACE CORRELATIONS WITH SELECTED FACTORS
(NUMBERS, SUCH AS 11, REFER TO FACTOR NUMBERS, SEE BELOW)

CORRELATION OF A-SPACE WITH + WEIGHTS,
POWER BASE DISTANCE

11	N= 60	P= .0232	R= .2900

CORRELATION OF A-SPACE WITH + WEIGHTS,
ECONOMIC DEVELOPMENT DISTANCE

1	N= 54	P= .0380	R= -.2800
21	N= 54	P= .0456	R= .2700

CORRELATION OF A-SPACE WITH + WEIGHTS,
POLITICAL DISTANCE

4	N= 65	P= .0017	R= .3900
14	N= 65	P= .0343	R= -.2600

CORRELATION OF A-SPACE WITH - WEIGHTS,
POWER BASE DISTANCE

1	N= 52	P= .0238	R= -.3100
2	N= 52	P= .0000	R= -.5900
16	N= 52	P= .0131	R= -.3400

CORRELATION OF A-SPACE WITH - WEIGHTS,
ECONOMIC DEVELOPMENT DISTANCE

1	N= 57	P= .0220	R= -.3000
20	N= 57	P= .0398	R= .2700

CORRELATION OF A-SPACE WITH - WEIGHTS,
POLITICAL DISTANCE

14	N= 46	P= .0478	R= -.2900
16	N= 46	P= .0478	R= .2900

INSERT 43

F-TEST OF - VS. + WEIGHTS,
POWER BASE DISTANCE

1	9.7895	.0026

```
     2     63.0251      .0000
     9      5.5583      .0190
GROUP MEANS  1 1     .3379     -.2261
GROUP MEANS  2 1     .7588     -.4451
GROUP MEANS  9 1     .1173     -.3186
```

F TEST OF - VS + WEIGHTS,
ECONOMIC DEVELOPMENT DISTANCE

```
     1     28.3096      .0000
     3      6.1900      .0137
     5      5.6530      .0181
     9      4.3081      .0379
GROUP MEANS  1 1     .4737     -.4243
GROUP MEANS  3 1    -.2128      .2378
GROUP MEANS  5 1     .2359     -.2126
GROUP MEANS  9 1     .0636     -.3233
```

F TEST OF - VS + WEIGHTS,
POLITICAL DISTANCE

```
     4      8.3675      .0048
    11      4.2692      .0387
    16      7.2758      .0080
GROUP MEANS  4 1    -.2995      .2667
GROUP MEANS 11 1     .2473     -.1302
GROUP MEANS 16 1    -.3452      .1610
```

INSERT 44

GENERAL MODEL, DISTANCE THEORY, WORLD SYSTEM

1. WORLD	1.26	.66	1.21	.18	-1.11	-.93	-.60	.22	-1.83	-1.58
	-1.74	.88	-2.73	2.53	-1.46	-.83	.01	-1.08	-2.05	-.69
	.16	-1.54	.99	-1.17	.94	-.62	.35	.22	-.59	-.15
	.42	2.33	1.61							

INSERT 45

CONTRIBUTIONS OF THE FACTORS TO CONFLICT
IN DISTANCE OR CLOSENESS TERMS

FACTORS WHERE DISTANCE PREDICTS CONFLICT

01 POWER BASE
02 ECONOMIC DEVELOPMENT
03 POLITICAL
04 SCHOOL ENROLLMENT
06 INTERNAL VIOLENCE

08 DATE OF INDEPENDENCE
12 POPULATION SIZE
14 ENERGY PRODUCTION
16 FIXED PRICES GNP GROWTH RATE
19 ALL MAIL
20 POLITICAL PARTY FRACTIONALIZATION
21 DOMESTIC TURMOIL
22 TOTAL AREA
23 PER CAPITA ENERGY CONSUMPTION GROWTH RATE
24 INFANT MORTALITY
26 TOTAL HEALTH EXPENDITURE
30 CONCENTRATION OF EXPORT COMMODITIES
31 MEAN ELECTIONS
32 CONCENTRATION OF EXPORT RECEIVERS

FACTORS WHERE CLOSENESS PREDICTS CONFLICT

05 INTERNAL POLITICAL TURMOIL
07 MILITARISM
09 POPULATION GROWTH RATE
10 DENSITY
11 INTERNAL SECURITY FORCES
13 RELIGIOUS
15 GNP GROWTH RATE
17 ETHNO-LINGUISTIC FRACTIONALIZATION
18 PER CENT URBAN POPULATION
25 AGE OF CURRENCY
27 CRUDE DEATH RATE
28 REGULAR EXECUTIVE TRANSFERS
29 PER CAPITA ECONOMIC ACTIVE MALE POPULATION
33 ORTHODOX COMMUNITY

INSERT 46

VARIABLE LIST

001 TOTAL POPULATION
002 POPULATION GROWTH RATE,1960-65
003 POPULATION GROWTH RATE,1950-65
004 TOTAL AREA
005 DENSITY(PEOPLE PER SQUARE KILOMETER)
006 TOTAL AGRICULTURAL AREA
007 PEOPLE PER SQUARE KILOMETER OF AGRICULTURAL LAND AREA
008 CRUDE BIRTH RATES,1960
009 CRUDE DEATH RATES,1960
010 INFANT MORTALITY RATES
011 WORKING AGE POPULATION
012 ADULT POPULATION
013 CONCENTRATION OF POPULATION IN CITIES
014 NEWSPAPERS PER 1,000 POPULATION
015 RADIOS PER 1,000 POPULATION
016 TELEVISIONS PER 1,000 POPULATION

017 CINEMA ATTENDANCE PER CAPITA,1960
018 LITERACY RATES
019 UNADJUSTED SCHOOL ENROLLMENT RATIO
020 ADJUSTED SCHOOL ENROLLMENT RATIO
021 ETHNO-LINGUISTIC FRACTIONALIZATION
022 LINGUISTIC FRACTIONALIZATION,MULLER SCALE
023 CHRISTIAN COMMUNITY,% OF THE TOTAL POP.
024 MOSLEM,% OF THE TOTAL POP.
025 PROTESTANT,% OF THE TOTAL POP.
026 CATHOLIC,% OF THE TOTAL POP.
027 NUMBER OF SEPARATE CHRISTIAN CHURCHES
028 ORTHODOX COMMUNITY,% OF THE TOTAL POP.
029 ENERGY CONSUMPTION PER CAPITA GROWTH RATES
030 TOTAL GNP (IN MILLIONS U.S. DOLLARS)
031 GNP PER CAPITA (IN U.S. DOLLARS)
032 GNP AT FIXED PRICES FOR CALCULATING GROWTH RATES
033 GNP PER CAPITA AT FIXED PRICES (GROWTH RATES)
034 TOTAL GNP GROWTH RATES,ANNUAL AVERAGES, 1960-1965
035 TOTAL GNP PER CAPITA GROWTH RATES,ANNUAL AVERAGES, 1960-1965
036 TOTAL TRADE,1960 (IN MILLIONS U.S. DOLLARS)
037 TOTAL TRADE,% OF GNP, 1960
038 CONCENTRATION OF EXPORT COMMODITIES
039 CONCENTRATION OF EXPORT RECEIVING COUNTRIES
040 TOTAL SCIENTIFIC AND TECHNICAL SERIALS PUBLISHED
041 PERCENTAGE CONTRIBUTION TO WORLD TOTAL OF SCIENTIFIC AUTHORS
042 PERCENTAGE OF GROSS DOMESTIC PRODUCT ORIGINATING IN AGRICULTURE
043 PERCENTAGE OF GROSS DOMESTIC PRODUCT ORIGINATING IN INDUSTRY
044 GROSS DOMESTIC FIXED CAPITAL FORMATION,% OF GNP
045 TOTAL ECONOMICALLY ACTIVE MALE POP.,% OF TOTAL MALE POP.
046 CALORIES PER CAPITA PER DIEM,1960
047 PROTEINS PER CAPITA PER DIEM,1960
048 TOTAL NUMBER OF PHYSICIANS
049 PHYSICIANS PER ONE MILLION POPULATION,1965
050 TOTAL MILITARY MANPOWER
051 MILITARY MANPOWER PER ONE THOUSAND POPULATION
052 MILITARY MANPOWER PER ONE THOUSAND WORKING AGED POPULATION
053 MILITARY MANPOWER PER AREA
054 TOTAL DEFENSE EXPENDITURE (IN MILLIONS U.S. DOLLARS)
055 DEFENSE EXPENDITURE PER CAPITA (IN U.S. DOLLARS)
056 DEFENSE EXPENDITURE,% OF GNP
057 TOTAL EDUCATION EXPENDITURE (IN MILLION U.S. DOLLARS)
058 EDUCATION EXPENDITURE PER CAPITA (IN MILLION U.S. DOLLARS)
059 TOTAL EDUCATION EXPENDITURE,% OF GNP
060 TOTAL HEALTH EXPENDITURE (IN MILLIONS U.S. DOLLARS)
061 HEALTH EXPENDITURE PER CAPITA
062 TOTAL HEALTH EXPENDITURE AS A PERCENTAGE OF GNP
063 POLITICAL PARTY FRACTIONALIZATION BASED ON NUMBER OF SEATS,1964
064 ELECTORAL IRREGULARITY SCORE
065 PRESS FREEDOM INDEX
066 TOTAL INTERNAL SECURITY FORCES (IN UNITS)
067 INTERNAL SECURITY FORCES PER ONE THOUSAND WORKING AGE POP.
068 INTERNAL SECURITY FORCES PER ONE MILLION POPULATION
069 BEGINNING YEAR OF MODERNIZATION
070 DATE OF INDEPENDENCE(BANKS)
071 DATE OF INSTITUTIONAL FORMATION(HUDSON)
072 DATE OF INDEPENDENT IDENTIFICATION(RUSTOW)
073 DATE OF FOUNDING OF PRESENT CONSTITUTIONAL FORM(HUDSON)
074 MILITARY REGIME
075 MEAN NUMBER OF MAJOR CONSTITUTIONAL CHANGES,1962-1966
076 SELECTION OF EFFECTIVE EXECUTIVE
077 LEGISLATIVE EFFECTIVENESS
078 LEGISLATIVE SELECTION
079 MEAN NUMBER OF LEGISLATIVE ELECTIONS,1962-1966
080 POPULATION IN CITIES OF 100,000+
081 PER CAPITA POPULATION IN CITIES OF 100,000+
082 POPULATION IN CITIES OF 50,000+

083 PER CAPITA POPULATION IN CITIES OF 50,000+
084 NATIONAL GOVERNMENT REVENUE
085 NATIONAL GOVERNMENT REVENUE PER CAPITA
086 NATIONAL GOVERNMENT EXPENDITURE
087 NATIONAL GOVERNMENT EXPENDITURE PER CAPITA
088 RAILROAD MILEAGE
089 RAILROAD MILEAGE PER SQUARE MILE
090 ALL MAIL
091 ALL MAIL PER CAPITA
092 TOTAL TELEPHONES
093 TELEPHONES PER CAPITA
094 TOTAL IMPORTS
095 IMPORTS PER CAPITA
096 TOTAL EXPORTS
097 EXPORTS PER CAPITA
098 PROPORTION OF TOTAL WORLD TRADE
099 TOTAL PRIMARY SCHOOL ENROLLMENT
100 PRIMARY SCHOOL ENROLLMENT PER CAPITA
101 TOTAL SECONDARY SCHOOL ENROLLMENT
102 SECONDARY SCHOOL ENROLLMENT PER CAPITA
103 TOTAL PRIMARY AND SECONDARY ENROLLMENT
104 PRIMARY AND SECONDARY ENROLLMENT PER CAPITA
105 TOTAL UNIVERSITY ENROLLMENT
106 UNIVERSITY ENROLLMENT PER CAPITA
107 TOTAL SCHOOL ENROLLMENT
108 TOTAL SCHOOL ENROLLMENT PER CAPITA
109 RAIL PASSENGER KILOMETERS
110 TOTAL PASSENGER CARS
111 PASSENGER CARS PER CAPITA
112 TOTAL COMMERCIAL VEHICLES
113 COMMERCIAL VEHICLES PER CAPITA
114 TOTAL HIGHWAY VEHICLES
115 TOTAL HIGHWAY VEHICLES PER CAPITA
116 GROSS DOMESTIC PRODUCT PER CAPITA
117 TOTAL ENERGY PRODUCTION IN METRIC TONS COAL EQUIVALENT
118 ENERGY PRODUCTION IN KILOGRAMS PER CAPITA
119 TOTAL ENERGY CONSUMPTION IN METRIC TONS OF COAL EQUIVALENT
120 ENERGY CONSUMPTION IN KILOGRAMS PER CAPITA
121 BOOK PRODUCTION BY TITLES
122 BOOK PRODUCTION BY TITLES PER MILLION POPULATION
123 AGE OF CURRENCY IN MONTHS
124 RATIO OF BLACK MARKET TO OFFICIAL EXCHANGE RATE
125 SIZE OF LEGISLATURE (LOWER HOUSE)
126 SIZE OF LEGISLATURE/NUMBER OF SEATS HELD BY LARGEST PARTY
127 COMPETITIVENESS OF NOMINATING PROCESS
128 PARTY LEGITIMACY
129 AGGREGATE COMPETITION INDEX
130 MEAN NUMBER OF PROTEST DEMONSTRATIONS DURING 1963-1967
131 MEAN NUMBER OF RIOTS DURING 1963-1967
132 MEAN NUMBER OF ARMED ATTACKS DURING 1963-1967
133 MEAN NUMBER OF DEATHS FROM DOMESTIC VIOLENCE DURING 1963-1967
134 MEAN NUMBER OF REGULAR EXECUTIVE TRANSFERS DURING 1963-1967
135 MEAN NUMBER OF EXECUTIVE ADJUSTMENTS DURING 1963-1967
136 MEAN NUMBER OF IRREGULAR POWER TRANSFERS DURING 1963-1967
137 MEAN NUMBER OF POLITICAL ASSASSINATIONS DURING 1963-1967
138 MEAN NUMBER OF ELECTIONS DURING 1963-1967
139 MEAN NUMBER OF REGIME-SUPPORT DEMONSTRATIONS DURING 1963-1967
140 MEAN NUMBER OF POLITICAL STRIKES DURING 1963-1967
141 MEAN UNSUCCESSFUL REGULAR EXECUTIVE TRANSFERS,1963-1967
142 MEAN UNSUCCESSFUL IRREGULAR POWER TRANSFERS,1963-1967
143 MEAN NUMBER OF POLITICAL EXECUTIONS DURING 1963-1967
144 MEAN RELAXATIONS OF GOV. RETRICTIONS ON POL. ACTIVITY,1963-1967

INSERT 47

Z-SCORE DATA BANK ON 144 ATTRIBUTE VARIABLES

Country										
1 AFGHANISTAN	.80	1.72	1.39	-1.58	.20	1.10	-1.42	1.72	1.72	-1.72
	-1.72	.45	.58	1.34	-1.64	1.18	.34	-1.50	1.72	-.04
	1.72	.12	-.04	.39	-1.72	-.36	.66	1.39	1.72	-1.61
	.07	-1.45	1.72	1.72	1.64	-1.64	1.45	.93	-.80	.88
	.18	1.72	.42	.28	-1.72	-1.72	1.72	-.66	.69	1.72
	.34	1.72	-1.20	1.72	-1.10	1.31	.31	-1.61	1.72	.20
	-1.69	1.61	-.69	-1.72	-.74	-1.72	1.72	-1.72	1.72	-.53
	-.34	.26	-.66	-1.72	.39	.74	-.09	-1.26	-1.18	-.28
	-.96	-.23	-1.18	-1.10	-1.69	-.74	-1.66	-1.72	-1.72	-.12
	-1.20	-.93	-1.58	-1.23	-1.69	-1.02	-1.53	-1.15	-.53	-1.56
	-.50	-1.45	-.53	-1.56	-.55	-1.18	-.55	-1.56	.23	-.83
	-1.58	-.58	-1.47	-.77	-1.50	-1.58	-.91	-1.23	-.77	-1.47
	-1.26	-1.56	-1.18	-.50	-1.72	-1.72	-.55	-1.72	-.39	-1.72
	-.07	-1.72	-1.72	.83	-.15	-1.72	-1.72	-1.04	-1.72	-1.72
	1.20	-1.72	-1.72	-.88						
2 ALBANIA	-1.07	.74	.83	-1.26	.50	-1.20	.18	.69	.55	.91
	.01	.31	.61	.12	-.23	-1.23	.18	.58	.80	1.34
	-.96	-1.50	-.20	1.07	-1.69	-.31	-1.58	1.56	1.07	-.53
	.28	-1.12	-.88	.99	1.15	-1.15	-1.04	.34	.28	-.31
	-1.29	-.80	-.18	.72	.15	-.91	-.50	-.55	.34	-.04
	1.50	1.47	1.34	-.20	1.18	-1.72	-1.61	.50	-.20	-.45
	.42	.09	-1.61	-1.26	-1.72	.04	1.64	1.69	.04	-.28
	-.26	-.64	-.96	-1.69	-1.72	.77	-1.37	-1.23	.93	-.93
	-.69	-.91	-.80	.07	-.04	.04	-.07	-1.15	.04	-.07
	-.18	-.80	-.39	-1.02	-.07	-1.04	-.36	-1.10	-.66	1.64
	-.58	.04	-.72	1.50	-.04	1.04	-.69	1.39	-1.10	-1.50
	-.23	.26	-.12	-1.50	-.20	-.53	-.58	.50	-.53	.01
	-.77	1.10	.34	-.45	1.02	-.99	-1.72	-1.69	-1.39	-1.69
	-1.72	-1.69	-.36	-1.72	-.61	-1.69	-1.69	-1.02	-1.69	-1.69
	-1.72	-1.69	-1.69	-.47						
3 ALGERIA	.61	-.58	-.31	1.47	-1.26	1.29	-1.02	-.31	-.85	.55
	-.85	-.12	-.28	-.80	.31	.18	-.39	-1.02	-.74	-.91
	.23	.34	-1.10	1.39	-1.66	-.42	.23	-1.72	-.34	.31
	-.23	-1.69	.23	-1.37	.20	.42	1.18	-.31	1.66	.12
	.09	-.39	-.96	-1.15	-.04	.12	.31	-.31	-.80	.09
	-.01	-.12	-.83	.15	.15	.66	.53	.20	.80	-.61
	-1.26	-1.42	-1.72	-1.23	-1.66	1.07	1.31	1.23	-1.07	1.29
	1.29	1.26	.47	1.56	-1.69	.80	-1.72	-1.72	.96	.50
	-.04	.64	.07	.36	.12	.26	.01	.61	-.83	.50
	.18	.36	.09	.23	.18	.45	.28	.34	.53	.07
	.15	-.45	.31	-.31	-.18	-.72	.50	-.36	.28	.91
	.55	.80	.47	.91	.55	-.31	1.10	1.34	.26	-.15
	-1.18	-1.37	-.61	-.26	.26	-1.07	-1.69	-1.66	-1.37	1.29
	.26	1.12	.88	1.18	1.26	.88	1.20	1.07	1.15	1.45
	-1.69	.99	1.26	.72						
4 ARGENTINA	1.07	-.72	-.55	1.53	-1.15	1.58	-1.31	-.72	-.69	.45
	1.29	1.02	.93	.83	1.20	.93	.69	.09	.50	.01
	-.04	.74	1.26	-1.72	.01	1.39	1.53	.91	-.47	1.20
	.91	-.39	-1.12	-.83	-1.02	.99	-1.47	-.28	-1.37	1.10
	.99	-.77	1.12	.58	1.10	.91	1.02	.36	.64	.80
	.45	.20	-.42	.53	.28	-.66	1.23	.88	-.18	.31
	-.99	-1.69	-.01	-.36	.15	.42	-1.47	-1.29	-.91	-1.15
	-1.10	-1.42	-1.47	-1.66	.42	-1.72	-1.34	-1.20	.99	1.26
	1.10	1.10	.96	1.02	.53	1.10	.64	1.61	.77	1.02
	.83	1.29	.93	.93	-.09	1.10	.39	.96	1.12	.58
	.34	-.83	.85	.18	1.37	1.34	1.12	.26	1.29	1.29
	.88	1.45	1.34	1.37	.93	1.04	1.04	1.02	1.12	.83
	.91	.74	-1.42	-.15	.83	.96	.47	-.12	.72	1.37

	1.29	.99	.50	1.20	1.53	.91	.80	1.10	.47	1.61
	-1.66	1.02	-1.66	1.37						
5 AUSTRALIA	.55	-.42	-.09	1.58	-1.64	1.69	-1.56	-.85	-.83	-1.53
	1.02	1.07	1.64	1.47	.93	1.50	1.69	1.10	1.53	1.50
	-.01	-1.45	.72	-.04	1.47	.36	1.39	1.29	-.80	1.42
	1.53	1.34	1.07	-.04	-.26	1.10	-1.50	-.96	-1.12	1.23
	1.47	-1.29	.96	1.61	1.20	1.56	1.29	1.23	1.37	.36
	.42	.09	-1.23	1.07	1.47	.50	1.29	1.26	-.01	1.29
	1.12	-.58	1.10	.53	1.34	.55	-.53	-.18	-1.50	-.50
	-.47	-.74	-1.34	-1.64	-1.66	-.85	.72	-1.18	1.02	1.31
	1.72	1.34	1.72	1.45	1.50	1.42	1.39	1.58	-.01	1.39
	1.53	1.47	1.53	1.39	1.23	1.39	1.29	1.39	.74	.72
	1.26	1.58	.61	1.45	1.15	1.50	.83	1.45	1.39	1.53
	1.64	1.56	1.72	1.50	1.64	1.50	1.12	1.37	1.31	1.56
	.80	1.07	.85	.85	-.15	.66	.50	.99	1.07	.88
	-.72	-1.07	-1.69	-.18	-.58	-1.66	-1.66	1.66	-.04	.28
	-1.64	-1.66	-1.64	-.45						
6 AUSTRIA	.07	-1.56	-1.64	-.88	.74	-.42	.47	-1.37	.91	-1.02
	1.20	1.61	1.39	1.15	1.26	1.15	1.56	1.12	1.02	.88
	-.83	-1.56	1.31	-1.69	.64	1.23	-.15	1.10	-.53	.96
	1.18	-1.20	-1.18	-.55	1.31	1.15	.07	-1.58	-.74	1.26
	1.18	-.74	1.34	1.42	1.42	1.10	1.23	1.10	1.64	-.31
	-.12	-.39	.64	.09	.55	-1.20	.96	1.07	.09	1.23
	1.34	1.02	.74	.55	1.04	.39	-.04	-.28	-1.02	-.26
	-1.72	-.55	-1.02	-1.61	-1.64	-.83	.74	-1.15	1.04	.74
	1.47	.69	1.18	1.23	1.31	1.23	1.31	.96	1.37	1.07
	1.31	1.10	1.29	1.15	1.20	1.18	1.23	1.15	.20	-.36
	-.12	-.39	-.04	-.58	.69	1.02	.20	-.50	1.02	1.23
	1.31	1.29	1.50	1.20	1.31	1.23	.74	1.12	.93	1.07
	1.02	1.53	.72	1.69	.69	1.18	.53	1.02	1.10	-.47
	-.69	-1.04	-.72	.85	-.96	-1.64	-1.64	1.12	-1.66	-1.66
	-1.61	-1.64	-1.61	-.28						
7 BELGIUM	.42	-1.53	-1.58	-1.20	1.56	-1.07	1.37	-1.58	.83	-1.26
	1.23	1.56	.96	1.29	1.34	1.45	.99	1.23	1.56	1.56
	.50	.93	1.12	-1.66	-.69	1.42	.26	1.15	-1.10	1.18
	1.34	1.26	.91	-.15	.66	1.47	1.31	-1.10	-.45	1.53
	1.23	-1.61	1.07	.96	.74	1.31	1.12	1.12	1.45	.58
	1.04	.99	1.56	.85	1.26	.34	1.31	1.47	1.02	.42
	.07	-1.66	1.34	.58	1.37	.07	-.99	-.53	-1.61	-.93
	-.80	-1.18	-1.58	-1.58	-1.61	-.80	.77	-1.12	1.07	.45
	.23	.53	.18	1.34	1.39	1.37	1.58	.77	1.66	1.42
	1.61	1.31	1.37	1.47	1.66	1.47	1.72	1.47	.34	-.47
	.77	.99	.18	-.04	.96	1.26	.39	-.01	1.10	1.45
	1.39	1.18	1.31	1.39	1.37	1.34	.96	1.20	1.29	1.53
	.96	1.29	.88	.93	.99	1.58	.55	1.04	1.12	.58
	-.04	-.28	-1.66	-.15	-1.72	-1.61	-1.61	-.99	1.02	.66
	1.50	-1.61	-1.58	-1.72						
8 BOLIVIA	-.47	-.91	-.96	1.07	-1.37	.47	-1.04	.74	-.09	-.96
	-.50	-1.18	.23	-.45	.42	-.07	.04	-.50	-.50	-.53
	.83	1.18	1.53	-1.64	-.09	1.66	.55	-1.69	-.07	-.72
	-.55	.88	.88	-.01	.50	-.99	-.12	-.69	1.56	-.07
	-.74	.20	.55	.31	1.07	-.85	-.77	-.42	-.01	-.55
	.01	-.15	-.91	-.85	-.58	-.77	-.42	-.36	.39	.09
	.47	1.39	.01	-.34	1.26	-.80	-.50	-.47	-.36	-.99
	-.93	-1.26	-.91	1.58	1.12	.83	-1.69	-1.69	1.10	-.26
	.12	.01	.42	-1.29	-1.31	-1.29	-1.34	.50	-.39	.23
	-.20	-.34	-.47	-.83	-.45	-.74	-.55	-.83	-.04	.61
	-.15	.28	-.31	.55	-.09	.09	-.34	.39	-.15	-.77
	-.58	-1.18	-1.07	-.83	-.80	-.61	-.69	-.18	-.36	-.42
	.36	-.72	-1.56	.39	-1.69	-1.69	-1.66	-1.64	-1.72	.69
	1.12	1.18	1.18	1.23	.09	.93	1.45	.20	-1.64	1.64
	-1.58	1.04	-1.56	.64						
9 BRAZIL	1.53	1.10	1.15	1.61	-1.02	1.56	-.45	.88	-.07	-.93
	-.09	-.45	-.77	-.09	-.04	.61	.15	-.23	-.42	-.64
	-1.10	-1.02	1.64	-1.61	.77	1.29	1.61	.18	-.74	1.37
	-.01	1.39	-.50	-.31	.07	.96	-1.58	.07	-.55	1.34

	.88	.69	.58	-.39	.18	.83	.42	1.20	-.04	1.07
	-.45	-.47	-.72	.93	-.09	-.01	1.07	-.66	-1.39	1.42
	.36	.55	.39	-.31	.58	1.47	-.45	-.31	-.93	-1.04
	-.96	-1.31	1.47	1.39	.45	-.77	-1.31	-1.10	1.64	1.58
	.64	1.58	.55	.91	-.83	1.07	-.64	1.45	-.23	1.23
	.31	1.20	.34	.80	-1.34	1.15	-.85	.99	1.58	.34
	1.47	.09	1.50	.12	1.29	-.12	1.56	.07	1.37	1.37
	.45	1.58	.77	1.47	.53	-.12	.77	-.77	1.10	.04
	1.07	-.36	-1.53	1.07	-1.66	-1.66	-1.64	-1.61	-.64	.34
	1.23	.85	.34	.36	1.61	.96	.83	1.15	.50	1.47
	-1.56	-1.58	-1.53	1.15						
10 BULGARIA	.20	-1.37	-1.37	-.66	.64	-.12	.07	-1.42	-1.42	-.99
	1.69	1.45	-.12	.96	1.04	.45	1.47	.91	1.04	1.23
	-.36	-.66	.66	.61	-.88	-1.29	.09	1.69	1.50	.80
	.96	-1.53	-1.64	-1.64	.61	.93	1.23	-.93	1.29	.77
	1.07	1.04	1.45	-.20	1.50	.96	1.04	1.15	1.58	.88
	1.42	1.34	1.37	.34	.93	-.80	.88	.93	.26	.99
	1.10	.80	-1.58	-1.20	-1.42	1.10	1.45	1.61	-.53	-.55
	-.31	-.09	-.88	-1.56	-1.58	-.74	-1.29	-1.07	1.12	.36
	.36	.58	.50	1.26	1.29	1.26	1.29	.93	1.26	.96
	1.20	.69	.64	.91	.85	.96	.96	.88	.45	.69
	.09	-.34	.20	.34	1.07	1.61	.47	.61	.91	.61
	.69	.64	.42	.64	.64	.88	.80	1.15	.99	1.04
	.93	1.42	-1.26	-1.42	1.18	-.96	-1.61	-1.58	-1.34	-.45
	-.39	-.64	-.69	-1.07	-.93	-1.58	-1.58	-.96	-.01	-1.64
	-1.53	-1.56	.85	-.26						
11 BURMA	1.15	-.39	-.45	.80	.23	.55	.28	.64	-.04	1.37
	.36	.20	-1.56	-.93	-1.47	-.83	.42	.26	-.91	-.45
	.31	.55	-1.02	.15	.23	-1.04	-.69	-1.66	.58	.12
	-1.45	-.26	-1.02	-1.10	.88	-.36	-.77	1.18	-1.31	.23
	-.53	.99	-.42	-.01	-.09	-.26	-.91	-.18	-.83	.64
	.15	-.09	.18	-.01	-.36	1.12	-.12	-1.34	-1.10	-.18
	-1.50	-1.04	-.15	-1.18	-.18	.91	-.23	.09	.42	.20
	.31	.09	.50	1.61	.47	.85	-1.66	-1.66	-1.72	.64
	-.61	.55	-.64	-.07	-.93	-.15	-1.37	.28	-.15	-.83
	-1.45	-.64	-1.50	-.26	-1.45	-.15	-1.26	-.23	.85	-.96
	1.15	.50	.64	-.85	.31	-.69	.85	-.85	.64	-.50
	-1.42	-.12	-1.34	-.20	-1.42	-1.64	-.66	-.99	-.15	-1.12
	.66	.07	.91	-1.53	-1.64	-1.64	-1.58	-1.56	-1.69	.64
	1.31	1.02	1.10	-1.69	.12	-1.56	-1.56	-1.72	.80	-1.61
	-1.50	-1.53	-1.50	1.02						
12 BURUNDI	-.64	-.36	-.28	-1.31	1.04	-.91	.26	1.04	1.34	1.47
	-1.61	-.88	-.09	-1.72	-.88	-.85	-1.56	-1.10	-1.45	-1.45
	-1.50	.39	.09	.01	.66	.83	-.91	.20	-1.26	-1.45
	-1.72	.01	.34	-1.20	-1.47	-.26	.18	-.26	-.01	-1.72
	-1.58	-1.12	-1.69	-1.53	-1.26	-1.66	-1.69	-1.56	-1.69	-1.61
	-1.45	-1.47	-.55	-1.64	-1.64	-1.50	-1.34	-1.42	-.53	-1.69
	-.74	-.15	.04	-.28	-.07	-1.26	-1.45	-1.45	1.39	1.31
	1.31	1.29	1.20	-1.53	1.15	-.72	-.07	-1.04	-1.15	-1.72
	-1.72	-1.42	-1.39	-1.58	-1.66	-1.66	-1.69	-1.69	-1.69	-1.61
	-1.69	-1.45	-1.45	-1.64	-1.64	-1.64	-1.61	-1.02	-1.29	-1.37
	-1.69	-1.69	-1.29	-1.39	-1.58	-1.72	-1.29	-1.39	-1.72	-1.39
	-1.64	-1.61	-1.66	-1.42	-1.66	-1.02	-.34	-.61	-1.58	-1.61
	-1.58	-1.53	-1.64	-1.10	-.09	-.04	-.53	-.09	-.18	-1.66
	-1.69	-.26	.69	1.50	.15	1.42	1.23	-.93	-1.61	-1.58
	-1.47	1.53	1.61	-.85						
13 CAMBODIA	-.01	.07	.45	-.28	.18	-.53	.55	.53	1.20	1.34
	-.47	-.53	-1.04	-1.15	.55	-1.04	-1.31	-.15	-.34	-.50
	-.09	-.45	.20	-1.58	-1.64	.58	-1.47	-1.64	1.10	-.39
	-.72	-.42	.64	-.45	-.91	-1.07	-.93	1.20	-1.23	-1.69
	-.91	1.29	-.93	.34	-.34	-1.26	-1.18	-1.02	-1.23	-.23
	.26	.18	.20	-.31	.01	1.04	-.28	-.50	.28	-.77
	-1.12	-1.02	-1.56	-.26	-1.15	.31	-.01	-.80	.66	.47
	.45	.42	-.39	-1.50	-1.56	.88	-1.26	-1.02	1.15	-.23
	-.45	-.28	-.69	-.85	-1.23	-.83	-1.04	-.93	-.85	-.20
	-1.18	-1.07	-1.47	-.99	-1.10	-.80	-.96	-.96	.12	.04

	.01	-.09	-.07	-.20	-.36	-.61	.12	-.31	-.28	-.64
	-.85	-.83	-1.10	-.72	-1.04	-.80	.18	-.26	-.96	-1.15
	-.18	.55	.58	-1.45	-.50	-.93	-.50	-.07	-.36	-1.64
	-.66	.07	-1.64	.39	-.55	-1.53	-1.53	-.91	-1.58	1.04
	1.53	-1.50	-1.47	-.83						
14 CAMEROUN	-.09	-.23	-.07	.55	-.91	.66	-.85	.23	-.45	.20
	.45	.47	-.96	-1.37	-1.04	-.42	-.80	-1.29	.45	.26
	1.61	1.66	-.18	.72	.93	.31	-.34	-1.61	.61	-.58
	-.77	-1.50	.45	-1.07	-.04	-.74	.31	.66	.96	-1.66
	-.47	.23	-1.34	-.88	1.15	.50	-.15	-1.18	-1.26	-1.12
	-1.31	-1.34	-1.29	-.69	-.83	.69	-.66	-1.02	-.74	-1.61
	-.88	-.55	-1.53	-1.69	-1.34	-.20	.20	.61	.88	.72
	.72	.69	.28	-1.47	-1.53	-1.69	-1.23	-.99	-1.12	-.96
	-1.07	-.64	-1.04	-.83	-.99	-.91	-1.10	-.72	-.96	-.31
	-1.12	-1.18	-1.42	-.66	-.61	-.50	-.66	-.66	.18	.64
	-.66	-1.12	-.09	.20	-1.07	-1.15	-.09	.12	-.34	-.69
	-.74	-.23	-.20	-.50	-.58	-.74	-.99	-1.10	-.80	-.99
	-1.47	-1.66	-.50	.45	-.93	-.91	.58	-1.53	.20	-1.61
	-1.66	-1.66	1.64	-1.66	-.53	-1.50	-1.50	.23	-1.56	-1.56
	-1.45	-1.47	-1.45	-1.69						
15 CANADA	1.04	-.61	.12	1.69	-1.56	1.42	-.88	-.39	-1.47	-1.37
	.80	.85	1.02	1.07	1.69	1.69	.39	1.26	1.58	.58
	1.26	.77	.53	-1.56	1.23	.66	.96	1.45	-1.42	1.47
	1.64	1.47	1.18	.28	-.01	1.58	-.28	-1.50	1.50	1.29
	1.56	-1.58	.99	.85	-.26	1.23	1.39	1.39	1.10	.72
	.50	.31	-1.02	1.31	1.50	-.12	1.53	1.66	1.53	1.64
	1.66	1.18	.99	.61	1.61	-.58	-1.66	-1.61	-1.64	-.58
	-.58	-.83	-1.45	-1.45	-1.50	-.69	.80	-.96	1.66	1.15
	.93	1.23	.88	1.53	1.56	1.53	1.45	1.66	.36	1.50
	1.58	1.61	1.61	1.56	1.47	1.56	1.47	1.56	1.23	1.56
	1.45	1.61	1.23	1.66	1.04	.83	1.29	1.61	.88	1.58
	1.66	1.61	1.66	1.61	1.69	1.61	1.53	1.61	1.56	1.69
	.99	.88	-1.12	1.10	1.07	1.12	.61	1.07	1.50	1.02
	.96	.64	-.20	-1.04	1.56	-1.47	-1.47	-1.69	.53	1.53
	1.23	-1.45	-1.42	-.80						
16 CENTRAL AFRICAN REP	-1.23	-.55	-.85	.74	-1.53	.01	-1.12	-.12	-.66	-.39
	.74	.69	-.69	-.31	-1.02	-1.69	-1.53	-.99	-.88	-.99
	.88	-.36	-.28	.26	.85	.12	-.61	-1.58	-1.56	-1.56
	-1.10	.28	.26	-1.34	-1.20	-1.56	.36	.88	.85	-1.64
	-1.64	-.26	-1.53	-1.20	-1.56	-1.53	-1.53	-.07	-.58	-1.58
	-1.20	-1.29	-1.53	-1.47	-1.02	-1.56	-1.23	-.85	.50	-1.37
	-.28	.74	-.47	-1.15	-.42	-1.37	-1.04	-.91	.91	.74
	.74	.72	-.12	-1.42	.50	-.66	-.04	-.93	-1.10	-.99
	-.39	-.99	-.58	-1.39	-.72	-1.50	-.69	-1.66	-1.66	-.47
	-.74	-1.37	-.93	-1.58	-.99	-1.39	-.91	-1.56	-1.39	-.77
	-1.53	-1.34	-1.39	-1.04	-1.56	-1.69	-1.39	-1.04	-1.12	-1.20
	-.83	-1.15	-.18	-1.12	-.64	-.72	-.28	-.39	-1.53	-1.37
	-.31	-.34	-.47	.47	-.91	-.88	-1.56	-1.50	-1.31	-1.58
	-1.64	-1.64	-1.61	-1.64	-1.31	.99	-1.45	.26	-1.53	-1.53
	-1.42	-1.42	-1.39	-.42						
17 CEYLON	.53	.23	.20	-.99	1.34	-.93	1.39	.07	-1.04	.34
	-.23	-.07	-1.18	-.01	-.80	-1.66	-.15	.66	.72	.91
	.28	.31	-.72	.28	-.53	-.15	-.31	-1.56	-.96	.09
	-.69	.93	.07	-.91	-1.07	.01	.39	1.31	-.96	.15
	.07	1.34	-1.56	-.55	.07	-.45	-1.15	.45	-.31	.55
	-1.18	-1.20	.07	-.83	-1.39	-1.42	.07	-.42	.64	.45
	-.01	.58	1.37	.64	.45	-.34	-1.23	-1.12	.15	.23
	.23	-.01	-.85	-1.39	-1.47	-.64	.83	-.91	-1.07	-.34
	-.91	-.09	-.85	-.12	-.45	-.07	-.23	.04	.88	.77
	.80	-.07	-.72	-.15	-.66	.04	-.26	-.04	.80	.99
	1.31	1.66	.69	1.56	.04	-.39	.88	1.53	.69	.31
	-.20	.15	-.64	.31	-.31	-.64	-1.23	-1.50	-.12	-.77
	.31	.39	.93	-1.34	.61	1.34	.64	1.10	1.15	-1.56
	.34	-1.61	-.66	-.12	.36	-1.45	-1.42	-.88	-1.50	1.18
	1.26	-1.39	-1.37	.66						
18 CHAD	-.61	-1.02	-1.07	1.23	-1.47	1.37	-1.50	1.23	.12	1.50

	-.93	-1.56	-1.53	-1.69	-1.58	-1.64	-1.69	-1.64	-1.31	-1.34
	1.42	1.29	-.74	1.10	.18	-.45	-.88	-1.53	1.12	-1.18
	-1.39	-1.56	-.28	-1.56	-1.45	-1.53	-.99	1.50	1.07	-1.61
	-1.20	.26	-1.50	-.85	-.55	-1.56	-1.50	-1.53	-1.66	-1.72
	-1.72	-1.72	-1.72	-1.45	-1.45	-.88	-1.20	-1.37	-1.12	-1.34
	-1.31	-.53	-1.50	-1.66	-1.45	-1.07	-1.34	-1.31	.93	.77
	.77	.74	-.09	-1.37	-1.45	-.61	-1.20	-.88	-1.04	-1.69
	-1.69	-1.23	-1.34	-1.45	-1.42	-1.58	-1.50	-1.64	-1.64	-.42
	-1.02	-1.29	-1.37	-1.56	-1.50	-1.37	-1.31	-1.50	-1.15	-1.42
	-1.45	-1.50	-1.20	-1.42	-1.53	-1.66	-1.20	-1.42	-1.69	-1.29
	-1.50	-1.34	-1.12	-1.26	-1.31	-1.47	-.26	-.55	-1.50	-1.56
	-.39	-.91	-.45	.50	-.39	-.85	-1.53	-1.47	-1.29	-1.53
	.88	-1.02	.58	-1.61	-.91	-1.42	-1.39	-.85	-1.47	-1.50
	-1.39	-1.37	-1.34	-.77						
19 CHILE	.28	-.07	.04	.85	-.85	.39	-.42	.09	.85	1.20
	.20	.23	1.47	.77	.09	-.31	.64	.34	.53	.69
	-.74	-1.12	.93	-1.53	.80	1.02	1.07	-1.50	-.93	.61
	.74	.58	-.09	-.53	-.88	.36	-.80	1.34	-.23	.80
	.77	-1.42	.45	-.53	-.28	.23	.83	.64	.36	.04
	.36	.23	-.28	-.09	.26	-.34	.64	.64	-.58	.83
	.91	.45	1.23	.66	.53	.69	.88	1.07	-.88	-1.12
	-1.07	-1.39	-1.23	-1.34	-1.42	-1.66	.85	-.85	-1.02	.55
	.69	.66	.69	.72	.77	.80	.88	1.04	.45	-.72
	.23	.64	.58	.20	.31	.39	.58	.20	.58	1.07
	.53	.53	.36	1.04	.58	.53	.55	.99	.72	.36
	.23	.93	.72	.58	.47	.72	.61	.77	.66	.74
	.47	.77	-1.72	-.58	.31	.93	.66	1.12	1.18	.74
	.50	.23	-.01	-.09	.18	-1.39	-1.37	.28	.93	1.37
	-1.37	-1.34	-1.31	-.07						
20 CHINA,PR	1.72	-.80	-.83	1.66	.61	1.64	.74	-.04	.88	-1.3
	-.07	-1.39	-1.69	-.28	-1.39	-1.47	.45	.07	-.07	-.12
	-.85	.83	-1.50	.12	-1.20	-1.26	1.29	-1.47	1.34	1.56
	-.83	-1.64	.01	-1.53	-.58	1.26	-1.72	-.61	-.12	1.37
	.36	1.26	.15	1.20	-1.47	-.93	-.74	1.50	-.45	1.64
	-.09	-.28	.58	1.64	-.01	1.47	1.50	-.77	.31	1.53
	-.93	-.47	-1.47	-1.64	-1.58	1.72	-1.20	-1.07	-.15	-1.69
	-1.69	.28	-.64	-1.31	-1.39	.91	-1.18	-.83	-.99	1.50
	-.34	1.53	-.31	1.18	-.36	1.20	-.39	1.56	-.18	1.31
	-1.53	.77	-1.64	1.10	-1.72	1.23	-1.66	1.10	1.72	-.45
	1.64	-.58	1.69	-.74	1.61	-.47	1.72	-.72	1.64	.83
	-.93	.74	-.45	.88	-.69	-.09	1.66	.31	1.66	.18
	1.50	-.20	.64	-.74	1.64	-.83	-1.50	-1.45	-1.26	-.01
	1.64	1.66	1.37	-1.02	1.31	1.66	-1.34	.31	1.72	-1.47
	-1.34	-1.31	1.31	1.56						
21 COLOMBIA	.93	1.02	1.18	1.10	-.61	.80	-.31	-1.10	-1.37	.80
	-1.26	-1.15	.34	.26	.18	.31	.23	.45	-.66	-.31
	-1.15	-.61	.74	-1.50	-.66	1.18	1.34	-1.45	-.26	.66
	.12	.74	-.42	-.42	-.99	.18	-1.39	1.26	1.04	.50
	.23	.88	.23	.01	.53	-.23	-.61	.83	.42	.39
	-.31	-.26	-.31	-.07	-.26	-1.18	.58	-.23	-.88	.55
	-.34	-1.20	1.53	-.23	1.12	.99	.55	.50	-.83	-1.10
	-1.04	-1.15	.72	-1.29	-1.37	-1.64	-.01	-.80	1.18	1.23
	1.26	1.31	1.20	.18	-.47	.12	-.55	.47	-.47	-.85
	-1.23	.85	.47	.07	-.77	.20	-.53	.07	.99	.39
	.61	-.23	.66	.07	.64	-.01	.91	.04	.15	.58
	-.26	.96	.31	.69	-.15	.18	.88	.93	.74	.26
	-.34	-1.02	-1.69	-.85	.80	1.04	.69	-.04	.23	1.23
	.99	1.37	1.23	-.07	1.34	-1.37	-1.31	1.18	-1.45	.69
	-1.31	-1.29	-1.29	.09						
22 CONGO (BRA)	-1.39	-.66	-.93	.39	-1.50	-1.42	.04	.47	-.23	-.58
	.42	.53	-.18	-1.53	-.50	-1.20	-.53	-.80	.83	.61
	.74	-.20	.18	-.12	1.10	.69	-1.26	-1.42	-1.50	-1.47
	-.53	.26	.18	-1.47	-.39	-1.23	1.42	.80	.74	-1.58
	-1.02	.28	-.26	.04	-.74	-1.04	-.58	-1.42	-.96	-1.56
	-.91	-1.02	-1.47	-1.23	-.20	1.53	-1.45	-.88	-1.07	-1.47
	-.26	-.45	-1.45	-1.61	-1.07	-1.23	.72	.80	.96	.80

	.80	.77	-.07	-1.26	.53	-.58	-1.15	-.77	-.96	-.91
	.50	-.74	.72	-1.12	.26	-1.26	.07	-.74	-.91	-.15
	.04	-.96	-.09	-1.15	.36	-1.15	.12	-1.20	-1.12	1.72
	-1.18	.15	-1.12	1.64	-1.04	-.45	-1.12	1.56	-.31	-1.56
	.01	.20	-.07	-1.56	-.01	-.50	-1.02	-.83	-1.18	-.64
	-.09	.20	-.42	.53	-.74	-.80	-1.47	-1.42	-1.23	1.04
	1.02	.28	-.12	-.04	-.50	1.02	1.58	-1.66	-1.42	.31
	-1.29	1.07	-1.26	-.74						
23 CONGO (LEO)	.83	-.34	-.04	1.45	-1.18	1.34	-.91	.93	1.50	-.47
	.15	.61	-.66	-.26	-1.34	-1.61	-1.66	-.42	-.31	-.28
	1.66	1.64	.12	.09	.96	.53	1.50	-1.39	-1.64	-.07
	-1.26	.50	.36	-1.18	-.69	-.01	.69	1.29	1.18	-1.56
	-.28	.31	-1.31	-.36	-.72	.47	-1.20	-.77	-1.31	-.12
	-.53	-.58	-.88	-.23	-.42	-.93	.04	-.69	1.10	.34
	-.39	.83	-.36	-.20	-.58	.66	-.61	-.50	.99	.83
	.83	.80	1.50	1.42	1.58	-.55	-1.12	-.74	-.93	.34
	-.47	.26	-.47	-.66	-1.53	-.31	-1.39	.83	-.69	.04
	-.91	-.55	-1.23	-.12	-.96	-.04	-.77	-.07	.77	-.09
	-.01	-1.02	.47	-.55	-.50	-1.07	.66	-.64	.20	-.04
	-.91	.09	-.88	.07	-.93	-.69	-.80	-1.04	-.09	-.93
	.55	-.80	-1.20	-1.04	-1.61	-1.61	-1.45	-1.39	-1.66	.15
	1.15	1.64	1.58	1.53	.85	1.04	.85	1.56	1.18	.72
	1.29	1.10	1.72	1.23						
24 COSTA RICA	-1.20	1.53	1.58	-1.04	-.15	-1.12	-.23	1.29	-.80	.74
	-1.56	-1.29	.74	.47	-.07	.72	.07	.85	.47	.93
	-1.07	-.53	.28	-1.47	.09	.93	1.10	1.04	-1.29	-.74
	.42	-.74	-.18	-.28	-.66	-.77	.64	.15	1.37	-.04
	-.26	.80	-.55	.61	-.61	.34	.26	-.74	.23	-1.69
	-1.69	-1.69	-1.69	-1.53	-1.29	-1.61	-.58	.58	.01	.69
	1.37	1.69	.77	.69	1.50	-1.50	-1.18	-1.18	-.28	-.83
	-.77	-.96	-1.39	-1.23	-1.34	-1.61	.88	-.72	1.20	-.85
	-.12	-.55	.45	-.88	.18	-.96	.09	-.36	.66	.09
	.26	-.53	.28	-.47	.69	-.72	.55	-.64	-.93	1.61
	-.47	.77	-.85	1.53	-.39	.36	-.85	1.47	-.61	-.58
	.47	-.66	.53	-.64	.50	.42	-1.12	-.93	-.72	-.07
	-.99	.66	-1.02	.07	-.66	1.02	.72	.80	1.20	-1.50
	-1.61	-1.58	-1.58	-.99	-.88	-1.34	-1.29	-.83	-1.39	-1.45
	-1.26	-1.26	-1.23	-1.66						
25 CUBA	.12	-.04	-.01	-.55	.53	-.07	-.04	-1.18	-1.34	-.34
	.66	.58	.77	.80	.66	.99	.72	.36	.55	.72
	-1.42	-1.72	.64	-1.45	.34	1.04	.99	-1.37	-.20	.45
	.36	-1.58	.53	-.77	.15	.64	.77	1.58	.99	.64
	-.45	-1.10	.36	.99	.93	.77	.09	.66	.91	.69
	1.26	1.29	1.12	.39	1.04	1.26	.80	.91	1.69	.93
	1.07	1.50	-1.64	-1.58	-1.47	.45	-.15	.31	-.23	-.47
	-.45	.66	-.20	-1.20	-1.31	.93	-1.64	-1.64	-1.69	.66
	1.18	-.12	.99	.64	.39	.61	.45	1.47	1.72	.66
	.55	.58	.55	.39	.64	.36	.72	.47	.47	.96
	.18	.20	.28	.74	.36	.26	.42	.77	-.26	.72
	.61	.88	.88	.80	.69	.45	-1.18	-1.34	.58	.66
	-.26	.31	1.58	-1.64	-1.58	-1.58	-1.42	-1.37	-1.64	-1.47
	-1.58	1.10	1.07	-1.58	1.37	-1.31	1.26	-1.64	.83	-1.42
	-1.23	-1.23	1.69	1.47						
26 CYPRUS	-1.47	-1.50	-1.04	-1.53	.45	-1.45	-.15	-.47	-1.72	-1.04
	.55	.72	1.23	1.04	.91	.50	.93	.72	1.07	1.26
	.07	.36	.42	.74	-1.61	.77	-.85	1.64	1.15	-.99
	.88	-1.26	-.64	.45	.45	-1.04	.85	-.23	-.34	-.28
	-.88	-.04	.26	.07	.80	.72	.77	-.85	.77	-1.53
	-.72	-.80	-.07	1.26	.50	-.58	-.93	.69	-.85	-1.12
	.45	-.99	.53	-.18	.99	-.01	.23	.36	-.50	.85
	.85	.83	-.04	-1.18	-1.29	-1.58	-1.10	-.69	-1.66	-1.10
	.31	-1.12	-.01	-.93	.74	-1.12	.61	-1.61	-1.61	-1.26
	.53	-.23	.80	-.74	1.15	-.99	.77	-.91	-1.56	-.55
	-1.04	.88	-1.53	-.26	-1.50	-1.64	-1.53	-.34	-1.20	-.23
	.99	-.74	1.18	-.34	1.02	.77	.31	.83	-.61	.61
	-1.29	.64	.96	-.07	-.88	.58	.74	1.15	.74	.45

	.83	1.50	1.12	-1.56	-1.69	1.07	-1.26	-1.61	.85	-1.39
	-1.20	-1.20	-1.20	1.04						
27 CZECHOSLOVAKIA	.77	-1.47	-1.23	-.47	.99	.07	.58	-1.66	.26	-1.15
	1.39	1.31	-.36	1.26	1.10	1.37	1.34	1.29	.99	.85
	.34	.88	.23	-1.42	.99	.80	-.45	1.34	-.28	1.39
	1.29	-1.15	-1.37	-1.23	1.23	1.39	.55	-.88	.15	1.20
	1.42	-1.20	1.69	.36	-.18	1.45	.69	1.45	1.61	1.10
	1.34	1.20	1.47	1.23	1.56	.23	1.39	1.31	.96	1.50
	1.58	1.42	-1.42	-1.12	-1.37	1.02	.61	.99	-.99	-.23
	-.23	.12	-.77	-1.15	-1.26	.96	-1.07	-.66	-.91	.69
	-.01	.85	.12	1.39	1.23	1.39	1.23	1.18	1.56	1.18
	1.10	1.26	1.20	1.29	1.04	1.31	1.12	1.37	.93	1.02
	.12	-.72	.58	.66	1.31	1.45	.80	.83	1.45	1.31
	1.18	1.07	.64	1.29	1.15	.99	1.31	1.58	1.39	1.64
	1.42	1.64	-1.61	-1.58	1.10	-.77	-1.39	-1.34	-1.20	-.42
	.53	-.61	-.64	-.96	-.12	-1.29	-1.23	-.80	.55	.34
	-1.18	-1.18	-1.18	.80						
28 DAHOMEY	-.88	.61	.85	-.58	-.28	-.88	-.12	1.34	1.64	.18
	-1.29	-.34	-1.15	-1.58	-1.20	-.74	-1.58	-1.61	-1.29	-1.31
	.64	1.50	-.53	.69	-.26	.09	-1.42	-1.34	-1.72	-1.31
	-1.47	.07	.96	1.20	-1.56	-1.61	-.69	.83	1.42	-1.53
	-1.47	-.23	-1.47	-1.50	.39	-1.61	-1.56	-.01	-.69	-1.50
	-1.37	-1.37	-1.12	-1.26	-1.26	-.74	-1.31	-1.29	-.83	-1.04
	-.36	1.04	-.55	-1.10	-.47	-1.15	-1.07	-1.04	1.02	.88
	.88	.85	-.01	1.64	1.50	.99	-1.61	-1.61	-.88	-1.66
	-1.66	-.88	-.88	-1.34	-1.15	-1.47	-1.29	-.69	-.04	-.28
	-.77	-1.15	-.99	-1.47	-1.26	-1.61	-1.45	-1.58	-1.31	-1.29
	-1.31	-1.18	-1.31	-1.31	-1.47	-1.61	-1.34	-1.31	-.42	-1.02
	-.80	-1.31	-.91	-1.02	-.91	-1.34	-.12	-.45	-1.37	-1.42
	-.23	-.69	-.39	.55	-.61	-.74	-1.37	-1.31	-1.18	.72
	.58	-.23	.36	.42	-.47	1.69	-1.20	.34	-1.37	1.20
	-1.15	1.12	-1.15	-1.64						
29 DENMARK	-.20	-1.34	-1.50	-1.10	1.02	-.50	.20	-1.61	.36	-1.47
	1.42	1.42	.80	1.45	1.42	1.61	1.10	1.61	1.18	1.37
	-1.23	-1.18	1.37	-1.39	1.64	-1.07	.12	-1.31	-.18	.99
	1.56	1.50	1.61	-.12	.77	1.34	.72	-1.26	-.83	1.15
	1.20	-1.31	.85	1.15	1.53	1.66	1.50	.72	1.31	.18
	1.02	.93	1.23	.55	1.37	-.23	1.20	1.64	1.39	1.37
	1.69	1.31	1.50	.72	1.45	.26	.04	-.04	-1.39	-1.66
	-1.66	-1.47	-.42	-1.12	-1.23	-.53	.91	-.64	1.23	.47
	1.61	.47	1.45	1.12	1.47	.93	1.34	.64	1.47	1.10
	1.50	1.23	1.56	1.31	1.53	1.29	1.53	1.31	-.07	-.28
	.23	.93	-.23	.01	.72	1.39	-.20	.20	.80	1.15
	1.50	1.23	1.61	1.15	1.53	1.53	-.74	-.74	.96	1.45
	1.12	-1.69	.99	1.58	.74	1.37	.77	1.18	1.53	-.39
	-1.56	-1.56	-1.56	-.93	-.09	-1.26	-1.18	1.20	.01	-1.37
	1.56	-1.15	-1.12	-1.61						
30 DOMINICAN REPUBLIC	-.50	1.34	1.50	-1.07	.66	-1.18	.99	.15	-.20	-.91
	-1.42	-1.12	1.18	-.42	-.74	.20	-1.04	.42	.04	.04
	-1.47	-1.53	1.42	-1.37	-.04	1.61	.58	.23	.09	-.23
	-.04	-.45	-.53	-1.26	-.36	-1.02	-1.10	.85	1.72	-.26
	-1.23	.42	-.15	.39	-.85	-.42	-.53	-.20	.66	-.47
	.39	.34	.74	-.36	.07	.58	-.50	-.39	-.99	.01
	.39	.66	.36	-.15	.47	-.31	1.23	1.12	-.34	-.69
	-.64	-1.04	1.23	-1.10	1.18	1.02	-1.58	-1.58	1.26	-.45
	-.36	-.39	-.28	-.64	-.23	-.55	-.15	-.01	.91	.26
	.01	-.20	-.20	-1.10	-.74	-.64	-.39	-.93	.01	.91
	-.18	.34	-.26	.72	-.34	-.20	-.28	.69	-.36	-.20
	-.01	-.88	-.80	-.47	-.23	-.15	-1.64	-1.58	-.50	-.39
	.20	-.04	1.47	-.09	-1.56	-1.56	-1.34	-1.29	-1.61	1.42
	1.47	1.47	1.56	1.26	.64	1.45	-1.15	-.77	1.20	1.42
	-1.12	1.56	1.50	1.29						
31 ECUADOR	-.12	1.12	1.20	.18	-.45	-.26	-1.61	-.26	-.77	.96
	-.83	-.85	.36	.15	.04	-.15	-.23	.15	.15	.15
	.45	.09	.85	-1.34	-.85	1.20	.28	.26	-.45	-.15
	-.31	1.29	1.37	-.39	-.85	-.64	-.72	1.10	1.26	.26

	-.72	1.07	.18	-.66	.34	-.80	-.66	-.45	-.36	-.45
	-.07	-.18	-.26	-.61	-.31	-.72	-.23	-.20	-.39	-.36
	-.20	-.77	1.47	.74	1.07	-.64	-.96	-.88	-.55	-.91
	-.88	-1.23	1.53	1.66	.55	1.04	-1.56	-1.56	-1.64	.12
	.72	.36	.74	-.47	-.55	-.34	-.42	.09	.23	.34
	-.01	-.04	-.26	-.64	-.58	-.42	-.50	-.55	.23	.88
	-.28	-.36	-.01	.64	.07	.07	.15	.50	-.55	-.66
	-.69	-.28	-.31	-.55	-.61	-.39	-.77	-.85	-.23	-.31
	.61	-.18	-.96	.42	-1.53	-1.53	-1.31	-1.26	-1.58	.77
	1.04	.55	.07	.88	.39	1.47	-1.12	.36	-1.34	-1.34
	-1.10	1.15	-1.10	.12						
32 EL SALVADOR	-.69	1.37	1.02	-1.37	1.18	-1.29	.85	1.47	.66	.61
	-.72	-.74	.39	.18	.36	.07	.47	-.18	-.39	-.42
	-.58	-1.34	1.58	-1.31	.12	1.64	-.58	.28	-.31	-.42
	.01	-.53	-.47	.66	-.23	-.50	.66	.64	.31	-.01
	-.93	.91	-.39	-.18	.26	-.58	-.12	-.58	-.15	-.77
	-.64	-.61	.61	-1.02	-.61	-1.31	-.61	-.15	-.72	-.58
	.04	-.42	.85	.77	1.18	-1.04	-1.15	-1.15	.64	-.72
	-.74	-1.12	.53	-1.07	.58	-1.56	.01	-.61	1.29	-.36
	.18	-.34	.09	-.74	-.34	-.88	-.50	-.45	1.07	-1.39
	-1.50	-.58	-.42	-.42	.28	-.26	.36	-.39	-.58	.55
	-.45	-.26	-.61	.23	-.47	-.34	-.64	.18	-.09	-.47
	.07	-.64	-.26	-.53	-.07	.04	-1.20	-1.15	-.69	-.50
	-1.42	-1.34	1.56	.18	-.80	.53	.80	-.01	.50	-1.45
	-1.53	-.99	-1.53	-.01	-.45	-1.23	-1.10	1.23	-1.31	-1.31
	-1.07	-1.12	-1.07	-1.58						
33 ETHIOPIA	1.10	-.53	-.61	1.18	-.39	1.45	-.96	-.09	-.64	1.64
	.23	-1.66	-1.66	-1.50	-1.23	-1.45	-1.02	-1.58	-1.66	-1.64
	.93	1.53	-.09	.91	-.42	-1.39	1.02	1.58	1.53	-.18
	-1.69	-.36	-1.10	-.74	-.64	-.85	-.83	1.39	1.12	-1.50
	-.07	1.66	-1.64	-.64	-1.64	-.34	.66	-.91	-1.64	-.09
	-.77	-.83	-.66	-.50	-1.31	-.47	-.91	-1.64	-1.66	.61
	-.53	1.45	-1.69	-.12	-1.56	.88	-.77	-.61	.47	-1.64
	-1.64	-.88	-.36	-1.04	-1.20	1.07	-1.04	-.58	-.85	-.04
	-1.02	-.07	-1.29	-.50	-1.58	-.50	-1.61	-.12	-1.07	-1.56
	-1.72	-.42	-1.29	-.72	-1.61	-.69	-1.47	-.72	-.61	-1.66
	-.36	-1.47	-.58	-1.66	-.80	-1.58	-.61	-1.66	-.39	-.53
	-1.37	-.85	-1.64	-.66	-1.61	-1.69	-1.47	-1.72	-.91	-1.69
	.34	-.96	1.50	-.42	-1.50	-1.50	-.47	-1.23	-.61	-1.42
	-1.50	.72	.85	.01	-.85	-1.20	1.29	-1.58	-1.29	-1.29
	-1.04	-1.10	-1.04	-.39						
34 FINLAND	-.23	-1.31	-.42	.36	-.74	-.58	.31	-1.29	-.01	-1.58
	1.45	1.12	.91	1.23	1.45	1.42	.50	1.58	.85	.34
	-.64	.15	1.39	-1.29	1.61	-1.72	.31	1.20	.42	.88
	1.31	1.23	1.39	.34	1.20	1.07	-.09	-.80	-.93	1.04
	1.10	-.58	.61	1.39	.96	1.50	1.53	.15	.80	-.01
	.83	.53	-.01	.20	1.10	-.91	1.12	1.61	1.50	1.26
	1.47	1.23	1.61	.80	1.53	.23	.26	.07	-.80	-.18
	-.20	-.61	-1.26	-1.02	-1.18	-.50	.93	-.55	1.31	-.01
	.26	.20	.66	1.07	1.45	1.04	1.53	.85	.64	.88
	1.37	1.02	1.39	1.12	1.37	1.02	1.37	1.07	-.31	-.39
	.93	1.69	.01	.96	.61	1.23	.18	1.10	.61	1.04
	1.20	.72	1.20	.99	1.23	1.37	-.61	-.01	.83	1.12
	1.18	.36	.26	1.02	.88	1.69	.83	1.20	1.23	-1.39
	-1.47	-1.53	-1.50	.91	-.07	-1.18	-1.07	-.74	-1.26	-1.26
	-1.02	-1.07	-1.02	-1.56						
35 FRANCE	1.39	-.88	-1.15	.64	.77	1.07	.09	-1.34	.69	-1.39
	1.15	1.37	.83	1.10	1.31	1.29	.85	1.31	1.23	1.42
	-.20	-.99	.55	-.01	-.23	1.07	1.20	1.07	-.85	1.61
	1.45	-.96	-1.45	.18	1.12	1.64	-1.23	-1.69	-1.42	1.66
	1.61	-1.50	1.26	1.18	.88	1.42	1.66	1.58	1.07	1.50
	1.12	1.04	1.10	1.58	1.58	.91	1.58	1.29	.34	1.34
	.50	-1.39	1.12	.83	.96	1.58	.93	1.15	-1.66	-1.61
	-1.61	-1.58	-.28	-.99	.61	-1.53	.96	-.53	-.83	1.45
	.39	1.47	.61	1.66	1.53	1.66	1.56	1.53	1.34	1.61
	1.42	1.58	1.26	1.64	1.12	1.64	1.15	1.64	1.45	-.04

	1.56	1.50	1.42	.85	1.58	1.37	1.47	.91	1.58	1.69
	1.58	1.66	1.56	1.69	1.58	1.39	1.29	1.10	1.53	1.20
	1.58	1.34	-.58	1.72	1.42	1.23	.85	1.23	.93	1.39
	-.26	.20	-.53	-.91	-1.29	-1.15	-1.04	1.26	.04	.74
	-.99	-1.04	-.99	.93						
36 GABON	-1.56	-1.45	-1.34	.09	-1.61	-1.61	1.07	-.23	-.61	-.55
	.88	.77	-.23	-.07	-.12	-.72	-.34	-1.47	.39	.20
	.91	-.34	.26	-.09	1.07	.85	-1.39	-1.29	-.04	-1.50
	.04	.80	-1.66	-1.66	-.96	-1.18	1.64	.42	1.20	-1.47
	-.42	-.20	-.77	-.34	1.04	-1.18	-1.02	-1.39	-.42	-1.47
	-.58	-.69	-1.42	-1.42	-.15	.99	-1.07	.61	1.18	-1.02
	.80	1.34	-1.39	-1.56	-1.04	-1.42	1.26	1.34	1.04	.91
	.91	.88	.01	-.96	-1.15	-1.50	-1.02	-.50	-.80	-1.64
	-1.64	-1.66	-1.72	-1.31	.42	-1.42	.39	-1.58	-1.58	-.34
	-.04	-1.20	-.28	-1.18	.74	-.83	1.18	-1.12	-1.47	1.37
	-1.61	-.74	-1.47	.83	-1.45	-1.56	-1.47	.74	-1.66	-1.26
	-.34	-1.12	.83	-1.18	.34	.36	-.53	1.42	-1.20	-.23
	-1.69	-1.23	-.36	.58	-.99	-.09	-.45	-1.20	-.15	.50
	.36	-.20	.42	-.88	.42	1.50	-1.02	.39	-1.23	-1.23
	-.96	1.18	-.96	-1.53						
37 EAST GERMANY	.88	-1.69	-1.72	-.72	1.26	.04	.83	-1.56	.96	-1.23
	.99	1.66	-.07	1.58	1.47	1.56	1.42	1.34	1.61	1.69
	-1.58	.04	1.04	-1.26	1.56	.01	.50	.74	-.61	1.34
	1.15	-1.66	-1.72	-1.72	.39	1.37	-.85	-1.72	.72	1.31
	1.34	-1.18	1.72	.42	.64	1.18	.64	1.34	1.15	.66
	.55	.36	1.15	1.15	1.31	-.42	1.45	1.37	1.56	1.56
	1.53	1.53	-1.37	-1.07	-1.64	1.31	1.39	1.50	-1.47	.34
	-1.58	.31	-.61	-.93	-1.12	1.10	-.99	-.47	-.77	.88
	.15	1.29	-.04	1.10	.72	.99	.72	1.26	1.69	1.26
	1.15	1.34	1.15	1.26	.88	1.37	1.07	1.34	.96	.45
	1.10	.91	.74	.50	.93	.50	.99	.45	1.42	1.10
	.85	1.31	1.15	1.12	.85	1.10	1.39	1.50	1.47	1.61
	1.20	1.20	.23	-1.61	1.26	-.72	-1.29	-1.18	-1.15	-.36
	-.64	-.42	.04	-.85	.88	-1.12	-.99	-.72	.88	-1.20
	-.93	-1.02	.88	1.45						
38 WEST GERMANY	1.50	-.93	-1.12	.04	1.45	.45	1.20	-1.39	.72	-1.34
	1.50	1.69	-.47	1.42	1.66	1.58	1.04	1.37	1.45	1.39
	-1.56	.01	1.34	-1.23	1.45	.74	1.37	.77	-.72	1.66
	1.42	1.15	1.04	-.09	1.53	1.69	-.55	-1.23	-1.61	1.64
	1.64	-1.64	1.47	1.45	1.56	1.07	.91	1.64	1.50	1.45
	.69	.45	1.45	1.56	1.53	1.07	1.61	1.18	-.15	1.61
	1.15	-.39	.91	.85	1.29	1.50	.42	.88	-1.45	.36
	-1.56	-.77	-.58	-.91	-1.10	-.47	.99	-.45	-.74	1.61
	1.50	1.61	1.42	1.64	1.26	1.64	1.26	1.50	1.64	1.64
	1.39	1.64	1.34	1.69	1.26	1.69	1.34	1.69	1.42	-.74
	1.42	.47	1.34	-.61	1.47	.55	1.39	-.53	1.61	1.64
	1.45	1.53	.93	1.64	1.39	1.42	1.58	1.31	1.61	1.47
	1.64	1.39	-.93	1.12	1.45	1.15	.88	.83	.96	1.64
	.64	.42	-.34	.45	1.10	-1.10	-.96	-.69	1.42	-1.18
	-.91	-.99	-.93	.96						
39 GHANA	.18	.42	.47	-.04	.12	-.23	.15	1.53	1.45	.01
	-.66	-.23	-.93	-.34	-.20	-1.42	-1.10	-.77	.34	.39
	.99	.45	-.45	.53	.72	-.01	.36	-1.26	-1.47	.20
	.15	-.18	-.39	-1.04	-1.61	.04	-.42	1.42	-.88	-1.45
	.15	-.01	-.91	.45	-.66	-.55	-.85	-.69	-1.02	-.66
	-.88	-.91	-.47	-.34	-.34	-.31	.42	.31	.66	-1.31
	-1.58	-1.72	-.18	-1.04	-.20	.36	.74	.69	.80	.64
	.64	.61	1.26	-.88	-1.07	-.45	-.96	-1.37	-1.61	.04
	-.28	.12	-.26	.61	.69	.69	.85	-.04	.07	-.69
	.36	-.15	-.61	-.01	.12	-.09	-.20	-.01	.50	.93
	.83	1.26	.34	1.26	-.45	-.88	.53	1.18	.09	-.45
	-.64	-.42	-.85	-.31	-.77	.07	-1.61	-1.66	-.39	-.85
	-.93	-1.12	.39	-1.37	.85	-.69	-1.26	-1.15	-1.12	-1.37
	-.01	.15	.31	-.83	1.42	1.10	-.93	.42	1.47	-1.15
	-.88	-.96	1.10	1.39						
40 GREECE	.26	-1.58	-1.31	-.45	.47	.18	-.20	-1.26	-1.58	-.45

	1.47	1.34	1.34	.66	.12	.36	.74	.83	.74	.96
	-.12	-.72	1.07	.18	-1.04	-1.18	-.09	1.72	1.20	.74
	.85	-1.23	-1.26	1.07	1.56	.53	-.96	-.42	-1.07	.42
	.80	.47	.04	1.23	1.26	1.02	1.58	1.04	1.42	.91
	1.45	1.37	1.29	.36	.96	.45	.45	.26	-1.37	.64
	.23	-1.18	.28	.88	.66	.85	1.04	1.31	-.77	-.88
	-.85	-1.37	1.64	-.85	-1.04	-.42	1.02	-.42	1.34	.96
	1.56	.99	1.34	.74	.88	.74	.83	.26	.83	.53
	.69	.91	.88	.88	.72	-.07	-.15	.36	.31	-.07
	.91	1.29	.23	.28	.83	.99	.45	.28	.53	.47
	.31	.58	.55	.45	.36	.74	-.50	-.12	.47	.50
	.28	.58	.74	.34	1.12	1.39	.91	.85	.77	1.45
	1.18	.61	-.23	1.69	1.45	1.12	-.91	.45	1.39	.88
	1.66	1.20	-.91	1.64						
41 GUATEMALA	-.28	.93	1.23	-.69	.28	-.83	.61	1.31	1.10	1.04
	-1.04	-.99	.42	.20	-.34	.12	-.31	-.20	-1.07	-.96
	.69	1.45	1.45	-1.20	.20	1.58	-.07	.31	-1.23	-.01
	.23	-.31	-.31	.69	-.83	-.39	-.64	.45	.45	.01
	-.36	.61	-.36	-.61	.28	-.50	-.20	-.36	-.07	.45
	-.66	-.55	-.20	-.74	-.72	.26	-.55	-.61	-1.53	-.55
	-.23	-1.15	.88	-.09	.64	-.96	-1.39	-1.39	-.31	-.74
	-1.12	-1.29	1.29	1.45	1.20	1.12	-1.53	-1.53	-.72	-.20
	-.07	-.15	-.18	-.58	-.53	-.66	-.58	-.07	.42	.18
	-.28	-.39	-.53	-.34	-.12	-.31	-.04	-.28	-.42	-.69
	-.53	-.77	-.47	-.83	-.23	-.23	-.47	-.83	.34	-.31
	-.31	-.39	-.39	-.26	-.34	.28	-1.45	-1.47	-.34	-.45
	-.91	-.28	1.61	1.15	-1.47	-1.47	-1.23	-1.12	-1.56	-.34
	-.61	1.29	.72	-.80	-1.26	1.15	1.56	1.29	.07	-1.12
	-.85	-.93	1.47	.53						
42 GUINEA	-.53	.28	.88	.01	-.72	.20	-1.64	1.07	1.69	.93
	-1.53	.04	-1.39	-.58	-1.07	-.23	-.36	-1.26	-1.37	-1.39
	1.20	1.47	-.39	1.18	-1.18	-1.02	-1.23	-1.23	1.04	-1.12
	-1.34	.31	.72	.77	-.55	-1.34	-.04	.36	-.66	-1.42
	-1.45	.01	-.53	-1.47	-1.04	.18	-.88	.07	-.64	-.85
	-.83	-.77	-.80	-.93	-.74	-.09	-.80	-.74	1.20	-.88
	-.66	.85	-1.34	-1.02	-1.02	-1.20	-1.53	-1.47	.83	.69
	.69	.64	-.26	-.83	-1.02	-1.47	-.93	-.39	-.69	-1.04
	-.93	-1.04	-1.23	-.99	-1.04	-1.15	-1.15	-.50	-.61	-.18
	-.80	-1.02	-1.04	-1.26	-1.23	-1.12	-1.12	-1.29	-1.10	-1.31
	-1.15	-1.26	-1.10	-1.34	-1.02	-1.04	-1.10	-1.34	-1.15	-.93
	-.99	-.55	-.36	-.80	-.66	-.96	.23	-.09	-.85	-.88
	-1.72	-1.72	-.72	-.39	-.53	-.66	-.42	-1.10	-.58	-1.34
	-.58	-1.50	-1.47	-1.53	.20	-1.07	-.88	-.66	-1.20	-1.10
	-.83	-.91	-.88	.15						
43 HAITI	-.34	-1.07	-.53	-1.29	1.29	-1.39	1.23	-1.20	-1.39	-.88
	.69	.34	-1.12	-1.31	-1.26	-.96	-1.50	-1.23	-1.18	-1.20
	-1.64	.07	.47	-1.18	.91	.91	.69	.34	-.66	-1.04
	-1.31	-.07	-.61	-1.58	-.53	-1.42	-1.20	-.36	1.10	-.23
	-1.39	-1.07	-1.29	-1.39	1.18	-1.02	-.96	-.96	-1.04	-.83
	-.99	-1.10	.28	-1.69	-1.12	-.64	-1.29	-1.53	-1.64	-1.29
	-1.53	-.12	-1.31	-1.53	-.99	.09	1.12	1.20	-.42	-1.58
	-.66	-1.02	.88	-.80	.64	1.15	-.91	-.36	-1.58	-.66
	-.77	-.69	-.93	-1.42	-1.56	-1.56	-1.64	-.80	.58	-.26
	-.96	-1.12	-1.31	-1.45	-1.53	-1.29	-1.29	-1.42	-.85	-1.15
	-1.02	-1.15	-.91	-1.18	-.77	-.96	-.91	-1.18	-.93	-1.15
	-1.31	-1.56	-1.61	-1.29	-1.56	-1.20	.07	-.42	-1.12	-1.39
	-1.50	-1.64	1.64	1.18	-1.45	-1.45	-1.20	-1.07	-1.10	-1.31
	-.36	1.07	.74	-.77	-.42	1.18	.88	-1.56	.58	-1.07
	1.31	1.58	1.66	.74						
44 HONDURAS	-.93	1.15	1.26	-.61	-.34	-.34	-.58	-.80	-1.31	-.20
	-1.69	-1.45	-.45	-.61	-.45	-.64	-.47	-.26	-.83	-.66
	-.61	-1.26	.31	-1.15	.04	.96	.72	.36	-1.61	-.85
	-.26	-.58	-.36	-.85	-.93	-.91	.83	.01	1.45	.04
	-.69	1.37	-.23	-.50	.01	-.39	-.26	-1.04	-.77	-.80
	-.55	-.45	-.45	-1.10	-.80	-1.29	-.88	-.55	-1.04	-.93
	-.18	-.74	.64	-.07	.39	-1.02	-.91	-.96	.07	-.80

	-.72	-1.10	1.02	-.77	1.23	-.39	.04	-.34	-.66	-.83
	-.58	-.66	-.39	-.96	-.61	-1.18	-.66	-.15	.34	-1.20
	.12	-.91	-.64	-.85	-.04	-.61	.18	-.77	-.91	.36
	-1.12	-.80	-.93	-.09	-.74	-.66	-.93	-.26	-1.07	-.91
	-.55	-.93	-.50	-.93	-.50	-.26	-1.58	-1.45	-.83	-.61
	-.04	-.26	1.66	1.20	-.55	.69	.93	.01	.53	-1.29
	-1.45	-.04	-.42	-.74	-1.23	1.20	-.85	-.64	-1.18	-1.04
	-.80	-.88	-.85	-.04						
45 HUNGARY	.47	-1.64	-1.56	-.83	.96	.09	.12	-1.69	.53	-.07
	1.58	1.50	1.10	.99	1.02	1.10	1.39	1.15	.88	.99
	-.93	-.88	.69	-1.12	1.18	.88	-.55	1.31	.88	1.07
	1.10	-1.18	-1.29	-.26	1.47	1.04	.12	-1.61	-.26	.99
	1.26	-.36	1.66	.09	1.45	1.26	1.34	1.31	1.66	.61
	1.10	.96	1.26	.61	1.07	-.45	1.18	1.10	.88	1.31
	1.26	.96	-1.29	-.99	-1.23	1.04	1.18	1.39	-.96	-.20
	-.18	.15	-.55	-.74	-.99	1.18	-.88	-.31	-.64	.77
	.96	.91	.83	.99	1.04	.91	.99	1.07	1.50	.83
	.91	.96	.83	1.04	.93	1.12	.99	1.04	.66	.66
	.20	-.15	.39	.39	.77	.66	.58	.34	1.34	.45
	.12	.47	.07	.42	.12	1.15	1.02	1.23	1.07	1.18
	1.10	1.45	.42	-1.50	1.20	-.64	-1.18	-1.04	-1.07	-1.26
	-1.42	-.96	-1.45	.04	.45	-1.04	-.83	-1.53	.09	-1.02
	-.77	-.85	-.83	1.07						
46 ICELAND	-1.69	-.64	-.26	-.74	-1.58	-.72	-1.45	-.34	-1.66	-1.64
	.47	.80	1.66	1.61	1.29	1.04	1.23	1.64	1.69	1.72
	-1.20	.99	1.23	-1.10	1.58	-1.15	-.83	-1.20	-.83	-.93
	1.61	1.04	1.69	.31	.53	-.88	1.02	1.15	-.91	.28
	-.23	-1.04	1.02	1.47	1.47	.53	.47	-1.07	1.34	-1.66
	-1.66	-1.66	-1.66	-1.66	-1.69	-1.69	-.74	1.34	-.36	-.85
	1.31	-.20	1.39	.91	.93	-.12	.12	.34	-.58	.01
	-.15	-.53	-1.04	-.72	-.96	-.36	1.04	-.28	-.61	-1.61
	-1.61	-1.31	1.50	-.80	1.58	-.93	1.47	-1.56	-1.56	-1.37
	.77	.09	1.58	-.80	1.69	-.55	1.69	-.74	-1.69	.50
	-1.23	1.56	-1.66	1.34	.12	1.72	-1.61	1.72	-1.64	-.36
	1.42	-1.02	1.47	-.61	1.47	1.58	-1.07	.23	-.42	1.42
	-.53	1.37	-.99	.31	-1.07	1.47	.96	1.26	1.26	-.31
	-1.39	-1.47	-1.42	-.72	-1.66	-1.02	-.80	-.61	-1.15	-.99
	-.74	-.83	-.80	-1.50						
47 INDIA	1.69	.18	-.23	1.56	1.23	1.61	.93	.28	.99	1.39
	.18	.36	-1.64	-.88	-1.42	-1.58	-.01	-.64	-.64	-.80
	1.58	1.56	-1.20	.58	-.36	-.83	1.66	.80	-.50	1.50
	-.91	1.58	-.91	-.96	-.50	1.29	-1.66	-.72	-.20	1.42
	1.53	1.50	-.12	-1.10	.91	-.61	-.39	.77	-.47	1.61
	-.61	-.66	.66	1.47	-.45	.53	1.34	-1.23	-1.15	.96
	-1.61	-1.53	1.15	.93	.23	1.66	-.20	-.45	.09	.15
	.26	.01	-.53	-.69	-.93	-.34	1.07	-.26	-.58	1.64
	-.55	1.56	-.61	1.50	-1.29	1.50	-1.12	1.64	.74	1.58
	.28	1.04	-1.07	1.34	-1.66	1.20	-1.58	1.29	1.69	-.61
	1.72	1.10	1.66	-.12	1.66	.28	1.69	-.18	1.66	1.02
	-1.56	1.39	-1.53	1.07	-1.53	-1.12	1.34	-.72	1.42	-.47
	1.53	-1.18	1.02	-.72	1.47	.31	.99	1.29	1.56	1.66
	1.69	1.69	1.34	1.29	1.69	-.99	1.69	1.31	1.37	1.72
	-.72	-.80	-.77	1.61						
48 INDONESIA	1.61	-.01	-.15	1.29	.55	.69	1.42	.66	1.31	1.18
	.07	.09	-1.37	-1.12	-1.61	-1.26	-.50	-.09	-.61	-.61
	1.31	1.37	-.83	1.45	.39	-.80	1.47	-1.18	-.39	1.02
	-.99	.55	.55	-.72	-.34	.39	-1.42	.39	-.18	.53
	-.20	1.47	-.74	-1.07	.04	-.64	-1.66	.28	-.53	1.29
	-.28	-.34	.50	1.18	.04	1.42	.36	-1.56	-.12	-.07
	-1.66	-1.64	1.69	.96	-.53	1.53	-.88	-.74	.34	.39
	.36	.34	-.99	-.66	.66	-.31	-.85	-1.34	-1.56	.93
	-.50	.83	-.50	-.91	-1.72	-.69	-1.72	.99	-.12	.45
	-1.56	.47	-1.10	.26	-1.58	.42	-1.39	.31	1.61	.15
	1.18	-1.04	1.53	-.42	1.02	-.58	1.58	-.42	.93	.66
	-1.23	.99	-1.29	.77	-1.29	-1.31	1.07	.09	.77	-.80
	.74	-1.07	-1.31	-1.69	-1.42	-1.42	-.39	.04	-.34	1.47

	1.45	1.42	1.72	.47	1.58	1.23	-.77	-1.50	1.69	.36
	-.69	1.66	.91	1.10						
49 IRAN	1.12	.77	.15	1.34	-.69	.74	-.01	.99	.15	1.15
	-1.39	-.83	.18	-.04	-.31	-.50	-.45	-.72	-.85	-.88
	1.29	1.20	-1.53	1.37	-1.58	-1.53	-.04	.83	.77	.77
	-.09	-.91	-1.31	.47	.26	.83	-.18	1.61	-1.47	-.20
	.58	.83	.69	.64	.85	-.47	.07	.80	.04	.96
	.72	.88	-.04	.58	.34	.77	.72	-.09	-.50	.80
	.12	-.09	-.23	-.04	-1.12	.83	-.85	-.93	-.12	-1.56
	-1.53	-.36	-1.31	-.64	.69	1.20	.07	-.23	-.55	1.10
	.34	1.15	.26	.69	-.09	.64	-.09	.53	-.74	-.64
	-.42	.53	-.23	.85	.26	.85	.31	.83	.88	-.83
	1.02	.23	.72	-.80	.42	-.53	.93	-.77	.47	.64
	-.39	.39	-.96	.50	-.55	-.01	1.45	1.56	.69	.09
	.23	-.99	.50	.36	.91	.47	-.36	.07	.55	.61
	1.07	.09	.91	.07	.91	-.96	1.72	1.34	-1.12	-.96
	-.66	-.77	1.42	.18						
50 IRAQ	.23	1.61	1.29	.50	-.42	.61	-.61	1.58	.28	1.23
	-1.37	-.31	1.04	-.91	1.53	.39	-.20	-.91	-.58	-.26
	.12	-.01	-1.12	1.61	-1.15	-.74	-.20	1.23	1.02	.18
	-.15	-.20	-.69	.72	-.20	.45	1.26	.55	-.77	-.18
	.26	-1.02	1.53	-.31	.36	-.28	.15	-.28	-.39	.50
	.93	1.07	.23	.31	.91	1.50	.50	.42	1.42	-.04
	-.15	-.72	-.64	-.96	-1.18	.53	.58	-.01	.26	-.01
	.04	-.28	.91	1.69	1.26	1.23	-1.50	-1.50	-1.53	.58
	.85	.93	1.37	.47	.45	.09	.31	.15	-.09	-.80
	-.09	.12	-.31	.01	.01	.66	.74	.23	.36	.23
	.58	.85	.15	.26	.45	.39	.34	.23	-.04	.09
	-.28	.12	-.23	.20	-.26	.09	1.42	.26	.31	.34
	-.83	-.66	1.04	.15	-1.39	-1.39	-1.15	-1.02	-1.53	.53
	-1.37	1.04	1.53	1.61	1.64	1.61	.91	-1.47	-1.10	-.93
	-.64	1.72	1.64	1.66						
51 IRELAND	-.72	-1.61	-1.69	-.96	.34	-.31	-.50	-.99	.74	-1.18
	.58	.96	1.15	1.12	.85	1.23	1.53	1.07	1.47	1.64
	-1.31	.64	1.56	-1.07	.47	1.47	.39	.69	-.01	.34
	1.07	-.55	-.45	-.58	.47	.72	1.12	-1.18	1.64	.36
	.85	.04	.88	.74	.99	1.69	1.42	.39	.72	-.61
	.18	-.07	.42	-.42	.18	-1.26	.39	.96	-.28	.36
	.83	-.69	1.07	.99	1.20	-.61	.77	.83	-.66	-.04
	-.07	-.47	-1.10	-.61	-.91	-.28	1.10	-.20	-.53	-.09
	1.02	-.01	1.02	.53	1.18	.53	1.20	.20	.99	.58
	1.23	.55	1.07	.64	1.42	.28	1.20	.53	-.28	1.34
	.07	1.12	-.39	1.37	.09	.58	-.36	1.31	.18	.96
	1.23	.45	1.10	.93	1.20	1.12	-.47	.74	.45	.99
	-1.02	-.01	1.07	1.23	.28	1.07	1.02	1.31	1.58	.80
	-1.34	-.12	-1.39	-.69	-1.64	-.93	-.74	.47	.12	.39
	-.61	-.74	-.74	-.72						
52 ISRAEL	-.83	1.50	1.66	-1.39	1.12	-1.26	.66	-.36	-1.02	-1.12
	.83	.74	1.31	1.02	1.15	-.28	1.66	.99	.91	1.02
	-.42	1.23	-.99	.42	-1.02	-.47	1.04	1.12	.85	.47
	1.23	1.02	1.45	1.39	1.50	.34	-.39	-.45	-1.58	.31
	1.29	-.72	1.10	1.50	-.36	.85	1.10	.69	1.72	1.15
	1.69	1.66	1.66	.77	1.69	1.58	.69	1.20	.83	.39
	.96	-.96	1.58	1.02	.83	-.50	1.29	1.26	.18	.26
	.34	.18	-.74	-.58	-.88	-.26	1.12	-.18	-.50	.09
	1.58	.23	1.58	.66	1.34	.66	1.42	-.42	1.10	.42
	1.12	.61	1.18	.36	1.34	.01	1.02	.18	-.39	1.45
	-.23	.72	-.42	1.31	.53	1.58	-.42	1.37	-.01	.28
	.83	.28	.99	.28	.80	1.26	-.83	-.80	.42	.96
	.45	1.56	-1.07	.20	-.20	1.56	1.04	1.34	1.29	.93
	.39	.91	.12	.93	.93	-.91	-.72	-.58	.15	.77
	1.58	-.72	-.72	.55						
53 ITALY	1.42	-1.29	-1.47	.23	1.37	.91	.77	-1.31	.45	-.31
	1.56	1.47	-.20	.72	.80	1.26	1.58	.20	.58	.28
	-1.39	-1.29	.99	-1.04	-.83	1.37	.42	.39	.91	1.53
	1.12	1.64	.42	.20	1.34	1.53	-.88	-1.56	-1.39	1.56

	1.50	-1.15	.77	.77	.77	.80	.88	1.02	.85	1.37
	.66	.42	1.31	1.45	1.20	.04	1.56	1.15	1.26	1.39
	.53	-1.29	1.42	1.04	1.02	1.20	.15	-.07	-1.42	-.61
	-1.50	-.85	-.72	-.55	-.85	-.23	1.15	-.15	-.47	1.53
	1.37	1.45	1.12	1.58	1.12	1.61	1.15	1.31	1.31	1.53
	1.29	1.56	1.23	1.50	.83	1.53	.91	1.53	1.31	-.85
	1.50	1.20	1.31	-.36	1.50	.88	1.37	-.28	1.50	1.61
	1.29	1.47	.80	1.56	1.26	1.20	.99	.20	1.45	.91
	1.47	.91	1.10	1.50	1.53	1.42	1.07	1.37	1.31	1.31
	.93	.93	-.31	.50	-.39	-.88	-.69	.50	-1.07	1.39
	1.69	-.69	-.69	.36						
54 IVORY COAST	-.39	1.29	.50	.28	-.77	.34	-1.66	1.45	.31	1.45
	-.20	-1.53	-.74	-1.45	-1.18	-.91	-.61	-.88	-.96	-1.10
	1.50	-.09	-.47	.77	.07	-.07	-.53	-1.15	1.56	-.20
	-.12	.61	1.20	1.53	-.18	-.28	.91	1.07	.64	-1.39
	-.85	.34	-1.26	-1.31	-.01	.66	-.31	-1.15	-1.07	-.93
	-1.04	-1.07	-.99	-.80	-.64	-.39	-.20	.18	.12	-.74
	-.45	-1.12	-1.26	-.93	-.96	-1.12	-1.50	-1.42	1.07	.93
	.93	.91	.04	-.53	-.83	-1.45	-.83	-.12	-1.50	-.64
	-.72	-.58	-.72	-.53	-.12	-.58	-.31	-.53	-.77	-1.23
	-.72	-.66	-.58	-.31	.20	-.12	.50	-.15	-.55	-.42
	-.99	-1.10	-.69	-.77	-.72	-.85	-.72	-.80	.12	-.18
	-.04	-.18	.28	-.18	.07	-.20	-1.42	-1.37	-.58	-.58
	.01	-.09	-.34	.61	-.36	-.61	-.34	-.99	-.55	-1.23
	-1.31	-1.45	-.61	-.66	.66	-.85	-.66	-.55	.18	-.91
	-.58	-.66	-.66	.39						
55 JAMAICA	-1.10	-.31	-.58	-1.47	1.31	-1.47	1.10	.55	-.42	-.18
	-.04	.12	.64	.42	.77	.23	.26	.88	.23	.50
	-1.29	-1.69	.01	-1.02	1.37	-.12	1.15	-1.12	1.45	-.31
	.61	-1.02	-.80	.39	1.37	-.31	1.07	.47	1.02	-1.37
	.47	-1.26	.47	.88	-.15	-.04	-.07	-.53	.50	-1.26
	-1.02	-.99	.36	-1.20	-.88	-1.53	-.53	.28	-.80	-.34
	.55	.12	.50	1.07	1.10	-.72	1.20	1.18	.50	1.34
	1.34	1.31	.55	-.50	.72	-.20	1.18	-.09	-.45	-.74
	-.20	-.77	-.42	-.28	.64	-.42	.55	-.88	1.12	-.88
	.61	.01	.53	-.20	.99	-.18	.80	-.18	-.83	1.29
	-.96	-.50	-.88	.77	-.69	-.42	-.88	.80	-.53	.01
	.77	-.31	.66	-.04	.72	.58	-1.39	-1.20	-.04	.58
	-1.37	-1.20	1.12	-.61	-.07	.72	-.31	.09	.26	-1.20
	-.55	.26	-.09	.09	-1.20	-.83	-.64	-.53	.20	-.88
	-.55	-.64	-.64	-.69						
56 JAPAN	1.56	-1.10	-1.10	.42	1.50	.12	1.64	-1.53	-1.53	-1.50
	1.72	1.23	.45	1.64	.83	1.53	1.26	1.18	1.31	1.58
	-1.61	-1.47	-1.34	-.26	-.50	-1.37	1.69	.42	.45	1.58
	.99	1.42	-.58	1.34	1.69	1.56	-1.37	-1.31	-1.10	1.69
	1.58	-1.23	.64	1.72	1.31	-.15	.58	1.66	1.04	1.18
	-.39	-.64	.91	1.02	-.07	-1.15	1.64	1.04	.99	.91
	-1.04	-1.61	.93	1.10	1.31	1.61	-.74	.04	-.69	-1.53
	-1.47	-1.69	-.83	-.47	-.80	-.18	1.20	-.07	-.42	1.66
	1.66	1.66	1.69	1.61	.83	1.58	.77	1.42	1.39	1.66
	1.26	1.69	1.31	1.61	.45	1.61	.66	1.61	1.56	-.66
	1.66	1.72	1.56	1.20	1.64	1.42	1.61	1.26	1.72	1.50
	.66	1.69	1.53	1.58	.91	1.07	1.23	.45	1.58	.88
	1.61	1.02	1.45	.28	1.39	.55	1.10	1.39	1.61	.91
	.91	-.58	-1.37	-.64	1.29	-.80	-.61	-1.45	.91	-.85
	-.53	-.61	-.61	-.66						
57 JORDAN	-1.02	.96	.91	-.80	-.36	-1.23	.45	-1.12	-1.29	.23
	-1.34	-1.23	.07	-.99	.39	.01	.01	-.39	.18	.23
	-1.26	-1.23	-.88	1.31	-.64	-.99	.15	1.37	1.26	-.83
	-.07	-.83	-.66	1.37	1.61	-1.12	-.20	.58	-.47	-1.34
	-.83	.50	-1.45	-.47	-1.31	-.12	.20	-.88	-.34	.01
	1.47	1.53	.80	-.28	1.15	1.66	-.83	-.28	-.61	-1.10
	-.61	-1.10	-.42	-.01	-.64	-.77	1.15	1.02	.45	.04
	.18	-.07	-.47	-.45	.74	1.26	.09	-.04	-.39	-.39
	.74	-.26	1.07	-1.04	-.58	-.61	.34	-1.04	-.36	-1.34
	-.83	-.31	.15	-.55	.42	-1.45	-1.20	-1.07	-.88	.80

	.04	1.42	-.74	1.29	-.99	-.83	-.74	1.20	-.18	-.88
	-.42	-.91	-.34	-.88	-.39	-.23	.36	.15	-.47	-.18
	-1.10	.15	.83	1.26	-1.37	-1.37	-1.12	-.96	-1.04	1.34
	.66	-.18	.28	1.56	1.39	-.77	-.58	.53	.61	.42
	-.50	-.58	1.04	.88						
58 NORTH KOREA	.64	.31	.69	-.50	.88	-.09	1.15	.91	.01	-.69
	-.55	-1.34	-.15	.01	-.15	.15	-.07	-.45	-.23	-.39
	-1.72	-.18	-.80	-.23	.36	-.72	-1.56	-1.10	.12	.26
	-.42	-1.72	.74	.80	-.47	.28	.26	.23	.23	.45
	.04	-.99	-.34	-.83	-1.39	-1.07	-.72	.26	-.18	1.34
	1.61	1.58	1.53	.28	.47	1.23	.34	-.04	.15	-.20
	-1.07	-1.26	-1.23	-1.50	-1.69	.80	.66	.66	-.04	.28
	.12	.20	-.69	-.42	-.77	1.29	-.80	-.01	-.36	1.18
	1.07	1.12	.91	-1.72	-.64	-1.04	-.61	.88	1.18	-1.72
	-.23	-1.72	.31	.47	-.31	.55	.01	.58	1.02	1.66
	1.20	1.37	.80	1.72	1.39	1.66	1.07	1.69	1.18	-1.72
	.36	-1.72	.15	-1.72	.28	-1.07	1.26	.99	1.37	-.28
	1.04	-.23	.15	-1.02	1.66	-.58	-1.10	-.93	-1.02	-1.18
	-1.29	-.93	-.15	-.61	-1.18	-.74	-.55	-1.42	-1.04	-.83
	-.47	-.55	-.58	-1.47						
59 SOUTH KOREA	1.18	.55	.01	-.77	1.53	-.80	1.56	.42	1.02	-.85
	-.31	-.09	.53	.34	-.26	-.88	.09	.55	.36	.42
	-1.69	.20	-.66	-.99	.61	-.55	.74	-1.07	1.39	.42
	-.88	-.99	-1.39	1.04	.69	-.07	-1.26	-1.39	.69	.66
	.12	1.31	.20	-.15	-1.34	-.66	-.28	.99	.12	1.56
	1.53	1.50	1.64	.01	-.50	.55	.26	-1.04	-.45	.07
	-1.37	-1.07	.18	.01	-.15	.96	-.72	-.77	-.01	.31
	.15	.23	.58	-.39	.77	-1.42	-.77	.01	-.34	1.29
	.88	1.02	.53	-.01	-1.10	.31	-.72	.34	.96	.85
	.39	.66	-.12	.09	-1.12	-.36	-1.42	-.09	1.34	1.42
	1.39	1.07	1.29	1.39	1.20	.64	1.34	1.34	1.04	-.72
	-1.72	-.09	-1.42	-.39	-1.64	-1.10	.69	.18	.85	.15
	.77	.42	-1.29	-.36	.72	.61	-.28	.12	.28	1.61
	1.50	.53	.39	.12	1.47	-.72	-.53	1.58	.23	.80
	-.45	-.53	-.55	1.34						
60 LAOS	-.99	-.20	.36	-.09	-1.12	-1.10	-.09	-.18	-.58	-.83
	-.61	-1.50	-.85	-1.29	-.99	-.55	-1.72	-.96	-1.02	-1.07
	.61	.58	-1.31	-.96	-.99	-.93	-1.37	-1.04	1.61	-1.29
	-1.18	.47	.47	-1.02	-1.42	-1.69	-1.34	.12	.18	-1.31
	-1.18	-.18	-1.42	-1.29	-1.53	-1.50	-1.45	-1.61	-1.61	.34
	1.58	1.56	.47	-.55	.39	1.18	-1.18	-1.18	-.47	-.15
	.66	1.72	-.39	.04	-.61	-.55	1.47	1.47	.69	.50
	.47	.45	-.80	-.36	.80	1.31	-.74	.04	-.31	-1.07
	-.88	-1.10	-1.07	-1.61	-1.64	-1.31	-.91	-1.53	-1.53	-1.58
	-1.66	-1.53	-1.56	-1.50	-1.31	-1.72	-1.72	-1.64	-1.26	-1.18
	-1.58	-1.56	-1.26	-1.23	-1.42	-1.53	-1.26	-1.23	-1.18	-1.04
	-.96	-1.53	-1.45	-1.23	-1.20	-.85	-.04	-.28	-1.29	-1.20
	-1.64	-1.61	-1.50	-1.18	-.64	1.29	-.26	1.42	.58	-1.15
	-1.26	1.45	1.42	.15	-.04	1.26	1.61	.55	-1.02	-.80
	-.42	1.61	-.53	-.64						
61 LEBANON	-.80	.64	.53	-1.50	1.47	-1.50	1.47	-.91	-1.26	.53
	.53	-.42	1.56	.50	.20	.80	1.72	.93	-.12	-.15
	-.80	-.93	-.01	.93	-.55	.39	.77	1.50	-.23	-.12
	.45	1.07	.99	1.23	.28	-.34	.74	.18	-.99	.18
	.61	-.55	-.88	-.58	-1.15	.39	.53	-.26	.83	-.64
	.20	.04	1.18	-.47	.23	-.20	-.15	.53	-.34	-.53
	.15	-.93	1.72	1.12	.50	-.91	-.83	-.66	.20	.07

	.07	-.20	-1.20	-.34	-.74	-.15	.12	.07	-.28	-.15
	1.20	-.18	.80	-.36	.34	-.39	.42	-.39	1.42	-1.15
	.09	.28	.74	.12	1.10	-.91	-.31	-.12	-.74	.83
	-.09	1.15	-.55	1.02	.23	1.18	-.50	1.07	-.77	.42
	.91	-.53	.26	.26	.83	.26	-1.15	-1.07	-.01	.47
	-.85	.72	-1.58	1.66	-.31	1.66	1.12	.15	.61	.01
	.18	.18	.18	1.31	.69	-.69	.93	.58	-.99	1.34
	-.39	-.50	-.50	-.01						
62 LIBERIA	-1.31	-.69	-.77	-.64	-1.07	-.39	-.99	.36	-.18	-.01
	.72	.66	-.64	-1.34	.23	-.80	-1.29	-1.20	-1.10	-1.15
	1.45	1.26	-.50	.83	.88	-.77	.45	-1.02	1.58	-1.20
	-.45	.36	.12	-1.50	-.80	-.93	1.58	1.47	.50	-1.29
	-.66	.64	.72	-1.26	-.07	.36	-1.64	-1.34	-.99	-.91
	-.04	-.31	-.58	-1.39	-.85	-.85	-1.15	-.64	-.96	-1.26
	-.12	-.36	-1.20	-.91	-.93	-.66	1.58	1.66	-1.04	-.66
	-.61	-.99	-1.53	-.31	-.72	-1.39	-.72	.09	-.26	-1.58
	-1.58	-1.39	-.83	-1.18	-.01	-1.10	.04	-.96	-.31	-.39
	-.55	-1.26	-.77	-.96	.55	-.53	.83	-.80	-1.45	-.93
	-1.42	-.93	-1.45	-1.10	-.96	-.55	-1.45	-1.10	-1.61	-1.37
	-1.18	-1.45	-.42	-1.31	-.83	.15	.20	.12	-.93	-.20
	-1.66	-1.47	1.53	1.29	-1.02	-.55	-.23	-.91	-.53	-.28
	-1.23	-1.42	-1.34	-1.50	.23	-.66	-.50	.61	-.96	-.77
	-.36	-.47	-.47	-.61						
63 LIBYA	-1.18	1.45	1.53	1.37	.31	.31	-1.34	-.58	-.99	1.66
	-1.10	-.04	-.61	-1.26	-.91	.47	-.12	-.61	-.36	-.36
	-.28	.18	-1.26	1.56	-.96	-.66	-.66	-.99	.64	-.34
	.69	.77	1.26	1.58	-.31	.31	1.66	1.72	.80	-1.26
	-.64	-.53	-.61	-.80	-.99	-.77	-.64	-.99	-.28	-.69
	.31	.26	-1.37	-.53	.58	.36	-.47	.47	-.69	-1.23
	-.80	-1.50	.07	.07	-.04	-.04	1.66	1.72	.77	.45
	.42	.39	.74	-.28	-.69	1.34	-.69	.12	-.23	-.47
	.91	-.53	.36	-.20	.93	-.20	.91	-1.10	-1.26	-1.42
	-.88	-.72	-.18	-.09	1.07	.53	1.56	.12	-1.20	-.53
	-.69	-.18	-1.15	-.66	-.66	-.36	-1.15	-.69	-.74	-.07
	.80	-.26	.85	-.07	.77	.93	1.37	1.64	-.66	-.01
	-1.34	-1.04	.80	.04	-1.34	-1.34	-1.07	-.88	-.99	.55
	.01	.31	.15	1.34	.47	-.64	-.47	.64	.99	.91
	-.34	-.45	-.45	-1.45						
64 LUXEMBOURG	-1.58	-1.04	-1.45	-1.61	1.15	-1.58	.72	-1.64	.80	-1.29
	1.66	1.72	1.53	1.66	1.56	1.12	1.50	1.39	1.34	1.12
	-.69	-1.15	1.29	-.93	-.15	1.53	-1.20	-.96	-1.20	-.64
	1.47	-.72	.93	-.61	.01	.07	1.34	-1.07	-.31	.34
	-.61	-1.56	1.42	1.66	1.37	1.34	1.15	-.93	.99	-1.10
	.91	.74	1.20	-.99	1.12	-1.10	-.34	1.45	.69	-.66
	1.20	-.18	1.20	1.15	.85	-.09	-.09	-.26	-1.58	-1.50
	-.50	-.80	-1.42	-.26	-.66	-.12	1.23	.15	-.20	-1.56
	-1.56	-1.37	.39	-.34	1.61	-.47	1.61	-1.02	1.61	-.96
	1.34	.23	1.47	.58	1.39	.64	1.31	.66	-1.64	-.12
	-1.39	.31	-1.64	-.15	-.93	.18	-1.66	-.20	-.20	.20
	1.56	-.72	1.42	.04	1.56	1.47	-.45	.66	.01	1.39
	-1.20	1.26	1.15	.96	-.72	1.45	1.15	1.45	1.34	-1.12
	-1.20	-1.39	-1.31	.53	-1.61	-.61	-.45	-.50	-.93	-.74
	-.31	-.42	-.42	-.58						
65 MALAGASY REP	.01	1.39	.55	.72	-.93	1.18	-1.23	.58	.04	.77
	-1.45	-.96	-1.02	-.85	-.72	-.12	-1.39	-.36	-.72	-.85
	-1.12	-.47	-.07	.31	1.04	.34	-.80	.45	-1.04	-.77
	-1.12	.42	1.23	1.56	-.28	-.96	.09	-.01	1.23	-1.23
	-.18	-.96	-.85	-1.12	-.47	-.20	-.69	-.64	-.93	-1.07
	-1.34	.77	-1.34	-.91	-1.23	-1.37	-.26	-.47	1.37	-.50
	-.91	.26	-.66	-.88	-.66	-.42	-.18	-.39	1.10	.96
	.96	.93	-.18	-.23	-.64	-.09	.15	.18	-.18	-.53
	-.85	-.50	-.91	-.69	-.77	-.80	-.96	-.31	-.88	-1.02
	-.39	-1.50	-1.66	-.77	-.88	-.85	-1.04	-.85	.07	-.15
	-.31	-.64	-.15	-.47	-.64	-.99	-.18	-.55	-.23	-.15
	-.45	-.04	-.15	-.12	-.36	-.77	-1.56	-1.64	-.99	-1.29
	-1.12	-1.15	.66	.64	-.23	-.12	1.18	1.47	.64	-1.10

		-1.18	-1.37	-1.29	-1.47	-1.15	-.58	-.42	.66	-.91	-.72
		-.28	-.39	-.39	-1.42						
66	MALI	-.26	.01	-.39	1.12	-1.34	1.15	-1.69	1.69	1.61	.88
		-1.47	-1.20	-1.50	-1.56	-1.72	-.47	-.77	-1.56	-1.56	-1.56
		1.37	.69	-1.37	1.15	-.93	-.96	-1.02	-.93	.80	-1.07
		-1.50	.18	.58	-.69	-1.39	-1.50	-1.31	-.39	.04	-1.20
		-1.10	.07	-1.23	-1.58	-.91	-1.39	-1.39	-1.29	-1.42	-1.04
		-1.23	-1.26	-1.50	-.96	-1.07	.01	-.77	-1.07	.91	-1.64
		-.72	1.07	-1.18	-1.47	-.91	-1.34	-1.64	-1.64	1.12	.99
		.99	.96	.07	-.20	-.61	-1.37	-.66	.20	-.15	-.88
		-.99	-.85	-1.26	-1.26	-1.45	-1.37	-1.53	-.61	-1.20	-.23
		-.99	-1.10	-1.34	-1.37	-1.47	-1.50	-1.56	-1.47	-1.18	-1.50
		-.93	-1.29	-1.18	-1.47	-1.39	-1.50	-1.18	-1.47	-.50	-1.12
		-1.34	-1.29	-1.26	-1.10	-1.39	-1.39	.01	-.50	-1.23	-1.50
		-.20	-.88	-.31	.66	-.47	-.53	-.20	-.85	-.50	-.26
		-1.15	-.55	-.39	-1.45	-.36	-.55	-.39	-.47	-.88	-.69
		-.26	-.36	-.36	-1.39						
67	MAURITANIA	-1.34	1.66	1.64	1.04	-1.69	1.20	-1.53	1.20	1.47	1.58
		1.34	-1.64	-1.34	-.39	-.85	-.20	-.88	-1.69	-1.61	-1.61
		.04	.42	-1.47	1.50	-1.56	-1.12	-1.69	-.91	1.66	-1.53
		-.80	.39	1.42	1.66	-1.37	-1.47	1.04	1.66	.47	-1.18
		-1.61	-.45	-1.20	-1.64	-1.61	-1.37	-1.31	-1.66	-1.39	-1.45
		-1.10	-1.18	-1.58	-1.50	-1.15	1.02	-1.12	-.58	.45	-1.45
		-.77	-.07	-1.15	-1.45	-.88	-1.58	-1.42	-1.23	1.15	1.02
		1.02	.99	.09	-.18	-.58	-1.34	-.64	.23	-.12	-1.53
		-1.53	-1.64	-1.69	-1.50	-.74	-1.64	-.85	-.58	-1.18	-.61
		-1.10	-1.61	-1.39	-1.61	-.80	-1.07	.23	-1.37	-1.72	-1.61
		-1.72	-1.64	-1.72	-1.61	-1.37	-1.47	-1.72	-1.61	-1.58	-1.45
		-1.39	-1.47	-.66	-1.37	-1.15	-.88	-.23	-.23	-1.47	-1.10
		-.69	-.42	-.28	.69	-1.04	-.50	-1.04	-.83	-.96	-1.07
		-.15	-1.34	-1.26	-1.42	.72	-.53	-.36	1.37	-.85	.45
		-.23	-.34	-.34	-1.37						
68	MEXICO	1.37	1.56	1.45	1.39	-.26	1.53	-.77	1.10	.64	.47
		-1.23	-1.02	-.42	.74	.74	.77	1.15	.12	-.04	.12
		-.07	-.77	.77	-.91	-.12	1.15	1.42	-.88	-.64	1.29
		.53	-1.34	-1.56	.53	.31	1.02	-1.56	-1.37	1.39	.93
		.83	-.69	.91	.12	.23	.69	.72	1.37	.61	.47
		-.74	-.74	-.61	.23	-.55	-1.39	1.02	.04	-1.31	1.10
		.26	-.66	-.09	1.18	.69	1.12	.45	-.23	-.72	-1.07
		-1.02	-1.53	-1.29	-.15	-.55	-1.31	.18	.26	-.09	1.37
		.45	1.39	.20	1.04	.01	1.15	.12	1.37	.50	1.04
		.45	.99	.39	1.07	-.36	.93	-.61	1.02	1.53	1.10
		1.34	.26	1.39	.99	1.12	.31	1.45	.88	.83	1.18
		.58	1.42	.61	1.23	.58	.55	1.15	.91	1.23	.69
		1.15	.53	.69	1.47	.96	-.07	1.20	.18	.80	.36
		.42	.66	.66	-.58	-.34	-.50	-.34	-.45	.64	1.23
		-.20	-.31	-.31	.20						
69	MONGOLIA	-1.29	1.18	.58	1.31	-1.72	1.26	-1.72	.18	-.39	-.61
		.93	.99	-1.10	.55	.15	.66	.12	.64	-.20	.31
		.18	-.91	-1.58	.96	-1.53	-1.69	-1.66	.85	.15	-.88
		.50	.85	1.12	1.47	.34	-.23	-.15	.20	.20	-1.15
		-1.34	-.42	-.09	-.12	.20	-.88	-.47	-.12	.15	-.42
		1.37	1.39	-.96	-.58	.88	.96	-1.66	.74	-.09	-1.56
		-1.29	-1.58	-1.12	-1.42	-.85	.01	.96	.15	.28	-.09
		-.04	-.39	.12	-.12	-.53	1.37	-.61	.28	1.37	-.72
		.80	-.72	.23	.09	.09	.07	-.01	.01	-1.04	-.04
		.20	-.77	.12	-.58	.80	-.96	.42	-.88	-1.34	.18
		-1.34	-.85	-1.37	-.34	-.01	1.47	-1.31	-.07	-.99	-1.47
		.15	.31	.04	-1.47	.15	-1.61	.50	.69	.36	-.69
		-.07	.18	.28	-.99	1.69	-.47	-1.02	-.80	-.93	-1.04
		-.53	-1.31	-1.23	-.55	-1.12	-.47	-.31	-1.39	-.83	-.66
		-.18	-.28	-.28	-1.34						
70	MOROCCO	.72	.45	.61	.47	.04	.58	-.36	1.15	1.15	1.12
		-1.07	-1.10	-.04	-.74	-.61	-.77	-1.12	-1.07	-.99	-.93
		.47	.26	-1.23	1.34	-1.50	-.53	-.99	-.85	-1.39	.28
		-.47	-.12	-.77	-.88	-1.66	.15	-.36	-.50	.83	-1.12

	-.09	.93	.28	-.77	-.50	-.18	.45	-.34	-.91	.07
	-.26	-.23	-.09	-.04	-.12	.85	.01	-.07	.42	.15
	-.58	-.91	.12	.09	.26	.74	.28	.45	.61	-1.47
	.55	.53	.61	-.09	.83	1.39	-.58	.31	-.07	.91
	.61	.96	.34	-.09	-.39	-.09	-.53	.07	-.26	-.93
	-.93	.39	-.04	.04	-.47	.07	-.42	.04	.42	-.88
	.39	-.28	.26	-.91	-.07	-.64	.36	-1.02	.01	.74
	.34	.53	-.09	.66	.23	-.47	-.72	-.91	.12	-.55
	-.88	-1.26	-.85	.09	-1.31	-1.31	-.99	-.77	-1.50	.04
	.85	.34	.45	.96	.74	-.45	-.28	.69	1.50	.83
	-.15	-.26	1.34	.58						
71 NEPAL	.45	-.50	-.74	-.39	.58	-.99	1.34	.50	1.26	-.80
	.50	.42	.12	-1.42	-1.69	-1.39	-.85	-1.45	-1.47	-1.37
	.96	.80	-1.72	-.88	-1.47	-1.66	-1.18	-.83	1.47	-.50
	-1.37	.34	.28	-1.31	-1.34	-.20	.42	-.58	-.07	-1.10
	-1.26	-.15	-1.18	-1.45	1.02	-1.42	-1.37	-1.12	-1.45	-.39
	-.69	-.72	.15	-1.18	-1.58	-1.47	-1.53	-1.69	-1.69	-.64
	-1.10	-.34	-.50	-.85	-.69	.61	-.42	-.83	-1.10	-1.45
	-1.45	-1.64	.64	-.07	.85	1.42	-.55	.34	-.04	-.80
	-1.18	-.83	-1.42	.04	-.42	-.01	-.45	-1.18	-1.15	-.45
	-1.34	-1.34	-1.69	.61	-.42	.69	-.07	.69	-.64	-1.45
	-.26	-.96	-.50	-1.45	-.31	-.80	-.53	-1.45	-1.04	-1.58
	-1.02	.23	-.47	-1.58	-.72	-1.45	-.01	-.69	-1.26	-1.72
	-.15	-.15	-.69	-.88	-1.29	-1.29	-.18	-.74	-.47	.07
	-.34	-.91	.47	.18	1.12	-.42	-.26	-.42	-.80	1.07
	-.12	-.23	1.15	.42						
72 NETHERLANDS	.66	-.85	-.99	-1.18	1.64	-.74	1.29	-1.07	-1.50	-1.66
	1.07	1.10	.20	1.31	1.07	1.47	.28	1.42	1.26	1.45
	-.91	-1.39	.45	-.85	1.29	.61	1.12	.47	-.58	1.26
	1.26	1.61	1.47	.04	1.07	1.50	1.29	-1.66	-.58	1.39
	1.37	-1.47	1.37	1.26	.83	1.04	1.18	1.18	1.12	.77
	1.07	1.02	1.61	.96	1.39	.72	1.37	1.42	1.29	1.07
	1.04	-.64	1.66	1.20	1.66	.50	-.69	-.36	-1.56	-1.42
	-1.42	-1.72	-1.66	-.04	-.50	-.07	1.26	.36	-.01	1.04
	1.45	1.18	1.56	1.42	1.37	1.45	1.37	.39	1.53	1.47
	1.69	1.42	1.42	1.53	1.58	1.50	1.64	1.50	.61	.01
	1.12	1.31	.50	.36	1.23	1.53	.72	.53	1.07	1.39
	1.26	1.20	1.23	1.34	1.29	1.29	.85	1.07	1.26	1.26
	1.45	1.66	-.91	1.64	.34	1.64	1.23	1.50	1.37	.26
	-.31	.04	-1.20	.99	-1.10	-.39	-.23	1.39	-.77	-.64
	1.72	-.20	-.26	.45						
73 NEW ZEALAND	-.77	-.18	1.69	.12	-.99	.42	-1.15	-.42	-.36	-1.45
	.77	.88	1.42	1.56	.99	1.39	1.61	1.45	1.50	1.53
	.15	-1.31	.50	-.83	1.53	.15	.85	.50	-1.58	.72
	1.50	-.34	-.07	-.23	-.15	.80	.04	-.34	1.15	.83
	.93	.09	.31	1.37	.61	1.72	1.69	.42	1.56	-.58
	.28	.07	-.39	.04	1.23	-.55	.74	1.23	-.07	1.02
	1.61	1.37	.72	1.23	1.15	-.99	-1.10	-.99	-1.20	-.34
	-.36	-.66	-1.50	-.01	-.47	-.04	1.29	.39	1.39	.18
	1.64	.31	1.61	.85	1.64	.83	1.66	.66	.61	.99
	1.66	1.12	1.66	.72	1.45	.83	1.42	.74	-.34	1.53
	.26	1.45	-.28	1.61	.34	1.29	-.26	1.58	.31	1.12
	1.69	1.10	1.64	1.10	1.66	1.64	-.39	1.04	.53	1.02
	.50	1.58	1.18	.26	-.45	.88	1.26	1.53	1.64	.83
	-1.12	-.88	-1.18	-1.39	-.83	-.36	-.20	1.42	.26	-.61
	-.09	-.18	-.23	-1.31						
74 NICARAGUA	-1.12	1.04	1.04	-.42	-.80	-1.02	-.28	-.77	-1.23	.42
	-1.64	-1.31	1.20	.23	-.39	-.09	.20	.04	-.69	-.55
	-.55	-1.20	.83	-.80	.28	1.12	-.42	-.80	.74	-.80
	.26	-.77	-.26	1.12	.80	-.66	.96	.04	.58	-.15
	-1.07	1.12	-.31	.15	-.53	.28	.18	.20	.07	-.72
	.04	.12	-.34	-1.07	-.28	-.96	-1.64	-.45	-1.47	-.26
	.74	.88	.45	-.83	.20	-.85	.99	.91	-.07	-.77
	-.69	-1.07	.77	.01	-.45	-1.29	.20	.42	.01	-.61
	.28	-.42	.58	-1.02	-.31	-1.07	-.47	-.83	-.42	-.09
	-.12	-.85	-.34	-.53	.50	-.47	.64	-.53	-1.04	.28

	-1.10	-.55	-1.07	-.07	-.53	-.15	-1.07	-.12	-.58	-.80
	-.18	-1.26	-.69	-.91	-.28	.34	-1.34	-1.12	-.74	-.26
	.15	-.12	.55	.12	-.77	.42	-.15	.20	.31	.18
	.28	.45	.80	.55	-1.58	-.34	-.18	.72	-.74	-.58
	-.07	1.23	-.20	.01						
75 NIGER	-.58	1.20	1.31	1.20	-1.45	.72	-1.20	1.56	1.56	1.07
	-.80	-.39	-.58	-1.66	-1.31	-1.18	-.99	-1.66	-1.64	-1.69
	1.12	1.34	-1.56	1.23	-1.45	-1.34	-1.15	-.77	1.64	-1.15
	-1.29	-.01	1.15	1.50	-1.53	-1.45	-.91	1.04	1.58	-1.07
	-1.15	1.69	-1.72	-1.72	.09	-1.69	-1.72	-1.47	-1.58	-1.42
	-1.47	-1.45	-1.61	-1.15	-1.20	-1.23	-1.26	-1.45	-1.45	-.83
	-.42	.91	-1.10	-.80	-.83	-1.31	-1.56	-1.50	1.18	1.04
	1.04	1.02	.15	.04	-.42	-1.26	-.53	.45	.04	-1.50
	-1.50	-1.61	-1.66	-1.37	-1.39	-1.53	-1.47	-1.50	-1.50	-1.47
	-1.64	-1.42	-1.53	-1.39	-1.39	-1.42	-1.34	-1.45	-1.53	-1.64
	-1.64	-1.66	-1.58	-1.64	-1.34	-1.45	-1.58	-1.64	-1.56	-1.23
	-1.53	-1.23	-1.15	-1.20	-1.34	-1.29	-.31	-.58	-1.56	-1.58
	-.66	-.83	-.26	.72	-.85	-.45	-.96	-.72	-.91	-1.02
	-1.10	-.09	.26	-1.37	-1.07	-.31	1.47	-1.37	-.72	-.55
	-.04	-.15	1.20	-.55						
76 NIGERIA	1.47	-.28	-.20	.93	.39	.96	.80	1.61	.34	.58
	-.01	-.15	-1.31	-1.10	-1.50	-1.15	-1.64	-.47	-1.15	-1.23
	1.53	1.69	-.64	1.02	.42	-.28	1.23	-.74	-1.53	.64
	-1.23	.66	-.99	.01	.64	.58	-.58	-.64	.66	-1.04
	.74	1.58	-1.15	-1.37	.47	.45	-.42	-.23	-1.34	.93
	-1.58	-1.58	-1.07	-.26	-1.42	.47	.20	-1.39	-1.34	.77
	-.96	.18	-.12	.12	-.12	.77	-1.61	-1.56	1.20	1.07
	1.07	1.04	1.31	.07	1.29	-.01	.23	.47	.07	.53
	-1.04	.74	-1.15	-.04	-1.50	.15	-1.45	.31	-.34	.07
	-1.39	.15	-1.26	.34	-1.37	.47	-1.18	.42	1.07	-1.39
	.55	-1.31	.77	-1.37	-.12	-1.12	1.02	-1.37	.42	.15
	-1.47	-.01	-1.58	.18	-1.58	-1.50	.91	.07	.18	-1.18
	-.74	-1.45	-.53	-.04	1.15	.50	1.29	.23	.66	.66
	1.66	1.61	1.61	-.53	1.15	1.29	1.64	-.39	1.04	.93
	-.01	1.26	1.37	1.31						
77 NORWAY	-.42	-1.26	-.50	.31	-.83	-1.31	1.12	-1.50	.18	-1.61
	1.18	1.39	.66	1.53	1.18	1.31	1.18	1.66	1.29	1.47
	-1.37	-.85	1.61	-.77	1.69	-1.45	-.39	.93	-1.69	.83
	1.39	1.56	1.66	.36	1.02	1.12	.80	-1.47	-.42	.96
	1.12	-.93	.80	1.69	1.34	.99	.99	.55	1.20	-.15
	.85	.80	-.12	.50	1.45	.61	1.04	1.56	1.12	.88
	1.29	.20	1.31	1.26	1.69	.20	.31	.01	-1.37	-.39
	-.39	-.69	-1.64	.09	-.39	.01	1.31	.50	.09	-.12
	.42	-.04	.28	.88	1.42	.85	1.50	.72	.55	.93
	1.45	1.07	1.50	1.18	1.56	1.04	1.45	1.12	-.47	-.18
	.47	1.39	-.34	.45	.26	.72	-.31	.42	.58	1.07
	1.34	1.02	1.45	1.04	1.34	1.45	.58	1.18	.88	1.34
	.83	1.72	1.20	1.31	.36	1.31	1.31	1.56	1.39	.85
	-1.07	-.85	-1.15	.58	-.80	-.28	-.15	-.36	.28	-.53
	.01	-.12	-.18	-.23						
78 PAKISTAN	1.58	-.15	-.12	1.02	.85	.99	1.18	.83	1.23	1.42
	-1.02	-.28	-1.29	-.69	-1.66	-1.37	-1.23	-.85	-1.20	-1.18
	.72	1.31	-1.39	1.47	-.74	-1.31	1.31	-.72	.34	1.10
	-.85	1.10	-.85	.42	-.77	.66	-1.53	.74	-1.69	.55
	.66	1.42	-.83	.47	.66	-.36	-.99	1.26	-.61	1.23
	-.42	-.42	.53	.91	-.23	-.07	.66	-1.31	-1.50	.04
	-1.64	-1.56	.15	1.29	-.36	1.56	-.39	-.58	.12	.18
	.28	.04	1.72	.12	-.36	.04	.26	.53	1.42	1.39
	-.66	.61	-.66	.39	-1.61	.55	-1.56	1.12	.47	.91
	-.31	.34	-1.20	.66	-1.42	.18	-1.50	.50	1.50	-1.20
	1.53	.64	1.47	-1.07	1.42	.01	1.53	-1.07	1.23	.55
	-1.29	.50	-1.56	.47	-1.47	-.93	.26	-.96	.72	-.91
	.69	-1.31	.53	-.53	.39	.26	1.34	.26	.69	1.53
	1.58	.96	1.45	-1.34	1.18	-.26	1.31	.74	.66	1.50
	.04	-.09	-.15	1.42						
79 PANAMA	-1.26	1.23	.64	-.91	-.55	-1.15	-.26	.45	-.15	.12

	-.45	-.47	-.26	.53	1.61	.83	.31	.39	.66	.74
	-.15	-1.04	1.15	-.74	.45	1.31	-.12	.96	.36	-.69
	.58	-.69	-.12	1.10	.91	-.80	.47	.96	.93	-.12
	-1.31	.45	-.07	.18	-.23	.01	-.04	-.61	.55	-1.02
	-.50	-.53	-.50	-1.61	-1.50	-1.66	-.39	.72	.36	-.42
	.69	.28	1.29	1.31	.80	-.88	1.10	1.04	-.18	-.42
	-.42	-.72	-.93	.15	-.34	-1.23	.28	.55	.12	-.50
	1.31	-.45	1.26	-.77	.36	-.85	.47	-1.07	-.55	.36
	.64	-.01	.66	-.45	.96	-.93	.34	-.69	-1.07	1.23
	-.55	.80	-1.04	1.23	-.20	.91	-1.04	1.23	-.88	-.28
	.72	-.80	.45	-.45	.66	.61	.45	.88	-.07	.77
	.09	.45	1.69	1.34	-.96	1.53	1.37	.28	.83	1.10
	1.39	.36	.53	.20	-1.56	-.23	.96	-.34	.69	-.50
	.07	-.07	-.12	-.20						
80 PARAGUAY	-.96	.80	.23	.45	-1.23	.26	-1.18	-.83	.93	.85
	-1.31	-1.07	1.07	.04	-.42	-.39	-.04	.50	-.01	-.01
	-.72	.85	1.20	-.72	-.39	1.50	-.01	.53	1.42	-.96
	-.28	-.88	-.72	-.20	-1.50	-1.29	-1.07	.09	-.09	.07
	-.80	1.20	-.28	-.45	.12	.61	.34	-.09	-.12	-.36
	.96	1.10	-.36	-.77	-.18	-.61	-1.04	-.96	-1.42	-1.42
	-.09	-1.37	.61	-.77	.36	-.45	1.53	1.53	-1.12	-1.39
	-1.15	-1.50	1.56	.18	-.31	-1.20	-.50	.58	.15	-.58
	.09	-.61	-.12	-1.15	-.66	-1.39	-.99	-.09	-.53	-1.45
	-1.42	-.74	-.45	-1.31	-.85	-1.10	-.58	-1.26	-.72	1.50
	-.74	-.47	-.77	1.12	-.28	.12	-.77	1.04	-.66	-1.10
	-1.04	-1.10	-.72	-1.07	-.85	-.36	.15	-.07	-1.04	-.72
	-.01	-.55	.31	-1.15	-.58	.45	-.12	.31	.34	-.99
	-.50	-.15	-.28	-1.31	-1.53	-.20	-.12	.77	-.69	-.47
	.09	-.04	-.09	-1.29						
81 PERU	.58	.83	.26	1.26	-1.10	.85	-.53	-.20	-.55	1.02
	-.58	-.50	.69	.28	.69	.28	.58	.23	.12	.36
	.58	1.15	1.10	-.69	-.34	1.45	1.45	-.69	.99	.55
	.31	1.72	1.50	.83	.72	.50	-.47	-.74	.09	.72
	.20	-.34	.39	.91	-.58	-.09	-.09	.61	.45	.20
	.07	.01	-.53	.12	.09	-.04	.47	.07	-.93	.72
	.20	-.31	1.45	1.34	1.58	.58	-.26	-.20	-.39	-1.02
	-.99	-1.34	-1.61	.20	-.28	-1.18	1.34	.61	1.45	.85
	.66	.88	.47	.45	.15	.47	.20	.45	-.64	-.77
	-.45	.31	.07	.28	.15	.34	.15	.28	.83	1.15
	.69	.55	.55	1.15	.85	.61	.77	1.15	-.12	.69
	.39	.83	.50	.72	.39	-.04	.55	.34	.55	.36
	.12	.09	.20	-.01	.07	1.50	1.39	.88	.99	-.23
	-.12	1.20	1.20	1.02	.96	1.31	-.09	.80	.31	1.26
	1.34	-.01	-.07	-.36						
82 PHILIPPINES	1.34	1.26	1.34	.20	.93	.28	1.02	.72	.61	.64
	-1.15	-1.26	-.99	-.72	-.77	-.61	-1.26	.61	.26	1.10
	1.18	1.42	.58	.20	.83	.99	1.26	-.66	.50	.69
	-.58	1.20	-.15	-.07	.09	.69	-.53	-.85	1.31	.69
	.31	1.10	.12	-.28	-.88	-.83	-1.12	1.42	.74	-.07
	-.96	-.93	.01	-.18	-.99	-1.07	.93	.12	1.31	.26
	-1.23	-1.31	.47	1.37	1.47	.28	.07	-1.53	-.20	.09
	.20	-.04	-1.15	.23	-.26	-1.15	1.37	.64	.18	1.02
	-.23	.07	-.23	.15	-1.12	.01	-1.07	-.20	-.28	.55
	-.36	.42	-.55	.42	-.64	.50	-.72	.55	1.47	1.58
	1.37	.83	1.37	1.42	1.53	1.56	1.42	1.42	.45	.77
	-.47	.91	-.58	.83	-.47	-.07	-.85	-1.31	.50	-.34
	.18	-1.10	-.74	.83	-.26	.64	1.42	.91	1.42	1.26
	-.09	1.53	.93	-.50	-.77	-.18	1.34	1.45	1.07	-.45
	.12	.01	-.04	-.53						
83 POLAND	1.29	-.99	-.72	.26	.91	.88	.23	-.88	-1.56	.04
	1.04	.91	-.34	.93	.64	.88	.53	1.20	1.10	1.29
	-1.53	-1.07	1.02	-.66	-.20	1.34	-.50	1.18	-.99	1.45
	1.04	-.80	-1.34	.61	1.42	1.31	-1.29	-.55	-.39	1.47
	1.31	.36	1.61	.50	.55	1.64	1.47	1.53	1.23	1.26
	.88	.85	1.04	1.37	1.29	.28	1.47	1.12	1.34	1.58
	1.39	1.47	-1.07	-.74	-1.39	1.18	-.66	-.34	-.74	-.15

	-.12	-.15	-.45	.26	-.23	1.45	-.47	.66	.20	1.34
	.77	1.42	.85	1.31	.61	1.31	.58	1.39	1.45	1.15
	.72	1.18	.72	1.20	.34	1.26	.47	1.26	1.37	1.31
	.96	-.20	1.26	.91	1.45	1.15	1.31	.96	1.56	.93
	-.09	1.15	.20	.96	-.04	1.02	1.47	1.47	1.50	1.31
	1.39	1.12	.47	-1.66	1.34	-.42	-.93	-.69	-.88	.96
	-.23	-.39	.96	-.47	-.01	-.15	-.07	-.31	1.29	-.42
	.15	.04	.93	-.18						
84 PORTUGAL	.34	-1.23	-1.53	-.85	.83	-.36	.64	-.55	.58	.50
	1.10	1.15	-.72	.39	.28	.34	-.09	.18	.01	.18
	-1.66	-1.66	1.18	-.64	-.80	1.56	.01	-.64	-.15	.50
	.39	.45	-.20	.74	1.26	.55	.15	-1.42	-1.26	1.02
	.50	-.12	1.15	.20	1.64	.58	.74	.85	.93	.85
	1.31	1.23	1.39	.45	.99	1.15	.09	.01	-1.29	.47
	.09	-.88	-1.04	-.72	-1.20	.15	-.47	-.15	-1.23	-1.37
	-1.39	-.34	-1.18	.28	-.20	.07	-.45	.69	.23	.15
	-.15	.18	-.36	.26	.28	.23	.28	.58	1.15	.74
	.85	.93	.91	.45	.58	.23	.26	.39	.28	-.64
	.31	.01	.09	-.64	.50	.45	.28	-.61	.77	.88
	.64	.69	.58	.85	.61	.39	-.64	-.88	.34	.23
	1.29	1.61	1.23	1.61	-.12	-.39	-.91	-.66	-.85	.28
	-.20	-.01	-.50	-.45	-.31	-.12	.99	.83	.96	-.39
	.18	.07	-.01	.69						
85 ROMANIA	.99	-1.42	-1.20	-.07	.72	.50	-.07	-1.23	-.53	.09
	1.53	1.29	-.55	.91	.50	.55	.88	1.47	1.12	1.31
	-.26	-.74	1.66	-.20	.53	.07	-.77	1.66	.04	1.15
	.93	-.93	-1.23	1.26	1.72	.88	-.50	-.83	.39	.85
	1.15	.74	1.56	.80	1.69	1.37	1.45	1.47	1.39	1.04
	.99	.91	1.02	.83	1.02	-.83	1.26	1.02	1.07	1.45
	1.18	1.29	-1.02	-.69	-1.61	1.29	1.02	1.29	-.47	-.64
	-.55	.07	1.04	.31	-.18	1.47	-.42	.72	.26	.99
	.07	1.04	-.09	1.37	1.15	1.34	1.12	1.10	1.20	.72
	.42	.88	.50	.77	.09	.91	.20	.80	1.15	1.12
	.85	.07	.91	.93	1.18	1.07	1.15	.93	1.31	-.42
	-1.26	.04	-1.04	-.09	-1.23	.47	1.18	1.26	1.20	.93
	1.26	1.18	-1.37	-1.56	1.37	-.36	-.88	-.64	-.83	-.20
	-1.04	-.83	-1.12	.23	.26	-.09	-.04	-.28	.34	-.36
	.20	.09	.01	1.18						
86 RWANDA	-.66	.99	1.07	-1.34	1.07	-.96	.36	1.64	1.39	-.53
	-.18	-1.37	-.01	-.66	-.58	-.93	-1.47	-1.42	-.55	-.77
	-.77	-.80	-.12	.04	.50	.42	-.74	-.61	.69	-1.39
	-1.64	-.04	1.10	1.45	-1.31	-1.66	-1.12	1.23	.53	-1.02
	-1.53	-.66	-1.39	-1.04	-1.37	-1.58	-1.47	-1.64	-1.72	-1.23
	-1.26	-1.31	-.23	-1.58	-1.61	-1.45	-1.42	-1.47	-1.26	-1.66
	-.85	-.04	-.99	.15	-.80	-1.61	-1.69	-1.66	1.42	1.37
	1.37	1.34	.31	.34	.88	-1.12	-.39	.74	.28	-1.47
	-1.47	-1.58	-1.64	.20	-.28	.28	-.28	-1.47	-1.47	-.58
	-1.37	-1.58	-1.72	.69	-.26	.74	.04	.72	-.69	.09
	-1.56	-1.61	-.80	-.50	-1.31	-1.42	-.80	-.58	-1.53	-1.34
	-1.66	-1.58	-1.69	-1.39	-1.69	-.99	-.20	-.53	-1.45	-1.53
	-.64	-.07	-1.34	-1.31	.09	-1.04	-.85	-.61	-.31	-.96
	-1.02	.39	1.66	-1.29	-1.04	-.07	-.01	-1.34	-.66	-.34
	.23	.12	1.39	-1.26						
87 SAUDI ARABIA	.04	.04	-1.29	1.42	-1.42	1.47	-1.47	-1.04	-1.20	1.69
	.26	-1.58	-.83	-1.23	.01	-.53	-.55	-1.18	-1.50	-1.50
	-1.18	-1.64	-1.69	1.66	-1.42	-1.64	-1.64	-.58	-.55	.01
	-.20	.72	.61	-.66	-1.58	.74	1.56	-.91	-.72	-.99
	-.15	-.91	-.58	-1.56	-1.58	-1.15	-.93	.47	-.09	-.20
	.12	-.04	-.93	.18	.74	1.64	.28	.39	1.45	.53
	.28	.77	-.53	-.66	-.45	.34	-.12	.28	1.56	-.45
	.01	-.26	.66	.36	-.15	1.50	-1.47	-1.47	-1.47	.01
	-.18	.09	-.20	.55	.66	.45	.66	-.85	-1.23	-1.18
	-1.07	-.26	-.66	.74	.07	.80	.07	.77	-.96	-1.47
	-.91	-1.37	-.96	-1.50	-.61	-1.02	-.96	-1.50	.55	.07
	-.12	.34	.23	.23	.01	-.45	1.50	1.72	.09	-.04
	.39	.61	-.66	1.04	-1.26	-1.26	-.83	-.58	-1.47	-.93

	-.99	-.07	-1.10	-.42	.28	-.04	.01	-1.31	-.64	-.31
	.26	.15	1.45	-.34						
88 SENEGAL	-.55	.09	.07	-.18	-.47	-.20	-.47	1.37	1.07	1.10
	-.39	.18	.55	-1.20	-.47	-.04	-.74	-1.39	-1.23	-1.26
	1.07	.23	-.96	1.26	-1.12	-.26	-.96	-.55	1.18	-.55
	-.50	-1.47	.66	-.36	-.74	-.72	.28	.31	1.69	-.96
	.01	.39	-.72	-1.34	-.42	-1.23	-1.07	-1.20	-1.10	-.88
	-.93	-.96	-.77	-.66	-.39	1.29	-.45	-.31	-.31	-.80
	-.64	-.85	-.96	.18	-1.26	-.83	-.64	-.64	1.23	1.10
	1.10	1.07	.18	.39	.91	-1.10	-.36	.77	.31	-.42
	-.26	-.47	-.45	-.31	.07	-.45	-.04	-.91	-.80	.20
	-.15	-.36	-.36	-.50	-.18	-.58	-.23	-.61	-.99	-1.26
	-.64	-.69	-1.02	-1.20	-.58	-.77	-1.02	-1.20	-.07	-.34
	-.07	-.34	-.01	-.23	-.09	-.58	.28	.01	-.64	-.66
	.07	.12	-.23	.74	-.42	-.34	-.09	-.55	-.45	.09
	.77	-1.29	.09	.61	-.74	-.01	1.37	.85	-.61	1.29
	.28	1.29	.96	-1.23						
89 SIERRA LEONE	-.91	-.12	-.36	-.93	.07	-.04	-.80	.01	-.34	.31
	.61	.64	-1.26	-1.07	-.66	-1.12	-1.61	-1.15	-1.42	-1.47
	1.34	-.31	-.93	.80	.26	-.91	.18	-.53	.47	-1.02
	-.64	.23	.50	-.99	-.72	-.83	1.39	1.37	1.61	-.93
	-.50	.85	.50	-.09	.72	.26	-1.58	.01	-.22	-1.20
	-1.12	-1.15	-.69	-1.37	-1.34	-1.12	-.99	-.91	-.91	-.99
	-.31	-.28	-.28	-.64	-.28	-1.18	-1.31	-1.10	1.34	1.20
	1.20	1.18	.34	.42	-.12	.09	.31	.80	.34	-1.02
	-.83	-1.02	-1.02	-1.07	-.69	-1.23	-.77	-.66	.31	-1.31
	-1.04	-1.04	-.88	-.93	-.20	-.88	-.18	-1.04	-1.37	-1.34
	-1.20	-.99	-1.34	-1.29	-.91	-.93	-1.37	-1.29	-.69	-.99
	-.66	-1.42	-1.02	-.99	-.88	-.66	.09	-.20	-1.10	-1.04
	-1.56	-1.42	-1.39	-.83	-.04	-.01	-.07	.34	-.12	-.91
	.20	-1.26	-.26	.64	.50	1.34	.04	-.26	.72	-.28
	1.61	.18	.04	.04						
90 SOMALIA	-.85	1.64	-.34	.77	-1.31	.93	-1.39	-1.02	-1.18	1.26
	.28	-1.69	-1.47	-1.47	-1.29	-1.02	-1.42	-1.53	-1.69	-1.66
	-1.04	-.55	-1.61	1.64	-1.39	-1.50	-1.34	-.50	.26	-1.42
	-1.56	-.09	1.34	1.64	-.12	-1.37	1.10	.61	1.34	-.91
	-1.56	-.88	-1.12	-1.69	-1.66	-.99	-.34	-.04	-.72	-.74
	-.47	-.50	-1.10	1.53	-.53	.93	-1.50	-1.58	-1.58	-1.20
	-1.18	.36	-.20	-.61	-.23	-.74	.34	.55	1.26	1.12
	1.12	1.10	.20	.45	-.09	.12	.34	.83	.36	-1.45
	-1.45	-.93	-.96	-1.47	-1.26	-1.45	-1.31	-1.45	-1.45	-.36
	-.85	-1.23	-1.12	-1.29	-1.02	-1.31	-1.15	-1.34	-1.66	-1.72
	-1.37	-1.39	-1.69	-1.69	-1.29	-1.39	-1.69	-1.69	-1.50	-1.07
	-1.12	-1.07	-.83	-1.04	-1.02	-1.37	-.09	-.47	-1.34	-1.45
	-1.61	-1.58	.07	-.34	-.18	.28	-.04	1.58	1.02	-.88
	.23	-.36	-.07	-.39	-1.02	.01	.07	-.23	.74	-.26
	1.37	.20	.07	-.15						
91 SOUTH AFRICA	.91	.12	.18	1.15	-.64	1.50	-1.26	.20	-.31	-.50
	.31	.26	.09	.09	.47	-1.56	.36	-.34	-.18	-.34
	1.56	1.61	.15	.07	1.26	-.18	1.64	.55	-.91	1.04
	.80	.91	-.23	.50	.23	1.18	-.23	-1.53	.55	1.07
	1.02	-1.39	1.18	1.29	.50	.93	.93	.93	.58	-.28
	-.80	-.85	-.74	.64	.64	.39	.91	.55	-.77	.50
	-.50	-1.47	.20	-.58	.31	1.37	1.50	1.58	.01	-.31
	-.28	-.31	.36	.47	-.07	.15	1.39	.85	.39	1.12
	.99	1.20	1.15	.93	.58	1.02	.69	1.34	.72	1.12
	1.02	1.15	.96	1.23	.77	1.07	.61	1.18	1.04	1.04
	.99	.74	.88	1.07	.80	.20	1.10	1.02	1.15	1.34
	1.12	1.26	1.02	1.31	1.12	.69	1.20	1.29	1.34	1.15
	.53	.23	-.83	.23	.66	.36	1.45	.36	1.04	1.07
	.61	.69	.61	1.04	-.28	.04	1.02	1.47	1.45	1.10
	.31	.23	1.23	1.26						
92 SPAIN	1.31	-1.20	-1.26	.58	.42	1.12	-.34	-.96	-.28	-.15
	1.26	1.26	.01	.85	.45	.85	1.31	.31	.28	.53
	.26	.47	1.69	-.61	-1.10	1.72	-.18	-.47	-.42	1.23
	.72	1.37	.09	1.15	1.45	1.20	-1.15	-1.02	-1.45	1.12

	1.04	-.09	.74	.23	1.29	.88	.80	1.56	1.26	1.20
	.77	.50	.83	.88	.69	-.36	.83	-.01	-1.56	1.20
	.58	-.01	-.93	-1.39	-1.10	1.34	.36	.74	-1.31	-1.34
	-1.37	-.23	-1.07	.50	.93	1.53	-.34	-1.31	-1.45	1.47
	1.53	1.50	1.53	1.20	.55	1.18	.50	1.29	1.02	1.45
	1.18	1.45	1.12	1.37	.47	.72	-.47	1.20	1.18	-.34
	1.29	.61	.93	-.23	1.10	.47	1.18	-.23	1.20	1.20
	.74	1.37	.69	1.26	.74	.80	.83	.39	1.15	.72
	1.56	1.50	-.55	.99	1.50	-.31	-.80	-.53	-.80	1.56
	1.26	.74	-.47	-1.26	-.26	.07	.09	.88	1.34	.96
	.34	.26	.09	1.50						
93 SUDAN	.74	.58	.72	1.50	-1.20	1.04	-.72	1.39	1.29	.83
	-.99	-1.61	-1.45	-.12	-1.15	-1.10	-1.20	-1.04	-1.53	-1.53
	1.15	1.02	-1.15	1.12	-.31	-.61	-.64	-.45	.53	-.04
	-.93	-.85	-1.15	-.50	-.45	-.42	-.61	.50	-1.64	-.88
	.34	1.53	-1.66	-1.02	1.66	-.53	.61	-.83	-1.29	-.50
	-.85	-.88	-1.26	-.39	-.93	.80	-.04	-.93	.04	.23
	-.47	.47	1.26	.20	.91	-.28	-1.29	-1.34	.53	.58
	.58	.55	-.34	.53	.96	.18	.36	.88	.42	-.55
	-1.15	-.31	-1.12	-.23	-1.02	-.18	-.88	.91	-.72	.28
	-.61	-.12	-.80	-.39	-1.15	-.20	-1.10	-.31	-.45	-1.53
	-.04	-.91	-.45	-1.53	-.15	-.74	-.45	-1.53	-.91	-.55
	-1.20	-.36	-1.18	-.42	-1.26	-1.04	.42	-.15	-.26	-1.02
	.26	-.47	.45	-.18	-1.23	-1.23	-.01	-.50	-.28	1.50
	1.34	1.26	1.39	1.07	1.20	1.53	.12	-.20	1.10	.99
	1.39	1.31	.12	1.20						
94 SWEDEN	.15	-1.39	-1.42	.53	-.53	-.45	.53	-1.72	.50	-1.69
	1.61	1.64	.26	1.72	1.58	1.66	.61	1.69	1.37	1.15
	-1.02	-1.10	1.72	-.58	1.72	-1.23	.20	.58	-1.02	1.31
	1.66	1.66	1.64	.07	.93	1.45	.23	-1.29	-1.29	1.45
	1.39	-1.53	1.20	1.31	1.39	1.15	1.07	.88	1.02	1.02
	1.56	1.42	.77	1.10	1.64	.83	1.42	1.69	1.61	1.47
	1.64	1.10	1.18	1.39	1.64	.47	.18	-.09	-1.34	-.36
	-1.34	-1.56	-1.69	.55	-.04	.20	1.42	.91	.45	.42
	.55	.80	1.29	1.47	1.72	1.47	1.72	1.20	.93	1.29
	1.47	1.50	1.69	1.45	1.50	1.45	1.61	1.45	.26	-.31
	.36	.42	.07	-.28	.88	1.20	.26	-.09	.96	1.47
	1.61	1.04	1.12	1.45	1.61	1.66	.53	.80	1.18	1.50
	1.34	1.69	1.26	1.37	1.04	1.20	1.47	1.61	1.66	-.18
	.04	-1.23	-1.07	-1.23	-1.50	.09	.15	-.18	.36	.47
	.36	.28	.15	-1.20						
95 SWITZERLAND	-.04	-.09	-.69	-1.12	1.20	-.77	.91	-1.45	.47	-1.56
	1.64	1.58	.85	1.50	1.12	1.20	.77	1.72	.31	.07
	.36	.91	.80	-.55	1.39	.72	.34	.61	-1.31	1.12
	1.58	1.53	1.53	.26	.83	1.42	.58	-1.20	-1.56	1.50
	1.45	-.31	1.23	1.64	1.61	1.58	1.31	.91	1.53	1.58
	1.72	1.69	1.72	.66	1.34	-.28	1.15	1.39	.18	1.15
	1.42	.31	1.64	1.42	1.72	-.47	-.93	-.42	-1.53	-1.31
	-1.31	-.93	-1.37	.58	-.01	.23	1.45	.93	.47	.20
	.58	.42	.64	.80	1.10	.77	1.10	.80	1.58	1.34
	1.64	1.39	1.64	1.42	1.61	1.42	1.58	1.42	-.36	-1.10
	.66	1.34	-.18	-.53	.47	.74	-.15	-.45	1.12	1.26
	1.47	.77	.96	1.18	1.42	1.56	-.42	.36	.91	1.10
	1.31	.04	.77	1.56	.93	1.72	1.50	1.64	1.45	-.85
	-.47	-.53	-1.04	1.37	-.72	.12	.18	1.61	.39	-.23
	.39	.31	.18	-1.18						
96 SYRIA	-.07	.85	1.37	-.26	-.09	.36	-.74	-.61	-.96	.99
	-1.58	-.80	.88	-.55	1.39	.09	-.58	-.31	-.28	-.20
	-.31	-.50	-.61	1.20	-.91	-.23	-.28	1.42	-.12	-.09
	-.39	.53	.15	1.31	1.58	-.53	-.34	.26	-1.04	-.85
	-.77	1.18	-.69	.83	-1.45	.09	.50	-.39	-.23	.42
	1.15	1.18	.72	-.12	.66	1.61	.12	.45	1.58	.74
	.88	1.58	-.72	-1.37	-1.29	-.36	.64	.47	.23	.12
	.09	-.18	1.34	1.47	1.61	1.56	-1.45	-1.45	-1.42	.31
	1.04	.45	1.10	-.39	-.50	-.28	-.36	-.23	.01	-1.12
	-.53	.20	.26	-.36	-.28	-.39	-.45	-.42	.09	.42

	.42	1.04	.04	.58	.55	1.10	.23	.64	-.47	-.39
	-.50	-.50	-.74	-.36	-.53	-.55	-1.53	-1.61	.07	-.09
	-.80	.26	-1.15	-.69	-1.20	-1.20	-.77	-.47	-.77	1.12
	1.20	.80	1.31	1.66	.99	1.56	1.04	-1.29	1.53	1.58
	1.64	1.69	1.58	1.53						
97 THAILAND	1.23	1.47	1.10	.61	.36	.23	1.04	.04	-.93	-.12
	-.28	-.26	-1.07	-.83	-.55	-.26	-.42	.53	-.53	-.74
	.77	.72	-1.45	.23	-1.07	-1.20	-.36	-.42	1.37	.53
	-.74	1.69	1.29	.96	.74	.47	-.31	-.09	-.85	.39
	.42	1.02	-.50	1.34	.42	-.31	-1.10	.34	-.74	.83
	.09	-.01	.55	-.15	-.91	-.18	.23	-1.10	-1.02	.12
	-1.34	-1.23	-.04	.23	.04	1.23	.09	.42	.58	-1.29
	-1.29	-.91	1.66	1.50	.01	1.58	-.31	-1.29	-1.39	.80
	-.64	.77	-.77	.23	-.88	.18	-.93	.55	.26	-.54
	-1.47	.18	-.85	.31	-.83	.31	-.80	.26	1.29	.53
	.80	-.53	1.20	.15	.74	-.18	1.23	.09	.74	.23
	-1.07	.61	-.77	.39	-.99	-.91	-.93	-1.42	.23	-.83
	.72	-.45	.61	1.53	-1.18	-1.18	-.74	-.45	-.74	-.83
	-.96	.88	.64	-.36	-1.47	.15	.20	-1.26	-.58	-.20
	.42	.34	.20	.61						
98 TOGO	-1.15	.34	.66	-1.02	-.07	-.69	-.39	1.66	1.58	-.28
	-1.66	-.66	-.31	-1.18	-1.12	-.69	-.83	-1.37	-.93	-1.02
	1.02	1.39	-.31	.34	.55	.28	-1.10	-.39	1.29	-1.37
	-1.04	.12	.77	.85	.12	-1.39	.50	.72	.91	-.83
	-1.50	1.45	-1.10	-.07	-.64	.64	.04	-1.50	-1.37	-1.39
	-1.29	-1.23	-.85	-1.34	-1.18	.64	-1.39	-1.26	-1.23	-1.39
	-1.15	-.50	-.26	-.55	-.26	-1.47	-1.12	-1.20	1.29	1.15
	1.15	1.12	.23	.61	.04	.26	-.28	.96	.50	-1.42
	-1.42	-1.26	-1.10	-1.53	-1.20	-1.61	-1.20	-.77	.28	-1.50
	-1.61	-1.31	-.96	-1.34	-.69	-1.34	-.99	-1.39	-1.23	-.72
	-1.29	-.88	-1.23	-.88	-1.26	-1.37	-1.23	-.99	-.45	-1.42
	-1.69	-1.69	-1.72	-1.45	-1.72	-1.15	-.07	-.34	-1.31	-1.31
	-.45	-.61	-.20	.77	-.69	-.28	.01	-.42	-.26	-.15
	.07	-.50	-.58	.26	.01	1.58	1.39	-.15	-.55	-.18
	.45	1.34	.23	.26						
99 TRINIDAD	-1.37	.88	.93	-1.56	1.39	-1.56	1.31	.31	-1.45	-.36
	-.34	-.36	.47	.64	.58	.74	.91	.74	1.15	.64
	.53	.28	.39	-.53	1.31	.50	.80	-.36	.66	-.66
	.83	-.66	.04	.58	.85	.12	1.69	1.56	-.15	-.80
	-.01	-1.37	1.50	1.53	-.69	.55	.23	.18	.47	-1.37
	-1.07	-1.04	.45	-1.31	-.77	-1.58	-.69	.66	-.66	-.31
	.99	.69	.42	1.45	.18	-1.10	.83	.93	.85	1.39
	1.39	1.37	.69	.64	.07	.28	1.47	.99	.53	-1.12
	-.31	-1.15	-.53	-.42	.96	-.53	.93	-1.26	-.07	.31
	.66	-.09	.69	-1.07	.53	-.01	1.50	-.20	-1.02	1.69
	-.42	1.23	-.99	1.69	-.88	-.50	-.99	1.64	-1.23	.12
	1.04	-.45	1.07	.01	1.07	.85	.72	.85	.28	1.29
	-.36	.80	-.01	-.64	-.01	.74	.04	.39	.36	-.80
	-.93	-.80	-1.02	-1.20	-1.45	.18	.23	-.12	-.53	-.15
	.47	.36	.26	-1.15						
100 TUNISIA	-.31	-1.18	-.91	-.34	-.20	.15	-.66	.80	.07	.72
	-.15	.15	.99	-.64	-.28	.26	-1.07	-.58	.07	.09
	-.66	-.69	-1.18	1.29	-1.37	-1.42	.04	-.34	-1.15	-.26
	-.34	-.47	-.74	.09	1.18	-.55	-.07	-.99	-.50	.09
	-.34	.12	-.04	1.56	-.83	-.69	-.45	-.80	-.85	-.34
	.23	.15	.04	-.72	-.69	-1.04	-.09	.15	.53	-.09
	.18	.50	-.91	.26	-.72	-.39	.80	.72	.36	.61
	.61	.58	-.15	.66	.09	-1.07	.39	1.02	.55	.07
	.53	.28	.93	-.26	-.07	-.36	-.12	.18	.53	-1.10
	-.34	.04	.04	-.28	-.01	-.66	-.64	-.45	.15	1.18
	-.72	-1.07	-.12	.69	-.26	-.31	-.12	.66	.04	.04
	.26	.01	.39	.09	.26	-.42	-1.37	-1.39	-.31	-.36
	-1.04	-.77	-1.47	-.28	-.34	-.26	.07	-.39	-.23	.20
	.69	1.39	-.45	-1.18	.04	.20	.26	-.09	-.50	-.12

		.50	.39	.28	-.12						
101	TURKEY	1.26	.15	.39	.88	.26	1.39	-.55	1.02	1.04	1.53
		-.26	-.01	-.91	-.23	-.09	-1.34	-1.18	-.01	-.47	-.18
		-.23	-.64	-1.42	1.53	-1.34	-1.47	-1.07	.99	-1.12	.91
		.09	.99	-.55	-.34	.42	.23	-1.61	-.77	-1.18	.58
		.64	1.15	-.01	-.26	.45	1.53	1.64	.96	.09	1.42
		1.23	1.31	.85	.80	.42	.74	.77	-.12	-.64	.85
		.01	-.61	1.04	1.47	.74	.93	.01	-.55	-.09	-1.26
		-1.26	-.42	.39	.69	.12	.31	1.50	1.04	.58	1.20
		.04	1.26	.01	.77	-.20	.72	-.34	1.02	.39	.69
		.15	.80	.01	.18	-1.07	.12	-1.07	.09	1.26	.31
		1.07	-.07	1.18	.04	.99	.23	1.26	.01	.85	.34
		-.88	.85	-.55	.53	-.74	.12	.64	-.04	.80	.07
		1.23	.83	-1.45	-.20	1.31	.99	1.53	.93	.85	.99
		.45	-.34	.55	1.39	1.02	.23	.28	.91	1.31	1.12
		1.42	1.37	1.07	.91						
102	UGANDA	.09	.26	.28	-.12	.09	-.47	.50	.85	1.37	-.26
		.39	.07	-1.72	-.96	-.96	-1.07	-1.45	-.69	-1.12	-1.04
		1.64	1.72	.04	.36	1.15	.47	.07	.64	.55	-.61
		-1.15	-.64	-.96	-.64	-1.29	-.69	.45	.99	-.69	-.77
		.55	1.61	-.80	-1.23	-1.02	-.07	-.18	-1.26	-1.47	-1.18
		-1.50	-1.53	-1.15	1.20	-1.37	-1.02	-.31	-.80	.72	-.28
		-.69	.61	.31	1.50	.09	-.69	-1.37	-1.37	1.45	1.42
		1.42	1.39	1.58	.72	1.31	.34	.42	1.07	.61	-1.39
		-1.39	-1.34	-1.47	-.61	-.96	-.64	-1.02	-.47	-.50	.01
		-.66	-.61	-.83	-.91	-1.18	-.34	-.74	-.58	-.01	-1.12
		-.20	-.66	-.36	-1.15	-.85	-1.10	-.39	-1.15	-1.47	-.26
		-.61	-1.04	-1.50	-.58	-.96	-1.26	-1.10	-1.26	-.88	-1.26
		-.50	-.53	.01	-1.12	.12	.01	.09	.42	-.09	-.77
		1.53	.83	1.47	.66	.53	1.37	.31	-1.23	.42	.50
		.53	1.39	.31	.77						
103	U.S.S.R	1.66	-.77	-.66	1.72	-.96	1.72	-.83	-.53	-1.61	-1.07
		.96	1.18	-1.23	1.18	1.37	.91	1.64	1.50	1.20	1.04
		.80	1.12	-.36	.66	-.28	-.85	.83	1.53	.01	1.69
		1.20	-1.10	.83	.88	1.39	1.61	-1.64	-.53	-1.66	1.61
		1.66	.15	1.64	-.04	.69	1.39	1.20	1.72	1.69	1.69
		1.20	1.15	.09	1.66	1.66	1.56	1.69	1.53	1.66	1.72
		1.72	1.64	-.88	-.53	-1.50	1.64	-.36	-.12	-.85	-1.23
		-1.23	-.58	-1.12	.74	.15	1.61	-.26	1.10	1.47	1.72
		1.12	1.72	1.31	1.56	.31	1.56	.26	1.69	.18	1.56
		.58	1.53	.45	1.58	-.39	1.58	-.34	1.58	1.66	1.39
		1.61	.18	1.61	1.18	1.69	1.64	1.64	1.29	1.69	1.56
		.50	1.50	.36	1.53	.42	.96	1.69	1.45	1.69	1.37
		1.72	1.23	-.77	-1.47	1.61	-.23	-.72	-.36	-.72	.31
		.47	.12	.01	.69	1.72	.26	1.07	-.07	1.56	-.09
		.55	.42	1.56	1.58						
104	U.A.R.	1.20	.47	.31	.99	.01	-.64	1.53	1.18	1.18	1.31
		-.36	.01	.50	-.77	-.53	-.01	-.18	-.55	-.26	-.23
		-1.34	-1.37	-.55	1.42	-.72	-1.10	.88	1.47	-1.07	.58
		-.61	-.23	-1.07	.91	1.04	.61	-.45	1.02	-1.34	.47
		.91	-.85	.01	-.74	.58	.74	.85	1.07	.31	.99
		.47	.39	.31	.72	.36	1.37	.85	.09	1.23	1.12
		.64	1.56	-.85	-.50	-1.31	1.42	1.42	1.42	.39	.42
		-.01	-.45	.93	.77	1.34	-1.04	-.23	1.12	1.50	1.42
		1.34	1.37	1.04	.83	.04	.96	.18	.69	-.20	.61
		.07	.74	-.01	.55	-.55	.26	-.83	.45	1.20	.12
		1.23	.58	.96	.09	1.26	.69	1.20	.15	.99	.39
		-.72	-.07	-1.39	.34	-1.10	-.18	.66	.04	.64	-.12
		.88	.50	-1.10	-.77	-1.15	-1.15	.12	-.34	-.42	.39
		-.45	-.77	-.99	1.10	.61	.28	.34	.93	1.61	-.07
		.58	1.42	1.12	1.12						
105	UNITED KINGDOM	1.45	-1.15	-1.61	-.01	1.42	.83	.96	-1.47	.77	-1.42
		1.37	1.53	1.12	1.69	1.23	1.64	1.12	1.53	1.64	1.66
		.01	-1.42	.34	-.50	1.50	-.09	1.58	1.02	-1.45	1.64
		1.37	1.45	-.04	-.80	.36	1.66	-.66	-1.34	-1.72	1.58
		1.69	-1.72	1.39	.66	1.58	1.61	1.26	1.61	1.18	1.39

	.74	.47	1.42	1.61	1.61	1.20	1.66	1.50	1.04	1.66
	1.45	.93	.69	1.53	1.23	1.39	-.28	.39	-1.72	-1.20
	-1.20	-1.66	-1.56	.80	.18	.36	1.53	1.15	1.53	1.56
	1.39	1.64	1.64	1.69	1.66	1.69	1.64	1.23	1.29	1.69
	1.56	1.66	1.45	1.66	1.18	1.66	1.26	1.66	1.39	-.58
	1.58	1.47	1.45	.53	1.56	1.12	1.50	.55	1.53	1.66
	1.53	1.64	1.39	1.66	1.50	1.31	1.61	1.39	1.64	1.58
	1.66	1.47	1.29	1.39	1.56	1.10	1.56	1.66	1.69	1.58
	.80	.47	-.96	.28	1.50	.31	.36	.96	.45	-.04
	.61	.45	.34	.47						
106 UNITED STATES	1.64	-.74	-.64	1.64	-.31	1.66	-.69	-.64	.39	-1.20
	.85	.93	.28	1.37	1.72	1.72	1.29	1.56	1.66	1.61
	.39	-.58	.91	-.47	1.42	.64	1.72	1.26	-1.34	1.72
	1.72	-.61	-1.53	-.18	.04	1.72	-1.69	-1.45	-1.53	1.72
	1.72	-1.69	1.04	.53	.31	1.47	1.37	1.69	1.47	1.66
	1.29	1.26	.69	1.69	1.72	1.34	1.72	1.72	1.15	1.69
	1.50	.23	.55	1.56	1.56	1.69	.39	.64	-1.69	-1.18
	-1.18	-1.61	-1.72	.83	.20	-1.02	1.56	1.18	1.69	1.69
	1.23	1.69	1.39	1.72	1.69	1.72	1.69	1.72	1.04	1.72
	1.72	1.72	1.72	1.72	.61	1.72	.93	1.72	1.64	1.20
	1.69	1.53	1.64	1.58	1.72	1.69	1.66	1.66	1.47	1.72
	1.72	1.72	1.69	1.72	1.72	1.69	1.72	1.66	1.72	1.72
	1.69	1.15	1.72	1.42	1.29	.34	1.58	1.69	1.72	1.72
	1.72	1.56	.99	-.34	1.04	.34	1.10	.99	1.66	1.66
	.64	.47	.36	1.72						
107 UPPER VOLTA	-.18	.20	.34	.15	-.50	-.28	-.18	1.42	1.66	.36
	.04	.28	-1.20	-.20	-1.53	-1.31	-.96	-1.34	-1.58	-1.58
	.85	1.10	-.91	.85	-.61	-.34	-1.04	-.31	.93	-1.10
	-1.61	-1.61	.69	.12	-1.26	-1.58	-1.02	.91	.88	-.74
	-1.42	-.07	-1.37	-1.61	1.72	-1.47	-1.42	-1.45	-1.56	-1.34
	-1.56	-1.56	-1.45	-1.29	-1.53	1.10	-1.10	-1.50	-1.20	-1.07
	-1.39	.01	-1.66	-1.34	-1.53	-1.29	-1.58	-1.58	1.31	1.18
	1.18	1.15	1.61	.85	.99	-.99	-.20	1.20	.64	-1.37
	-1.37	-.96	-1.31	-1.23	-1.47	-1.34	-1.58	-.55	-.66	-.50
	-1.26	-1.39	-1.61	-1.42	-1.56	-1.53	-1.64	-1.53	-1.42	-1.58
	-1.50	-1.58	-1.42	-1.58	-1.23	-1.34	-1.42	-1.58	-1.45	-1.18
	-1.61	-1.20	-1.31	-1.15	-1.45	-1.66	-.18	-.66	-1.42	-1.66
	-.28	-.85	-.18	.80	-.83	-.20	-.69	-.31	-.69	.42
	-.91	-.31	-.55	-1.15	-.23	1.39	.39	-1.20	-.47	-.01
	.66	.50	.39	-1.12						
108 URUGUAY	-.74	-.83	-.88	-.23	-.66	.64	-1.29	-.66	-.91	.07
	1.31	1.20	1.69	1.39	1.50	.96	1.07	1.02	.93	1.07
	-.45	-.42	.61	-.45	-.18	1.10	.61	.66	-.88	.04
	.77	-.28	-.01	-1.45	-1.69	-.58	-1.18	-.66	-1.02	.74
	.28	-.83	.53	-.72	1.12	1.12	1.56	.23	.39	-.53
	.53	.28	-.15	-.64	-.04	-.99	-.64	-.26	-1.61	-.23
	.31	-.83	.80	1.58	1.42	.12	-.58	.23	-1.18	-.96
	-.91	-1.45	1.37	.88	.23	-.96	1.58	1.23	-1.37	.23
	1.69	.39	1.66	.58	.80	.58	.80	.36	.69	.64
	.93	.50	.99	-.69	.04	-.23	.45	-.47	-.77	.26
	-.07	1.02	-.66	.31	.18	.96	-.58	.31	.39	.53
	.93	.66	1.37	.55	1.04	.66	-1.04	-1.02	.15	.64
	-1.15	-.50	-1.66	-1.72	-.28	1.26	1.61	1.72	1.47	.23
	.72	-.47	-.93	1.58	-.20	.36	.42	-.04	-.45	1.31
	.69	1.45	.42	-1.10						
109 VENEZUELA	.31	1.31	1.56	.91	-1.04	.77	-.64	-.93	-1.15	.15
	-.91	-.93	1.29	.45	.72	1.02	.96	.77	.20	.45
	-.88	-.83	.88	-.42	-.58	1.26	.53	.88	1.23	.85
	1.02	.96	.20	.15	.96	1.23	.93	.77	.77	.61
	.72	.66	1.31	1.02	-.31	.04	.01	.74	.88	-.18
	-.15	-.20	-.64	.26	.83	-.53	.99	.99	.74	1.18
	1.23	1.26	1.56	.28	1.39	-.26	-.80	-.85	-.64	-.85
	-.83	-1.20	-.23	.91	.26	-.93	1.61	1.26	.66	.83
	1.29	1.07	1.47	.96	1.07	.88	1.07	-.28	-1.02	.47
	.47	.72	.61	1.02	.91	1.34	1.39	1.23	.64	1.26
	.50	.36	.42	1.10	.66	.77	.61	1.12	-.64	.99

		.96	1.12	1.26	1.02	.88	1.18	1.64	1.69	1.02	1.23
		.85	.93	-1.23	.88	.77	1.61	1.64	.45	.88	-.12
		1.10	1.58	.83	.31	.55	.39	1.50	-.01	1.23	1.15
		.72	1.47	.45	.83						
110	NORTH VIETNAM	.96	1.42	1.47	-.36	1.10	-.85	1.50	-.50	-.88	-.66
		-.96	-1.42	1.37	-.47	-.18	.04	-.28	-.53	-.15	-.47
		-.18	-.39	-1.07	-.18	-1.31	-.39	-1.53	-.28	.28	.15
		-.96	-1.29	-1.47	-1.12	-.61	-.04	.61	.69	.34	-.09
		-.58	-.50	-.47	-.69	-1.42	-1.10	-.83	.31	-.50	1.31
		1.39	1.45	1.50	.69	.80	1.72	.61	-.18	1.64	.18
		-1.02	-.26	-.83	-.47	-.77	1.45	1.61	1.64	.72	.53
		.50	.47	.26	.93	.28	.39	-.18	1.29	1.56	.26
		-.74	.15	-.74	-1.69	-.85	-1.02	-.80	-.26	.12	-1.69
		-.64	-1.69	.20	.50	-.53	.58	-.12	.61	.69	-.80
		.64	-.42	1.58	-.72	-1.61	-.07	.74	-.66	.66	-1.69
		.18	-1.66	.09	-1.69	.18	-1.56	-.55	.64	-1.02	-.53
		.42	-.39	.12	-.96	1.23	-.18	-.66	-.28	-.66	-.74
		-.88	-1.20	1.26	-1.12	-.69	.42	.45	.01	.77	.01
		.74	.53	.99	-1.07						
111	SOUTH VIETNAM	.85	.50	1.12	-.31	.80	-.01	.88	.96	.20	-.23
		-.53	-.20	1.45	.07	-.36	-.18	-1.15	-.04	-.09	-.09
		-.47	-.15	-.58	-.07	-.77	-.04	-.72	-.26	.83	.23
		-.66	-1.31	-1.50	.23	.18	-.47	-1.45	1.45	.42	.20
		-.39	.96	-.66	-1.18	-.12	-1.20	-1.04	.12	-.26	1.53
		1.64	1.61	1.58	.47	.53	1.69	.18	-.53	-.26	-.39
		-1.47	-1.34	-.34	-.45	-.55	1.26	1.34	1.37	.74	.55
		.53	.50	1.39	1.72	.31	1.64	-1.42	-1.42	.69	.72
		-.09	-.20	-.15	.50	-.15	.42	-.18	-.18	.20	-.91
		-1.31	-.47	-1.15	-.07	-.91	-1.26	-1.69	-.36	.72	-.50
		.88	.45	.53	-.45	.39	-.26	.69	-.47	-.72	-.12
		-1.10	.07	-.93	-.01	-1.12	-.83	-1.50	-1.69	-.20	-.96
		-.42	-.93	-1.04	-1.39	-1.12	-1.12	-.64	-.26	-1.45	1.69
		1.61	1.72	1.69	1.72	1.66	1.72	1.66	1.69	1.64	1.69
		1.45	1.50	1.29	1.69						
112	YEMEN	-.15	-1.66	-1.39	-.20	-.23	-1.34	1.26	-1.15	-1.12	1.72
		.34	-1.72	-.88	-.50	-.64	-1.29	-.26	-1.72	-1.72	-1.72
		-1.45	-1.61	-1.66	1.69	-1.29	-1.61	-1.61	-.23	1.31	-.91
		-1.02	-.15	-1.69	-1.69	-1.64	-.18	.34	-1.04	-.28	-.72
		-1.37	1.64	-.45	-1.66	-1.69	-1.12	-.80	.50	-.55	-1.15
		-1.39	-1.39	-1.04	-.88	-1.04	-.50	-1.58	-1.66	-1.72	.58
		.61	1.66	-.58	-.42	-.50	-.23	.47	.58	1.47	-.07
		-.09	-.50	1.07	.96	1.37	1.66	-1.39	-1.39	-1.34	-1.34
		-1.34	-1.29	-1.45	-1.66	-.80	-.99	-.74	-1.42	-1.42	-1.66
		-.58	-1.66	.23	.53	-.50	.61	-.09	.64	-1.50	-1.69
		-1.66	-1.72	-1.56	-1.72	-1.20	-1.31	-1.56	-1.72	-1.42	-1.66
		.20	-1.64	.12	-1.66	.20	-1.53	-.15	-.64	-1.39	-1.64
		-.47	-.31	.36	-.93	-1.10	-1.10	-.61	-.23	-1.42	-.72
		.09	1.31	1.50	1.64	1.23	1.64	1.53	-1.18	-.42	.04
		.77	1.64	1.53	.28						
113	YUGOSLAVIA	1.02	-.96	-1.02	.07	.69	.53	.01	-.69	-1.10	.66
		1.12	1.04	-.80	.58	.53	.64	.66	.47	.69	.80
		1.23	.53	.96	.50	-.47	.45	-.26	1.61	.96	.93
		.47	-1.42	-1.58	1.18	1.66	.91	-.74	-1.64	-1.50	1.18
		.96	.72	1.29	1.58	1.23	1.29	1.61	1.29	.96	1.12
		1.18	1.12	1.07	.74	.85	.88	1.10	.80	.93	1.04
		.77	.64	-.80	-1.31	-.31	1.15	.50	.77	-.45	-.12
		-.53	-.12	.80	.99	1.02	.42	.45	1.31	1.58	.61
		-.42	.72	-.34	1.15	.85	1.12	.74	1.15	1.23	1.20
		1.04	.83	.42	.99	.23	.88	.09	.93	1.10	.85
		.45	-.61	.83	.47	1.34	1.31	1.04	.58	1.26	.85
		.09	.55	-.53	.74	-.12	.83	.93	.96	1.04	.80
		1.37	1.31	-.80	-.12	1.58	-.15	1.66	-.20	-.07	-.69
		-.28	-.45	-.18	-1.10	.31	.45	1.12	.04	-.39	.53
		.80	.55	.47	.85						
114	BOTSWANA	-1.50	.66	.74	.66	-1.66	1.23	-1.58	-.28	-.74	-.77
		-.88	-.61	.15	-1.64	-1.56	-1.72	-.72	-.83	-.80	-.72

	.42	1.07	-.42	-.39	1.12	-.69	-.47	-.20	.18	-1.66
	-1.53	.09	1.02	1.29	-1.18	-.15	-.01	.28	.26	-.69
	-1.69	-.28	-1.07	-.99	-.96	-1.31	-1.26	-1.69	-1.15	.23
	-.20	.72	.34	1.42	-1.72	.07	-1.69	-1.72	.07	-1.53
	-.83	.99	-.45	1.61	-.39	-1.64	-.55	-.69	-1.15	1.64
	1.64	1.61	1.10	1.02	1.64	.45	.47	1.34	-1.31	-1.31
	-1.31	-1.56	-1.61	.01	-.18	-.04	-.20	-.64	-.99	-.53
	-.50	-1.47	-.74	-1.69	-.93	-1.56	-.69	-1.69	-.26	-1.07
	-.88	-.12	.99	-1.02	-1.64	.04	-.07	-.96	-1.39	-1.61
	-.53	.18	-.28	-1.61	-.45	.01	-.88	.61	-1.64	.28
	-.61	.01	-.15	-1.29	.42	.04	.15	.47	-.04	-.66
	-.85	-.74	-.91	.72	-.99	.47	.47	.07	-.36	.07
	.83	.58	.50	-1.04						
115 GAMBIA	-1.61	-.26	-.80	-1.45	-.04	-1.53	.34	-.01	-.50	.69
	-1.12	.50	.04	-.53	.34	-.36	-.69	-1.12	-1.34	-1.42
	1.10	-.28	-1.04	1.04	-.07	-.64	-1.31	-.18	-.36	-1.69
	-1.20	.20	.39	-1.15	-1.15	-1.72	1.50	1.12	1.53	-.66
	-.99	.18	-1.04	-1.42	-.80	-1.34	-1.29	-1.72	-1.18	.12
	-.23	.64	.26	1.12	-.47	.09	-1.56	-.99	.20	-1.72
	-.07	.15	.23	1.64	.07	-1.66	.69	.53	1.61	1.56
	1.56	1.56	.83	1.04	1.39	.47	1.64	1.37	1.61	-1.29
	-1.29	-1.53	-1.58	-1.64	-1.18	-1.72	-1.18	-1.39	-1.39	-.55
	-.47	-1.56	-.69	-1.66	-.15	-1.58	-.01	-1.66	-.23	-1.04
	-.85	-.01	1.02	-.99	.15	-.09	-.04	-.93	-.85	-1.31
	-.36	-1.50	.34	-1.34	-.18	-1.23	-.36	-.36	-1.61	-1.34
	-.58	-.58	1.31	-1.26	.45	.77	.18	.50	.39	-.64
	-.83	-1.18	-.88	-.31	-.66	.50	.50	1.02	-.34	.55
	.85	.61	.53	-1.02						
116 KUWAIT	-1.53	1.69	1.72	-1.42	-.01	-1.69	1.58	.39	-.12	.28
	.91	.55	1.50	-.36	1.64	1.34	1.20	.01	.42	.47
	-.50	-1.58	-1.29	1.58	-.45	-.88	-1.29	-.15	1.69	.07
	1.69	1.31	1.56	1.69	1.10	.26	1.20	1.64	-.04	-.64
	-.96	-.64	.93	.93	-.93	.31	.39	-.72	1.29	-1.64
	-1.64	-1.64	-1.64	-.45	1.42	-.69	-.01	1.58	-.42	.28
	1.56	.39	.09	.31	-.01	-.07	1.69	.12	-1.29	1.23
	1.23	1.20	.42	1.07	1.04	1.69	.50	1.39	.72	-1.18
	.83	-1.20	.31	.42	1.20	.20	1.18	-1.37	-1.37	-1.53
	-1.15	-.28	.85	-.04	1.72	-1.23	.69	-.26	-1.58	-.26
	-.61	1.64	-1.50	.80	-1.18	-1.29	-1.50	.72	-1.29	.18
	1.37	-.20	1.58	.12	1.45	1.72	1.56	1.53	.39	1.66
	-1.23	.99	-.88	-.31	.01	.07	.20	.53	-.01	-.61
	-.80	-1.15	-.85	1.42	.77	.53	.53	1.64	-.31	.09
	.88	.64	.55	-.99						
117 LESOTHO	-1.42	1.58	.09	-1.23	-.18	-.55	-.93	1.50	1.42	-.74
	-.74	-.77	-.53	-1.61	-.93	-.58	-.66	-.28	.61	.66
	-.34	.66	.36	-.36	1.20	.55	-.93	-.12	.31	-1.64
	-1.58	.15	1.31	1.61	-1.12	-.12	.01	-.07	.07	-.61
	-1.66	-.47	-1.02	-.96	-1.23	-1.29	-1.23	-1.58	-1.12	.26
	-.18	.83	.39	1.50	-.66	.12	-1.47	-1.20	.55	-1.50
	-1.20	.42	.58	.34	.34	-1.56	-1.02	-1.02	-1.26	1.66
	1.66	1.64	1.42	1.10	1.66	.50	.53	1.42	-1.29	-1.26
	-1.26	-1.50	-1.56	-1.56	-.91	-1.69	-1.23	-1.23	-1.10	-1.64
	-1.58	-1.64	-.07	-1.53	-.34	-1.66	-1.37	-1.61	-.20	-1.02
	-.83	-.31	1.04	-.96	-1.72	-.04	-.01	-.91	-1.37	-1.64
	.04	-1.39	-.04	-1.64	.04	.23	-1.66	.58	-1.66	.39
	-.55	-.64	-.64	-1.23	.47	.09	.23	.55	.01	-.09
	.31	-.72	-.04	.74	-.64	.55	1.15	1.50	-.28	.12
	.91	.66	.58	.07						
118 MALAWI	-.36	.36	.42	-.53	.15	-1.04	.69	-.15	-.47	-.09
	-1.18	-.55	-1.61	-.18	-1.10	-1.53	-.93	-1.31	-1.04	-1.12
	.66	-.26	-.15	.45	1.02	.23	-.23	-.09	.20	-1.26
	-1.66	-1.39	-1.42	-1.42	-1.72	-1.31	.88	-.04	1.47	-.58
	-.55	1.39	-1.61	-.42	-1.18	-1.64	-1.61	-1.37	-1.53	-1.31
	-1.53	-1.50	-1.18	-1.56	-1.66	-1.34	-.85	-1.12	1.47	-1.18
	-1.45	.04	-.77	-1.29	-.09	-.93	-1.26	-1.26	1.58	1.47
	1.47	1.47	1.45	1.12	1.53	.53	.55	1.45	.85	-1.15

	-1.10	-1.18	-1.37	-1.20	-1.34	-1.20	-1.26	-.99	-.45	-1.29
	-1.29	-.99	-1.02	-1.20	-1.29	-1.20	-1.23	-1.31	-.80	-.91
	-1.26	-1.42	-.83	-1.12	-1.15	-1.26	-.83	-1.12	-1.26	-.96
	-1.15	-.99	-.99	-.96	-1.18	-1.72	.04	-.31	-1.15	-1.23
	-1.45	-1.50	1.34	-1.07	.15	.12	.26	.58	.04	-.58
	.74	.77	.23	1.45	.80	.58	1.18	.09	-.26	.58
	.93	.69	1.02	-.09						
119 MALTA	-1.64	-1.72	-1.66	-1.72	1.69	-1.66	1.69	-.45	-.72	-.42
	.64	.83	1.61	.88	.96	1.07	1.37	.80	.77	.55
	-.99	.96	1.47	-.34	-1.26	1.69	-1.45	-.07	-.09	-1.34
	.66	-1.37	-.83	-1.39	.55	-1.20	1.37	-.47	-.64	-.55
	-.12	-1.45	.66	1.04	-1.10	-.01	.12	.04	.26	.28
	.64	.58	.96	.99	.72	.15	-1.02	.83	.77	-.96
	1.02	1.15	.66	.36	.42	-1.53	1.37	1.45	.31	1.50
	1.50	1.50	.96	1.15	1.07	.55	1.66	1.47	.88	-1.23
	-1.23	-1.47	-1.53	.34	.99	.39	1.02	-1.34	-1.34	.15
	.99	-.45	1.04	-1.04	1.29	-1.47	.53	-1.18	-1.61	.74
	-1.47	.12	-1.61	.61	-.83	.34	-1.64	.47	-1.34	-.61
	1.15	-.96	1.29	-.69	1.18	.53	.12	.47	-1.07	.45
	-1.31	.96	1.37	1.45	.04	.80	.28	.61	.42	.47
	.12	-.69	-.83	-.28	-1.42	.61	.55	1.04	-.23	.15
	.96	.72	.61	-.50						
120 TANZANIA	.50	-.47	-.47	.96	-.88	1.31	-1.10	1.12	1.53	1.56
	.12	-.18	-1.58	-.15	-1.45	-1.50	-1.37	-.93	-1.26	-1.29
	1.69	.61	-.26	.88	.74	.26	.47	-.04	-.77	-.47
	-1.42	-1.07	-1.20	-.93	-1.10	-.61	.20	-.15	-1.15	-.53
	-.04	1.56	-1.58	-.23	-1.12	.42	.55	.09	-.66	-1.29
	-1.61	-1.61	-1.56	-1.12	-1.56	-1.64	-.36	-1.15	.23	-.72
	-1.42	-.80	-.74	.39	.12	-1.45	-1.72	-1.69	1.37	1.26
	1.26	1.23	1.12	1.18	1.42	-.91	.58	1.50	.74	-.69
	-1.12	-1.69	-1.20	-.72	-1.37	-.77	-1.42	.23	-.58	.12
	-.69	-.50	-.91	-.61	-1.20	-.28	-.93	-.50	.04	-1.23
	-.80	-1.53	-.20	-1.26	-1.12	-1.23	-.23	-1.26	-.96	-.09
	-.77	-.77	-1.37	-.28	-1.07	-1.42	-1.31	-1.56	-.45	-1.07
	-.72	-.74	.09	-.91	.20	.15	.31	.64	.07	.12
	-.42	.50	.20	.34	.58	.64	.58	.12	1.12	.61
	.99	.74	1.18	.99						
121 ZAMBIA	-.45	.69	.77	.83	-1.29	1.02	-1.37	.12	-.26	-.64
	-.64	-.72	.31	-1.04	-1.37	-.66	-.64	-.12	-.77	-.83
	1.39	-.23	-.34	-.15	.58	.20	.91	-.01	-1.37	-.45
	-.36	-1.04	-1.04	.55	-.09	.09	1.53	1.69	-.53	-.50
	-.31	-1.34	1.58	1.07	-1.20	1.20	.96	-1.23	-1.20	-.99
	-1.15	-1.12	-1.39	1.29	-.96	-.26	-.72	-.72	-1.18	-.47
	-.04	-.23	.26	.42	.28	.18	.53	.20	1.64	1.53
	1.53	1.53	.99	1.20	1.10	.58	-.15	1.53	.91	-.18
	-.53	-1.72	-.55	-.15	.50	-.23	.23	-.34	-.93	-1.07
	-.07	-.18	-.15	-.18	.39	.15	.88	.15	-.50	-.23
	-1.07	-1.23	-.64	-.69	-1.10	-1.20	-.66	-.74	.36	-.01
	.28	-.61	-.61	-.15	.09	-.28	-1.29	-1.29	.04	.20
	-1.39	-1.39	1.39	-.66	.18	-1.02	-.58	-.18	-.20	-.55
	1.37	1.23	1.29	.77	.34	.66	.61	1.53	-.20	1.56
	1.02	.77	.64	.23						
122 KENYA	.36	.72	.96	.69	-.58	-.18	.39	1.26	1.12	1.61
	-1.50	-1.04	-1.42	-1.02	-.83	-.99	-1.34	-.74	-.45	-.69
	1.47	1.58	-.23	.55	.69	.04	.93	.72	-.69	-.36
	-1.07	-.50	-.93	-.47	-1.04	-.45	.53	-.18	-1.20	-.47
	.39	1.23	-.64	-.93	-1.29	-.74	.36	-.47	-.88	-.96
	-1.42	-1.42	-1.31	-1.04	-1.47	1.45	-.18	-.83	.58	-.12
	-.55	.53	-.61	.45	.55	-.18	-.34	-.72	1.50	1.45
	1.45	1.45	.85	1.23	1.56	-.88	.61	1.56	.77	-.31
	-.80	-.36	-.99	-.45	-1.07	-.26	-.83	.42	.15	.39
	-.26	.07	-.50	-.23	-.72	-.45	-1.02	-.34	.39	.20
	-.39	-1.20	.12	-.39	-.42	-.91	.31	-.39	.07	.26
	-.15	-.69	-1.23	.15	-.42	-1.18	-1.26	-1.53	-.18	-.74
	-1.07	-1.29	.04	-.80	.23	.18	.34	.66	.09	-.07
	1.42	1.15	1.02	1.47	.83	.69	1.42	1.72	1.58	1.02

	1.04	.80	.66	.31						
123 W. SAMOA	-1.04	.39	1.61	-1.64	1.72	-1.72	1.72	.26	-1.69	-1.10
	-.77	-.64	1.72	1.20	.88	.69	1.45	.28	.96	1.18
	.20	1.04	-.69	.64	.15	-.20	-1.50	.01	-1.66	-.28
	.64	1.18	.80	.93	-.07	.85	1.72	-1.15	-.36	-.45
	.45	-1.66	.07	.69	-.20	-.72	-.36	-.50	.53	.53
	.80	.66	.99	1.34	.77	.31	-.07	.85	.85	-.01
	.85	.72	.34	.47	.88	-.53	1.56	1.56	1.66	1.58
	1.58	1.58	1.15	1.26	1.45	.61	.64	1.58	-1.26	-.07
	.01	-1.07	-.07	-.55	.47	-.72	.36	-1.20	.80	-.99
	.50	.26	.77	.96	1.64	.77	1.66	.85	-.18	-.20
	.28	.39	1.07	-.18	.28	.42	.01	-.15	.50	.50
	1.07	-.15	.74	.36	.99	.64	.39	.42	-.28	.31
	-.96	.47	-.12	-.55	.50	.20	.36	.69	.12	-.04
	-.18	-1.12	-.80	.80	-1.39	.72	.64	-1.15	-.18	.18
	1.07	.83	.69	-.96						
124 SINGAPORE	-1.45	.53	.80	-.15	-1.39	-.61	-1.07	.61	.42	.39
	-1.20	-.91	-.50	.61	.26	.42	.80	.96	1.39	1.20
	.55	-.04	.07	.47	1.34	.18	.64	.04	.72	-1.23
	.20	.69	.85	1.02	.58	-1.10	1.47	.53	.12	-.42
	-1.12	.53	.83	1.10	-.77	.07	.28	-1.10	.18	.31
	.58	.69	.88	1.39	.20	.18	-.96	.36	.47	-.91
	.72	1.12	1.02	1.66	.72	-1.39	.85	.85	.55	1.69
	1.69	1.66	1.18	1.29	1.69	.64	1.69	1.61	-1.23	-.77
	1.15	-.80	.77	-.18	.23	-.12	.15	-1.12	-1.12	-1.04
	.88	-.88	.36	-.88	1.02	-.77	1.04	-.99	-.15	.47
	-.34	-.04	1.10	.42	.20	.15	.04	.36	-1.02	-1.53
	.42	.36	.18	-1.53	.31	.31	.34	.72	-.55	.53
	-.12	.28	-.09	-.23	.53	.83	.39	.72	.45	1.15
	.55	1.34	1.04	1.12	1.07	.74	.66	.15	-.15	.85
	1.47	.85	.72	.50						
125 GUYANA	.39	.91	.99	.34	-.12	-.15	.42	.77	.09	.26
	-.42	-.58	-.39	.31	-.69	-.34	1.02	-.07	.09	-.07
	1.04	-.12	-.85	.99	-.01	-.50	1.18	.07	-1.18	.39
	.18	.04	-.34	.64	.99	.77	1.15	-.12	-.61	-.39
	.53	.77	.09	.55	-.45	.20	-.23	.53	.01	-.26
	-.36	-.36	-.18	.07	.31	-.15	.55	.34	.61	.66
	.34	.34	.96	1.69	.77	.72	.91	.96	1.53	.66
	.66	1.42	-.31	1.31	.34	.66	.66	1.64	.80	.28
	.47	.04	.15	.12	.20	.50	.53	.12	.09	-.66
	.34	-.83	-1.18	.83	.66	.99	.85	.91	.55	.77
	.74	.96	.45	.88	.01	-.28	.64	.85	.26	.80
	.53	.42	.01	.61	.45	.20	-.96	-1.18	.20	.12
	.04	.34	1.42	.91	.64	.91	1.69	.96	.91	1.18
	1.56	.58	.77	1.15	.07	.77	.69	.18	1.26	.64
	1.10	.88	.74	.34						
126 MALAYSIA	-1.72	-.45	-.18	-1.69	1.58	-.66	1.66	-.74	-1.07	1.29
	.09	-1.47	1.58	-1.39	-.01	.58	-.91	-.66	-1.39	-.58
	-.53	-.96	-1.64	1.72	-1.23	-1.58	-1.72	.09	.23	-1.72
	.55	.83	.31	-1.29	-1.23	-.09	.99	-.20	.01	-.36
	-1.72	-.61	-.99	-.91	-1.50	-1.45	-1.34	-.15	-1.50	.74
	-.34	.61	.12	1.04	.45	.42	-1.72	.77	-.04	-1.58
	-1.72	.07	-.31	-.39	-.34	-.15	-.31	.26	1.69	1.61
	1.61	1.69	1.69	1.34	1.47	1.72	.69	1.66	-1.20	-1.20
	-1.20	-1.45	-1.50	1.29	1.02	1.29	1.04	-1.31	-1.31	1.37
	1.07	1.37	1.10	-1.72	-1.04	-1.69	-.88	-1.72	-.12	-.99
	-.77	.66	1.12	-.93	-1.69	.93	.07	-.88	-1.31	1.42
	1.02	1.34	.91	1.42	.96	.91	-1.72	.53	-1.72	.85
	-1.53	1.04	-.07	-1.20	.55	.23	.42	.74	.15	1.20
	.15	-.66	-.77	-.26	-1.37	.80	.72	-1.12	-.12	.20
	1.12	.91	.77	-.93						
127 MALDIVE ISLANDS	-1.66	-1.12	-1.18	-1.66	1.66	-1.64	1.45	-.07	.23	-.04
	-.12	.39	1.26	.69	.61	.53	.83	1.04	1.42	.83
	-.39	-.07	1.50	-.31	1.66	-1.56	-1.12	.12	.07	-1.58
	.34	.64	-1.61	-1.61	-.42	-1.26	1.61	1.53	.61	-.34
	-1.04	.55	-.20	1.12	-.39	-.96	-.55	-1.31	.20	.15

	.61	.55	.93	-1.72	.12	.20	-1.37	.23	-.23	-1.15
	.93	1.20	.83	1.72	.61	-1.69	1.07	1.10	-.61	1.72
	1.72	1.72	.45	1.37	1.72	.69	1.72	1.69	1.72	.39
	.20	.34	.04	.28	.91	.34	.96	-1.29	-1.29	-.01
	.96	-.69	1.02	-1.12	1.31	-1.18	1.10	-1.23	-.09	-.01
	.72	.69	1.15	-.01	-1.66	.85	.09	-.04	-.83	-.74
	1.10	-1.37	1.04	-.85	1.10	.50	-1.69	.55	-1.69	.55
	.58	.85	-.04	-.47	.58	.85	.45	.77	.47	-.53
	-.77	-1.10	-.74	-.23	-1.34	.83	.74	-1.10	-.09	.23
	1.15	.93	.80	-.91						
128 BARBADOS	.69	1.07	1.42	-1.15	1.61	-1.37	1.61	.34	-1.64	-.72
	-.69	-.69	.72	.36	.07	-.45	.55	.69	.64	.77
	.09	.50	-.77	-.28	.31	-.58	1.56	.15	.39	.36
	-.18	1.12	1.58	1.42	1.29	.20	-.26	-1.12	.36	.91
	.69	.58	.34	.26	-1.07	.15	-.01	.58	.28	1.47
	1.66	1.64	1.69	.42	.61	1.39	.15	-.34	-.55	-.69
	-1.56	-1.45	-.07	.50	.01	.64	-.07	.18	-.26	-1.72
	.39	.36	-.50	1.53	.36	.72	-.12	1.72	.83	1.07
	1.42	.50	1.23	.31	-.26	.36	-.26	.74	.85	.80
	.74	.45	.18	.15	-.23	.09	-.28	.01	.91	1.47
	1.04	1.18	1.72	1.47	.91	.80	.96	1.50	-.80	-.85
	-1.45	-.47	-1.20	-.74	-1.37	-.34	.47	.28	.61	.42
	.64	.69	.18	.01	1.72	.39	1.72	-.15	.18	-.50
	-.74	.01	1.15	-.20	-.18	.85	.77	-1.07	-.07	.26
	1.18	.96	.83	-.31						

INSERT 48

CORRELATION OF 144 ATTRIBUTE VARIABLES WITH WEIS CONFLICT SCORES (CORRELATIONS ARE RANK SORTED,+ OR - .16 IS SIGNIFICANT AT THE .05 LEVEL AND + OR - .21 AT THE .01 LEVEL)

050	TOTAL MILITARY MANPOWER	.42
056	DEFENSE EXPENDITURE,% OF GNP	.42
080	POPULATION IN CITIES OF 100,000+	.36
082	POPULATION IN CITIES OF 50,000+	.36
054	TOTAL DEFENSE EXPENDITURE (IN MILLIONS U.S. DOLLARS)	.35
055	DEFENSE EXPENDITURE PER CAPITA (IN U.S. DOLLARS)	.35
057	TOTAL EDUCATION EXPENDITURE (IN MILLION U.S. DOLLARS)	.35
066	TOTAL INTERNAL SECURITY FORCES (IN UNITS)	.35
048	TOTAL NUMBER OF PHYSICIANS	.34
051	MILITARY MANPOWER PER ONE THOUSAND POPULATION	.34
101	TOTAL SECONDARY SCHOOL ENROLLMENT	.34
030	TOTAL GNP (IN MILLIONS U.S. DOLLARS)	.33
099	TOTAL PRIMARY SCHOOL ENROLLMENT	.33
105	TOTAL UNIVERSITY ENROLLMENT	.33
107	TOTAL SCHOOL ENROLLMENT	.33
109	RAIL PASSENGER KILOMETERS	.33
139	MEAN NUMBER OF REGIME-SUPPORT DEMONSTRATIONS DURING 1963-1967	.33
060	TOTAL HEALTH EXPENDITURE (IN MILLIONS U.S. DOLLARS)	.32
103	TOTAL PRIMARY AND SECONDARY ENROLLMENT	.32
119	TOTAL ENERGY CONSUMPTION IN METRIC TONS OF COAL EQUIVALENT	.32
121	BOOK PRODUCTION BY TITLES	.32
144	MEAN RELAXATIONS OF GOV . RETRICTIONS ON POL. ACTIVITY,1963-1967	.32
052	MILITARY MANPOWER PER ONE THOUSAND WORKING AGED POPULATION	.31
001	TOTAL POPULATION	.30
094	TOTAL IMPORTS	.30
135	MEAN NUMBER OF EXECUTIVE ADJUSTMENTS DURING 1963-1967	.30
041	PERCENTAGE CONTRIBUTION TO WORLD TOTAL OF SCIENTIFIC AUTHORS	.29

Variable	r
053 MILITARY MANPOWER PER AREA	.29
086 NATIONAL GOVERNMENT EXPENDITURE	.29
036 TOTAL TRADE,1960 (IN MILLIONS U .S. DOLLARS)	.28
088 RAILROAD MILEAGE	.28
098 PROPORTION OF TOTAL WORLD TRADE	.28
106 UNIVERSITY ENROLLMENT PER CAPITA	.28
040 TOTAL SCIENTIFIC AND TECHNICAL SERIALS PUBLISHED	.27
059 TOTAL EDUCATION EXPENDITURE,% OF GNP	.27
083 PER CAPITA POPULATION IN CITIES OF 50,000+	.27
081 PER CAPITA POPULATION IN CITIES OF 100,000+	.26
096 TOTAL EXPORTS	.26
084 NATIONAL GOVERNMENT REVENUE	.25
092 TOTAL TELEPHONES	.25
117 TOTAL ENERGY PRODUCTION IN METRIC TONS COAL EQUIVALENT	.25
017 CINEMA ATTENDANCE PER CAPITA,1960	.24
049 PHYSICIANS PER ONE MILLION POPULATION,1965	.23
027 NUMBER OF SEPARATE CHRISTIAN CHURCHES	.23
090 ALL MAIL	.22
108 TOTAL SCHOOL ENROLLMENT PER CAPITA	.22
120 ENERGY CONSUMPTION IN KILOGRAMS PER CAPITA	.22
122 BOOK PRODUCTION BY TITLES PER MILLION POPULATION	.22
125 SIZE OF LEGISLATURE (LOWER HOUSE)	.22
035 TOTAL GNP PER CAPITA GROWTH RATES,ANNUAL AVERAGES, 1960-1965	.21
104 PRIMARY AND SECONDARY ENROLLMENT PER CAPITA	.21
114 TOTAL HIGHWAY VEHICLES	.21
130 MEAN NUMBER OF PROTEST DEMONSTRATIONS DURING 1963-1967	.21
058 EDUCATION EXPENDITURE PER CAPITA (IN MILLION U.S. DOLLARS)	.20
100 PRIMARY SCHOOL ENROLLMENT PER CAPITA	.20
110 TOTAL PASSENGER CARS	.20
112 TOTAL COMMERCIAL VEHICLES	.20
028 ORTHODOX COMMUNITY,% OF THE TOTAL POP.	.20
018 LITERACY RATES	.19
019 UNADJUSTED SCHOOL ENROLLMENT RATIO	.19
020 ADJUSTED SCHOOL ENROLLMENT RATIO	.19
043 PERCENTAGE OF GROSS DOMESTIC PRODUCT ORIGINATING IN INDUSTRY	.19
131 MEAN NUMBER OF RIOTS DURING 1963-1967	.19
089 RAILROAD MILEAGE PER SQUARE MILE	.18
102 SECONDARY SCHOOL ENROLLMENT PER CAPITA	.18
015 RADIOS PER 1,000 POPULATION	.18
047 PROTEINS PER CAPITA PER DIEM,1960	.18
132 MEAN NUMBER OF ARMED ATTACKS DURING 1963-1967	.17
143 MEAN NUMBER OF POLITICAL EXECUTIONS DURING 1963-1967	.17
046 CALORIES PER CAPITA PER DIEM,1960	.16
118 ENERGY PRODUCTION IN KILOGRAMS PER CAPITA	.16
068 INTERNAL SECURITY FORCES PER ONE MILLION POPULATION	.16
*********************	
070 DATE OF INDEPENDENCE(BANKS)	-.16
073 DATE OF FOUNDING OF PRESENT CONSTITUTIONAL FORM(HUDSON)	-.17
010 INFANT MORTALITY RATES	-.19
071 DATE OF INSTITUTIONAL FORMATION(HUDSON)	-.19
037 TOTAL TRADE,% OF GNP, 1960	-.29
039 CONCENTRATION OF EXPORT RECEIVING COUNTRIES	-.30

INSERT 49

CORRELATION OF 144 ATTRIBUTE VARIABLES WITH WEIS
COOPERATION SCORES (SIGNIFICANCE LEVELS REMAIN THE SAME)

Variable	r
057 TOTAL EDUCATION EXPENDITURE (IN MILLION U.S. DOLLARS)	.37
030 TOTAL GNP (IN MILLIONS U.S. DOLLARS)	.36
048 TOTAL NUMBER OF PHYSICIANS	.36
050 TOTAL MILITARY MANPOWER	.36

066	TOTAL INTERNAL SECURITY FORCES (IN UNITS)	.36
080	POPULATION IN CITIES OF 100,000+	.36
082	POPULATION IN CITIES OF 50,000+	.36
099	TOTAL PRIMARY SCHOOL ENROLLMENT	.36
101	TOTAL SECONDARY SCHOOL ENROLLMENT	.36
107	TOTAL SCHOOL ENROLLMENT	.36
036	TOTAL TRADE,1960 (IN MILLIONS U .S. DOLLARS)	.35
054	TOTAL DEFENSE EXPENDITURE (IN MILLIONS U.S. DOLLARS)	.35
001	TOTAL POPULATION	.35
060	TOTAL HEALTH EXPENDITURE (IN MILLIONS U.S. DOLLARS)	.35
086	NATIONAL GOVERNMENT EXPENDITURE	.35
094	TOTAL IMPORTS	.35
103	TOTAL PRIMARY AND SECONDARY ENROLLMENT	.35
105	TOTAL UNIVERSITY ENROLLMENT	.35
119	TOTAL ENERGY CONSUMPTION IN METRIC TONS OF COAL EQUIVALENT	.35
084	NATIONAL GOVERNMENT REVENUE	.34
088	RAILROAD MILEAGE	.34
098	PROPORTION OF TOTAL WORLD TRADE	.34
109	RAIL PASSENGER KILOMETERS	.34
121	BOOK PRODUCTION BY TITLES	.34
040	TOTAL SCIENTIFIC AND TECHNICAL SERIALS PUBLISHED	.33
041	PERCENTAGE CONTRIBUTION TO WORLD TOTAL OF SCIENTIFIC AUTHORS	.33
055	DEFENSE EXPENDITURE PER CAPITA (IN U.S. DOLLARS)	.33
092	TOTAL TELEPHONES	.33
096	TOTAL EXPORTS	.33
114	TOTAL HIGHWAY VEHICLES	.33
090	ALL MAIL	.32
110	TOTAL PASSENGER CARS	.32
112	TOTAL COMMERCIAL VEHICLES	.32
117	TOTAL ENERGY PRODUCTION IN METRIC TONS COAL EQUIVALENT	.31
139	MEAN NUMBER OF REGIME-SUPPORT DEMONSTRATIONS DURING 1963-1967	.30
144	MEAN RELAXATIONS OF GOV . RETRICTIONS ON POL. ACTIVITY,1963-1967	.30
106	UNIVERSITY ENROLLMENT PER CAPITA	.29
056	DEFENSE EXPENDITURE,% OF GNP	.28
120	ENERGY CONSUMPTION IN KILOGRAMS PER CAPITA	.28
049	PHYSICIANS PER ONE MILLION POPULATION,1965	.27
027	NUMBER OF SEPARATE CHRISTIAN CHURCHES	.27
058	EDUCATION EXPENDITURE PER CAPITA (IN MILLION U.S. DOLLARS)	.27
018	LITERACY RATES	.27
125	SIZE OF LEGISLATURE (LOWER HOUSE)	.27
006	TOTAL AGRICULTURAL AREA	.26
020	ADJUSTED SCHOOL ENROLLMENT RATIO	.26
015	RADIOS PER 1,000 POPULATION	.26
019	UNADJUSTED SCHOOL ENROLLMENT RATIO	.26
130	MEAN NUMBER OF PROTEST DEMONSTRATIONS DURING 1963-1967	.26
051	MILITARY MANPOWER PER ONE THOUSAND POPULATION	.25
083	PER CAPITA POPULATION IN CITIES OF 50,000+	.25
031	GNP PER CAPITA (IN U.S. DOLLARS)	.25
118	ENERGY PRODUCTION IN KILOGRAMS PER CAPITA	.25
004	TOTAL AREA	.24
046	CALORIES PER CAPITA PER DIEM,1960	.24
016	TELEVISIONS PER 1,000 POPULATION	.24
116	GROSS DOMESTIC PRODUCT PER CAPITA	.24
135	MEAN NUMBER OF EXECUTIVE ADJUSTMENTS DURING 1963-1967	.24
059	TOTAL EDUCATION EXPENDITURE,% OF GNP	.23
014	NEWSPAPERS PER 1,000 POPULATION	.23
081	PER CAPITA POPULATION IN CITIES OF 100,000+	.23
047	PROTEINS PER CAPITA PER DIEM,1960	.23
052	MILITARY MANPOWER PER ONE THOUSAND WORKING AGED POPULATION	.23
091	ALL MAIL PER CAPITA	.23
093	TELEPHONES PER CAPITA	.23
017	CINEMA ATTENDANCE PER CAPITA,1960	.23
043	PERCENTAGE OF GROSS DOMESTIC PRODUCT ORIGINATING IN INDUSTRY	.23
122	BOOK PRODUCTION BY TITLES PER MILLION POPULATION	.23
061	HEALTH EXPENDITURE PER CAPITA	.22
085	NATIONAL GOVERNMENT REVENUE PER CAPITA	.22

087 NATIONAL GOVERNMENT EXPENDITURE PER CAPITA	.22
028 ORTHODOX COMMUNITY,% OF THE TOTAL POP.	.22
102 SECONDARY SCHOOL ENROLLMENT PER CAPITA	.22
108 TOTAL SCHOOL ENROLLMENT PER CAPITA	.22
104 PRIMARY AND SECONDARY ENROLLMENT PER CAPITA	.21
111 PASSENGER CARS PER CAPITA	.21
115 TOTAL HIGHWAY VEHICLES PER CAPITA	.21
131 MEAN NUMBER OF RIOTS DURING 1963-1967	.21
089 RAILROAD MILEAGE PER SQUARE MILE	.20
113 COMMERCIAL VEHICLES PER CAPITA	.20
012 ADULT POPULATION	.19
079 MEAN NUMBER OF LEGISLATIVE ELECTIONS,1962-1966	.19
053 MILITARY MANPOWER PER AREA	.19
132 MEAN NUMBER OF ARMED ATTACKS DURING 1963-1967	.19
011 WORKING AGE POPULATION	.18
128 PARTY LEGITIMACY	.16
************************	
008 CRUDE BIRTH RATES,1960	-.16
042 PERCENTAGE OF GROSS DOMESTIC PRODUCT ORIGINATING IN AGRICULTURE	-.19
070 DATE OF INDEPENDENCE(BANKS)	-.20
072 DATE OF INDEPENDENT IDENTIFICATION(RUSTOW)	-.21
010 INFANT MORTALITY RATES	-.21
038 CONCENTRATION OF EXPORT COMMODITIES	-.22
073 DATE OF FOUNDING OF PRESENT CONSTITUTIONAL FORM(HUDSON)	-.23
071 DATE OF INSTITUTIONAL FORMATION(HUDSON)	-.24
069 BEGINNING YEAR OF MODERNIZATION	-.25
039 CONCENTRATION OF EXPORT RECEIVING COUNTRIES	-.28
037 TOTAL TRADE,% OF GNP, 1960	-.29

INSERT 50

Interpretation of factors in terms of whether
closeness or distance contributes to conflict

Factors where distance predicts conflict

01 Power base
02 Economic development
03 Political
04 School enrollment
06 Internal violence
08 Date of independence
12 Population size
14 Energy production
16 Fixed prices gnp growth rate
19 All mail
20 Political party fractionalization
21 Domestic turmoil
22 Total area
23 Per capita energy consumption growth rate
24 Infant mortality
26 Total health expenditure
30 Concentration of export commodities
31 Mean elections

32 Concentration of export receivers

Factors where closeness predicts conflict

05 Internal political turmoil
07 Militarism
09 Population growth rate
10 Density
11 Internal security forces
13 Religious
15 Gnp growth rate
17 Ethno-linguistic fractionalization
18 Per cent urban population
25 Age of currency
27 Crude death rate
28 Regular executive transfers
29 Per capita economic active male population
33 Orthodox community

INSERT 51

Interpretation of major factors in terms of closeness or distance prediction

	economic development	power base	non-competitive political system
01 Power base	closeness	closeness	
02 Economic development	closeness	closeness	
03 Political			
04 School enrollment			
05 Internal political turmoil			
06 Internal violence			
07 Militarism	closeness		
08 Date of independence			
09 Population growth rate			
10 Density			
11 Internal security forces		distance	
12 Population size		closeness	
13 Religious			
14 Energy production	closeness	closeness	
15 Gnp growth rate			
16 Fixed prices gnp growth rate			closeness
17 Ethno-linguistic fractionalization			
18 Per cent urban population	distance	distance	
19 All mail	closeness		
20 Political party fractionalization			
21 Domestic turmoil			distance
22 Total area			
23 Per capita energy consumption growth rate			distance
24 Infant mortality	closeness	closeness	
25 Age of currency			
26 Total health expenditure			
27 Crude death rate	distance	distance	
28 Regular executive transfers			closeness
29 Per capita economic active male population			
30 Concentration of export commodities			
31 Mean elections			

32 Concentration of export receivers
33 Orthodox community

closeness

INSERT 52

DISTANCE THEORY, WORLD MODEL

1. WORLD	1.26	.66	1.21	.18	-1.11	-.93	-.60	.22	-1.83	-1.58
	-1.74	.88	-2.73	2.53	-1.46	-.83	.01	-1.08	-2.05	-.69
	.16	-1.54	.99	-1.17	.94	-.62	.35	.22	-.59	-.15
	.42	2.33	1.61							

INSERT 53

THE GROUPS AND THEIR MEMBERS

WORLD 1
1 AFGHANISTAN
2 ALBANIA
3 ALGERIA
4 ARGENTINA
5 AUSTRALIA
6 AUSTRIA
7 BELGIUM
8 BOLIVIA
9 BRAZIL
10 BULGARIA
11 BURMA
12 BURUNDI
13 CAMBODIA
14 CAMEROUN
15 CANADA
16 CENERAL AFICAN REP.
17 CEYLON
18 CHAD
19 CHILE
20 CHINA, PR
21 COLOMBIA
22 CONGO (BRA)
23 CONGO (LEO)
24 COSTA RICA
25 CUBA

26 CYPRUS
27 CZECHOSLOVAKIA
28 DAHOMEY
29 DENMARK
30 DOMINICAN REP.
31 ECUADOR
32 EL SALVADOR
33 ETHIOPIA
34 FINLAND
35 FRANCE
36 GABON
37 EAST GERMANY
38 WEST GERMANY
39 GHANA
40 GREECE
41 GUATEMALA
42 GUINEA
43 HAITI
44 HONDURAS
45 HUNGARY
46 ICELAND
47 INDIA
48 INDONESIA
49 IRAN
50 IRAQ
51 IRELAND
52 ISRAEL
53 ITALY
54 IVORY COAST
55 JAMAICA
56 JAPAN
57 JORDAN
58 NORTH KOREA
59 SOUTH KOREA
60 LAOS
61 LEBANON
62 LIBERIA
63 LIBYA
64 LUXEMBOURG
65 MALAGASY REP.
66 MALI
67 MAURITANIA
68 MEXICO
69 MONGOLIA
70 MOROCCO
71 NEPAL
72 NETHERLANDS
73 NEW ZEALAND
74 NICARAGUA
75 NIGER
76 NIGERIA
77 NORWAY
78 PAKISTAN
79 PANAMA
80 PARAGUAY
81 PERU
82 PHILIPPINES
83 POLAND
84 PORTUGAL
85 ROMANIA
86 RUANDA
87 SAUDI ARABIA
88 SENEGAL
89 SIERRA LEONE
90 SOMALIA
91 SOUTH AFRICA

```
92 SPAIN
93 SUDAN
94 SWEDEN
95 SWITZERLAND
96 SYRIA.
97 THAILAND
98 TOGO
99 TRINIDAD
100 TUNISIA
101 TURKEY
102 UGANDA
103 U.S.S.R.
104 U.A.R.
105 UNITED KINGDOM
106 U.S.A.
107 UPPER VOLTA
108 URUGUAY
109 VENEZUELA
110 NORTH VIETNAM
111 SOUTH VIETNAM
112 YEMEN
113 YUGOSLAVIA
114 BOTSWANA
115 GAMBIA
116 KUWAIT
117 LESOTHO
118 MALAWI
119 MALTA
120 TANZANIA
121 ZAMBIA
122 KENYA
123 WEST SAMOA
124 SINGAPORE
125 GUYANA
126 MALAYSIA
127 MALDIVE ISLAND
128 BARBADOS

NATO 2
001 BELGIUM 007
002 CANADA 015
003 DENMARK 029
004 FRANCE 035
005 W. GERMANY 038
006 GREECE 040
007 ICELAND 046
008 ITALY 053
009 LUXEMBORG 064
010 NETHERLANDS 072
011 NORWAY 077
012 PORTUGAL 089
013 TURKEY 101
014 UNITED KINGDOM 105
015 U.S.A. 106

SEATO 3
001 AUSTRALIA 005
002 FRANCE 035
003 NEW ZEALAND 073
004 PAKISTAN 078
005 PHILIPPINES 082
006 THAILAND 097
007 UNITED KINGDOM 105
008 U.S.A. 106

EUROPEAN ECONOMIC COM. 4
```

```
001 BELGIUM 007
002 DENMARK 029
003 FRANCE 035
004 W. GERMANY 038
005 IRELAND 051
006 ITLAY 053
007 LUXEMBOURG 064
008 NETHERLANDS 072
009 NORWAY 077
010 UNITED KINGDOM 105

CENTRAL TREATY ORG. 5
001 IRAN 049
002 PAKISTAN 078
003 TURKEY 101
004 UNITED KINGDOM 105
005 U.S.A. 106

OAS 6
001 ARGENTINA 004
002 BOLIVIA 008
003 BRAZIL 009
004 CHILE 019
005 COLOMBIA 021
006 COSTA RICA 024
007 DOMMICAN REP. 030
008 ECUADOR 031
009 EL SALVADOR 032
010 GUATEMALA 041
011 HAITI 043
012 HONDURAS 044
013 JAMAICA 055
014 MEXICO 068
015 NICARAGUA 074
016 PANAMA 079
017 PARAGUAY 080
018 PERU 081
019 TRINIDAD 099
020 U.S.A. 106
021 URUGUAY 108
022 VENEZUELA 109
023 BARBADOS 128

THE ARAB LEAGUE 7
001 ALGERIA 003
002 IRAQ 050
003 JORDAN 057
004 LEBANON 061
005 LIBYA 063
006 MOROCCO 070
007 SAUDI ARABIA 087
008 SUDAN 093
009 SYRIA 096
010 TUNISIA 100
011 U.A.R. 104
012 YEMEN 112
013 KUWAIT 116

ORGANIZATION OF AFRICAN UNITY 8
001 ALGERIA 003
002 BURUNDI 012
003 CAMEROON 014
004 CEN. AFRICAN REP. 016
005 CHAD 018
006 CONGO (BRA) 022
007 CONGO (LEO) 023
```

```
008 DAHOMEY 028
009 ETHIOPIA 033
010 GABON 036
011 GHANA 039
012 GUINEA 042
013 IVORY COAST 054
014 LIBERIA 062
015 LIBYA 063
016 MALAGASY REP. 065
017 MALI 066
018 MAURITANIA 067
019 MOROCCO 070
020 NIGER 075
021 NIGERIA 076
022 RWANDA 086
023 SENEGAL 088
024 SIERRA LEONE 089
025 SOMALIA 090
026 SUDAN 093
027 TOGO 098
028 TUNISIA 100
029 UGANDA 102
030 U.A.R. 104
031 UPPER VOLTA 107
032 BOTSWANA 114
033 GAMBIA 115
034 LESOTHO 117
035 MALAWI 118
036 TANZANIA 120
037 ZAMBIA 121
038 KENYA 122

ANZUS 9
001 AUSTRALIA 005
002 NEW ZEALAND 073
003 U.S.A. 106

ODECA 10
001 COSTA RICA 024
002 EL SALVADOR 032
003 GUATEMALA 041
004 HONDURAS 044
005 NICARAGUA 074


COMMONWEALTH 11
001 AUSTRALIA 005
002 CANADA 015
003 CEYLON 017
004 CYPRUS 026
005 GHANA 039
006 INDIA 047
007 JAMAICA 055
008 NEW ZEALAND 073
009 NIGERIA 076
010 PAKISTAN 078
011 SIERRA LEONE 089
012 TRINIDAD 099
013 UGANDA 102
014 UNITED KINGDOM 105
015 BOTSWANA 114
016 GAMBIA 115
017 LESOTHO 117
018 MALAWI 118
019 MALTA 119
020 TANZANIA 120
```

021 ZAMBIA 121
022 KENYA 122
023 SINGAPORE 124
024 GUYANA 125
025 MALAYSIA 126
026 BARBADOS 128

COMECON 12
001 BULGARIA 010
002 CZECHOSLOVAKIA 027
003 EAST GERMANY 037
004 HUNGARY 045
005 MONGOLIA 069
006 POLAND 083
007 RUMANIA 085
008 U.S.S.R. 103

LAFTA 13
001 ARGENTINA 004
002 BOLIVIA 008
003 BRAZIL 009
004 CHILE 019
005 COLOMBIA 021
006 ECUADOR 031
007 MEXICO 068
008 PARAGUAY 080
009 PERU 081
010 URUGUAY 108
011 VENEZUELA 109

WARSAW PACT 14
001 BULGARIA 010
002 CZECHOSLOVAKIA 027
003 EAST GERMANY 037
004 HUNGARY 045
005 POLAND 083
006 RUMANIA 085
007 U.S.S.R. 103

EUROPEAN COAL & STEEL COM. 15
001 BELGIUM 007
002 FRANCE 035
003 WEST GERMANY 038
004 ITALY 053
005 LUXEMBOURG 064
006 NETHERLANDS 072

COUNCIL OF EUROPE 16
001 AUSTRIA 006
002 BELGIUM 007
003 CYPRUS 026
004 DENMARK 029
005 FRANCE 035
006 WEST GERMANY 038
007 ICELAND 046
008 IRELAND 051
009 ITALY 053
010 LUXEMBOURG 064
011 NETHERLANDS 072
012 NORWAY 077
013 SWEDEN 094
014 SWITZERLAND 095
015 TURKEY 101
016 UNITED KINGDOM 105
017 MALTA 119

OPEC 17
001 ALGERIA 003
002 INDONESIA 048
003 IRAN 049
004 IRAQ 050
005 LIBYA 063
006 NIGERIA 076
007 SAUDI ARABIA 087
008 VENEZUELA 109
009 KUWAIT 116

ASIA & PACIFIC COUNCIL 18
001 AUSTRALIA 005
002 JAPAN 056
003 SOUTH KOREA 059
004 NEW ZEALAND 073
005 PHILIPPINES 082
006 THAILAND 097
007 SOUTH VIETNAM 111
008 MALAYSIA 126

FRENCH COM. 19
001 CAMEROON 014
002 CEN. AFRICAN REP. 016
003 CHAD 018
004 CONGO (BRA) 022
005 DAHOMEY 028
006 FRANCE 035
007 GABON 036
008 IVORY COAST 054
009 MALAGASY REP. 065
010 MALI 066
011 NIGER 075
012 SENEGAL 088
013 TOGO 098
014 UPPER VOLTA 107

WEU 20
001 BELGIUM 007
002 FRANCE 035
003 WEST GERMANY 038
004 ITALY 053
005 LUXEMBOURG 064
006 NETHERLANDS 072
007 UNITED KINGDOM 105

LATIN AMERICA 21
001 ARGENTIAN 004
002 BOLIVIA 008
003 BRAZIL 009
004 CHILE 019
005 COLOMBIA 021
006 COSTA RICA 024
007 CUBA 025
008 DOMINICAN REP. 030
009 ECUADOR 031
010 EL SALVADOR 032
011 GUATEMALA 041
012 HAITI 043
013 HONDURAS 044
014 JAMAICA 055
015 MEXICO 068
016 NICARAGUA 074
017 PANAMA 079
018 PARAGUAY 080

```
019 PERU 081
020 TRINIDAD 099
021 URUGUAY 108
022 VENEZUELA 109
023 GUYANA 125
024 BARBADOS 128

ASIA 22
001 AFGHANISTAN 001
002 AUSTRALIA 005
003 BURMA 011
004 CAMBODIA 013
005 CEYLON 017
006 CHINA, PR 020
007 INDIA 047
008 INDONESIA 048
009 JAPAN 056
010 NORTH KOREA 058
011 SOUTH KOREA 059
012 LAOS 060
013 MONGOLIA 069
014 NEPAL 071
015 NEW ZEALAND 073
016 PAKISTAN 078
017 PHILIPPINES 082
018 THAILAND 097
019 NORTH VIETNAM 110
020 SOUTH VIETNAM 111
021 WEST SAMOA 123
022 SINGAPORE 124
023 MALAYSIA 126
024 MALDIVE ISLANDS 127

AFRICA 23
001 ALGERIA 003
002 BURRUNDI 012
003 CAMEROUN 014
004 CEM9 AFRICAN REP9 016
005 CHAD 018
006 CONGO (BRA) 022
007 CONGO (LEO) 023
008 DAHOMEY 028
009 ETHIOPIA 033
010 GABON 036
011 GHANA 039
012 GUINEA 042
013 IVORY COAST 054
014 LIBERIA 062
015 LIBYA 063
016 MALAGASY REP. 065
017 MALI 066
018 MAURITANIA 067
019 MOROCCO 070
020 NIGER 075
021 NIGERIA 076
022 RWANDA 086
023 SENEGAL 088
024 SIERRA LEONE 089
025 SOMALIA 090
026 SOUTH AFRICA 091
027 SUDAN 093
028 TOGO 098
029 TUNISICA 100
030 UGANDA 102
031 U.A.R. 104
032 UPPER VOLTA 107
```

033 BOTSWANA 114
034 GAMBIA 115
035 LESOTHO 117
036 MALAWI 118
037 TANZANIA 120
038 ZAMBIA 121
039 KENYA 122

WESTERN EUROPE 24
001 AUSTRIA 006
002 BELGIUM 007
003 DENMARK 029
004 FINLAND 034
005 FRANCE 035
006 WEST GERMANY 038
007 GREECE 040
008 ICELAND 046
009 IRELAND 051
010 ITALY 053
011 LUXEMBOURG 064
012 NETHERLANDS 072
013 NORWAY 077
014 PORTUGAL 084
015 SPAIN 092
016 SWEDEN 094
017 SWITZERLAND 095
018 UNITED KINGDOM 105

ALL EUROPE 25
001 ALBANIA 002
002 AUSTRIA 006
003 BELGIUM 007
004 BULGARIA 010
005 CZECHOSLOVAKIA 027
006 DENMARK 029
007 FINLAND 034
008 FRANCE 035
009 EAST GERMANY 037
010 WEST GERMANY 038
011 GREECE 040
012 HUNGARY 045
013 ICELAND 046
014 IRELAND 051
015 ITALY 053
016 LUXEMBOURG 064
017 NETHERLANDS 072
018 NORWAY 077
019 POLAND 083
020 PORTUGAL 084
021 ROMANIA 085
022 SPAIN 092
023 SWEDEN 094
024 SWITZERLAND 095
025 TURKEY 101
026 U.S.S.R. 103
027 UNITED KINGDOM 105
028 YUGOSLAVIA 113
029 MALTA 119

SOVIET BLOC EUROPE 26
001 ALBANIA 002
002 BULGARIA 010
003 CZECHOSLOVAKIA 027
004 EAST GERMANY 037
005 HUNGARY 045
006 POLAND 083

007 ROMANIA 085
008 U.S.S.R. 103
009 YUGOSLAVIA 113

MIDDLE EAST 27
001 CYPRUS 026
002 IRAN 049
003 IRAQ 050
004 ISRAEL 052
005 JORDAN 057
006 LEBANON 061
007 SAUDI ARABIA 087
008 SYRIA 096
009 TURDEY 101
010 U.A.R. 104
011 YEMEN 112
012 DUWAIT 116

AFRO-ASIAN THIRD WORLD 29
001 AFGHANISTAN 001
002 ALGERIA 003
003 BURMA 011
004 BURUNDI 012
005 CAMBODIA 013
006 CAMEROUN 014
007 CEN. AFRICAN REP. 016
008 CEYLON 017
009 CHAD 018
010 CHINA, PR 020
011 CONGO (BRA) 022
012 CONGO (LEO) 023
013 DAHOMEY 028
014 ETHIOPIA 033
015 GABON 036
016 GHANA 039
017 GUINEA 042
018 INDIA 047
019 INDONESIA 048
020 IRAN 049
021 IRAQ 050
022 IVORY COAST 054
023 JORDAN 057
024 NORTH KOREA 058
025 LAOS 060
026 LEBANON 061
027 LIBERIA 062
028 LIBYA 063
029 MALAGASY REP. 065
030 MALI 066
031 MAURITANIA 067
032 MOROCCO 070
033 NEPAL 071
034 NIGER 075
035 NIGERIA 076
036 PAKISTAN 078
037 PHILIPPINES 082
038 RWANDA 086
039 SAUDI ARABIA 087
040 SENEGAL 088
041 SIERRA LEONE 089
042 SOMALIA 090
043 SUDAN 093
044 SYRIA 096
045 THAILAND 097
046 TOGO 098
047 TUNISIA 100

048 UGANDA 102
049 U.A.R. 104
050 UPPER VOLTA 107
051 NORTH VIETNAM 110
052 YEMEN 112
053 BOTSWANA 114
054 GAMBIA 115
055 KUWAIT 116
056 LESOTHO 117
057 MALAWI 118
058 MALTA 119
059 TANZANIA 120
060 ZAMBIA 121
061 KENYA 122
062 WEST SAMOA 123
063 SINGAPORE 124
064 MALAYSIA 126
065 MALDIVE ISLANDS 127

(THE ABOVE CODES ARE:REGIONAL CODES, SUCH AS SEATO 3;COUNTRY CODES, SUCH AS AUSTRALIA 005 AND THE SEQUENCE CODE WITHIN A GROUP, SUCH AS 001 FOR AUSTRALIA, THE FIRST COUNTRY LISTED IN SEATO.)

INSERT 54

LIST SORT OF THE WORLD MODEL WITH THE GROUP MODELS ON SELECTED FACTORS

POWER BASE DISTANCE

29.THIRD WORLD	3.08
8. ORGAN. OF AFRICAN UNITY	2.03
23.AFRICA	1.99
1. WORLD	1.26
11.COMMONWEALTH	1.11
21.LATIN AMERICA	.95
6. OAS	.87
22.ASIA	.52
7. ARAB LEAGUE	.50
27.MID. EAST REGIONAL	.22
10.CEN. AMER. COMMON MARKET	.21
13.LAFTA	.16
17.OPEC	.12
19.FRENCH COMMUNITY	-.00
18.ASIA AND PACIFIC COUNCIL	-.11
9. ANZUS	-.23
5. CENTO	-.50
26.EASTERN EUROPE	-.75
12.COMECON	-.81
3. SEATO	-.81
14.WARSAW PACT	-.88
15.EUROPEAN COAL AND STEEL COM	-1.03
16.COUNCIL OF EUROPE	-1.35
4. EUROPEAN ECON. COM.	-1.37
20.W. EUROPEAN UNION	-1.38
24.WESTERN EUROPE	-1.60
2. NATO	-1.61
25.EUROPE	-2.22

ECONOMIC DEVELOPMENT DISTANCE

29.THIRD WORLD	1.53
8. ORGAN. OF AFRICAN UNITY	.91
23.AFRICA	.91
1. WORLD	.66
7. ARAB LEAGUE	.52
22.ASIA	.46
27.MID. EAST REGIONAL	.34
21.LATIN AMERICA	.26
6. OAS	.24
11.COMMONWEALTH	.21
13.LAFTA	.12
5. CENTO	.11
18.ASIA AND PACIFIC COUNCIL	.09
10.CEN. AMER. COMMON MARKET	.08
17.OPEC	.01
3. SEATO	-.13
9. ANZUS	-.14
12.COMECON	-.26
14.WARSAW PACT	-.26
2. NATO	-.29
15.EUROPEAN COAL AND STEEL COM	-.30
26.EASTERN EUROPE	-.31
20.W. EUROPEAN UNION	-.32
19.FRENCH COMMUNITY	-.44
4. EUROPEAN ECON. COM.	-.50
16.COUNCIL OF EUROPE	-.57
24.WESTERN EUROPE	-.73
25.EUROPE	-.94

POLITICAL DISTANCE

1. WORLD	1.21
7. ARAB LEAGUE	.74
29.THIRD WORLD	.70
17.OPEC	.59
27.MID. EAST REGIONAL	.54
6. OAS	.35
21.LATIN AMERICA	.32
13.LAFTA	.31
14.WARSAW PACT	.27
26.EASTERN EUROPE	.27
12.COMECON	.23
25.EUROPE	.19
8. ORGAN. OF AFRICAN UNITY	.14
23.AFRICA	.13
5. CENTO	.06
22.ASIA	.04
20.W. EUROPEAN UNION	.03
15.EUROPEAN COAL AND STEEL COM	.02
24.WESTERN EUROPE	.02
9. ANZUS	.02
3. SEATO	-.06
10.CEN. AMER. COMMON MARKET	-.07
18.ASIA AND PACIFIC COUNCIL	-.07
4. EUROPEAN ECON. COM.	-.07
11.COMMONWEALTH	-.10
16.COUNCIL OF EUROPE	-.12
2. NATO	-.14
19.FRENCH COMMUNITY	-.49

MILITARISM DISTANCE

13.LAFTA	.56
21.LATIN AMERICA	.54
6. OAS	.44
11.COMMONWEALTH	.39
23.AFRICA	.36
8. ORGAN. OF AFRICAN UNITY	.27
18.ASIA AND PACIFIC COUNCIL	.25
7. ARAB LEAGUE	.20
17.OPEC	.04
29.THIRD WORLD	.02
27.MID. EAST REGIONAL	-.03
9. ANZUS	-.03
10.CEN. AMER. COMMON MARKET	-.08
22.ASIA	-.10
3. SEATO	-.12
15.EUROPEAN COAL AND STEEL COM	-.19
19.FRENCH COMMUNITY	-.22
20.W. EUROPEAN UNION	-.22
4. EUROPEAN ECON. COM.	-.30
5. CENTO	-.34
14.WARSAW PACT	-.44
12.COMECON	-.45
16.COUNCIL OF EUROPE	-.46
24.WESTERN EUROPE	-.58
1. WORLD	-.60
26.EASTERN EUROPE	-.62
2. NATO	-.70
25.EUROPE	-1.32

INSERT 55

01 ECONOMIC DEVELOPMENT

085 NATIONAL GOVERNMENT REVENUE PER CAPITA	.92
087 NATIONAL GOVERNMENT EXPENDITURE PER CAPITA	.91
095 IMPORTS PER CAPITA	.91
031 GNP PER CAPITA (IN U.S. DOLLARS)	.90
058 EDUCATION EXPENDITURE PER CAPITA (IN MILLION U.S. DOLLARS)	.89
115 TOTAL HIGHWAY VEHICLES PER CAPITA	.89
111 PASSENGER CARS PER CAPITA	.88
116 GROSS DOMESTIC PRODUCT PER CAPITA	.88
097 EXPORTS PER CAPITA	.87
093 TELEPHONES PER CAPITA	.87
113 COMMERCIAL VEHICLES PER CAPITA	.86
015 RADIOS PER 1,000 POPULATION	.86
120 ENERGY CONSUMPTION IN KILOGRAMS PER CAPITA	.85
016 TELEVISIONS PER 1,000 POPULATION	.80
017 CINEMA ATTENDANCE PER CAPITA, 1960	.78
061 HEALTH EXPENDITURE PER CAPITA	.77
049 PHYSICIANS PER ONE MILLION POPULATION, 1965	.76
091 ALL MAIL PER CAPITA	.76

****

INSERT 56

CORRELATION OF GROUP ATTRIBUTES
WITH GROUP MODELS

	1	2	3	4	5	6	7	8	9	10	11	12	13	14	15	16	17	18	19	20	21	22
VAR 1	-.79	-.64	.45	.16	-.55	.32	.13	.22	-.25	-.06	.55	-.30	.05	.28	.19	-.21	.06	.12	.02	.20	-.11	.10
VAR 2	-.73	-.49	.48	.12	-.53	.23	.26	.18	-.32	-.03	.36	-.30	.04	.19	.28	-.19	-.01	.13	-.03	.14	-.04	.12
VAR 3	-.12	-.12	.53	.37	-.31	.03	.30	-.08	-.27	-.19	.19	.08	-.24	-.02	.54	.18	-.10	.26	-.32	.34	.12	.43
VAR 4	.43	.01	-.38	-.42	.49	-.36	-.03	-.07	-.08	.58	-.39	.04	.30	-.80	-.07	-.06	-.37	-.54	-.45	-.45	.08	-.12
VAR 5	.39	.29	-.33	-.17	.22	-.06	-.01	-.23	.01	.18	-.31	-.04	.18	-.25	-.18	.17	-.21	-.35	-.02	-.30	.17	-.02
VAR 6	-.01	.11	.49	.02	-.54	.17	-.06	-.32	-.32	-.33	.36	-.22	-.04	.26	.23	.07	.07	.31	.05	.37	.20	.14
VAR 7	-.51	-.41	.37	-.08	-.67	.35	-.09	-.08	-.49	.09	.55	-.51	.36	.24	.13	-.22	-.03	-.01	.14	.24	.21	.09
VAR 8	-.45	-.29	.34	.22	-.04	.09	.39	.70	.03	-.01	.17	-.05	-.17	-.06	.10	.00	.02	.21	-.26	.00	-.46	-.03
VAR 9	-.36	-.16	.36	.04	-.55	.33	.07	-.04	-.23	-.19	.39	-.36	.09	.35	-.00	-.06	.04	.07	.16	.11	.12	-.03
VAR 10	.39	.44	-.17	-.07	.09	.07	-.06	-.15	.14	-.05	-.19	-.10	.01	-.04	-.24	.13	.10	-.07	.02	-.18	.17	-.15
VAR 11	.43	.51	-.13	-.02	.07	-.05	-.07	-.18	.16	-.21	-.20	.04	-.10	.12	-.19	.17	.08	.13	.21	.03	.10	-.10
VAR 12	-.17	-.54	.22	.38	.09	.04	.16	.33	.09	-.11	.28	.33	-.30	-.14	.10	-.09	-.03	.10	-.48	.15	-.08	.32
VAR 13	.42	.39	-.20	-.16	.22	-.07	.09	-.07	.09	.04	-.31	-.01	.04	-.16	-.23	.11	-.13	-.20	.02	-.30	.08	-.17
VAR 14	-.59	-.56	.13	-.18	-.33	.11	-.10	.11	-.30	.29	.33	-.30	.29	.08	.16	-.41	.01	-.06	.11	.09	-.04	-.07
VAR 15	.14	.16	-.10	-.19	-.17	.10	-.01	-.20	-.13	.16	-.01	-.33	.27	-.05	-.15	.02	-.15	-.32	.07	-.20	.22	-.17
VAR 16	-.42	-.24	.47	.58	-.50	.34	.07	-.04	.13	-.67	.56	.06	-.34	.55	.08	.08	.27	.35	.07	.38	.05	.31
VAR 17	.21	.28	.02	.15	-.28	.02	-.09	-.59	-.03	-.28	-.04	.00	-.10	.25	.13	.17	.05	.08	.12	.20	.40	.15
VAR 18	.61	.62	-.40	.11	.55	-.29	-.23	-.00	.60	-.33	-.39	.47	-.35	.02	-.29	.22	.25	.25	.17	.03	-.16	-.09
VAR 19	.49	.41	-.41	-.14	.30	-.05	-.31	-.26	.24	-.03	-.21	.10	.07	-.05	-.31	.14	.08	-.12	.17	-.13	.10	-.09
VAR 20	.07	.15	.16	.17	-.46	.06	-.15	-.39	-.06	-.27	.29	-.13	.02	.26	.08	.12	-.05	.15	.21	.37	.26	.16
VAR 21	.35	.28	-.25	.50	.38	-.02	-.41	-.03	.66	-.42	.06	.53	-.44	.14	-.13	.33	.45	.43	-.04	.34	-.13	.25
VAR 22	-.44	-.19	.42	.12	-.55	.50	.09	-.05	-.24	-.21	.47	-.40	.09	.35	.02	.05	.14	.05	.06	.07	.10	.07
VAR 23	-.25	-.08	.23	.50	-.08	-.02	.06	.16	.24	-.35	.15	.29	-.46	.27	.29	.09	.32	.58	.08	.45	-.24	.29
VAR 24	.61	.64	-.55	-.24	.54	-.27	-.12	.05	.36	.12	-.59	.14	-.02	-.12	-.34	.10	.04	-.06	.24	-.28	-.08	-.38
VAR 25	-.28	-.21	.33	.22	-.07	.21	-.03	.21	-.16	-.11	.31	.10	-.10	.12	.24	.17	.21	.38	-.11	.34	-.24	.36
VAR 26	.36	.49	.27	.42	-.03	-.04	.27	-.12	.28	-.61	-.12	.33	-.57	.31	.14	.23	.16	.43	.08	.21	.13	.10
VAR 27	-.52	-.20	.63	.37	-.46	.17	.46	.26	-.18	-.28	.27	-.09	-.30	.27	.42	.11	-.01	.41	-.06	.28	-.22	.21
VAR 28	.02	.20	.08	.70	.17	-.01	.24	.25	.35	-.45	-.15	.50	-.60	.31	.16	.26	.28	.56	.06	.39	-.09	.47
VAR 29	-.28	-.24	.29	.16	-.04	.16	.41	.58	-.13	.04	.11	-.15	-.07	-.11	.04	.05	-.14	.00	-.29	-.08	-.23	.06
VAR 30	.43	.65	-.18	.24	.49	-.04	-.15	.08	.53	-.33	-.31	.40	-.47	.21	-.01	.30	.52	.55	.29	.12	-.26	-.00
VAR 31	-.17	-.09	.27	.16	-.53	-.13	.22	-.35	-.30	-.09	.05	-.09	-.02	.15	.38	.03	-.32	.06	.06	.30	.29	.19
VAR 32	-.41	-.32	.12	.24	-.21	.15	-.33	.14	.11	-.17	.45	.02	-.08	.37	.11	-.17	.40	.37	.19	.46	-.12	.13
VAR 33	.04	.07	.08	.57	.33	-.04	.10	.34	.49	-.51	-.03	.63	-.61	.22	.04	.17	.35	.49	-.07	.27	-.26	.29

INSERT 57

Summary of theories

	subjects	predictors	that predicted
attribute theory	nation monads	a-space factor scores	total behavior
social field theory	nation dyads	a-space distances	dyadic behavior
status field	nation dyads	a-space distances	dyadic behavior

theory			
relative status field theory	nation dyads	partitioned a-space distances	partitioned dyadic behavior
distance theory	nation dyads	d-space factor scores	dyadic behavior
deviance theory	nation monads	means of d-space factor scores	total behavior

INSERT 58

Basic Steps

Step 1. Construct a-space.

Step 2. Construct d-space.

Step 3. Construct the monadic conflict vector.

Step 4. Construct the dyadic conflict vectors.

Step 5. Construct the monadic cooperation vector.

Step 6. Construct the dyadic cooperation vectors.

Step 7. Correlate a-space factor scores with the monadic conflict vector (attribute theory).

Step 8. Correlate a-space factor scores with the monadic cooperation vector (attribute theory).

Step 9. Correlate the 128 a-space distance sets with 128 dyadic conflict vector sets (social field and status-field theories).

Step 10. Correlate the 128 a-space distance sets with 128 dyadic cooperation vector sets (social field and status-field theory).

Step 11. Correlate the 128 d-space dyadic factor sets with the 128 dyadic conflict vector sets (distance theory).

Step 12. Correlate the 128 d-space dyadic factor sets with the 128 dyadic cooperation vector sets (distance theory).

Step 13. Partition the a-space distances into tt, ut, tu and uu matrices (for relative status-field theory tests).

Step 14. Correlate the 128 tt a-space distances matrices with the 128 conflict vector sets (relative status-field theory).

Step 15. Correlate the 128 ut a-space distance matrices with the 128 dyadic conflict vector sets (relative status-field theory).

Step 16. Correlate the 128 tu a-space distance matrices with the 128 dyadic conflict vector sets (relative status field theory).

Step 17. Correlate the 128 uu a-space distance matrices with the 128 dyadic conflict vector sets (relative status-field theory).

Step 18. Correlate the 128 tt a-space distance matrices with the 128 dyadic cooperation vector sets (relative status-field theory).

Step 19. Correlate the 128 ut a-space distance matrices with the 128 dyadic cooperation vector sets (relative status-field theory).

Step 20. Correlate the 128 tu distance matrices with the 128 dyadic cooperation vector sets (relative status-field theory).

Step 21. Correlate the 128 uu a-space distance matrices with the 128 dyadic cooperation vector sets (relative status-field theory).

Step 22. Partition the negative weight subjects from the positive weight subjects on each dimension, such as economic development, for each test i.e., for the outcomes generated from the steps 9-12, 14-21.

Step 23. Correlate the a-space factor scores with the magnitude of the positive weights generated for each step 9-12, 14-21 (to provide a basis for comparing theories and to generate descriptive information concerning the characteristics of those with large vs. small positive parameter weights).

Step 24. Correlate a-space factor scores with the magnitude of the negative weights for steps 9-12, 14-21 (for the same purpose as in the case of the positive weights).

Step 25. Perform a discriminant function analysis on positive weight vs. negative weight subjects from steps 9-12, 14-21 (to compare positive vs. negative weight subjects across the theories i.e., in contrast to the magnitude of weights analysis as performed in steps 23-24).

Step 26. Compute the means of d-space factor scores, dyadic set by dyadic set, to create a matrix of means of d-space (for deviance theory).

Step 27. Correlate the means of d-space with the monadic conflict vector (deviance theory).

Step 28. Correlate the means of d-space with the monadic cooperation vector (deviance theory).

Step 29. Generate predictive models for the theories for various groupings such as OAS, Africa, NATO, etc., spanning the international relations system.

Step 30. Compare the theoretic models, generated in step 29, (in respect to the implications for conflict and cooperation exportation between regional groupings) for major dimensions, such as economic development.

INSERT 59

Selected illustrative findings on steps that have been completed (step numbers correspond with previous step numbers).

Step 1. 22 factors are generated from 144 attribute variables. Economic development, power base, and non-competitive political system are among the largest factors.

Step 2. 33 factors are generated from a 144 distance matrix. Economic development, power base and political distance are among the largest factors.

Step 3. The USSR, US, Chinese Peoples' Republic and Israel are among the highest conflict exporting states.

Step 3. Iceland, Afghanistan, and Nigeria are among the lowest conflict exporting states.

Step 5. The US, USSR, United Kingdom and France are among the highest cooperation exporting states.

Step 5. Paraguay, Iceland and Dahomey, are among the lowest cooperation exporting states.

Step 7. Power base and military personal per capita are the best predictors of high conflict exportation (attribute theory).

Step 8. Power base is the best predictor of high cooperation exportation (attribute theory).

Step 9. In the system as a whole, i's tend to export most conflict to j's above them in respect to economic development and power (social field theory).

Step 10. In the system as a whole, i's tend to export most cooperation to j's above them in respect to economic development and power (social field theory).

Step 11. In the system as a whole, i's tend to export most conflict to j's distant from them in respect to power base, economic development and political system (distance theory).

Step 12. In the system as a whole, i's tend to export most cooperation to j's distant from them in respect to power base, economic development and political systems (distance theory).

Step 14. TT i's tend to export most conflict to j's close to them in respect to economic development and power (tt, relative status-field theory).

Step 15. UT i's tend to export most conflict to j's close to them in respect to economic development and power (ut, relative status-field theory).

Step 16. TU i's tend to export most conflict to j's close to them in respect to economic devlopment but distant from them in respect to power (tu, relative status-field theory).

Step 17. UU i's tend to export most conflict to j's distant from them in respect to economic development and power (uu, relative status-field theory).

Step 18. TT i's tend to export most cooperation to j's close to them in respect to economic development and power (tt, relative status-field theory).

Step 19. UT i's tend to export most cooperation to j's close to them in respect to economic development and power (ut, relative status-field theory).

Step 20. TU i's tend to export most cooperation to j's close to them in respect to economic development and distant from them in respect to power (tu, relative status-field theory).

Step 21. UU i's tend to export most cooperation to j's distant from them in respect to economic development and power (uu, relative status-field theory).

Step 26. The most deviant national actors in terms of their attributes are the U.S., United kingdom and Sweden.

Step 27. High deviance in respect to militarism and power tends to predict high conflict (deviance theory).

Step 28. High deviance in respect to economic development and power tends to predict high cooperation (deviance theory).

Step 30. On the basis of limited testing, distinct regional patterns are apparent. For example, European states tend to export high levels of conflict to states close to them in respect to power while African states tend to export high conflict to states distant from them in respect to power.

INSERT 60

CANONICAL CORRELATIONS FOR 128 STATES

31	ECUADOR	.96
63	LIBYA	.92
61	LEBANON	.90
104	U.A.R.	.85
126	MALAYSIA	.84
87	SAUDI ARABIA	.84
96	SYRIA	.81
19	CHILE	.77
84	PORTUGAL	.74
83	POLAND	.74
52	ISRAEL	.70
56	JAPAN	.69
50	IRAQ	.66

106	UNITED STATES	.65
3	ALGERIA	.65
92	SPAIN	.64
109	VENEZUELA	.64
103	U.S.S.R	.62
73	NEW ZEALAND	.62
38	WEST GERMANY	.62
10	BULGARIA	.61
4	ARGENTINA	.61
72	NETHERLANDS	.60
15	CANADA	.60
85	ROMANIA	.60
95	SWITZERLAND	.59
39	GHANA	.59
35	FRANCE	.58
45	HUNGARY	.58
94	SWEDEN	.56
7	BELGIUM	.56
53	ITALY	.56
37	EAST GERMANY	.53
29	DENMARK	.52
27	CZECHOSLOVAKIA	.52
91	SOUTH AFRICA	.51
105	UNITED KINGDOM	.50
5	AUSTRALIA	.45

INSERT 61

CANONICAL WEIGHTS

3 ALGERIA	.01	-.35	-.12	-.26	.20	.19	-.05	.06	.39	.00
	.36	-.04	-.23	.10	-.21	.29	-.19	-.20	.02	.15
	-.06	-.13	.88							
4 ARGENTINA	-.32	-.33	.36	.23	.06	-.28	.03	.13	.05	.05
	-.13	.19	.03	-.14	-.20	-.11	.16	-.23	-.09	.20
	-.27	-.23	.88							
5 AUSTRALIA	.12	-.07	-.29	-.31	.02	.12	-.04	.01	.42	.06
	.39	.08	-.25	.14	-.20	.25	-.20	-.22	.08	.24
	-.15	-.12	.93							
7 BELGIUM	.13	-.28	-.26	-.27	-.14	-.24	.34	-.25	.21	-.37
	-.18	.10	.12	.06	-.06	.35	.02	-.16	.23	.26
	.13	-.15	1.04							
10 BULGARIA	-.09	-.26	.04	.21	-.44	-.06	-.11	.18	.37	.17
	.11	-.33	-.30	-.02	-.09	.23	-.17	-.14	-.02	-.08
	-.17	.06	.89							
15 CANADA	-.29	-.27	-.02	-.45	-.01	.15	.12	-.17	-.21	.08
	.10	.14	.06	-.07	.04	.06	.07	-.30	.31	-.21
	-.13	.36	.90							
19 CHILE	.01	-.01	-.23	-.23	-.10	-.17	.39	.33	.14	-.41
	-.07	.07	.31	-.12	-.05	-.13	-.11	.15	-.20	-.01
	.28	-.28	.96							
27 CZECHOSLOVAKIA	-.53	-.37	-.11	.21	-.24	.26	.10	.10	-.15	-.28
	.34	-.24	-.05	.22	-.02	.03	.03	.17	.27	.02
	.37	-.02	1.19							
29 DENMARK	-.01	-.55	-.03	.24	-.22	.23	-.08	.06	.21	.29
	.35	-.17	-.17	.05	-.33	.09	-.31	-.18	.14	-.16
	-.15	.06	1.10							
31 ECUADOR	.30	.13	-.29	-.27	-.53	.13	.33	.17	-.03	-.08
	-.04	-.10	-.21	-.16	-.19	-.10	.17	.10	.25	-.22
	-.37	.31	1.22							
35 FRANCE	-.31	-.40	.13	.11	-.27	.05	.07	-.14	.11	-.12

		-.06	-.12	-.01	.24	-.26	-.12	.14	.08	.17	.05
		-.30	.02	.72							
37	EAST GERMANY	-.13	-.41	-.06	-.35	-.18	-.04	-.07	-.08	-.22	.23
		-.10	-.23	.07	-.30	-.08	.10	-.02	-.30	.03	.10
		-.06	-.15	.76							
38	WEST GERMANY	-.40	-.19	-.12	.00	-.32	.03	-.24	.20	.40	.23
		.29	-.43	-.10	-.10	.04	.23	-.28	-.14	.05	-.19
		-.14	-.27	1.20							
39	GHANA	.14	-.04	.44	-.31	.34	-.14	-.28	-.09	-.26	.00
		.15	.04	.08	.28	.08	-.02	.08	.14	.16	.21
		.06	-.17	.84							
45	HUNGARY	-.10	.19	.45	-.31	.12	.16	-.29	.13	-.22	.25
		.13	-.18	-.06	-.31	-.07	-.07	-.15	-.19	-.25	.04
		-.05	.04	.88							
50	IRAQ	-.12	-.42	-.38	-.17	.16	-.08	-.32	.04	.29	-.17
		.23	-.13	.32	-.07	.04	.24	.37	.20	.11	-.19
		-.26	-.26	1.21							
52	ISRAEL	-.15	.12	-.03	-.19	.17	.03	-.25	.12	.41	.10
		.33	-.36	-.10	-.17	-.13	.02	.16	.17	.10	.03
		-.37	.21	.90							
53	ITALY	-.33	-.23	-.07	.22	-.32	.02	-.17	.13	.29	.37
		.33	-.25	-.29	-.03	-.19	.11	-.30	-.18	.07	-.11
		-.11	-.01	1.04							
56	JAPAN	.12	-.30	.01	-.14	.14	.30	-.05	-.05	-.33	-.19
		.35	.34	-.09	-.24	-.12	-.42	.09	-.06	.23	.00
		.00	-.02	.94							
61	LEBANON	-.30	-.13	.07	.01	.20	.13	-.34	.08	.46	.19
		.35	-.28	-.03	-.28	-.14	.09	.06	.20	.06	.19
		-.24	.19	1.02							
63	LIBYA	-.12	-.10	.13	-.23	.19	.04	-.27	.09	.48	.09
		.25	-.15	.00	-.19	-.15	.20	.10	.13	.15	.09
		-.31	.29	.87							
72	NETHERLANDS	-.19	-.43	-.14	.16	-.18	.20	-.17	.10	.15	.18
		-.05	-.36	-.06	.03	-.19	.27	-.25	.25	.06	-.06
		-.05	.27	.89							
73	NEW ZEALAND	-.24	-.30	.18	.18	.14	.10	-.19	.06	.26	-.16
		.31	-.25	-.06	-.22	.07	.10	.18	-.07	.34	-.10
		.14	-.27	.86							
83	POLAND	-.43	-.41	-.07	-.17	-.30	.10	-.02	.09	-.20	.36
		-.04	-.40	.03	-.09	-.10	-.11	-.18	-.16	-.14	-.09
		-.02	-.25	1.01							
84	PORTUGAL	-.28	.00	-.08	-.01	.14	-.20	.09	-.23	.18	-.03
		-.25	-.04	-.05	.30	-.25	.30	-.15	-.22	.27	-.11
		.15	.26	.79							
85	ROMANIA	-.29	-.15	-.32	-.27	.09	.05	-.17	.01	.25	-.01
		.31	-.24	.20	-.16	.04	.33	.27	.07	.14	-.22
		-.21	-.33	1.01							
87	SAUDI ARABIA	.00	.04	-.27	-.03	-.11	.18	-.32	.33	.24	.21
		-.35	.33	.42	.35	-.18	-.13	.07	-.10	.09	-.46
		-.29	-.12	1.35							
91	SOUTH AFRICA	-.23	-.16	-.28	-.20	-.35	-.19	.01	-.46	-.10	-.09
		.24	.01	-.27	-.39	-.24	.05	-.07	-.12	-.20	.03
		-.25	-.10	1.06							
92	SPAIN	-.20	-.16	-.16	-.34	.15	-.16	-.13	-.17	.10	.05
		-.10	.43	-.41	.31	-.12	.12	-.25	.22	.09	-.10
		.10	-.12	.95							
94	SWEDEN	-.09	-.26	.08	.22	-.29	-.09	-.21	.23	.40	.29
		.15	-.38	-.29	.07	-.12	.12	-.19	-.26	-.04	-.05
		-.10	-.08	.97							
95	SWITZERLAND	-.10	.29	.05	-.11	.24	.01	-.25	.04	.40	.15
		.33	-.20	.00	-.28	-.09	-.08	.11	.22	.03	.15
		-.30	.28	.91							
96	SYRIA	-.28	.13	.02	.00	.17	-.03	-.27	.04	.48	.25
		.29	-.17	-.11	-.27	-.28	.08	.04	.08	.13	.18
		-.30	.14	.94							
103	U.S.S.R	-.41	-.49	-.04	.09	-.28	.30	-.30	.13	-.03	.21

	.04	-.39	-.07	-.24	-.04	.05	.00	-.25	-.07	.08
	-.27	-.16	1.13							
104 U.A.R.	-.21	.09	-.18	-.10	-.14	.15	-.37	.27	.24	.14
	-.32	.20	.41	.36	-.13	-.16	.03	.00	.02	-.35
	-.25	-.04	1.09							
105 UNITED KINGDOM	-.22	-.39	-.40	-.20	-.47	.12	-.16	.15	.31	.11
	-.14	-.14	-.15	.42	-.17	.24	.07	.07	-.16	-.20
	-.16	-.02	1.22							
106 UNITED STATES	.04	-.35	-.02	-.05	.29	.31	.06	-.16	-.33	.06
	.48	.30	.09	-.08	-.29	-.29	-.18	-.02	.20	-.06
	-.14	.19	1.08							
109 VENEZUELA	-.31	-.31	.00	-.34	.17	.04	.21	-.05	.03	.02
	.11	.13	.02	-.16	.16	.30	.22	-.18	.34	-.20
	-.11	.40	.97							
126 MALAYSIA	-.35	-.13	-.27	.31	.22	-.18	-.03	-.27	.21	-.17
	.10	-.17	.32	-.08	-.25	-.07	.18	-.22	-.06	.14
	.22	.08	.91							
COLUMN SUM OF SQUARES	2.28	3.00	1.67	1.93	2.22	1.01	1.74	1.13	3.03	1.48
	2.35	2.26	1.50	1.79	1.02	1.37	1.14	1.19	1.08	1.09
	1.70	1.54								

INSERT 62

HIGHEST AND LOWEST
WEIGHTS FOR SELECTED FACTORS

01 ECONOMIC DEVELOPMENT

31	ECUADOR	.30
39	GHANA	.14
7	BELGIUM	.13
5	AUSTRALIA	.12
56	JAPAN	.12
106	UNITED STATES	.04
3	ALGERIA	.01
29	DENMARK	-.01
10	BULGARIA	-.09
94	SWEDEN	-.09
45	HUNGARY	-.10
95	SWITZERLAND	-.10
63	LIBYA	-.12
50	IRAQ	-.12
37	EAST GERMANY	-.13
52	ISRAEL	-.15
72	NETHERLANDS	-.19
92	SPAIN	-.20
104	U.A.R.	-.21
105	UNITED KINGDOM	-.22
91	SOUTH AFRICA	-.23
73	NEW ZEALAND	-.24
84	PORTUGAL	-.28
96	SYRIA	-.28
85	ROMANIA	-.29

15	CANADA	-.29
61	LEBANON	-.30
35	FRANCE	-.31
109	VENEZUELA	-.31
4	ARGENTINA	-.32
53	ITALY	-.33
126	MALAYSIA	-.35
38	WEST GERMANY	-.40
103	U.S.S.R	-.41
83	POLAND	-.43
27	CZECHOSLOVAKIA	-.53

02 POWER BASE

95	SWITZERLAND	.29
45	HUNGARY	.19
31	ECUADOR	.13
96	SYRIA	.13
52	ISRAEL	.12
104	U.A.R.	.09
87	SAUDI ARABIA	.04
19	CHILE	-.01
39	GHANA	-.04
5	AUSTRALIA	-.07
63	LIBYA	-.10
61	LEBANON	-.13
126	MALAYSIA	-.13
85	ROMANIA	-.15
91	SOUTH AFRICA	-.16
92	SPAIN	-.16
38	WEST GERMANY	-.19
53	ITALY	-.23
10	BULGARIA	-.26
94	SWEDEN	-.26
15	CANADA	-.27
7	BELGIUM	-.28
56	JAPAN	-.30
73	NEW ZEALAND	-.30
109	VENEZUELA	-.31
4	ARGENTINA	-.33
106	UNITED STATES	-.35
3	ALGERIA	-.35
27	CZECHOSLOVAKIA	-.37
105	UNITED KINGDOM	-.39
35	FRANCE	-.40
37	EAST GERMANY	-.41
83	POLAND	-.41
50	IRAQ	-.42
72	NETHERLANDS	-.43
103	U.S.S.R	-.49
29	DENMARK	-.55

04 NON-COMPETITIVE POLITICAL SYSTEM

126	MALAYSIA	.31
29	DENMARK	.24
4	ARGENTINA	.23
53	ITALY	.22
94	SWEDEN	.22
10	BULGARIA	.21
27	CZECHOSLOVAKIA	.21
73	NEW ZEALAND	.18
72	NETHERLANDS	.16
35	FRANCE	.11
103	U.S.S.R	.09
61	LEBANON	.01
84	PORTUGAL	-.01
87	SAUDI ARABIA	-.03
106	UNITED STATES	-.05
104	U.A.R.	-.10
95	SWITZERLAND	-.11
56	JAPAN	-.14
50	IRAQ	-.17
83	POLAND	-.17
52	ISRAEL	-.19
91	SOUTH AFRICA	-.20
105	UNITED KINGDOM	-.20
63	LIBYA	-.23
19	CHILE	-.23
3	ALGERIA	-.26
31	ECUADOR	-.27
7	BELGIUM	-.27
85	ROMANIA	-.27
45	HUNGARY	-.31
39	GHANA	-.31
5	AUSTRALIA	-.31
92	SPAIN	-.34
109	VENEZUELA	-.34
37	EAST GERMANY	-.35
15	CANADA	-.45

INSERT 63

A-SPACE CORRELATIONS WITH SELECTED FACTORS
(NUMBERS, SUCH AS 10, REFER TO FACTOR NUMBERS, SEE BELOW)

CORRELATION OF A-SPACE WITH + WEIGHTS,
ECONOMIC DEVELOPMENT

1	10	N= 8	P= .0473	R= .7100
2	16	N= 8	P= .0389	R= -.7300

CORRELATION OF A-SPACE WITH + WEIGHTS,
POWER BASE

(NO SIGNIFICANT ASSOCIATIONS)

CORRELATION OF A-SPACE WITH + WEIGHTS,
NON-COMPETITIVE POLITICAL SYSTEM

1	12	N= 12	P= .0126	R= -.6900
2	14	N= 12	P= .0337	R= -.6100

CORRELATION OF A-SPACE WITH - WEIGHTS,

ECONOMIC DEVELOPMENT

```
   1           8    N=   29 P=      .0298 R=    -.4000
```

CORRELATION OF A-SPACE WITH - WEIGHTS,
POWER BASE

```
   1           2    N=   30 P=      .0362 R=    -.3800
   2          11    N=   30 P=      .0143 R=     .4400
   3          13    N=   30 P=      .0121 R=     .4500
```

CORRELATION OF A-SPACE WITH - WEIGHTS,
NON-COMPETITIVE POLITICAL SYSTEM

```
   1           7    N=   24 P=      .0389 R=     .4200
   2          18    N=   24 P=      .0124 R=    -.5000
```

INSERT 64

CORRELATIONS, SUMMARY

TYPE OF STATE WITH BIG + WEIGHT,
ECONOMIC DEVELOPMENT

(TENDS TO EXPORT CONFLICT TO THOSE DISTANT)

LARGE GNP GROWTH RATE AT FIXED PRICES

LOW ENERGY PRODUCTION

TYPE OF STATE WITH BIG + WEIGHT,
POWER BASE

(TENDS TO EXPORT CONFLICT TO THOSE DISTANT)

(NO SIGNIFICANT ASSOCIATION)

TYPE OF STATE WITH BIG + WEIGHT,
NON-COMPETITIVE POLITICAL SYSTEM

(TENDS TO EXPORT CONFLICT TO THOSE BELOW)

LOW GNP GROWTH RATE

LOW PER CAPITA SCHOOL ENROLLMENT

TYPE OF STATE WITH BIG - WEIGHT,
ECONOMIC DEVELOPMENT

(TENDS TO EXPORT MOST CONFLICT TO THOSE CLOSE)

RECENT NATIONAL INDEPENDENCE

TYPE OF STATE WITH BIG - WEIGHT,
POWER BASE

(TENDS TO EXPORT MOST CONFLICT TO THOSE CLOSE)

HIGH POWER BASE

MANY MILITARY PERSONNEL PER CAPITA

LARGE HEALH EXPENDITURES AS A PERCENTAGE OF GNP

TYPE OF STATE WITH BIG - WEIGHT,
NON-COMPETITIVE POLITICAL SYSTEM

(TENDS TO EXPORT MOST CONFLICT TO THOSE ABOVE)

LARGE CHRISTIAN COMMUNITY

HIGH RATIO OF BLACK MARKET TO OFFICIAL EXCHANGE

INSERT 65

F-TEST OF - VS. + WEIGHTS,
ECONOMIC DEVELOPMENT

1		12	6.8715	.0124
2	G MEA	12 1	.1749	-.8143

F-TEST OF - VS + WEIGHTS,
POWER BASE

1		16	6.7472	.0131
2	G MEA	16 1	.1804	-.7461

F-TEST OF - VS + WEIGHTS,
NON-COMPETITIVE POLITICAL SYSTEM

(NO SIGNIFICANT ASSOCIATIONS FOUND)

INSERT 66

F-TEST OF MEANS, SUMMARY

TYPE OF STATE WITH + WEIGHT,
ECONOMIC DEVELOPMENT

(TENDS TO EXPORT MOST CONFLICT TO THOSE DISTANT)

SMALL GNP GROWTH RATE

TYPE OF STATE WITH - WEIGHT,
ECONOMIC DEVELOPMENT
(TENDS TO EXPORT MOST CONFLICT TO THOSE CLOSE)

LARGE GNP GROWTH RATE

TYPE OF STATE WITH + WEIGHT,
POWER BASE

(TENDS TO EXPORT MOST CONFLICT TO THOSE DISTANT)

LOW ENERGY PRODUCTION

TYPE OF STATE WITH - WEIGHT,
POWER BASE

(TENDS TO EXPORT MOST CONFLICT TO THOSE CLOSE)

HIGH ENERGY PRODUCTION

TYPE OF STATE WITH + WEIGHT,
NON-COMPETITIVE POLITICAL SYSTEM

(TENDS TO EXPORT MOST CONFLICT TO THOSE BELOW)

(NO SIGNIFICANT ASSOCIATIONS)

TYPE OF STATE WITH - WEIGHT,
NON-COMPETITIVE POLITICAL SYSTEM

(TENDS TO EXPORT MOST CONFLICT TO THOSE ABOVE)

(NO SIGNIFICANT ASSOCIATIONS)

INSERT 67

CONTRIBUTIONS OF THE DISTANCES ON THE FACTORS TO CONFLICT

01 ECONOMIC DEVELOPMENT	J'S CLOSE BELOW
02 POWER BASE	J'S CLOSE BELOW
03 POLITICAL INSTABILITY	J'S FAR ABOVE
04 NON-COMPETITIVE POLITICAL SYSTEM	J'S FAR ABOVE
05 SMALL POPULATION GROWTH RATE	J'S FAR ABOVE
06 SMALL POPULATION DENSITY	J'S FAR BELOW
07 SMALL CHRISTIAN COMMUNITY	J'S FAR ABOVE
08 RECENT NATIONAL INDEPENDENCE	J'S FAR BELOW
09 LITTLE DOMESTIC VIOLENCE	J'S FAR BELOW
10 LARGE GNP GROWTH RATE AT FIXED PRICES	J'S FAR BELOW
11 FEW MILITARY PERSONNEL PER CAPITA	J'S FAR BELOW
12 LARGE GNP GROWTH RATE	J'S FAR ABOVE
13 SMALL HEALTH EXPENDITURE AS PERCENT OF GNP	J'S FAR ABOVE
14 HIGH PER CAPITA SCHOOL ENROLLMENT	J'S FAR ABOVE
15 HIGH PER CAPITA INTERNAL SECURITY FORCE	J'S FAR ABOVE
16 HIGH ENERGY PRODUCTION	J'S FAR BELOW
17 MANY ELECTIONS	J'S FAR ABOVE
18 HIGH RATIO OF BLACK MARKET TO OFFICIAL EXCHANGE	J'S FAR ABOVE

19 FEW EXECUTIVE ADJUSTMENTS	J'S FAR BELOW
20 LOW CRUDE DEATH RATE	J'S FAR ABOVE
21 LITTLE ETHNO-LINGUISTIC FRACTIONALIZATION	J'S FAR ABOVE
22 NEW CURRENCY	J'S FAR BELOW

INSERT 68

A-space factors.

01. Economic development
02. Power base
03. Political instability
04. Non-competitive political system
05. Small population growth rate
06. Small population density
07. Small Christian community
08. Recent national independence
09. Little domestic violence
10. Large GNP growth rate at fixed prices
11. Few military personnel per capita
12. Large GNP growth rate
13. Small health expenditure as percent of GNP
14. High per capita school enrollment
15. High per capita internal security force
16. High energy production
17. Many elections
18. High ratio of black market to official exchange
19. Few executive adjustments
20. Low crude death rate
21. Little ethno-linguistic fractionalization
22. New currency

INSERT 69

D-space factors.

01. Power base distance
02. Economic development distance
03. Political distance
04. School enrollment distance
05. Internal political turmoil distance
06. Internal violence closeness
07. Militarism distance
08. Date of independence distance
09. Population growth rate distance
10. Density distance
11. Internal security forces distance
12. Population size distance
13. Religious distance
14. Energy production distance
15. GNP growth rate distance
16. Fixed prices GNP growth rate closeness
17. Ethno-linguistic fractionalization closeness
18. Per cent urban population distance
19. All mail closeness
20. Political party fractionalization closeness
21. Domestic turmoil distance
22. Total area closeness
23. Per capita energy consumption growth rate distance

24. Infant mortality closeness
25. Age of currency closeness
26. Total health expenditure closeness
27. Crude death rate closeness
28. Regular executive transfers closeness
29. Per capita economic active male population distance
30. Concentration of export commodities closeness
31. Mean elections distance
32. Concentration of export receivers distance
33. Orthodox community closeness

INSERT 70

Frequency and direction of a-space discrimination across the d-space dimensions in the case of closeness.

01. Economic development	hhlllhhlh
02. Power base	hhhhh
03. Political instability	lhhllh
04. Non-competitive political system	lhl
05. Small population growth rate	hlhlllhhh
06. Small population density	llhhh
07. Small Christian community	hlh
08. Recent national independence	lhl
09. Little domestic violence	hhllhllh
10. Large GNP growth rate at fixed prices	lllhl
11. Few military personnel per capita	hlll
12. Large GNP growth rate	h
13. Small health expenditure as percent of GNP	lhlllh
14. High per capita school enrollment	hhh
15. High per capita internal security force	hll
16. High energy production	lhlhhh
17. Many elections	lll
18. High ratio of black market to official exchange	lhhh
19. Few executive adjustments	lllhhll
20. Low crude death rate	hll
21. Little ethno-linguistic fractionalization	hll
22. New currency	ll

INSERT 71

Frequency and direction of a-space predictions of weight magnitudes for closeness.

01. Economic development	lhhhhhhhhl
02. Power base	lhhhhhlhh
03. Political instability	llhh
04. Non-competitive political system	lh
05. Small population growth rate	lh
06. Small population density	hlll
07. Small Christian community	hh
08. Recent national independence	hl
09. Little domestic violence	l
10. Large GNP growth rate at fixed prices	lll
11. Few military personnel per capita	hlhh
12. Large GNP growth rate	hhh
13. Small health expenditure as percent of GNP	lhh
14. High per capita school enrollment	hhlh

15. High per capita internal security forc%	
16. High energy production	hhlhll
17. Many elections	lllh
18. High ratio of black market to official exchange	h
19. Few executive adjustments	hhl
20. Low crude death rate	llhl
21. Little ethno-linguistic fractionalization	lh
22. New currency	hhl

INSERT 72

Frequency and direction of a-space predictions of weight magnitudes for distance.

01. Economic development	lh
02. Power base	lllh
03. Political instability	hh
04. Non-competitive political system	hh
05. Small population growth rate	h
06. Small population density	hhh
07. Small Christian community	ll
08. Recent national independence	hhhl
09. Little domestic violence	hllhll
10. Large GNP growth rate at fixed prices	hllhhlhh
11. Few military personnel per capita	hhhhhlhh
12. Large GNP growth rate	ll
13. Small health expenditure as percent of GNP	lhh
14. High per capita school enrollment	llhl
15. High per capita internal security force	hhh
16. High energy production	lhl
17. Many elections	l
18. High ratio of black market to official exchange	
19. Few executive adjustments	lllh
20. Low crude death rate	hhhhl
21. Little ethno-linguistic fractionalization	hlhh
22. New currency	hl

INSERT 73

An inventory of findings for distance theory, conflict, a-space factor means for positive weight nations.

I's that tend to export high conflict to j's distant from them on power base

tend to exhibit the characteristics of:

low economic development -.2261 (mean group score in a-space)

small power base -.4451 (mean group score in a-space)

much domestic violence -.3186 (mean group score in a-space)

I's that tend to export high conflict to J's distant from them on economic development tend to exhibit the characteristics of:

low economic development -.4243 (mean group score in a-space)

political instability .2378 (mean group score in a-space)

large population growth rate -.2126 (mean group score in a-space)

much domestic violence -.3233 (mean group score in a-space)

I's that tend to export high conflict to J's distant from them on political system tend to exhibit the characteristics of:

non-competitive political system .2667 (mean group score in a-space)

many military personnel per capita -.1302 (mean group score in a-space)

high energy production .1610 (mean group score in a-space)

I's that tend to export high conflict to J's distant from them on school enrollment tend to exhibit the characteristics of:

low per capita school enrollment -.5211 (mean group score in a-space)

high crude death rate -.1733 (mean group score in a-space)

I's that tend to export high conflict to J's distant from them on internal political turmoil tend to exhibit the characteristics of:

little political instability -.5316 (mean group score in a-space)

small population growth rate .2484 (mean group score in a-space)

large gnp growth rate at fixed prices .3124 (mean group score in a-space)

few executive adjustments .2150 (mean group score in a-space)

I's that tend to export high conflict to J's close to them on internal violence tend to exhibit the characteristics of:

low economic development -.1802 (mean group score in a-space)

political instability .2418 (mean group score in a-space)

much domestic violence -.5329 (mean group score in a-space)

few elections   -.1389 (mean group score in a-space)

many executive adjustments   -.2319 (mean group score in a-space)

I's that tend to export high conflict to J's distant from them on militarism
tend to exhibit the characteristics of:

large christian community   -.2398 (mean group score in a-space)

few military personnel per capita   .5363 (mean group score in a-space)

I's that tend to export high conflict to J's distant from them on date of independence
tend to exhibit the characteristics of:

recent national independence   .5162 (mean group score in a-space)

much ethno-linguistic fractionalization   -.2026 (mean group score in a-space)

I's that tend to export high conflict to J's distant from them on population growth rate
tend to exhibit the characteristics of:

political instability   .3357 (mean group score in a-space)

large population growth rate   -.6670 (mean group score in a-space)

small population density   .2909 (mean group score in a-space)

few executive adjustments   .2585 (mean group score in a-space)

I's that tend to export high conflict to J's distant from them on density
tend to exhibit the characteristics of:

small population density   .3505 (mean group score in a-space)

I's that tend to export high conflict to J's distant from them on internal security forces
tend to exhibit the characteristics of:

low per capita internal security force   -.4368 (mean group score in a-space)

I's that tend to export high conflict to J's distant from them on population size
tend to exhibit the characteristics of:

high economic development   .2657 (mean group score in a-space)

small power base   -.2583 (mean group score in a-space)

low per capita school enrollment   -.1674 (mean group score in a-space)

many executive adjustments   -.2176 (mean group score in a-space)

I's that tend to export high conflict to J's distant from them on religion
tend to exhibit the characteristics of:

high economic development .3979 (mean group score in a-space)

small population growth rate .3780 (mean group score in a-space)

I's that tend to export high conflict to J's distant from them on energy production
tend to exhibit the characteristics of:

low economic development -.1910 (mean group score in a-space)

small power base -.0405 (mean group score in a-space)

large population density -.1813 (mean group score in a-space)

low energy production -.4746 (mean group score in a-space)

I's that tend to export high conflict to J's distant from them on gnp growth rate
tend to exhibit the characteristics of:

little domestic violence .2328 (mean group score in a-space)

small gnp growth rate -.3471 (mean group score in a-space)

I's that tend to export high conflict to J's close to them on fixed prices gnp growth rate
tend to exhibit the characteristics of:

non-competitive political system .2669 (mean group score in a-space)

small gnp growth rate at fixed prices -.5007 (mean group score in a-space)

I's that tend to export high conflict to J's close to them on ethno-linguistic fractionalization
tend to exhibit the characteristics of:

I's that tend to export high conflict to J's distant from them on per cent urban population
tend to exhibit the characteristics of:

large power base .4082 (mean group score in a-space)

little domestic violence .3348 (mean group score in a-space)

small gnp growth rate at fixed prices -.4337 (mean group score in a-space)

large health expenditure as percent of gnp -.4271 (mean group score in a-space)

old currency -.2915 (mean group score in a-space)

I's that tend to export high conflict to J's close to them on all mail
tend to exhibit the characteristics of:

high economic development .3257 (mean group score in a-space)

small population density .2767 (mean group score in a-space)

high per capita school enrollment .2803 (mean group score in a-space) low per capita internal security force -.2329 (mean group score in a-space)

low ratio of black market to official exchange -.2478 (mean group score in a-space)

few executive adjustments .3741 (mean group score in a-space)

I's that tend to export high conflict to J's close to them on political party fractionalization

tend to exhibit the characteristics of:

large population growth rate -.2301 (mean group score in a-space)

few elections -.1714 (mean group score in a-space)

I's that tend to export high conflict to J's distant from them on domestic turmoil

tend to exhibit the characteristics of:

long national independence -.2455 (mean group score in a-space)

little domestic violence .1424 (mean group score in a-space)

large health expenditure as percent of gnp -.2184 (mean group score in a-space)

high energy production .1820 (mean group score in a-space)

low crude death rate .2423 (mean group score in a-space)

I's that tend to export high conflict to J's close to them on total area

tend to exhibit the characteristics of:

low economic development -.1645 (mean group score in a-space)

large power base .3734 (mean group score in a-space)

large population growth rate -.2434 (mean group score in a-space)

small population density .4796 (mean group score in a-space)

much domestic violence -.3321 (mean group score in a-space)

I's that tend to export high conflict to J's distant from them on per capita energy consumption growth rate

tend to exhibit the characteristics of:

high energy production .1786 (mean group score in a-space)

many elections .2310 (mean group score in a-space)

few executive adjustments .1304 (mean group score in a-space)

I's that tend to export high conflict to J's close to them on infant mortality

tend to exhibit the characteristics of:

high economic development .3183 (mean group score in a-space)

little political instability -.2240 (mean group score in a-space) small population growth rate .2355 (mean group score in a-space)

large gnp growth rate at fixed prices .1823 (mean group score in a-space)

many military personnel per capita -.2776 (mean group score in a-space)

old currency -.2681 (mean group score in a-space)

I's that tend to export high conflict to J's close to them on age of currency
tend to exhibit the characteristics of:

large health expenditure as percent of gnp -.1877 (mean group score in a-space)

high energy production .1367 (mean group score in a-space)

high ratio of black market to official exchange .1893 (mean group score in a-space)

I's that tend to export high conflict to J's close to them on total health expenditure
tend to exhibit the characteristics of:

large health expenditure as percent of gnp -.3556 (mean group score in a-space)

low per capita internal security force -.1745 (mean group score in a-space)

I's that tend to export high conflict to J's close to them on crude death rate
tend to exhibit the characteristics of:

political instability .1687 (mean group score in a-space)

high ratio of black market to official exchange .2485 (mean group score in a-space)

many executive adjustments -.2873 (mean group score in a-space)

I's that tend to export high conflict to J's close to them on regular executive transfers
tend to exhibit the characteristics of:

long national independence -.2573 (mean group score in a-space)

large health expenditure as percent of gnp -.2568 (mean group score in a-space)

I's that tend to export high conflict to J's distant from them on per capita economic active male population
tend to exhibit the characteristics of:

small christian community .3599 (mean group score in a-space)

large health expenditure as percent of gnp -.3197 (mean group score in a-space)

I's that tend to export high conflict to J's close to them on concentration of export commodities
tend to exhibit the characteristics of:

small population growth rate .3412 (mean group score in a-space)

I's that tend to export high conflict to J's distant from them on mean elections

tend to exhibit the characteristics of:

1#ew elections -.1914 (mean group score in a-space)

little ethno-linguistic fractionalization .2408 (mean group score in a-space)

I's that tend to export high conflict to J's distant from them on concentration of export receivers

tend to exhibit the characteristics of:

non-competitive political system .2229 (mean group score in a-space)

large christian community -.2777 (mean group score in a-space)

few military personnel per capita .2469 (mean group score in a-space)

low crude death rate .2483 (mean group score in a-space)

I's that tend to export high conflict to J's close to them on orthodox community

tend to exhibit the characteristics of:

small population growth rate .1754 (mean group score in a-space)

little domestic violence .0888 (mean group score in a-space)

small gnp growth rate at fixed prices -.2978 (mean group score in a-space)

high ratio of black market to official exchange .1336 (mean group score in a-space)

much ethno-linguistic fractionalization -.1621 (mean group score in a-space)

INSERT 74

An inventory of findings for distance theory, conflict, a-space factor means for negative weight nations.

I's that tend to export high conflict to J's close to them on power base

tend to exhibit the characteristics of:

high economic development .3379 (mean group score in a-space)

large power base .7588 (mean group score in a-space)

little domestic violence .1173 (mean group score in a-space)

I's that tend to export high conflict to J's close to them on economic development

tend to exhibit the characteristics of:

high economic development .4737 (mean group score in a-space)

little political instability -.2128 (mean group score in a-space) small population growth rate .2359 (mean group score in a-space)

little domestic violence .0636 (mean group score in a-space)

I's that tend to export high conflict to J's close to them on political system

tend to exhibit the characteristics of:

competitive political system -.2995 (mean group score in a-space)

few military personnel per capita .2473 (mean group score in a-space)

low energy production -.3452 (mean group score in a-space)

I's that tend to export high conflict to J's close to them on school enrollment

tend to exhibit the characteristics of:

high per capita school enrollment .4609 (mean group score in a-space)

low crude death rate .2854 (mean group score in a-space)

I's that tend to export high conflict to J's close to them on internal political turmoil

tend to exhibit the characteristics of:

political instability .2855 (mean group score in a-space)

large population growth rate -.1407 (mean group score in a-space)

small gnp growth rate at fixed prices -.2539 (mean group score in a-space)

many executive adjustments -.1743 (mean group score in a-space)

I's that tend to export high conflict to J's distant from them on internal violence

tend to exhibit the characteristics of:

high economic development .2604 (mean group score in a-space)

little political instability -.2680 (mean group score in a-space)

little domestic violence .3068 (mean group score in a-space)

many elections .2397 (mean group score in a-space)

few executive adjustments .1812 (mean group score in a-space)

I's that tend to export high conflict to J's close to them on militarism

tend to exhibit the characteristics of:

small christian community .2521 (mean group score in a-space)

many military personnel per capita -.4501 (mean group score in a-space)

I's that tend to export high conflict to J's close to them on date of independence

tend to exhibit the characteristics of:

long national independence -.5492 (mean group score in a-space)

little ethno-linguistic fractionalization .2526 (mean group score in a-space)

I's that tend to export high conflict to J's close to them on population growth rate tend to exhibit the characteristics of:

little political instability -.1430 (mean group score in a-space)

small population growth rate .3407 (mean group score in a-space)

large population density -.1484 (mean group score in a-space)

many executive adjustments -.1826 (mean group score in a-space)

I's that tend to export high conflict to J's close to them on density tend to exhibit the characteristics of:

large population density -.1711 (mean group score in a-space)

I's that tend to export high conflict to J's close to them on internal security forces tend to exhibit the characteristics of:

high per capita internal security force .2480 (mean group score in a-space)

I's that tend to export high conflict to J's close to them on population size tend to exhibit the characteristics of:

low economic development -.2599 (mean group score in a-space)

large power base .5923 (mean group score in a-space)

high per capita school enrollment .2350 (mean group score in a-space)

few executive adjustments .1997 (mean group score in a-space)

I's that tend to export high conflict to J's close to them on religion tend to exhibit the characteristics of:

low economic development -.0676 (mean group score in a-space)

large population growth rate -.0876 (mean group score in a-space)

I's that tend to export high conflict to J's close to them on energy production tend to exhibit the characteristics of:

high economic development .3618 (mean group score in a-space)

large power base .3482 (mean group score in a-space)

small population density .2493 (mean group score in a-space)

high energy production .4974 (mean group score in a-space)

I's that tend to export high conflict to J's close to them on gnp growth rate

tend to exhibit the characteristics of:

much domestic violence -.2896 (mean group score in a-space)

large gnp growth rate .1420 (mean group score in a-space)

I's that tend to export high conflict to J's distant from them on fixed prices gnp growth rate

tend to exhibit the characteristics of:

competitive political system -.1645 (mean group score in a-space)

large gnp growth rate at fixed prices .3499 (mean group score in a-space)

I's that tend to export high conflict to J's distant from them on ethno-linguistic fractionalization

tend to exhibit the characteristics of:

I's that tend to export high conflict to J's close to them on per cent urban population

tend to exhibit the characteristics of:

small power base -.0546 (mean group score in a-space)

much domestic violence -.3823 (mean group score in a-space)

large gnp growth rate at fixed prices .2095 (mean group score in a-space)

small health expenditure as percent of gnp .2221 (mean group score in a-space)

new currency .1980 (mean group score in a-space)

I's that tend to export high conflict to J's distant from them on all mail

tend to exhibit the characteristics of:

low economic development -.1050 (mean group score in a-space)

large population density -.1484 (mean group score in a-space)

low per capita school enrollment -.1592 (mean group score in a-space)

high per capita internal security force .2077 (mean group score in a-space)

high ratio of black market to official exchange .1726 (mean group score in a-space)

many executive adjustments -.2909 (mean group score in a-space)

I's that tend to export high conflict to J's distant from them on political party fractionalization

tend to exhibit the characteristics of:

small population growth rate .1769 (mean group score in a-space)

many elections .2189 (mean group score in a-space)

I's that tend to export high conflict to J's close to them on domestic turmoil

tend to exhibit the characteristics of:

recent national independence .1458 (mean group score in a-space)

much domestic violence -.4300 (mean group score in a-space)

small health expenditure as percent of gnp .2488 (mean group score in a-space)

low energy production -.3176 (mean group score in a-space)

high crude death rate -.1690 (mean group score in a-space)

I's that tend to export high conflict to J's distant from them on total area

tend to exhibit the characteristics of:

high economic development .2610 (mean group score in a-space)

small power base -.1134 (mean group score in a-space)

small population growth rate .2473 (mean group score in a-space)

large population density -.4062 (mean group score in a-space)

little domestic violence .1178 (mean group score in a-space)

I's that tend to export high conflict to J's close to them on per capita energy consumption growth rate

tend to exhibit the characteristics of:

low energy production -.3237 (mean group score in a-space)

few elections -.2313 (mean group score in a-space)

many executive adjustments -.2556 (mean group score in a-space)

I's that tend to export high conflict to J's distant from them on infant mortality

tend to exhibit the characteristics of:

low economic development -.1658 (mean group score in a-space)

political instability .1743 (mean group score in a-space)

large population growth rate -.1815 (mean group score in a-space)

small gnp growth rate at fixed prices -.2165 (mean group score in a-space)

few military personnel per capita .3030 (mean group score in a-space)

new currency .2097 (mean group score in a-space)

I's that tend to export high conflict to J's distant from them on age of currency

tend to exhibit the characteristics of:

small health expenditure as percent of gnp .2085 (mean group score in a-space)

low energy production -.2704 (mean group score in a-space)

low ratio of black market to official exchange -.2314 (mean group score in a-space)

I's that tend to export high conflict to j's distant from them on total health expenditure
tend to exhibit the characteristics of:

small health expenditure as percent of gnp .3417 (mean group score in a-space)

high per capita internal security force .2271 (mean group score in a-space)

I's that tend to export high conflict to j's distant from them on crude death rate
tend to exhibit the characteristics of:

little political instability -.2545 (mean group score in a-space)

low ratio of black market to official exchange -.3469 (mean group score in a-space)

few executive adjustments .3103 (mean group score in a-space)

I's that tend to export high conflict to j's distant from them on regular executive transfers
tend to exhibit the characteristics of:

recent national independence .2134 (mean group score in a-space)

small health expenditure as percent of gnp .3187 (mean group score in a-space)

I's that tend to export high conflict to j's close to them on per capita economic active male population
tend to exhibit the characteristics of:

large christian community -.1991 (mean group score in a-space)

small health expenditure as percent of gnp .2070 (mean group score in a-space)

I's that tend to export high conflict to j's distant from them on concentration of export commodities
tend to exhibit the characteristics of:

large population growth rate -.3044 (mean group score in a-space)

I's that tend to export high conflict to j's close to them on mean elections
tend to exhibit the characteristics of:

many elections .3034 (mean group score in a-space)

much ethno-linguistic fractionalization -.1473 (mean group score in a-space)

I's that tend to export high conflict to j's close to them on concentration of export receivers
tend to exhibit the characteristics of:

competitive political system -.2300 (mean group score in a-space)

small christian community .4428 (mean group score in a-space)

many military personnel per capita -.2189 (mean group score in a-space) high crude death rate -.2012 (mean group score in a-space)

I's that tend to export high conflict to J's distant from them on orthodox community

tend to exhibit the characteristics of:

large population growth rate -.2373 (mean group score in a-space)

much domestic violence -.3465 (mean group score in a-space)

large gnp growth rate at fixed prices .1694 (mean group score in a-space)

low ratio of black market to official exchange -.2167 (mean group score in a-space)

little ethno-linguistic fractionalization .2994 (mean group score in a-space)

INSERT 75

An inventory of findings for distance theory, conflict, a-space factor correlations with positive weights.

I's most likely to export high conflict to J's distant from them on power base

tend to exhibit the characteristics of:

few military personnel per capita n= 60 p= .0232 r= .2900

I's most likely to export high conflict to J's distant from them on economic development

tend to exhibit the characteristics of:

low economic development n= 54 p= .0380 r= .2800

little ethno-linguistic fractionalization n= 54 p= .0456 r= .2700

I's most likely to export high conflict to J's distant from them on political system

tend to exhibit the characteristics of:

non-competitive political system n= 65 p= .0017 r= .3900

low per capita school enrollment n= 65 p= .0343 r= .2600

I's most likely to export high conflict to J's distant from them on school enrollment

tend to exhibit the characteristics of:

large gnp growth rate at fixed prices n= 53 p= .0399 r= .2800

I's most likely to export high conflict to J's distant from them on internal political turmoil

tend to exhibit the characteristics of:

small power base n= 40 p= .0149 r= .3800

low energy production n= 40 p= .0488 r= .3100

I's most likely to export high conflict to J's close to them on internal violence

tend to exhibit the characteristics of:

much domestic violence n= 57 p= .0220 r= .3000

I's most likely to export high conflict to J's distant from them on militarism

tend to exhibit the characteristics of:

few military personnel per capita n= 53 p= .0122 r= .3400

high energy production n= 53 p= .0184 r= .3200

I's most likely to export high conflict to J's distant from them on date of independence

tend to exhibit the characteristics of:

political instability n= 49 p= .0131 r= .3500

recent national independence n= 49 p= .0004 r= .5100

few military personnel per capita n= 49 p= .0131 r= .3500

low per capita school enrollment n= 49 p= .0236 r= .3200

high per capita internal security force n= 49 p= .0341 r= .3000

many executive adjustments n= 49 p= .0057 r= .3900

I's most likely to export high conflict to J's distant from them on population growth rate

tend to exhibit the characteristics of:

recent national independence n= 36 p= .0401 r= .3400

few military personnel per capita n= 36 p= .0060 r= .4500

I's most likely to export high conflict to J's distant from them on density

tend to exhibit the characteristics of:

small population density n= 36 p= .0401 r= .3400

I's most likely to export high conflict to J's distant from them on internal security forces

tend to exhibit the characteristics of:

high per capita school enrollment n= 34 p= .0043 r= .4800

I's most likely to export high conflict to J's distant from them on population size

tend to exhibit the characteristics of:

small population growth rate n= 63 p= .0103 r= .3200

little domestic violence n= 63 p= .0161 r= .3000

large health expenditure as percent of gnp n= 63 p= .0454 r= .2500

low crude death rate n= 63 p= .0304 r= .2700

I's most likely to export high conflict to J's distant from them on religion

tend to exhibit the characteristics of:

much domestic violence n= 23 p= .0194 r= .4800

small gnp growth rate at fixed prices n= 23 p= .0295 r= .4500

I's most likely to export high conflict to J's distant from them on energy production

tend to exhibit the characteristics of:

few military personnel per capita n= 63 p= .0454 r= .2500

small gnp growth rate n= 63 p= .0454 r= .2500

low energy production n= 63 p= .0051 r= .3500

I's most likely to export high conflict to J's distant from them on gnp growth rate

tend to exhibit the characteristics of:

small population density n= 35 p= .0164 r= .4000

much domestic violence n= 35 p= .0230 r= .3800

much ethno-linguistic fractionalization n= 35 p= .0432 r= .3400

I's most likely to export high conflict to J's close to them on fixed prices gnp growth rate

tend to exhibit the characteristics of:

small power base n= 51 p= .0305 r= .3000

I's most likely to export high conflict to J's close to them on ethno-linguistic fractionalization

tend to exhibit the characteristics of:

few executive adjustments n= 63 p= .0247 r= .2800

I's most likely to export high conflict to J's distant from them on per cent urban population

tend to exhibit the characteristics of:

non-competitive political system n= 42 p= .0085 r= .4000

small gnp growth rate at fixed prices n= 42 p= .0218 r= .3500

new currency n= 42 p= .0104 r= .3900

I's most likely to export high conflict to J's close to them on all mail

tend to exhibit the characteristics of:

I's most likely to export high conflict to J's close to them on political party fractionalization

tend to exhibit the characteristics of:

much ethno-linguistic fractionalization n= 52 p= .0238 r= .3100

I's most likely to export high conflict to J's distant from them on domestic turmoil

tend to exhibit the characteristics of:

little domestic violence n= 60 p= .0049 r= .3600

many military personnel per capita n= 60 p= .0423 r= .2600

many executive adjustments n= 60 p= .0062 r= .3500

I's most likely to export high conflict to J's close to them on total area

tend to exhibit the characteristics of:

little political instability n= 51 p= .0208 r= .3200

small population density n= 51 p= .0060 r= .3800

I's most likely to export high conflict to J's distant from them on per capita energy consumption growth rate

tend to exhibit the characteristics of:

low per capita school enrollment n= 64 p= .0236 r= .2800

I's most likely to export high conflict to J's close to them on infant mortality

tend to exhibit the characteristics of:

high economic develdpment n= 49 p= .0087 r= .3700

large power base n= 49 p= .0341 r= .3000

competitive political system n= 49 p= .0046 r= .4000

large health expenditure as percent of gnp n= 49 p= .0284 r= .3100

high crude death rate n= 49 p= .0485 r= .2800

I's most likely to export high conflict to J's close to them on age of currency

tend to exhibit the characteristics of:

few military personnel per capita n= 58 p= .0001 r= .5500

new currency n= 58 p= .0071 r= .3500

I's most likely to export high conflict to J's close to them on total health expenditure

tend to exhibit the characteristics of:

I's most likely to export high conflict to J's close to them on crude death rate

tend to exhibit the characteristics of:

few elections n= 65 p= .0343 r= .2600

I's most likely to export high conflict to J's close to them on regular executive transfers

tend to exhibit the characteristics of:

little political instability n= 63 p= .0082 r= .3300

large population density n= 63 p= .0373 r= .2600

small christian community n= 63 p= .0161 r= .3000

recent national independence n= 63 p= .0304 r= .2700

high per capita school enrollment n= 63 p= .0304 r= .2700

I's most likely to export high conflict to J's distant from them on per capita economic active male population

tend to exhibit the characteristics of:

recent national independence n= 47 p= .0068 r= .3900

low crude death rate n= 47 p= .0382 r= .3000

I's most likely to export high conflict to J's close to them on concentration of export commodities

tend to exhibit the characteristics of:

large power base n= 51 p= .0075 r= .3700

high energy production n= 51 p= .0114 r= .3500

I's most likely to export high conflict to J's distant from them on mean elections

tend to exhibit the characteristics of:

small gnp growth rate n= 55 p= .0362 r= .2800

few elections n= 55 p= .0299 r= .2900

many executive adjustments n= 55 p= .0164 r= .3200

little ethno-linguistic fractionalization n= 55 p= .0201 r= .3100

I's most likely to export high conflict to J's distant from them on concentration of export receivers

tend to exhibit the characteristics of:

few military personnel per capita n= 64 p= .0097 r= .3200

high per capita internal security force n= 64 p= .0357 r= .2600

low crude death rate n= 64 p= .0236 r= .2800

I's most likely to export high conflict to J's close to them on orthodox community

tend to exhibit the characteristics of:

large power base n= 59 p= .0129 r= .3200

small gnp growth rate at fixed prices n= 59 p= .0129 r= .3200

large gnp growth rate n= 59 p= .0364 r= .2700

INSERT 76

An inventory of findings for distance theory, conflict, a-space factor correlations with negative weights.

I's most likely to export high conflict to J's close to them on power base

tend to exhibit the characteristics of:

high economic development n= 52 p= .0238 r= .3100

large power base n= 52 p= .0000 r= .5900

high energy production n= 52 p= .0131 r= .3400

I's most likely to export high conflict to j's close to them on economic development
tend to exhibit the characteristics of:

high economic development n= 57 p= .0220 r= .3000

high crude death rate n= 57 p= .0398 r= .2700

I's most likely to export high conflict to j's close to them on political system
tend to exhibit the characteristics of:

high per capita school enrollment n= 46 p= .0478 r= .2900

low energy production n= 46 p= .0478 r= .2900

I's most likely to export high conflict to j's close to them on school enrollment
tend to exhibit the characteristics of:

large population growth rate n= 58 p= .0028 r= .3900

high per capita school enrollment n= 58 p= .0011 r= .4300

I's most likely to export high conflict to j's close to them on internal political turmoil
tend to exhibit the characteristics of:

large population density n= 71 p= .0171 r= .2800

recent national independence n= 71 p= .0171 r= .2800

I's most likely to export high conflict to j's distant from them on internal violence
tend to exhibit the characteristics of:

small power base n= 54 p= .0380 r= .2800

large gnp growth rate at fixed prices n= 54 p= .0010 r= .4500

I's most likely to export high conflict to j's close to them on militarism
tend to exhibit the characteristics of:

high economic development n= 57 p= .0270 r= .2900

many military personnel per capita n= 57 p= .0024 r= .4000

I's most likely to export high conflict to j's close to them on date of independence
tend to exhibit the characteristics of:

much domestic violence n= 62 p= .0259 r= .2800

small health expenditure as percent of gnp n= 62 p= .0136 r= .3100

new currency n= 62 p= .0259 r= .2800

I's most likely to export high conflict to j's close to them on population growth rate
tend to exhibit the characteristics of:

high economic development n= 74 p= .0459 r= .2300

large power base n= 74 p= .0020 r= .3600

small population growth rate n= 74 p= .0000 r= .5600

few executive adjustments n= 74 p= .0298 r= .2500

I's most likely to export high conflict to J's close to them on density

tend to exhibit the characteristics of:

small power base n= 74 p= .0043 r= .3300

few military personnel per capita n= 74 p= .0371 r= .2400

few elections n= 74 p= .0298 r= .2500

low crude death rate n= 74 p= .0072 r= .3100

I's most likely to export high conflict to J's close to them on internal security forces

tend to exhibit the characteristics of:

few military personnel per capita n= 76 p= .0346 r= .2400

low per capita school enrollment n= 76 p= .0430 r= .2300

I's most likely to export high conflict to J's close to them on population size

tend to exhibit the characteristics of:

large power base n= 49 p= .0000 r= .6700

few elections n= 49 p= .0236 r= .3200

old currency n= 49 p= .0284 r= .3100

I's most likely to export high conflict to J's close to them on religion

tend to exhibit the characteristics of:

little ethno-linguistic fractionalization n= 88 p= .0229 r= .2400

I's most likely to export high conflict to J's close to them on energy production

tend to exhibit the characteristics of:

high economic development n= 47 p= .0267 r= .3200

large power base n= 47 p= .0453 r= .2900

non-competitive political system n= 47 p= .0183 r= .3400

high energy production n= 47 p= .0124 r= .3600

high ratio of black market to official exchange n= 47 p= .0453 r= .2900

I's most likely to export high conflict to J's close to them on gnp growth rate

tend to exhibit the characteristics of:

political instability n= 72 p= .0398 r= .2400

small gnp growth rate at fixed prices n= 72 p= .0029 r= .3500

large gnp growth rate n= 72 p= .0258 r= .2600

I's most likely to export high conflict to J's distant from them on fixed prices gnp growth rate

tend to exhibit the characteristics of:

large gnp growth rate at fixed prices   n=   59 p=   .0006 r=   .4500

little ethno-linguistic fractionalization   n=   59 p=   .0066 r=   .3500

I's most likely to export high conflict to J's distant from them on ethno-linguistic fractionalization

tend to exhibit the characteristics of:

small power base   n=   43 p=   .0115 r=   .3800

few executive adjustments   n=   43 p=   .0052 r=   .4200

low crude death rate   n=   43 p=   .0095 r=   .3900

I's most likely to export high conflict to J's close to them on per cent urban population

tend to exhibit the characteristics of:

high economic development   n=   68 p=   .0023 r=   .3700

high per capita school enrollment   n=   68 p=   .0459 r=   .2400

low energy production   n=   68 p=   .0156 r=   .2900

many executive adjustments   n=   68 p=   .0374 r=   .2500

I's most likely to export high conflict to J's distant from them on all mail

tend to exhibit the characteristics of:

political instability   n=   68 p=   .0374 r=   .2500

I's most likely to export high conflict to J's distant from them on political party fractionalization

tend to exhibit the characteristics of:

high crude death rate   n=   57 p=   .0117 r=   .3300

I's most likely to export high conflict to J's close to them on domestic turmoil

tend to exhibit the characteristics of:

large population density   n=   50 p=   .0387 r=   .2900

small christian community   n=   50 p=   .0182 r=   .3300

low energy production   n=   50 p=   .0042 r=   .4000

I's most likely to export high conflict to J's distant from them on total area

tend to exhibit the characteristics of:

I's most likely to export high conflict to J's close to them on per capita energy consumption growth rate

tend to exhibit the characteristics of:

high economic development   n=   48 p=   .0301 r=   .3100

I's most likely to export high conflict to J's distant from them on infant mortality

tend to exhibit the characteristics of:

large power base   n=   61 p=   .0271 r=   .2800

much domestic violence n= 61 p= .0271 r= .2800

small health expenditure as percent of gnp n= 61 p= .0332 r= .2700

I's most likely to export high conflict to J's distant from them on age of currency

tend to exhibit the characteristics of:

large christian community n= 52 p= .0289 r= .3000

long national independence n= 52 p= .0131 r= .3400

small gnp growth rate at fixed prices n= 52 p= .0289 r= .3000

few military personnel per capita n= 52 p= .0349 r= .2900

old currency n= 52 p= .0011 r= .4500

I's most likely to export high conflict to J's distant from them on total health expenditure

tend to exhibit the characteristics of:

small population density n= 55 p= .0299 r= .2900

small health expenditure as percent of gnp n= 55 p= .0299 r= .2900

I's most likely to export high conflict to J's distant from them on crude death rate

tend to exhibit the characteristics of:

high per capita internal security force n= 46 p= .0478 r= .2900

I's most likely to export high conflict to J's distant from them on regular executive transfers

tend to exhibit the characteristics of:

large christian community n= 47 p= .0320 r= .3100

much domestic violence n= 47 p= .0320 r= .3100

I's most likely to export high conflict to J's close to them on per capita economic active male population

tend to exhibit the characteristics of:

low economic development n= 62 p= .0472 r= .2500

political instability n= 62 p= .0259 r= .2800

long national independence n= 62 p= .0021 r= .3900

large gnp growth rate n= 62 p= .0472 r= .2500

small health expenditure as percent of gnp n= 62 p= .0318 r= .2700

I's most likely to export high conflict to J's distant from them on concentration of export commodities

tend to exhibit the characteristics of:

high economic development n= 59 p= .0129 r= .3200

I's most likely to export high conflict to J's close to them on mean elections

tend to exhibit the characteristics of:

many elections n= 54 p= .0141 r= .3300

I's most likely to export high conflict to J's close to them on concentration of export receivers

tend to exhibit the characteristics of:

small gnp growth rate at fixed prices n= 47 p= .0267 r= .3200

high crude death rate n= 47 p= .0183 r= .3400

I's most likely to export high conflict to J's distant from them on orthodox community

tend to exhibit the characteristics of:

large gnp growth rate at fixed prices n= 49 p= .0160 r= .3400

INSERT 77

I'S WITH + SCORES TEND TO EXPORT HIGH
CONFLICT TO J'S WITH THE CHARACTERISTICS, RELATIVE TO I, OF:

VARIABLE CLUSTER 1

14	ENERGY PRODUCTION DISTANCE	.81
01	POWER BASE DISTANCE	.75
02	ECONOMIC DEVELOPMENT DISTANCE	.55

THESE I'S ARE:

VARIABLE CLUSTER 1

39	GHANA	2.16
122	KENYA	2.06
125	GUYANA	1.91
120	TANZANIA	1.63
17	CEYLON	1.59
115	GAMBIA	1.53
22	CONGO (BRA)	1.50
11	BURMA	1.46
13	CAMBODIA	1.44
93	SUDAN	1.44
112	YEMEN	1.43
100	TUNISIA	1.37
82	PHILIPPINES	1.34
41	GUATEMALA	1.32
70	MOROCCO	1.29
126	MALAYSIA	1.28
89	SIERRA LEONE	1.23
110	NORTH VIETNAM	1.22
121	ZAMBIA	1.22
40	GREECE	1.22
74	NICARAGUA	1.01
102	UGANDA	.98

```
 51  IRELAND                                   .95
 67  MAURITANIA                                .95
 42  GUINEA                                    .91
 43  HAITI                                     .89
119  MALTA                                     .89
 28  DAHOMEY                                   .87
111  SOUTH VIETNAM                             .85
 90  SOMALIA                                   .83
108  URUGUAY                                   .83
 31  ECUADOR                                   .82
 55  JAMAICA                                   .82
 71  NEPAL                                     .69
  2  ALBANIA                                   .64
 76  NIGERIA                                   .56
 25  CUBA                                      .54
 95  SWITZERLAND                               .54
 96  SYRIA                                     .51
 36  GABON                                     .50
 97  THAILAND                                  .47
101  TURKEY                                    .40
124  SINGAPORE                                 .37
 12  BURUNDI                                   .33
 29  DENMARK                                   .31
 30  DOMINICAN REPUBLIC                        .27
 23  CONGO (LEO)                               .23
118  MALAWI                                    .20
 50  IRAQ                                      .20
  9  BRAZIL                                    .12
 80  PARAGUAY                                  .12
 84  PORTUGAL                                  .11
104  U.A.R.                                    .07
  7  BELGIUM                                   .07
 81  PERU                                      .06
 63  LIBYA                                     .03
 52  ISRAEL                                    .03

THEY TEND TO HAVE THE CHARACTERISTICS OF:

 LOW ECONOMIC DEVELOPMENT
 SMALL POWER BASE
 LOW ENERGY PRODUCTION

I'S WITH - SCORES TEND TO EXPORT HIGH
CONFLICT TO J'S WITH THE CHARACTERISTICS, RELATIVE TO I, OF:

 VARIABLE CLUSTER      1

 14 ENERGY PRODUCTION CLOSENESS                .81
 01 POWER BASE CLOSENESS                       .75
 02 ECONOMIC DEVELOPMENT CLOSENESS             .55

THESE I'S ARE:

 79  PANAMA                                   -.01
 61  LEBANON                                  -.01
 62  LIBERIA                                  -.05
 64  LUXEMBOURG                               -.05
 65  MALAGASY REP                             -.05
 66  MALI                                     -.05
 75  NIGER                                    -.05
 86  RWANDA                                   -.05
```

88	SENEGAL	-.05
46	ICELAND	-.05
1	AFGHANISTAN	-.05
14	CAMEROUN	-.05
107	UPPER VOLTA	-.05
114	BOTSWANA	-.05
117	LESOTHO	-.05
123	W. SAMOA	-.05
127	MALDIVE ISLANDS	-.05
128	BARBADOS	-.05
34	FINLAND	-.05
58	NORTH KOREA	-.08
48	INDONESIA	-.09
3	ALGERIA	-.12
54	IVORY COAST	-.13
69	MONGOLIA	-.14
73	NEW ZEALAND	-.18
16	CENTRAL AFRICAN REP	-.21
33	ETHIOPIA	-.30
59	SOUTH KOREA	-.32
53	ITALY	-.36
78	PAKISTAN	-.37
21	COLOMBIA	-.37
99	TRINIDAD	-.40
47	INDIA	-.41
56	JAPAN	-.43
57	JORDAN	-.43
116	KUWAIT	-.44
44	HONDURAS	-.47
32	EL SALVADOR	-.48
26	CYPRUS	-.53
68	MEXICO	-.59
98	TOGO	-.62
92	SPAIN	-.62
94	SWEDEN	-.63
87	SAUDI ARABIA	-.65
8	BOLIVIA	-.65
77	NORWAY	-.71
6	AUSTRIA	-.77
60	LAOS	-.80
91	SOUTH AFRICA	-.82
24	COSTA RICA	-.83
20	CHINA, PR	-.93
106	UNITED STATES	-.94
49	IRAN	-.98
85	ROMANIA	-1.02
72	NETHERLANDS	-1.03
109	VENEZUELA	-1.03
45	HUNGARY	-1.20
4	ARGENTINA	-1.31
19	CHILE	-1.33
18	CHAD	-1.34
113	YUGOSLAVIA	-1.44
10	BULGARIA	-1.62
105	UNITED KINGDOM	-1.86
27	CZECHOSLOVAKIA	-1.93
5	AUSTRALIA	-1.99
35	FRANCE	-2.03
103	U.S.S.R	-2.07
15	CANADA	-2.18
38	WEST GERMANY	-2.32
83	POLAND	-2.43
37	EAST GERMANY	-2.83

THEY TEND TO HAVE THE CHARACTERISTICS OF:

HIGH ECONOMIC DEVELOPMENT
LARGE POWER BASE
HIGH ENERGY PRODUCTION

I'S WITH + SCORES TEND TO EXPORT HIGH
CONFLICT TO J'S WITH THE CHARACTERISTICS, RELATIVE TO I, OF:

VARIABLE CLUSTER 2

11	INTERNAL SECURITY FORCES DISTANCE	.67
28	REGULAR EXECUTIVE TRANSFERS CLOSENESS	.63
23	PER CAPITA ENERGY CONSUMPTION GROWTH RATE DISTANCE	.58
21	DOMESTIC TURMOIL DISTANCE	.56

THESE I'S ARE:

VARIABLE CLUSTER 2

118	MALAWI	2.53
83	POLAND	2.20
67	MAURITANIA	2.12
103	U.S.S.R	1.98
45	HUNGARY	1.86
24	COSTA RICA	1.68
42	GUINEA	1.66
61	LEBANON	1.62
17	CEYLON	1.55
33	ETHIOPIA	1.40
13	CAMBODIA	1.40
20	CHINA, PR	1.37
31	ECUADOR	1.24
90	SOMALIA	1.09
39	GHANA	1.06
81	PERU	1.06
85	ROMANIA	.98
34	FINLAND	.97
71	NEPAL	.92
56	JAPAN	.90
4	ARGENTINA	.88
58	NORTH KOREA	.87
10	BULGARIA	.87
124	SINGAPORE	.85
80	PARAGUAY	.85
29	DENMARK	.84
40	GREECE	.78
12	BURUNDI	.75
69	MONGOLIA	.75
2	ALBANIA	.71
125	GUYANA	.71
112	YEMEN	.67
74	NICARAGUA	.58
73	NEW ZEALAND	.56
95	SWITZERLAND	.56
36	GABON	.56
49	IRAN	.52
110	NORTH VIETNAM	.50
89	SIERRA LEONE	.50
25	CUBA	.49

72	NETHERLANDS	.49
105	UNITED KINGDOM	.47
27	CZECHOSLOVAKIA	.47
113	YUGOSLAVIA	.46
82	PHILIPPINES	.45
50	IRAQ	.43
79	PANAMA	.38
41	GUATEMALA	.36
109	VENEZUELA	.36
15	CANADA	.33
59	SOUTH KOREA	.31
47	INDIA	.27
76	NIGERIA	.27
120	TANZANIA	.24
21	COLOMBIA	.23
11	BURMA	.23
87	SAUDI ARABIA	.21
106	UNITED STATES	.15
97	THAILAND	.08
51	IRELAND	.07

THEY TEND TO HAVE THE CHARACTERISTICS OF:

LOW PER CAPITA INTERNAL SECURITY FORCE
HIGH RATIO OF BLACK MARKET TO OFFICIAL EXCHANGE

I'S WITH - SCORES TEND TO EXPORT HIGH
CONFLICT TO J'S WITH THE CHARACTERISTICS, RELATIVE TO I, OF:

VARIABLE CLUSTER 2

11	INTERNAL SECURITY FORCES CLOSENESS	.67
28	REGULAR EXECUTIVE TRANSFERS DISTANCE	.63
23	PER CAPITA ENERGY CONSUMPTION GROWTH RATE CLOSENESS	.58
21	DOMESTIC TURMOIL CLOSENESS	.56

THESE I'S ARE:

37	EAST GERMANY	-.00
62	LIBERIA	-.01
64	LUXEMBOURG	-.01
65	MALAGASY REP	-.01
66	MALI	-.01
75	NIGER	-.01
86	RWANDA	-.01
88	SENEGAL	-.01
46	ICELAND	-.01
14	CAMEROUN	-.01
107	UPPER VOLTA	-.01
114	BOTSWANA	-.01
117	LESOTHO	-.01
1	AFGHANISTAN	-.01
123	W. SAMOA	-.01
127	MALDIVE ISLANDS	-.01
128	BARBADOS	-.01
68	MEXICO	-.05
93	SUDAN	-.05
5	AUSTRALIA	-.06
115	GAMBIA	-.07
96	SYRIA	-.11
28	DAHOMEY	-.19

92	SPAIN	-.25
19	CHILE	-.28
111	SOUTH VIETNAM	-.32
22	CONGO (BRA)	-.33
63	LIBYA	-.34
53	ITALY	-.37
55	JAMAICA	-.41
116	KUWAIT	-.41
94	SWEDEN	-.55
84	PORTUGAL	-.59
119	MALTA	-.63
102	UGANDA	-.64
57	JORDAN	-.68
101	TURKEY	-.69
98	TOGO	-.75
77	NORWAY	-.85
18	CHAD	-.88
108	URUGUAY	-.88
70	MOROCCO	-.91
38	WEST GERMANY	-.97
48	INDONESIA	-1.00
60	LAOS	-1.00
9	BRAZIL	-1.03
43	HAITI	-1.07
3	ALGERIA	-1.11
35	FRANCE	-1.11
8	BOLIVIA	-1.12
30	DOMINICAN REPUBLIC	-1.20
6	AUSTRIA	-1.22
126	MALAYSIA	-1.23
52	ISRAEL	-1.31
7	BELGIUM	-1.48
78	PAKISTAN	-1.51
44	HONDURAS	-1.52
122	KENYA	-1.55
54	IVORY COAST	-1.59
32	EL SALVADOR	-1.62
121	ZAMBIA	-1.69
100	TUNISIA	-1.80
104	U.A.R.	-1.84
16	CENTRAL AFRICAN REP	-1.85
26	CYPRUS	-1.87
23	CONGO (LEO)	-1.94
99	TRINIDAD	-2.22
91	SOUTH AFRICA	-2.42

THEY TEND TO HAVE THE CHARACTERISTICS OF:

HIGH PER CAPITA INTERNAL SECURITY FORCE
LOW RATIO OF BLACK MARKET TO OFFICIAL EXCHANGE

I'S WITH + SCORES TEND TO EXPORT HIGH
CONFLICT TO J'S WITH THE CHARACTERISTICS, RELATIVE TO I, OF:

VARIABLE CLUSTER 3

06 INTERNAL VIOLENCE CLOSENESS	.74
22 TOTAL AREA CLOSENESS	.64
27 CRUDE DEATH RATE CLOSENESS	.52

THESE I'S ARE:

VARIABLE CLUSTER 3

20	CHINA, PR	2.77
47	INDIA	2.37
4	ARGENTINA	2.26
48	INDONESIA	1.88
3	ALGERIA	1.81
9	BRAZIL	1.79
57	JORDAN	1.64
92	SPAIN	1.64
61	LEBANON	1.52
96	SYRIA	1.37
103	U.S.S.R	1.34
91	SOUTH AFRICA	1.32
68	MEXICO	1.29
122	KENYA	1.28
76	NIGERIA	1.24
54	IVORY COAST	1.23
39	GHANA	1.03
105	UNITED KINGDOM	.97
118	MALAWI	.96
21	COLOMBIA	.94
49	IRAN	.93
80	PARAGUAY	.91
89	SIERRA LEONE	.89
30	DOMINICAN REPUBLIC	.89
93	SUDAN	.88
51	IRELAND	.86
78	PAKISTAN	.82
81	PERU	.79
82	PHILIPPINES	.78
52	ISRAEL	.69
120	TANZANIA	.68
109	VENEZUELA	.67
40	GREECE	.63
33	ETHIOPIA	.61
43	HAITI	.60
70	MOROCCO	.58
111	SOUTH VIETNAM	.58
38	WEST GERMANY	.54
101	TURKEY	.51
121	ZAMBIA	.48
8	BOLIVIA	.44
50	IRAQ	.43
60	LAOS	.37
106	UNITED STATES	.36
37	EAST GERMANY	.34
41	GUATEMALA	.34
119	MALTA	.32
24	COSTA RICA	.27
90	SOMALIA	.23
31	ECUADOR	.17
125	GUYANA	.14
126	MALAYSIA	.10
11	BURMA	.10
104	U.A.R.	.09
62	LIBERIA	.08
64	LUXEMBOURG	.08
65	MALAGASY REP	.08
66	MALI	.08
75	NIGER	.08
86	RWANDA	.08

88	SENEGAL	.08
1	AFGHANISTAN	.08
46	ICELAND	.08
107	UPPER VOLTA	.08
114	BOTSWANA	.08
117	LESOTHO	.08
14	CAMEROUN	.08
123	W. SAMOA	.08
127	MALDIVE ISLANDS	.08
128	BARBADOS	.08
15	CANADA	.06

THEY TEND TO HAVE THE CHARACTERISTICS OF:

LOW ECONOMIC DEVELOPMENT
LARGE POWER BASE
SMALL POPULATION DENSITY
MUCH DOMESTIC VIOLENCE
SMALL GNP GROWTH RATE AT FIXED PRICES

I'S WITH - SCORES TEND TO EXPORT HIGH
CONFLICT TO J'S WITH THE CHARACTERISTICS, RELATIVE TO I, OF:

VARIABLE CLUSTER 3

06	INTERNAL VIOLENCE DISTANCE	.74
22	TOTAL AREA DISTANCE	.64
27	CRUDE DEATH RATE DISTANCE	.52

THESE I'S ARE:

35	FRANCE	-.00
36	GABON	-.03
102	UGANDA	-.04
112	YEMEN	-.13
108	URUGUAY	-.13
19	CHILE	-.15
84	PORTUGAL	-.16
56	JAPAN	-.16
67	MAURITANIA	-.20
115	GAMBIA	-.20
42	GUINEA	-.21
83	POLAND	-.21
18	CHAD	-.22
25	CUBA	-.26
124	SINGAPORE	-.35
63	LIBYA	-.40
5	AUSTRALIA	-.43
26	CYPRUS	-.45
85	ROMANIA	-.52
113	YUGOSLAVIA	-.52
79	PANAMA	-.52
32	EL SALVADOR	-.55
44	HONDURAS	-.59
17	CEYLON	-.61
55	JAMAICA	-.65
74	NICARAGUA	-.70
69	MONGOLIA	-.73
16	CENTRAL AFRICAN REP	-.83
116	KUWAIT	-.83
23	CONGO (LEO)	-.84

12	BURUNDI	-.94
73	NEW ZEALAND	-1.01
100	TUNISIA	-1.02
45	HUNGARY	-1.03
59	SOUTH KOREA	-1.07
87	SAUDI ARABIA	-1.10
97	THAILAND	-1.11
71	NEPAL	-1.16
99	TRINIDAD	-1.18
53	ITALY	-1.20
98	TOGO	-1.21
110	NORTH VIETNAM	-1.25
2	ALBANIA	-1.37
27	CZECHOSLOVAKIA	-1.39
13	CAMBODIA	-1.41
28	DAHOMEY	-1.45
22	CONGO (BRA)	-1.46
29	DENMARK	-1.47
10	BULGARIA	-1.53
72	NETHERLANDS	-1.56
58	NORTH KOREA	-1.58
6	AUSTRIA	-1.76
7	BELGIUM	-1.85
95	SWITZERLAND	-1.86
77	NORWAY	-2.03
34	FINLAND	-2.06
94	SWEDEN	-2.26

THEY TEND TO HAVE THE CHARACTERISTICS OF:

HIGH ECONOMIC DEVELOPMENT
SMALL POWER BASE
LARGE POPULATION DENSITY
LITTLE DOMESTIC VIOLENCE
LARGE GNP GROWTH RATE AT FIXED PRICES

I'S WITH + SCORES TEND TO EXPORT HIGH
CONFLICT TO J'S WITH THE CHARACTERISTICS, RELATIVE TO I, OF:

VARIABLE CLUSTER 4

17 ETHNO-LINGUISTIC FRACTIONALIZATION CLOSENESS	.55
33 ORTHODOX COMMUNITY DISTANCE	.78

THESE I'S ARE:

VARIABLE CLUSTER 4

81	PERU	2.25
87!	SAUDI ARABIA	2.00
53	ITALY	1.89
20	CHINA, PR	1.73
56	JAPAN	1.72
22	CONGO (BRA)	1.67
47	INDIA	1.56
21	COLOMBIA	1.52
72	NETHERLANDS	1.49
82	PHILIPPINES	1.45

78	PAKISTAN	1.43
90	SOMALIA	1.35
97	THAILAND	1.32
38	WEST GERMANY	1.30
63	LIBYA	1.24
19	CHILE	1.21
92	SPAIN	1.16
9	BRAZIL	1.14
55	JAMAICA	1.03
109	VENEZUELA	.99
125	GUYANA	.96
13	CAMBODIA	.96
67	MAURITANIA	.93
44	HONDURAS	.92
105	UNITED KINGDOM	.89
18	CHAD	.83
32	EL SALVADOR	.81
68	MEXICO	.79
74	NICARAGUA	.79
29	DENMARK	.78
94	SWEDEN	.78
5	AUSTRALIA	.72
17	CEYLON	.67
110	NORTH VIETNAM	.67
31	ECUADOR	.63
116	KUWAIT	.62
111	SOUTH VIETNAM	.61
70	MOROCCO	.61
79	PANAMA	.59
59	SOUTH KOREA	.55
58	NORTH KOREA	.49
112	YEMEN	.45
101	TURKEY	.33
124	SINGAPORE	.33
48	INDONESIA	.32
25	CUBA	.31
54	IVORY COAST	.30
98	TOGO	.27
3	ALGERIA	.25
100	TUNISIA	.22
99	TRINIDAD	.18
93	SUDAN	.18
115	GAMBIA	.14
7	BELGIUM	.13
57	JORDAN	.12
42	GUINEA	.10
11	BURMA	.06
37	EAST GERMANY	.01
62	LIBERIA	.01
64	LUXEMBOURG	.01
65	MALAGASY REP	.01
66	MALI	.01
14	CAMEROUN	.01
75	NIGER	.01
1	AFGHANISTAN	.01
86	RWANDA	.01
88	SENEGAL	.01
46	ICELAND	.01
107	UPPER VOLTA	.01
114	BOTSWANA	.01
117	LESOTHO	.01
123	W. SAMOA	.01
127	MALDIVE ISLANDS	.01
128	BARBADOS	.01
102	UGANDA	.00

THEY TEND TO HAVE THE CHARACTERISTICS OF:

LARGE POWER BASE
COMPETITIVE POLITICAL SYSTEM
LARGE POPULATION GROWTH RATE
LARGE GNP GROWTH RATE AT FIXED PRICES

I'S WITH - SCORES TEND TO EXPORT HIGH
CONFLICT TO J'S WITH THE CHARACTERISTICS, RELATIVE TO I, OF:

VARIABLE CLUSTER 4

17	ETHNO-LINGUISTIC FRACTIONALIZATION DISTANCE	.55
33	ORTHODOX COMMUNITY CLOSENESS	.78

THESE I'S ARE:

103	U.S.S.R	-.01
76	NIGERIA	-.01
73	NEW ZEALAND	-.02
60	LAOS	-.04
24	COSTA RICA	-.04
30	DOMINICAN REPUBLIC	-.05
77	NORWAY	-.06
106	UNITED STATES	-.06
23	CONGO (LEO)	-.09
35	FRANCE	-.10
119	MALTA	-.14
91	SOUTH AFRICA	-.16
84	PORTUGAL	-.18
40	GREECE	-.19
12	BURUNDI	-.21
39	GHANA	-.29
69	MONGOLIA	-.43
49	IRAN	-.60
71	NEPAL	-.61
28	DAHOMEY	-.71
27	CZECHOSLOVAKIA	-.71
34	FINLAND	-.75
104	U.A.R.	-.80
41	GUATEMALA	-.81
108	URUGUAY	-.84
85	ROMANIA	-.87
95	SWITZERLAND	-.87
26	CYPRUS	-.88
61	LEBANON	-1.03
15	CANADA	-1.07
6	AUSTRIA	-1.08
51	IRELAND	-1.10
80	PARAGUAY	-1.12
89	SIERRA LEONE	-1.16
122	KENYA	-1.24
8	BOLIVIA	-1.25
120	TANZANIA	-1.34
96	SYRIA	-1.34
52	ISRAEL	-1.37
36	GABON	-1.37
118	MALAWI	-1.38
50	IRAQ	-1.47
43	HAITI	-1.49
4	ARGENTINA	-1.52

2	ALBANIA	-1.75
83	POLAND	-1.77
45	HUNGARY	-1.78
10	BULGARIA	-1.94
121	ZAMBIA	-1.98
113	YUGOSLAVIA	-2.05
126	MALAYSIA	-2.15
33	ETHIOPIA	-2.24
16	CENTRAL AFRICAN REP	-2.37

THEY TEND TO HAVE THE CHARACTERISTICS OF:

SMALL POWER BASE
NON-COMPETITIVE POLITICAL SYSTEM
SMALL POPULATION GROWTH RATE
SMALL GNP GROWTH RATE AT FIXED PRICES

I'S WITH + SCORES TEND TO EXPORT HIGH
CONFLICT TO J'S WITH THE CHARACTERISTICS, RELATIVE TO I, OF:

VARIABLE CLUSTER 5

10 DENSITY CLOSENESS	.83

THESE I'S ARE:

VARIABLE CLUSTER 5

54	IVORY COAST	2.26
18	CHAD	2.07
61	LEBANON	1.91
92	SPAIN	1.83
40	GREECE	1.77
26	CYPRUS	1.76
79	PANAMA	1.76
16	CENTRAL AFRICAN REP	1.69
112	YEMEN	1.62
68	MEXICO	1.53
19	CHILE	1.32
119	MALTA	1.31
36	GABON	1.16
81	PERU	1.15
78	PAKISTAN	1.12
108	URUGUAY	1.11
74	NICARAGUA	1.09
30	DOMINICAN REPUBLIC	1.02
72	NETHERLANDS	1.01
10	BULGARIA	.98
101	TURKEY	.96
97	THAILAND	.94
43	HAITI	.94
11	BURMA	.91
37	EAST GERMANY	.91
17	CEYLON	.87
31	ECUADOR	.85
4	ARGENTINA	.84
100	TUNISIA	.80
102	UGANDA	.80

29	DENMARK	.74
6	AUSTRIA	.73
77	NORWAY	.73
95	SWITZERLAND	.70
48	INDONESIA	.67
98	TOGO	.66
21	COLOMBIA	.65
99	TRINIDAD	.64
55	JAMAICA	.60
71	NEPAL	.58
2	ALBANIA	.55
47	INDIA	.52
42	GUINEA	.48
41	GUATEMALA	.46
82	PHILIPPINES	.44
56	JAPAN	.40
45	HUNGARY	.38
94	SWEDEN	.34
34	FINLAND	.33
126	MALAYSIA	.32
9	BRAZIL	.25
118	MALAWI	.24
57	JORDAN	.20
85	ROMANIA	.18
52	ISRAEL	.17
104	U.A.R.	.14
122	KENYA	.08
105	UNITED KINGDOM	.07
28	DAHOMEY	.02
51	IRELAND	.01
113	YUGOSLAVIA	.00

THEY TEND TO HAVE THE CHARACTERISTICS OF:

LARGE POPULATION DENSITY
LONG NATIONAL INDEPENDENCE
FEW MILITARY PERSONNEL PER CAPITA
FEW EXECUTIVE ADJUSTMENTS

I'S WITH - SCORES TEND TO EXPORT HIGH
CONFLICT TO J'S WITH THE CHARACTERISTICS, RELATIVE TO I, OF:

VARIABLE CLUSTER 5

10 DENSITY DISTANCE .83

THESE I'S ARE:

59	SOUTH KOREA	-.00
39	GHANA	-.00
83	POLAND	-.00
63	LIBYA	-.09
116	KUWAIT	-.10
27	CZECHOSLOVAKIA	-.11
53	ITALY	-.11
49	IRAN	-.20
93	SUDAN	-.27
32	EL SALVADOR	-.27
109	VENEZUELA	-.27
8	BOLIVIA	-.27
111	SOUTH VIETNAM	-.33

75	NIGER	-.36
14	CAMEROUN	-.36
64	LUXEMBOURG	-.36
1	AFGHANISTAN	-.36
86	RWANDA	-.36
88	SENEGAL	-.36
62	LIBERIA	-.36
46	ICELAND	-.36
107	UPPER VOLTA	-.36
114	BOTSWANA	-.36
66	MALI	-.36
117	LESOTHO	-.36
65	MALAGASY REP	-.36
123	W. SAMOA	-.36
127	MALDIVE ISLANDS	-.36
128	BARBADOS	-.36
73	NEW ZEALAND	-.38
124	SINGAPORE	-.41
38	WEST GERMANY	-.42
96	SYRIA	-.43
12	BURUNDI	-.45
25	CUBA	-.48
67	MAURITANIA	-.50
80	PARAGUAY	-.58
33	ETHIOPIA	-.60
35	FRANCE	-.65
84	PORTUGAL	-.65
50	IRAQ	-.68
24	COSTA RICA	-.73
115	GAMBIA	-.81
58	NORTH KOREA	-.82
13	CAMBODIA	-.85
69	MONGOLIA	-.86
15	CANADA	-.86
120	TANZANIA	-.93
70	MOROCCO	-.98
44	HONDURAS	-1.02
22	CONGO (BRA)	-1.03
20	CHINA, PR	-1.10
87	SAUDI ARABIA	-1.16
76	NIGERIA	-1.20
60	LAOS	-1.21
91	SOUTH AFRICA	-1.31
89	SIERRA LEONE	-1.46
103	U.S.S.R	-1.48
90	SOMALIA	-1.51
110	NORTH VIETNAM	-1.51
3	ALGERIA	-1.51
125	GUYANA	-1.57
5	AUSTRALIA	-2.12
7	BELGIUM	-2.28
106	UNITED STATES	-2.44
23	CONGO (LEO)	-2.77
121	ZAMBIA	-2.99

THEY TEND TO HAVE THE CHARACTERISTICS OF:

SMALL POPULATION DENSITY
RECENT NATIONAL INDEPENDENCE
MANY MILITARY PERSONNEL PER CAPITA
MANY EXECUTIVE ADJUSTMENTS

I'S WITH + SCORES TEND TO EXPORT HIGH
CONFLICT TO J'S WITH THE CHARACTERISTICS, RELATIVE TO I, OF:

VARIABLE CLUSTER 6

03 POLITICAL CLOSENESS	.51
04 SCHOOL ENROLLMENT CLOSENESS	.81

THESE I'S ARE:

VARIABLE CLUSTER 6

2	ALBANIA	2.16
32	EL SALVADOR	2.10
79	PANAMA	1.95
17	CEYLON	1.83
44	HONDURAS	1.71
125	GUYANA	1.67
23	CONGO (LEO)	1.62
11	BURMA	1.51
82	PHILIPPINES	1.50
68	MEXICO	1.50
22	CONGO (BRA)	1.48
24	COSTA RICA	1.47
81	PERU	1.43
85	ROMANIA	1.41
113	YUGOSLAVIA	1.38
8	BOLIVIA	1.33
19	CHILE	1.32
101	TURKEY	1.28
16	CENTRAL AFRICAN REP	1.22
118	MALAWI	1.22
83	POLAND	1.12
61	LEBANON	1.10
15	CANADA	1.09
18	CHAD	1.08
58	NORTH KOREA	.96
69	MONGOLIA	.94
59	SOUTH KOREA	.87
115	GAMBIA	.82
106	UNITED STATES	.80
52	ISRAEL	.78
102	UGANDA	.75
5	AUSTRALIA	.65
33	ETHIOPIA	.59
80	PARAGUAY	.55
39	GHANA	.55
99	TRINIDAD	.54
78	PAKISTAN	.52
97	THAILAND	.52
96	SYRIA	.41
109	VENEZUELA	.40
28	DAHOMEY	.39
54	IVORY COAST	.39
57	JORDAN	.38
93	SUDAN	.30
70	MOROCCO	.29
56	JAPAN	.28
87	SAUDI ARABIA	.27
55	JAMAICA	.26
103	U.S.S.R	.25
100	TUNISIA	.24

46	ICELAND	.19
62	LIBERIA	.19
64	LUXEMBOURG	.19
65	MALAGASY REP	.19
66	MALI	.19
75	NIGER	.19
14	CAMEROUN	.19
86	RWANDA	.19
88	SENEGAL	.19
1	AFGHANISTAN	.19
107	UPPER VOLTA	.19
114	BOTSWANA	.19
117	LESOTHO	.19
123	W. SAMOA	.19
127	MALDIVE ISLANDS	.19
128	BARBADOS	.19
40	GREECE	.07

THEY TEND TO HAVE THE CHARACTERISTICS OF:

HIGH PER CAPITA SCHOOL ENROLLMENT
FEW EXECUTIVE ADJUSTMENTS

I'S WITH - SCORES TEND TO EXPORT HIGH
CONFLICT TO J'S WITH THE CHARACTERISTICS, RELATIVE TO I, OF:

VARIABLE CLUSTER 6

03 POLITICAL DISTANCE	.51
04 SCHOOL ENROLLMENT DISTANCE	.81

THESE I'S ARE:

119	MALTA	-.02
73	NEW ZEALAND	-.03
47	INDIA	-.03
122	KENYA	-.04
31	ECUADOR	-.10
91	SOUTH AFRICA	-.13
13	CAMBODIA	-.16
7	BELGIUM	-.17
120	TANZANIA	-.18
60	LAOS	-.24
35	FRANCE	-.26
98	TOGO	-.27
84	PORTUGAL	-.32
111	SOUTH VIETNAM	-.33
36	GABON	-.36
21	COLOMBIA	-.41
30	DOMINICAN REPUBLIC	-.42
27	CZECHOSLOVAKIA	-.43
26	CYPRUS	-.45
10	BULGARIA	-.46
76	NIGERIA	-.49
72	NETHERLANDS	-.53
121	ZAMBIA	-.54
89	SIERRA LEONE	-.59
6	AUSTRIA	-.66
48	INDONESIA	-.69
104	U.A.R.	-.76
41	GUATEMALA	-.77

4	ARGENTINA	-.78
53	ITALY	-.82
34	FINLAND	-.83
20	CHINA, PR	-.84
37	EAST GERMANY	-.90
90	SOMALIA	-.96
116	KUWAIT	-.99
124	SINGAPORE	-.99
9	BRAZIL	-.99
105	UNITED KINGDOM	-1.03
50	IRAQ	-1.10
74	NICARAGUA	-1.12
49	IRAN	-1.19
94	SWEDEN	-1.19
77	NORWAY	-1.19
108	URUGUAY	-1.20
43	HAITI	-1.24
51	IRELAND	-1.25
112	YEMEN	-1.26
110	NORTH VIETNAM	-1.27
126	MALAYSIA	-1.32
45	HUNGARY	-1.33
95	SWITZERLAND	-1.37
71	NEPAL	-1.41
25	CUBA	-1.46
67	MAURITANIA	-1.49
92	SPAIN	-1.57
3	ALGERIA	-1.64
29	DENMARK	-1.65
12	BURUNDI	-1.73
42	GUINEA	-1.80
63	LIBYA	-1.85
38	WEST GERMANY	-2.77

THEY TEND TO HAVE THE CHARACTERISTICS OF:

LOW PER CAPITA SCHOOL ENROLLMENT
MANY EXECUTIVE ADJUSTMENTS

I'S WITH + SCORES TEND TO EXPORT HIGH
CONFLICT TO J'S WITH THE CHARACTERISTICS, RELATIVE TO I, OF:

VARIABLE CLUSTER 7

24 INFANT MORTALITY DISTANCE	.52
19 ALL MAIL DISTANCE	.62
13 RELIGIOUS CLOSENESS	.77

THESE I'S ARE:

VARIABLE CLUSTER 7

19	CHILE	2.25
96	SYRIA	2.09
59	SOUTH KOREA	2.06
50	IRAQ	2.06
55	JAMAICA	1.97
116	KUWAIT	1.87

121	ZAMBIA	1.78
71	NEPAL	1.41
21	COLOMBIA	1.36
58	NORTH KOREA	1.34
12	BURUNDI	1.32
74	NICARAGUA	1.24
81	PERU	1.19
37	EAST GERMANY	1.17
100	TUNISIA	1.16
18	CHAD	1.07
102	UGANDA	1.06
11	BURMA	1.05
45	HUNGARY	1.04
49	IRAN	1.03
83	POLAND	1.00
13	CAMBODIA	.99
31	ECUADOR	.96
79	PANAMA	.89
57	JORDAN	.89
97	THAILAND	.89
63	LIBYA	.87
4	ARGENTINA	.86
91	SOUTH AFRICA	.81
113	YUGOSLAVIA	.81
10	BULGARIA	.78
25	CUBA	.78
87	SAUDI ARABIA	.69
23	CONGO (LEO)	.66
110	NORTH VIETNAM	.66
3	ALGERIA	.64
32	EL SALVADOR	.63
40	GREECE	.63
52	ISRAEL	.62
29	DENMARK	.60
43	HAITI	.58
98	TOGO	.57
41	GUATEMALA	.57
89	SIERRA LEONE	.55
120	TANZANIA	.54
115	GAMBIA	.52
78	PAKISTAN	.50
104	U.A.R.	.48
99	TRINIDAD	.47
70	MOROCCO	.43
111	SOUTH VIETNAM	.41
44	HONDURAS	.36
61	LEBANON	.30
76	NIGERIA	.28
47	INDIA	.28
68	MEXICO	.26
5	AUSTRALIA	.25
122	KENYA	.24
109	VENEZUELA	.18
33	ETHIOPIA	.14
15	CANADA	.12
67	MAURITANIA	.10
94	SWEDEN	.09
34	FINLAND	.09
24	COSTA RICA	.06

THEY TEND TO HAVE THE CHARACTERISTICS OF:

NON-COMPETITIVE POLITICAL SYSTEM
LARGE POPULATION GROWTH RATE
HIGH RATIO OF BLACK MARKET TO OFFICIAL EXCHANGE

MANY EXECUTIVE ADJUSTMENTS

I'S WITH - SCORES TEND TO EXPORT HIGH
CONFLICT TO J'S WITH THE CHARACTERISTICS, RELATIVE TO I, OF:

VARIABLE CLUSTER 7

24	INFANT MORTALITY CLOSENESS	.52
19	ALL MAIL CLOSENESS	.62
13	RELIGIOUS DISTANCE	.77

THESE I'S ARE:

112	YEMEN	-.03
7	BELGIUM	-.08
39	GHANA	-.13
16	CENTRAL AFRICAN REP	-.18
84	PORTUGAL	-.23
85	ROMANIA	-.27
42	GUINEA	-.31
69	MONGOLIA	-.34
54	IVORY COAST	-.36
8	BOLIVIA	-.38
80	PARAGUAY	-.40
60	LAOS	-.41
48	INDONESIA	-.41
92	SPAIN	-.44
28	DAHOMEY	-.52
30	DOMINICAN REPUBLIC	-.53
93	SUDAN	-.56
27	CZECHOSLOVAKIA	-.56
90	SOMALIA	-.58
108	URUGUAY	-.62
9	BRAZIL	-.65
119	MALTA	-.66
88	SENEGAL	-.66
65	MALAGASY REP	-.66
86	RWANDA	-.66
14	CAMEROUN	-.66
107	UPPER VOLTA	-.66
75	NIGER	-.66
66	MALI	-.66
114	BOTSWANA	-.66
46	ICELAND	-.66
117	LESOTHO	-.66
1	AFGHANISTAN	-.66
62	LIBERIA	-.66
64	LUXEMBOURG	-.66
123	W. SAMOA	-.66
127	MALDIVE ISLANDS	-.66
128	BARBADOS	-.66
124	SINGAPORE	-.67
20	CHINA, PR	-.79
53	ITALY	-.80
106	UNITED STATES	-.82
103	U.S.S.R	-.94
101	TURKEY	-.96
51	IRELAND	-.96
38	WEST GERMANY	-.99
2	ALBANIA	-1.03
118	MALAWI	-1.05
77	NORWAY	-1.15

22	CONGO (BRA)	-1.24
95	SWITZERLAND	-1.25
17	CEYLON	-1.29
72	NETHERLANDS	-1.33
35	FRANCE	-1.43
56	JAPAN	-1.44
73	NEW ZEALAND	-1.56
105	UNITED KINGDOM	-1.59
125	GUYANA	-1.86
36	GABON	-1.92
126	MALAYSIA	-2.09
26	CYPRUS	-2.35
82	PHILIPPINES	-2.37
6	AUSTRIA	-2.38

THEY TEND TO HAVE THE CHARACTERISTICS OF:

COMPETITIVE POLITICAL SYSTEM
SMALL POPULATION GROWTH RATE
LOW RATIO OF BLACK MARKET TO OFFICIAL EXCHANGE
MANY EXECUTIVE ADJUSTMENTS

I'S WITH + SCORES TEND TO EXPORT HIGH
CONFLICT TO J'S WITH THE CHARACTERISTICS, RELATIVE TO I, OF:

VARIABLE CLUSTER 8

20 POLITICAL PARTY FRACTIONALIZATION CLOSENESS	.78
09 POPULATION GROWTH RATE DISTANCE	.58

THESE I'S ARE:

VARIABLE CLUSTER 8

26	CYPRUS	2.43
79	PANAMA	2.40
69	MONGOLIA	2.35
49	IRAN	2.12
67	MAURITANIA	1.97
99	TRINIDAD	1.75
60	LAOS	1.69
33	ETHIOPIA	1.61
70	MOROCCO	1.56
55	JAMAICA	1.34
41	GUATEMALA	1.32
5	AUSTRALIA	1.30
68	MEXICO	1.27
42	GUINEA	1.17
87	SAUDI ARABIA	1.13
50	IRAQ	1.09
98	TOGO	1.07
74	NICARAGUA	.93
82	PHILIPPINES	.85
63	LIBYA	.81
25	CUBA	.79
51	IRELAND	.77
109	VENEZUELA	.76
124	SINGAPORE	.74

116	KUWAIT	.72
93	SUDAN	.68
31	ECUADOR	.66
27	CZECHOSLOVAKIA	.61
21	COLOMBIA	.57
30	DOMINICAN REPUBLIC	.57
15	CANADA	.55
24	COSTA RICA	.55
90	SOMALIA	.53
122	KENYA	.51
36	GABON	.46
34	FINLAND	.45
111	SOUTH VIETNAM	.42
77	NORWAY	.41
78	PAKISTAN	.40
121	ZAMBIA	.34
2	ALBANIA	.33
3	ALGERIA	.32
48	INDONESIA	.32
61	LEBANON	.31
32	EL SALVADOR	.30
43	HAITI	.29
9	BRAZIL	.29
81	PERU	.29
62	LIBERIA	.28
64	LUXEMBOURG	.28
65	MALAGASY REP	.28
66	MALI	.28
14	CAMEROUN	.28
75	NIGER	.28
46	ICELAND	.28
86	RWANDA	.28
88	SENEGAL	.28
1	AFGHANISTAN	.28
107	UPPER VOLTA	.28
114	BOTSWANA	.28
117	LESOTHO	.28
123	W. SAMOA	.28
127	MALDIVE ISLANDS	.28
128	BARBADOS	.28
12	BURUNDI	.24
119	MALTA	.18
73	NEW ZEALAND	.16
28	DAHOMEY	.13
85	ROMANIA	.12
118	MALAWI	.08
54	IVORY COAST	.05
91	SOUTH AFRICA	.04
17	CEYLON	.03

THEY TEND TO HAVE THE CHARACTERISTICS OF:

SMALL POWER BASE
LARGE POPULATION GROWTH RATE

I'S WITH - SCORES TEND TO EXPORT HIGH
CONFLICT TO J'S WITH THE CHARACTERISTICS, RELATIVE TO I, OF:

VARIABLE CLUSTER 8

20 POLITICAL PARTY FRACTIONALIZATION DISTANCE	.78
09 POPULATION GROWTH RATE CLOSENESS	.58

THESE I'S ARE:

94	SWEDEN	-.05
83	POLAND	-.06
72	NETHERLANDS	-.08
44	HONDURAS	-.09
19	CHILE	-.12
84	PORTUGAL	-.16
23	CONGO (LEO)	-.19
126	MALAYSIA	-.29
101	TURKEY	-.29
18	CHAD	-.29
4	ARGENTINA	-.31
95	SWITZERLAND	-.32
103	U.S.S.R	-.33
8	BOLIVIA	-.34
104	U.A.R.	-.39
89	SIERRA LEONE	-.40
10	BULGARIA	-.41
7	BELGIUM	-.43
80	PARAGUAY	-.47
125	GUYANA	-.52
57	JORDAN	-.52
35	FRANCE	-.53
115	GAMBIA	-.61
58	NORTH KOREA	-.64
29	DENMARK	-.65
47	INDIA	-.65
110	NORTH VIETNAM	-.67
108	URUGUAY	-.69
20	CHINA, PR	-.69
112	YEMEN	-.72
13	CAMBODIA	-.88
16	CENTRAL AFRICAN REP	-.91
71	NEPAL	-.92
76	NIGERIA	-.94
59	SOUTH KOREA	-.99
92	SPAIN	-1.03
102	UGANDA	-1.11
100	TUNISIA	-1.19
45	HUNGARY	-1.20
6	AUSTRIA	-1.22
52	ISRAEL	-1.23
97	THAILAND	-1.29
56	JAPAN	-1.53
37	EAST GERMANY	-1.55
105	UNITED KINGDOM	-1.62
96	SYRIA	-1.62
113	YUGOSLAVIA	-1.66
120	TANZANIA	-1.69
11	BURMA	-1.80
22	CONGO (BRA)	-1.81
39	GHANA	-1.84
38	WEST GERMANY	-2.21
106	UNITED STATES	-2.37
53	ITALY	-2.45
40	GREECE	-2.65

THEY TEND TO HAVE THE CHARACTERISTICS OF:

LARGE POWER BASE

SMALL POPULATION GROWTH RATE

I'S WITH + SCORES TEND TO EXPORT HIGH
CONFLICT TO J'S WITH THE CHARACTERISTICS, RELATIVE TO I, OF:

VARIABLE CLUSTER 9

25	AGE OF CURRENCY DISTANCE	.53
32	CONCENTRATION OF EXPORT RECEIVERS CLOSENESS	.67
07	MILITARISM CLOSENESS	.72

THESE I'S ARE:

VARIABLE CLUSTER 9

101	TURKEY	2.21
48	INDONESIA	1.72
98	TOGO	1.69
32	EL SALVADOR	1.68
119	MALTA	1.66
96	SYRIA	1.55
40	GREECE	1.54
95	SWITZERLAND	1.48
94	SWEDEN	1.47
44	HONDURAS	1.46
11	BURMA	1.42
78	PAKISTAN	1.38
49	IRAN	1.36
111	SOUTH VIETNAM	1.32
125	GUYANA	1.29
52	ISRAEL	1.28
103	U.S.S.R	1.28
104	U.A.R.	1.26
87	SAUDI ARABIA	1.22
50	IRAQ	1.19
29	DENMARK	1.09
69	MONGOLIA	1.08
83	POLAND	.97
35	FRANCE	.93
70	MOROCCO	.88
93	SUDAN	.84
59	SOUTH KOREA	.83
105	UNITED KINGDOM	.80
13	CAMBODIA	.77
57	JORDAN	.76
67	MAURITANIA	.75
113	YUGOSLAVIA	.73
24	COSTA RICA	.67
36	GABON	.64
126	MALAYSIA	.64
47	INDIA	.59
39	GHANA	.56
16	CENTRAL AFRICAN REP	.54
60	LAOS	.51
85	ROMANIA	.51
106	UNITED STATES	.51
53	ITALY	.50
77	NORWAY	.47
79	PANAMA	.45
25	CUBA	.42
18	CHAD	.34

71	NEPAL	.31
42	GUINEA	.31
90	SOMALIA	.29
122	KENYA	.26
34	FINLAND	.22
27	CZECHOSLOVAKIA	.21
110	NORTH VIETNAM	.21
5	AUSTRALIA	.18
84	PORTUGAL	.18
92	SPAIN	.17
72	NETHERLANDS	.15
62	LIBERIA	.10
64	LUXEMBOURG	.10
65	MALAGASY REP	.10
66	MALI	.10
75	NIGER	.10
86	RWANDA	.10
88	SENEGAL	.10
1	AFGHANISTAN	.10
46	ICELAND	.10
107	UPPER VOLTA	.10
14	CAMEROUN	.10
114	BOTSWANA	.10
117	LESOTHO	.10
123	W. SAMOA	.10
127	MALDIVE ISLANDS	.10
128	BARBADOS	.10
115	GAMBIA	.07

THEY TEND TO HAVE THE CHARACTERISTICS OF:

SMALL CHRISTIAN COMMUNITY
MANY MILITARY PERSONNEL PER CAPITA
HIGH CRUDE DEATH RATE

I'S WITH - SCORES TEND TO EXPORT HIGH
CONFLICT TO J'S WITH THE CHARACTERISTICS, RELATIVE TO I, OF:

VARIABLE CLUSTER 9

25 AGE OF CURRENCY CLOSENESS	.53
32 CONCENTRATION OF EXPORT RECEIVERS DISTANCE	.67
07 MILITARISM DISTANCE	.72

THESE I'S ARE:

28	DAHOMEY	-.05
58	NORTH KOREA	-.12
41	GUATEMALA	-.17
108	URUGUAY	-.18
26	CYPRUS	-.19
30	DOMINICAN REPUBLIC	-.22
7	BELGIUM	-.23
20	CHINA, PR	-.23
97	THAILAND	-.28
124	SINGAPORE	-.29
54	IVORY COAST	-.36
51	IRELAND	-.36
4	ARGENTINA	-.38
38	WEST GERMANY	-.39
63	LIBYA	-.41

121	ZAMBIA	-.44
45	HUNGARY	-.48
43	HAITI	-.48
74	NICARAGUA	-.54
61	LEBANON	-.58
2	ALBANIA	-.68
102	UGANDA	-.68
109	VENEZUELA	-.74
33	ETHIOPIA	-.75
17	CEYLON	-.77
31	ECUADOR	-.79
68	MEXICO	-.87
3	ALGERIA	-.95
15	CANADA	-.95
76	NIGERIA	-.97
80	PARAGUAY	-.99
9	BRAZIL	-1.05
100	TUNISIA	-1.06
120	TANZANIA	-1.07
19	CHILE	-1.20
89	SIERRA LEONE	-1.27
37	EAST GERMANY	-1.27
55	JAMAICA	-1.29
81	PERU	-1.37
10	BULGARIA	-1.38
21	COLOMBIA	-1.39
116	KUWAIT	-1.39
23	CONGO (LEO)	-1.42
112	YEMEN	-1.57
56	JAPAN	-1.66
12	BURUNDI	-1.73
73	NEW ZEALAND	-1.81
82	PHILIPPINES	-1.85
118	MALAWI	-1.87
8	BOLIVIA	-1.88
99	TRINIDAD	-1.91
22	CONGO (BRA)	-2.07
6	AUSTRIA	-2.16
91	SOUTH AFRICA	-2.29

THEY TEND TO HAVE THE CHARACTERISTICS OF:

LARGE CHRISTIAN COMMUNITY
FEW MILITARY PERSONNEL PER CAPITA
LOW CRUDE DEATH RATE

I'S WITH + SCORES TEND TO EXPORT HIGH
CONFLICT TO J'S WITH THE CHARACTERISTICS, RELATIVE TO I, OF:

VARIABLE CLUSTER 10

05 INTERNAL POLITICAL TURMOIL DISTANCE	.75
18 PER CENT URBAN POPULATION CLOSENESS	.57

THESE I'S ARE:

VARIABLE CLUSTER 10

22	CONGO (BRA)	3.09
52	ISRAEL	2.70
104	U.A.R.	2.41
19	CHILE	2.16
96	SYRIA	1.73
40	GREECE	1.70
5	AUSTRALIA	1.56
8	BOLIVIA	1.45
69	MONGOLIA	1.44
21	COLOMBIA	1.43
97	THAILAND	1.41
4	ARGENTINA	1.37
26	CYPRUS	1.31
60	LAOS	1.22
23	CONGO (LEO)	1.08
36	GABON	1.06
15	CANADA	1.05
13	CAMBODIA	1.00
53	ITALY	1.00
90	SOMALIA	.99
42	GUINEA	.95
9	BRAZIL	.91
80	PARAGUAY	.91
34	FINLAND	.87
50	IRAQ	.85
38	WEST GERMANY	.81
31	ECUADMR	.81
109	VENEZUELA	.81
11	BURMA	.81
7	BELGIUM	.79
57	JORDAN	.78
71	NEPAL	.76
116	KUWAIT	.70
56	JAPAN	.68
29	DENMARK	.61
16	CENTRAL AFRICAN REP	.60
72	NETHERLANDS	.56
73	NEW ZEALAND	.55
33	ETHIOPIA	.55
108	URUGUAY	.48
105	UNITED KINGDOM	.47
28	DAHOMEY	.47
61	LEBANON	.37
49	IRAN	.36
124	SINGAPORE	.33
70	MOROCCO	.26
67	MAURITANIA	.26
81	PERU	.20
93	SUDAN	.19
79	PANAMA	.14
6	AUSTRIA	.09
18	CHAD	.07
103	U.S.S.R	.06
25	CUBA	.05
63	LIBYA	.04
101	TURKEY	.02

THEY TEND TO HAVE THE CHARACTERISTICS OF:

LITTLE POLITICAL INSTABILITY
SMALL POPULATION DENSITY
MUCH DOMESTIC VIOLENCE
LARGE GNP GROWTH RATE AT FIXED PRICES
NEW CURRENCY

I'S WITH - SCORES TEND TO EXPORT HIGH
CONFLICT TO J'S WITH THE CHARACTERISTICS, RELATIVE TO I, OF:

VARIABLE CLUSTER 10

05 INTERNAL POLITICAL TURMOIL CLOSENESS	.75
18 PER CENT URBAN POPULATION DISTANCE	.57

THESE I'S ARE:

120	TANZANIA	-.01
14	CAMEROUN	-.02
62	LIBERIA	-.02
64	LUXEMBOURG	-.02
65	MALAGASY REP	-.02
66	MALI	-.02
1	AFGHANISTAN	-.02
46	ICELAND	-.02
75	NIGER	-.02
86	RWANDA	-.02
88	SENEGAL	-.02
107	UPPER VOLTA	-.02
114	BOTSWANA	-.02
117	LESOTHO	-.02
123	W. SAMOA	-.02
127	MALDIVE ISLANDS	-.02
128	BARBADOS	-.02
17	CEYLON	-.03
2	ALBANIA	-.06
3	ALGERIA	-.06
39	GHANA	-.08
126	MALAYSIA	-.09
77	NORWAY	-.15
12	BURUNDI	-.18
122	KENYA	-.22
48	INDONESIA	-.23
55	JAMAICA	-.30
24	COSTA RICA	-.34
98	TOGO	-.36
51	IRELAND	-.37
95	SWITZERLAND	-.41
76	NIGERIA	-.41
121	ZAMBIA	-.42
47	INDIA	-.46
94	SWEDEN	-.51
74	NICARAGUA	-.52
45	HUNGARY	-.66
87	SAUDI ARABIA	-.67
54	IVORY COAST	-.78
20	CHINA, PR	-.87
118	MALAWI	-.89
92	SPAIN	-.91
78	PAKISTAN	-.92
30	DOMINICAN REPUBLIC	-.93
91	SOUTH AFRICA	-.93
102	UGANDA	-.93
113	YUGOSLAVIA	-.95
58	NORTH KOREA	-.98
41	GUATEMALA	-.99
89	SIERRA LEONE	-1.06
83	POLAND	-1.07
32	EL SALVADOR	-1.09

85	ROMANIA	-1.16
68	MEXICO	-1.18
43	HAITI	-1.19
125	GUYANA	-1.19
35	FRANCE	-1.22
59	SOUTH KOREA	-1.22
44	HONDURAS	-1.25
27	CZECHOSLOVAKIA	-1.25
82	PHILIPPINES	-1.30
84	PORTUGAL	-1.33
119	MALTA	-1.40
10	BULGARIA	-1.40
99	TRINIDAD	-1.48
100	TUNISIA	-1.51
111	SOUTH VIETNAM	-1.52
112	YEMEN	-1.52
115	GAMBIA	-1.70
106	UNITED STATES	-1.92
37	EAST GERMANY	-2.00
110	NORTH VIETNAM	-2.45

THEY TEND TO HAVE THE CHARACTERISTICS OF:

MUCH POLITICAL INSTABILITY
LARGE POPULATION DENSITY
LITTLE DOMESTIC VIOLENCE
SMALL GNP GROWTH RATE AT FIXED PRICES
OLD CURRENCY

I'S WITH + SCORES TEND TO EXPORT HIGH
CONFLICT TO J'S WITH THE CHARACTERISTICS, RELATIVE TO I, OF:

VARIABLE CLUSTER 11

25	AGE OF CURRENCY CLOSENESS	.57
15	GNP GROWTH RATE CLOSENESS	.83

THESE I'S ARE:

VARIABLE CLUSTER 11

101	TURKEY	3.24
93	SUDAN	2.25
26	CYPRUS	2.22
99	TRINIDAD	2.11
83	POLAND	2.05
8	BOLIVIA	1.84
40	GREECE	1.58
45	HUNGARY	1.57
76	NIGERIA	1.50
124	SINGAPORE	1.42
21	COLOMBIA	1.39
103	U.S.S.R	1.32
89	SIERRA LEONE	1.31
113	YUGOSLAVIA	1.31
38	WEST GERMANY	1.30
23	CONGO (LEO)	1.27
125	GUYANA	1.26

111	SOUTH VIETNAM	1.23
27	CZECHOSLOVAKIA	1.18
121	ZAMBIA	1.00
74	NICARAGUA	.96
85	ROMANIA	.96
109	VENEZUELA	.93
116	KUWAIT	.88
120	TANZANIA	.87
48	INDONESIA	.80
55	JAMAICA	.79
13	CAMBODIA	.69
42	GUINEA	.65
81	PERU	.63
102	UGANDA	.62
119	MALTA	.54
52	ISRAEL	.53
104	U.A.R.	.50
10	BULGARIA	.49
6	AUSTRIA	.48
49	IRAN	.47
115	GAMBIA	.46
90	SOMALIA	.45
71	NEPAL	.38
112	YEMEN	.37
31	ECUADOR	.35
82	PHILIPPINES	.33
72	NETHERLANDS	.32
105	UNITED KINGDOM	.32
47	INDIA	.22
19	CHILE	.19
96	SYRIA	.18
18	CHAD	.17
9	BRAZIL	.13
67	MAURITANIA	.12
20	CHINA, PR	.10
57	JORDAN	.10
97	THAILAND	.10
7	BELGIUM	.08
37	EAST GERMANY	.04
68	MEXICO	.02
69	MONGOLIA	.02

THEY TEND TO HAVE THE CHARACTERISTICS OF:

LARGE GNP GROWTH RATE
LARGE HEALTH EXPENDITURE AS PERCENT OF GNP
HIGH RATIO OF BLACK MARKET TO OFFICIAL EXCHANGE

I'S WITH - SCORES TEND TO EXPORT HIGH
CONFLICT TO J'S WITH THE CHARACTERISTICS, RELATIVE TO I, OF:

VARIABLE CLUSTER 11

25 AGE OF CURRENCY DISTANCE	.57
15 GNP GROWTH RATE DISTANCE	.83

THESE I'S ARE:

16	CENTRAL AFRICAN REP	-.03
110	NORTH VIETNAM	-.04
28	DAHOMEY	-.07

84	PORTUGAL	-.13
64	LUXEMBOURG	-.18
65	MALAGASY REP	-.18
66	MALI	-.18
46	ICELAND	-.18
75	NIGER	-.18
62	LIBERIA	-.18
86	RWANDA	-.18
88	SENEGAL	-.18
1	AFGHANISTAN	-.18
107	UPPER VOLTA	-.18
14	CAMEROUN	-.18
114	BOTSWANA	-.18
117	LESOTHO	-.18
123	W. SAMOA	-.18
127	MALDIVE ISLANDS	-.18
128	BARBADOS	-.18
60	LAOS	-.20
92	SPAIN	-.20
77	NORWAY	-.22
17	CEYLON	-.26
34	FINLAND	-.28
2	ALBANIA	-.30
54	IVORY COAST	-.31
126	MALAYSIA	-.32
70	MOROCCO	-.34
51	IRELAND	-.36
63	LIBYA	-.36
59	SOUTH KOREA	-.37
36	GABON	-.40
25	CUBA	-.47
11	BURMA	-.52
95	SWITZERLAND	-.52
73	NEW ZEALAND	-.52
122	KENYA	-.53
12	BURUNDI	-.55
33	ETHIOPIA	-.62
78	PAKISTAN	-.62
53	ITALY	-.63
118	MALAWI	-.65
58	NORTH KOREA	-.74
41	GUATEMALA	-.74
80	PARAGUAY	-.76
79	PANAMA	-.78
29	DENMARK	-.79
30	DOMINICAN REPUBLIC	-.81
106	UNITED STATES	-.85
32	EL SALVADOR	-.91
5	AUSTRALIA	-.94
100	TUNISIA	-.95
91	SOUTH AFRICA	-.98
94	SWEDEN	-1.02
24	COSTA RICA	-1.07
22	CONGO (BRA)	-1.12
3	ALGERIA	-1.26
35	FRANCE	-1.29
87	SAUDI ARABIA	-1.36
44	HONDURAS	-1.46
50	IRAQ	-1.58
98	TOGO	-1.59
56	JAPAN	-1.82
43	HAITI	-1.88
39	GHANA	-2.08
108	URUGUAY	-2.14
61	LEBANON	-2.29
15	CANADA	-2.32

4	ARGENTINA	-2.35

THEY TEND TO HAVE THE CHARACTERISTICS OF:

SMALL GNP GROWTH RATE
SMALL HEALTH EXPENDITURE AS PERCENT OF GNP
LOW RATIO OF BLACK MARKET TO OFFICIAL EXCHANGE

I'S WITH + SCORES TEND TO EXPORT HIGH
CONFLICT TO J'S WITH THE CHARACTERISTICS, RELATIVE TO I, OF:

VARIABLE CLUSTER 12

31 MEAN ELECTIONS DISTANCE	.84

THESE I'S ARE:

VARIABLE CLUSTER 12

112	YEMEN	2.16
17	CEYLON	2.10
43	HAITI	2.06
104	U.A.R.	1.80
93	SUDAN	1.74
58	NORTH KOREA	1.69
20	CHINA, PR	1.61
30	DOMINICAN REPUBLIC	1.55
12	BURUNDI	1.44
36	GABON	1.38
6	AUSTRIA	1.35
45	HUNGARY	1.34
50	IRAQ	1.34
92	SPAIN	1.31
106	UNITED STATES	1.18
49	IRAN	1.18
26	CYPRUS	1.16
44	HONDURAS	1.14
7	BELGIUM	1.13
109	VENEZUELA	1.13
56	JAPAN	1.10
25	CUBA	1.08
87	SAUDI ARABIA	.97
8	BOLIVIA	.92
19	CHILE	.83
111	SOUTH VIETNAM	.79
96	SYRIA	.75
31	ECUADOR	.75
32	EL SALVADOR	.72
103	U.S.S.R	.70
13	CAMBODIA	.69
59	SOUTH KOREA	.68
80	PARAGUAY	.66
42	GUINEA	.66
23	CONGO (LEO)	.60
2	ALBANIA	.56
41	GUATEMALA	.55
100	TUNISIA	.54
52	ISRAEL	.51

101	TURKEY	.38
84	PORTUGAL	.30
10	BULGARIA	.28
110	NORTH VIETNAM	.25
79	PANAMA	.24
70	MOROCCO	.24
68	MEXICO	.23
78	PAKISTAN	.21
74	NICARAGUA	.17
89	SIERRA LEONE	.16
24	COSTA RICA	.12
62	LIBERIA	.11
64	LUXEMBOURG	.11
65	MALAGASY REP	.11
66	MALI	.11
46	ICELAND	.11
75	NIGER	.11
86	RWANDA	.11
88	SENEGAL	.11
14	CAMEROUN	.11
107	UPPER VOLTA	.11
1	AFGHANISTAN	.11
114	BOTSWANA	.11
117	LESOTHO	.11
123	W. SAMOA	.11
127	MALDIVE ISLANDS	.11
128	BARBADOS	.11
27	CZECHOSLOVAKIA	.09
38	WEST GERMANY	.08
57	JORDAN	.08
4	ARGENTINA	.07
97	THAILAND	.05
47	INDIA	.04

THEY TEND TO HAVE THE CHARACTERISTICS OF:

NON-COMPETITIVE POLITICAL SYSTEM
LARGE POPULATION DENSITY
LONG NATIONAL INDEPENDENCE
FEW ELECTIONS

I'S WITH - SCORES TEND TO EXPORT HIGH
CONFLICT TO J'S WITH THE CHARACTERISTICS, RELATIVE TO I, OF:

VARIABLE CLUSTER 12

31 MEAN ELECTIONS CLOSENESS	.84

THESE I'S ARE:

61	LEBANON	-.04
48	INDONESIA	-.05
90	SOMALIA	-.06
22	CONGO (BRA)	-.07
71	NEPAL	-.07
98	TOGO	-.08
126	MALAYSIA	-.09
9	BRAZIL	-.13
102	UGANDA	-.14
83	POLAND	-.15
77	NORWAY	-.16

122	KENYA	-.20
72	NETHERLANDS	-.21
108	URUGUAY	-.33
55	JAMAICA	-.43
67	MAURITANIA	-.45
33	ETHIOPIA	-.47
120	TANZANIA	-.47
82	PHILIPPINES	-.48
60	LAOS	-.49
99	TRINIDAD	-.52
94	SWEDEN	-.55
76	NIGERIA	-.55
116	KUWAIT	-.59
39	GHANA	-.66
16	CENTRAL AFRICAN REP	-.70
35	FRANCE	-.72
73	NEW ZEALAND	-.74
91	SOUTH AFRICA	-.75
34	FINLAND	-.75
113	YUGOSLAVIA	-.76
69	MONGOLIA	-.77
105	UNITED KINGDOM	-.79
53	ITALY	-.84
95	SWITZERLAND	-.84
11	BURMA	-.85
18	CHAD	-.85
37	EAST GERMANY	-.88
85	ROMANIA	-.94
125	GUYANA	-1.09
3	ALGERIA	-1.20
5	AUSTRALIA	-1.26
28	DAHOMEY	-1.32
118	MALAWI	-1.33
21	COLOMBIA	-1.45
40	GREECE	-1.50
54	IVORY COAST	-1.65
63	LIBYA	-1.65
81	PERU	-1.66
121	ZAMBIA	-1.73
124	SINGAPORE	-1.79
15	CANADA	-2.01
115	GAMBIA	-2.20
119	MALTA	-2.41
29	DENMARK	-2.65
51	IRELAND	-3.03

THEY TEND TO HAVE THE CHARACTERISTICS OF:

COMPETITIVE POLITICAL SYSTEM
SMALL POPULATION DENSITY
RECENT NATIONAL INDEPENDENCE
MANY ELECTIONS

I'S WITH + SCORES TEND TO EXPORT HIGH
CONFLICT TO J'S WITH THE CHARACTERISTICS, RELATIVE TO I, OF:

VARIABLE CLUSTER 13

29 PER CAPITA ECONOMIC ACTIVE MALE POPULATION CLOSENESS	.87

THESE I'S ARE:

VARIABLE CLUSTER 13

35	FRANCE	2.62
40	GREECE	2.29
101	TURKEY	2.02
41	GUATEMALA	1.78
60	LAOS	1.76
108	URUGUAY	1.73
113	YUGOSLAVIA	1.64
2	ALBANIA	1.57
84	PORTUGAL	1.55
91	SOUTH AFRICA	1.54
92	SPAIN	1.40
22	CONGO (BRA)	1.36
5	AUSTRALIA	1.32
49	IRAN	1.28
74	NICARAGUA	1.24
97	THAILAND	1.18
4	ARGENTINA	1.12
68	MEXICO	1.07
43	HAITI	1.04
76	NIGERIA	1.04
111	SOUTH VIETNAM	1.02
38	WEST GERMANY	.93
36	GABON	.85
20	CHINA, PR	.85
53	ITALY	.84
23	CONGO (LEO)	.83
31	ECUADOR	.81
9	BRAZIL	.72
80	PARAGUAY	.71
95	SWITZERLAND	.69
32	EL SALVADOR	.67
21	COLOMBIA	.66
28	DAHOMEY	.64
121	ZAMBIA	.63
51	IRELAND	.61
13	CAMBODIA	.61
55	JAMAICA	.57
10	BULGARIA	.56
18	CHAD	.56
69	MONGOLIA	.55
85	ROMANIA	.54
78	PAKISTAN	.52
89	SIERRA LEONE	.51
58	NORTH KOREA	.51
79	PANAMA	.42
24	COSTA RICA	.41
120	TANZANIA	.36
19	CHILE	.34
47	INDIA	.28
30	DOMINICAN REPUBLIC	.22
59	SOUTH KOREA	.17
12	BURUNDI	.14
44	HONDURAS	.13
33	ETHIOPIA	.10
67	MAURITANIA	.06
126	MALAYSIA	.05
7	BELGIUM	.04
110	NORTH VIETNAM	.03
63	LIBYA	.03
39	GHANA	.02
62	LIBERIA	.02
1	AFGHANISTAN	.02

64	LUXEMBOURG	.02
65	MALAGASY REP	.02
66	MALI	.02
75	NIGER	.02
46	ICELAND	.02
86	RWANDA	.02
88	SENEGAL	.02
107	UPPER VOLTA	.02
114	BOTSWANA	.02
117	LESOTHO	.02
14	CAMEROUN	.02
123	W. SAMOA	.02
127	MALDIVE ISLANDS	.02
128	BARBADOS	.02

THEY TEND TO HAVE THE CHARACTERISTICS OF:

LARGE CHRISTIAN COMMUNITY
LONG NATIONAL INDEPENDENCE
SMALL HEALTH EXPENDITURE AS PERCENT OF GNP

I'S WITH - SCORES TEND TO EXPORT HIGH
CONFLICT TO J'S WITH THE CHARACTERISTICS, RELATIVE TO I, OF:

VARIABLE CLUSTER 13

29 PER CAPITA ECONOMIC ACTIVE MALE POPULATION DISTANCE .87

THESE I'S ARE:

83	POLAND	-.02
29	DENMARK	-.04
124	SINGAPORE	-.11
34	FINLAND	-.25
54	IVORY COAST	-.28
26	CYPRUS	-.29
45	HUNGARY	-.32
73	NEW ZEALAND	-.34
122	KENYA	-.37
98	TOGO	-.43
81	PERU	-.50
125	GUYANA	-.55
94	SWEDEN	-.55
56	JAPAN	-.55
93	SUDAN	-.55
8	BOLIVIA	-.56
112	YEMEN	-.56
90	SOMALIA	-.56
61	LEBANON	-.58
87	SAUDI ARABIA	-.59
42	GUINEA	-.62
27	CZECHOSLOVAKIA	-.66
11	BURMA	-.74
99	TRINIDAD	-.78
115	GAMBIA	-.78
16	CENTRAL AFRICAN REP	-.91
72	NETHERLANDS	-.92
100	TUNISIA	-.95
104	U.A.R.	-1.02
17	CEYLON	-1.04
105	UNITED KINGDOM	-1.15
118	MALAWI	-1.16
103	U.S.S.R	-1.18

25	CUBA	-1.18
116	KUWAIT	-1.20
37	EAST GERMANY	-1.22
50	IRAQ	-1.25
71	NEPAL	-1.26
6	AUSTRIA	-1.30
82	PHILIPPINES	-1.33
106	UNITED STATES	-1.37
77	NORWAY	-1.39
96	SYRIA	-1.55
109	VENEZUELA	-1.56
52	ISRAEL	-1.68
48	INDONESIA	-1.68
3	ALGERIA	-1.84
119	MALTA	-1.89
57	JORDAN	-1.91
15	CANADA	-2.12
102	UGANDA	-2.19
70	MOROCCO	-2.22

THEY TEND TO HAVE THE CHARACTERISTICS OF:

SMALL CHRISTIAN COMMUNITY
RECENT NATIONAL INDEPENDENCE
LARGE HEALTH EXPENDITURE AS PERCENT OF GNP